GAMES
PEOPLE PLAYED

GAMES
PEOPLE PLAYED

A GLOBAL HISTORY OF SPORT

WRAY VAMPLEW

REAKTION BOOKS

To Janice, who continues to appreciate how much sport means to me, Peter, who learned to play soccer from a book, and Ailsa, who has inherited both my hairy legs and my love of large databases.

Published by Reaktion Books Ltd
Unit 32, Waterside
44–48 Wharf Road
London N1 7UX, UK
www.reaktionbooks.co.uk

First published 2021
Copyright © Wray Vamplew 2021

Printed and bound in Great Britain by Bell & Bain, Glasgow

A catalogue record for this book is available from the British Library

ISBN 978 1 78914 457 4

CONTENTS

INTRODUCTION:
PRE-MATCH INSTRUCTIONS

S port is more than mere games. It can promote socialization, moral education and, occasionally, political indoctrination, all preparing citizens for duties and responsibilities beyond the playing arenas. The inference in the title of this book is that it will consider not just physical performance but also other reasons for involvement in the watching and playing of sport. Why sport was and is practised is a major theme that runs through the book, although with different motives emphasized at different times to reflect historical shifts in mentality. The analysis will not ignore the ludic aspect of sport: that sport could be an end in itself, with people participating simply for personal fun and enjoyment. However, additionally – or alternatively – it will show that play could be a means of displaying masculinity (or femininity), or of affirming social status by demonstrating that one had the time, money and energy to devote to activities other than work. Sport could be undertaken to promote health and welfare, to create loyalty to a group or nation, or for a plethora of other reasons. It can also be associated with carnival, where the normal goals of society are set aside and individuals are free to use their time in displays of non-utilitarian activities, often with the roles of authority and social position reversed.

Sport is an immensely important part of any serious attempt to re-construct a nation's collective life. Although sport exists outside the daily urgency of livelihood and sustenance, it is simultaneously highly popular, compulsive and a compelling stage for national, local and community drama and glory: a narrative that is hard to resist. It is important to millions of people across the globe, and the arena (I would suggest) of more male voluntary activity than any other. It can be big business or family recreation; be discriminatory but also integrative; produce triumphs and tragedies as well as heroes and villains; and encourage the best and worst of nationalism. Such cultural, political, social and economic significance warrants a study to add to our historical understanding of society and the individuals and communities within it. Indeed, the analysis of the history of sport and sporting traditions can offer rewarding insights that are not available from other sources. While acknowledging that sport can be fun, any attempt at sports history should also look at more than the ludic and contextualize events in wider social, political, economic and cultural scenarios. It gains relevance when it does not focus solely on past results but looks at how sport was associated historically with class, gender and other socio-cultural indicators.

Playing or watching sport was influenced by age, social and economic status, gender, time and locality. This book shows how sport was practised, experienced and made meaningful by a variety of groups and individuals in different historical periods. There is significant generalization, since space does not allow for a full discussion of differences and outliers. Nor are there chapters on sport in specific countries, although global examples will be used to illustrate the arguments. We will reference not only the privileged but also those people whose lives did not generate much documentation. The focus is not on elite sportspeople, but some such individuals will be mentioned, although a few of them may not be that well known to a British audience.

A wide definition of sport is taken. But obviously the line must be drawn somewhere, and while I can admire the athletic performance of contemporary dancers such as the BalletBoyz and the gymnastic skills of circus artists, I would not class them as sportspeople. (I still cannot quite comprehend that one of the books in the British Sports and Sportsmen series on my shelves is titled *Industry and Commerce!*) Sport for the purposes of this history is what people at the time considered it to be. This, of course, raises the question of translating various terms and deciding that they mean sport, a problem that applies as much to nineteenth-century Europe as it does to classical Rome (incidentally, there is no Latin word for sport). Not all sports will have their history outlined. Some are looked at in Part Two, which deals with various categories of sport; others may be covered elsewhere, such as in the chapters dealing with time periods and political and social effects on and of sport; some scarcely feature; and several are not mentioned at all. This is not a comprehensive encyclopaedia of sports but an analytical history of sport in various societies at varying times.

Recent revisions in our knowledge of sports history are assessed, and explanations are made of the abuse of sports history and the creation of sporting myths. There is an acknowledgement of our historical ignorance in some areas, noting that it is sometimes as important to say what we do not know as to state what we do know.

All book introductions should include a personal statement by the author to enlighten readers about where they are coming from and what baggage they are carrying. So here goes. I like sport and have participated in it throughout my life. I played my last game aged 69, scoring 20 not out and taking 5 wickets for 11 runs. It took all those intervening years for me to realize that as a bowler I should pitch the ball where I would not like it as a batsman. Now in my seventies, I play golf, confusing my partners by switching from my right to my left hand for putting and chipping, and amazing myself by achieving a hole-in-one – but one unseen by anyone, including myself, because of the layout of the course. My other sport is lawn bowls, which I took up with my wife as two of the youngest members of the group at a local rink, where after twelve ends we up and off to enjoy drinks and cakes.

I hope this book will show that I am a fan of sport, but not an uncritical one. What about my sporting prejudices? I support Hibernian and Barnsley football clubs (fortunately, they never have to play each other) and Yorkshire County cricket team, but I prefer watching sport on television to being there. I enjoy following the Tour de France (despite the drugs) but have given up on athletics (because of the drugs). I do not like (or perhaps do not understand) American sports. The scores in basketball are too high and I cannot fathom why in baseball a hit over the fence can score 1, 2, 3 or 4 rather than the undisputed 6 in cricket. However, I am ambivalent about gridiron, admiring the strategies but wondering why a 'touchdown' doesn't actually involve touching down. I am not a fan of Rangers or Celtic, corrupt and incompetent sporting officialdom (that doesn't leave many unscathed) or the claimed 'Olympic spirit'.

Since at least Greek antiquity a variety of social thinkers have championed sport as a force for good, while a few persistent critics have always taken the opposing position. Generally, the opposition to sport has not exhibited blanket coverage. Critics tend to focus on particular sports, on who has played them and where and when they were played. Hunting has been subjected to hostility from several quarters, including animal activists and farmers fearful that their crops will be trampled. Sports such as horse racing, in which gambling plays a central role, have drawn fire on moral grounds, as have blood sports, both human and animal. A long-running debate, with a class undertone, has focused on whether players should be paid for participating in sport, even when thousands of people have paid to watch them. The propriety of sporting contests invading the contested territories of public space, both geographical and calendrical, has produced enduring debates. For example, in the West, playing or even watching sport on 'holy days' such as Sunday (the Christian Sabbath) has been a subject of constant controversy. Nevertheless, there is a general premise by those involved in promoting sport that sport is mainly a force for good. I have been a notable sceptic on this. I don't think sport is good for neighbourliness; it often sets one community against another, one nation against another. Nor do I think sport is good for health; swimmers drown, joggers have heart attacks and all sportspeople suffer injuries.

Looking backwards at sport has become an industry in its own right, as nostalgia catering to both individual and collective memory has become an earner. Spectators pay to watch former stars in seniors' events, and for participants, particularly golfers, there are retro-heritage tournaments in which players use old-fashioned equipment. Sports marketers offer merchandise and memories for sale to the sports fan. Sporting memorabilia has become part of a growing, lucrative business, and several auction houses now employ sports history specialists. The numbers of sports museums and sporting halls of fame are at an all-time high. Clearly there is a growing interest in sports history.

This book is a personal record of what I believe has been significant in the development of sport, and of course others might have selected different issues. I have written it for the intelligent sports fan, who is not the oxymoron depicted by many commentators in high and even popular culture. The intention is to entertain but also inform and perhaps educate. Enjoy.

PART ONE

SPORTS HISTORY: FIRING BOTH BARRELS

In the first chapter of this section we explore the nature of sports history, its several guises, and some of the dangers that can be associated with each form. This is followed by a look at the type of evidence sports historians draw on, and how they use it to interpret the past.

At this early stage of the book I will push a personal academic barrow and argue that the study of sport can contribute to major historical debates on race, ethnicity, gender, international relations and other topics (providing that so-called mainstream historians are willing to read what these studies have to say). However, I also maintain that there is no longer such an entity as mainstream history, simply a heterogeneous group of sub-disciplines including political history, social history, cultural history, economic history, black history, gender history, military history and, of course, sports history, none of which should be privileged above any other. Sports history is as 'mainstream' and as relevant as any of these. The only real mainstreamers are those generalists who study periods rather than themes, but as non-specialists they are jacks of all trades, with the obvious corollary. Read on.

1

KNOW THE SCORE: UNDERSTANDING SPORTS HISTORY

Sports history is all around us, although sometimes we do not recognize it as such. Street names in Newmarket, the centre of the British horse-racing industry, pay tribute to long-dead jockeys, trainers, horses and turf administrators. Elsewhere, and of more recent vintage, Mancunians can drive down the Sir Matt Busby Way and the Sir Alex Ferguson Way, named after Manchester United football managers; Biel, the Swiss town where the tennis player trained as a junior, has Roger-Federer-Allee; and French Lick, the Indiana home town of legendary Boston Celtics basketballer Larry Bird, has a boulevard named in his honour. More generally, there is the heritage of sporting language. Some sporting terminology has become so much part of the vernacular that it is now used in non-sporting contexts. Most of us are conversant with such expressions of fair play as 'it's not cricket', 'a level playing field' and not 'moving the goalposts', but how many of these others can you recognize, and from what sport do they come?

1. 'come up to scratch'
2. 'throw in the towel'
3. 'having bottle'
4. 'rub of the green'
5. 'fast and loose'
6. 'stickler for the rules'
7. 'crestfallen'
8. 'on one's tod'

The first three originated in pugilism, a sport in which a fighter would lose the bout if he failed to be ready for combat by not having his foot on a line scratched in the centre of the ring. Sometimes a competitor's second decided that for him by throwing in the towel they had used to treat their man between rounds. More often they gave their fighter a swig from a brandy bottle to give him the courage to carry on. The rub of the green emanates from golf, although it does not refer to the grain on the putting surface which causes a ball to come up short or shoot past the hole, but to the whole course, including the pot bunkers liberally sprinkled around links courses to trap the unlucky golfer. A clue to this is that, more than a century after their profession began, golf course curators – the people responsible for maintaining the fairways, culling the rough and mowing the putting areas – are still called greenkeepers. Playing fast and loose in one's love life can be almost as dangerous as not knowing when to hold fast or to loose one's arrow in archery. Referees in traditional wrestling carried thin sticks that they attempted to push under the shoulders of a pinned wrestler to assess whether he had been fully pressed to the floor in a legitimate fall. 'Crestfallen' describes the state of the losing bird savaged in a cockfight. Finally, we have a phrase that came from racing in the early twentieth century, when American jockeys invaded the British turf and used their 'monkey on a stick' riding style to great advantage against home riders who stuck to an upright riding position with greater wind resistance. The Americans also brought with them different racing tactics. British jockeys had often raced almost half-paced in the earlier stages of a race and then swooped in for the final furlong or so. In contrast, the Americans often raced from the front if they felt their mount could cope with the pace. Prime among these riders was Tod Sloan, who was often so far in front that commentators spoke of him and his mount as being 'on their tod', possibly derived from rhyming slang of 'Tod Sloan, out alone'.

THE FUNCTION OF SPORTS HISTORY

Sports history's major contribution to the study of sport itself is the dimension of time. It can be considered the sports memory of a nation; without sports history there is sporting amnesia. It can explain why some things changed and others continued unamended. History can provide the evidence to set events and incidents in their proper context and help

Tod Sloan, American jockey who revolutionized riding styles.

to explain them by giving an awareness of underlying forces. If we want to know where sport is heading, it is useful to know where it has been. It provides the benchmarks for measuring progress and change (or the lack of it). It can help us to appreciate the difference between trend and fluctuation, to realize that not everything deemed 'important' in sport at a particular time need have a permanent influence, and that not everything in modern sport is new. Indeed, the sporting past has shaped the sporting present, since all sports have some inheritance from the past, be it rules, governing bodies, styles of play, competitions or equipment. As one of my favourite novelists, the late Henning Mankell (creator of the Swedish policeman Inspector Wallander), noted, history is not something that is behind us; it accompanies us into the future.

One function of sports history is simply to set the sporting record straight. By this I do not necessarily mean providing what I term basic 'sportifacts' confirming who won what, where and by how many, although historically these results can change. Many revisions have taken place, for example, when blood and urine samples were tested long after the event with new procedures and processes, and in 1987 assiduous research by Max and Reet Howell revealed that the Australian marksman Donald Mackintosh had been left off the official Olympic gold medal list for the Paris Games of 1900.

The sports historian can (as can historians in other areas) explore beyond the obvious and add context to the events being described. Let us head south to the Antipodes, to the picturesque Adelaide Oval in South Australia, where in 1932 a cricket Test match was played between Australia and England. This was the infamous Bodyline Test match in which, to counter the brilliance of the Australian batsmen, the English bowlers operated a strategy of bowling short-pitched deliveries aimed at the batsmen's bodies. This led to hostile crowd protests and a telegram from the Australian Cricket Board to Marylebone Cricket Club, complaining about the tactics. However, it was not just about cricket. The accusation of unsporting behaviour on the part of the English cricket team becomes much more meaningful when it is noted that there was an international economic depression at the time. Many Australians, fearful that imperial preference was being undermined in trade negotiations, thought Britain was not 'playing the game' politically and economically. The Test series became a convenient avenue for unorganized public protest.

Sports historians can also explain why, when and how sport has changed, or – equally important – why some sports did not change. Both may be seen in the experience of football in one English county. A prime example of continuity coexisting with change comes from Leicestershire in the 1890s, where every week during the Football League season Leicester Fosse played their home games at Filbert Street, a ground in the industrial city of Leicester surrounded by houses with a defined playing area of about 7,000 sq. m (75,300 sq. ft). An average attendance of around 6,000 paying spectators paid the wages of the fully professional male playing staff, only eleven of whom were allowed to participate in any match. On the pitch, their royal-blue shirts and stockings with white shorts were easily distinguishable from those of their opponents, who, by regulation of the football authorities, had to wear different colours. Games lasted just ninety minutes, with teams changing ends at half-time to ensure equal use of any prevailing weather or terrain conditions. All this contrasted with a

Douglas Jardine leads the England team out
to field during the Bodyline Test series.

folk football match played every Easter Monday between the inhabitants of the Leicestershire agricultural villages of Medbourne and Hallaton, a tradition dating back to 1796. It was a sporting event suitable for an agrarian economy, played once a year when there was time to spare from work, and making use of the natural environment by being played entirely across open countryside, with steeply sloping ground and a number of obstacles – hedges, fences and ponds – obstructing the mile (1.6 km) between the two goals. The 'ball' (a barrel filled with 5 litres/9 pints of ale) was not kicked into the opponent's territory, as at Filbert Street, but was carried to one's own goal, and that the match did not end until one set of villagers had brought two barrels home. There were no rules about the number of players or their gender, no requirements for the teams to be of equal size and no team colours were worn.

This can be contrasted with the contemporaneous football matches being played every second week during the season at Filbert Street, home of Leicester Fosse Football Club, just 21 km (13 mi.) away. The ground was surrounded by houses, and the pitch itself was in a defined area of about 7,000 sq. m (75,300 sq. ft). The club had been formed in 1884 by old boys of Wyggeston Grammar School, and for several years had a nomadic existence involving mainly friendly matches, before moving to Filbert Street stadium in 1891, when it joined the Midland League. After finishing second in that competition, the club was elected to the national Football League in 1894. As Leicester became an important centre for the manufacture of hosiery, textiles and footwear and, towards the end of the century, also for engineering, its population had risen from 68,000 in 1861 to 217,000 by 1901. This provided the base for a regular football crowd, with an average attendance of around 6,000 even in the lower reaches of the league. This gate money paid the wages of the fully professional male playing staff, only eleven of whom were allowed to participate in any match. On the pitch, their uniforms of royal-blue shirts and stockings with white shorts were easily distinguishable from those of their opponents, who, by regulation of the football authorities, had to wear different colours. The players, unlike those involved in the rough-and-tumble at Hallaton, had specialized roles, some offensive, some defensive. Games lasted just ninety minutes, with teams changing ends at half-time to ensure equal use of any prevailing weather or terrain conditions. A bureaucratic structure in the form of the league, the rules it imposed on the team, the specialization of playing roles and the efforts to ensure equality – none of them visible at Hallaton – are all features of modern sport. Nevertheless, despite there being almost a century between their origins, the two forms of football coexisted, a prime example of historical continuity and change in sport.

SPORTING MYTHS

A major role of the sports historian is to expose the myths that bedevil the public's conception of sports history. Myths too often pervade sport because a situation has not been properly investigated by historians. Much of what appears to be historical evidence is actually recycled. It simply becomes accepted over time as the 'truth', but often it is no more than conventional wisdom that falls apart when subjected to serious historical research. Sporting myths develop as nostalgia clouds memory. Indeed, all sports appear to have a 'golden age', usually beyond living memory. Many sports commentators allude to a previous era in particular sports, or in sport generally, in which money played a less prominent role than it does now and in which genuine amateurism prevailed, drugs, violence and corruption were non-existent, and everyone – both on and off the pitch – 'played the game'. Sports historians have shown that this was never really the case, that in the days before commercialized sport violence towards animals and fellow players featured strongly and corruption was not uncommon because of the gambling that underwrote much sport. Research has also suggested that the rhetoric of public-school sport was not always matched by behaviour on the field of play. Sport became commercialized during the so-called Golden Age of late Victorian Britain – another myth pricked – and shamateurism, foul play, drug use, gamesmanship and crowd trouble followed. It should be noted that the 'Golden Age' was also one of class discrimination and sexism, with half the population of Britain excluded from participation simply because of their gender.

Some myths, however, are deliberately constructed. In the 1980s the historians Eric Hobsbawm and Terence Ranger put together a ground-breaking collection of essays on modern historical context, detailing how modern societies 'invented traditions' to promote fealty to the nation and to centralize power in the hands of the upper and middle classes. Sports history, like all brands of history, has its own version of such 'fake news', which occurs when, for various reasons, a rewritten and untrue version of sporting history is presented as the truth. Of course, rewriting history is what sports history researchers do all the time, but generally it is because new and reliable information has been unearthed; the 'invented tradition' is rather a deliberate misrepresentation of history, a 'remembering' of things that did not exist and imposing that 'memory' on others. Unfortunately, such false history, when promoted assiduously, sometimes becomes the new conventional wisdom on the topic and gives an erroneous perception of continuity. At times, for example, the promoters of Highland games in Scotland and of several martial arts in Asia have falsely claimed that these had ancient origins. The two dominant invented traditions, however, lie in rugby football and baseball.

According to a commemorative plaque erected at Rugby School in 1900, in 1823 William Webb Ellis, a pupil at the school, 'with a fine disregard for the rules of football, as played in his time, first took the ball in his arms and ran with it, thus originating the distinctive feature of the rugby game'. Yet there is not a shred of evidence that this occurred. Two facts are true. Perhaps obviously from the school's name, the game of rugby was developed there, and Ellis was a pupil at the school between

1816 and 1825. The rest is conjecture, myth and outright fabrication. The idea that Ellis created sporting history first emerged in the 1870s when an old boy, Matthew Holbeche Bloxam, claimed that he had ascertained (from a fellow Old Rugbeian, since he himself had left the school in 1821) that Ellis had made his transgression in 1824. In 1880 Bloxam, now 75 years old, reiterated his claim, but changed the date to 1823. However, it did not receive official blessing until 1897 with the publication of a report by a committee of Old Rugbeians, which, undaunted by the lack of any first-hand witness, concluded that Ellis had indeed created running with the ball in hand as the distinctive feature of the rugby game. It was this committee that recommended the erection of the commemorative plaque.

That the myth became fully formulated at the turn of the twentieth century suited both Rugby School, which wanted to cement its position in the public-school hierarchy by showing that it had created a sport that had nothing to do with association football, and the Rugby Football Union (RFU), the governing body of the sport, which was under challenge from elements who wanted to commercialize rugby and emphasize the spectator aspect. Such was the strength of this myth that when the Rugby World Cup was inaugurated in 1987, the official trophy for the winning team was called the Webb Ellis Cup. Although a replica of the cup is on show at the Twickenham Rugby Museum, the schoolboy's role in inventing the game is now qualified by a note that it is 'generally believed',

Rugby Union 150 years after William Webb Ellis.

and that Bloxam, the octogenarian whose evidence is often cited, only 'thought that' he recalled the incident. Indeed, when the museum was pressurized by the RFU public relations department to accept the gift of a statue of Webb Ellis from Rugby Town Council, the curator turned it down because it would have contradicted his educational remit. Yet the myth endures.

Less enduring, but still accepted by many Americans, is the idea that Abner Doubleday invented baseball. Again, context is important. Concerned about stories that baseball was not actually an American game but a British one, and possibly one associated with females, the sports entrepreneur Albert Goodwill Spalding commissioned an enquiry in 1905 into the origins of the sport. Business reasons demanded that the game for which he supplied bats, balls and uniforms be an American one. The Mills Commission, composed of baseball figures, none of whom were historians, duly reported in 1907 that Doubleday had invented the game, titled it 'baseball', designed the diamond, indicated fielders' positions and written the rules. They added that this had occurred in rural Cooperstown, New York, in 1839. There is no evidence for this claim except for the 'memory' of a man who was five years old at the time and whose reliability can be questioned because he ended his life in a mental asylum. Even in his autobiography Doubleday himself never made such a claim; his many letters and papers contain no description of baseball or any suggestion that he considered himself prominent in the game's history. He was at West Point in 1839 and did not visit Cooperstown in that year, or possibly ever. Perhaps he was chosen by the commissioners because he was a military hero who they felt would not have his integrity challenged. The panel chair, Abraham G. Mills, was an old friend of Doubleday and had organized his funeral and memorial service in 1893. Nevertheless, despite the Doubleday legend not holding up to scrutiny, where is the National Baseball Hall of Fame and Museum? On Main Street, Cooperstown, and it advertises the town as the place 'where some say baseball was invented'.

PUBLIC SPORTS HISTORY

The public face of sports history does not reside in academic books and journals, but in such areas as sports museums, official club histories and television documentaries. In recent decades a sports heritage industry has developed based on sports museums (which house and exhibit some of the material culture of sport) and sports tourism (which uses the historical sporting landscape). The sports museum in particular has proliferated in recent years partly because entrepreneurs have realized that fans are pre-pared to pay (for) homage to their sporting heroes. Others have resulted from a genuine desire to exhibit the history of a sport and its participants. Unfortunately, the majority of the Hall of Fame variety, like the more overtly commercially orientated ventures associated with professional sports clubs, tend to emphasize ludic rather than social history.

Museums are involved in cultural production, although all too often it is cultural reproduction. Sports museums can be the best places to replicate the performance, drama, romance, passion and emotion of sport, and they have done much to educate through entertainment. Sadly, too often in the past sports museums have catered to the nostalgia market and, in so doing, have perpetuated myths, lacked historical objectivity and subtlety of argument, failed to contextualize artefacts, eschewed the controversial, had an obsession with winners and winning, and concen-trated on sport that was competitive, adult and male-dominated. With some notable exceptions, sports museums still resort to traditional heroic narratives in order to attract visitors and generally present the expected

Exhibit at the Musée National du Sport commemorating France's 1998 FIFA World Cup triumph.

(and uncontroversial) narrative to an undiscerning public. Champions are presented without warts and championships without political context. The controversial is ignored. Rags-to-riches stories abound but the aftermath of the descent into poverty, alcoholism or social dysfunction is rarely presented. Curators may argue that the fact a star player was a wife-beater is no concern of theirs unless it affected his performance on the field, but this attitude serves to reinforce the 'sport breeds good character' mythology.

That said, some sports museums are establishing themselves with associated research facilities and developing a symbiotic relationship with sports historians. Supply-side changes, particularly the emergence of lottery heritage funds, have forced museums to become more inclusive in their presentation of exhibits. They no longer see themselves as catering to the cognoscenti but to a broader clientele, some of whom need the basics of the sport and its history explained to them. On the more positive side, the primacy of the display case is being undermined by electronic touchscreens and interactivity. This has enabled some museums to deal with the paradox of static material culture and the mobility and passion of sport. Moreover, all sports museums contribute a visual impact, something that is often missing in the world of scholarship. One communication problem with sports museums is that display panels do not have the space to accommodate nuance. However, the growing use of portable audio commentaries has allowed more explanation to be offered to visitors.

Club museums especially, like many enthusiastic amateur sports historians, have a fascination with 'firsts', such as arguing that their particular club was the first to achieve something in its field or that a particular sport was first played in this or that place. To my mind, 'firsts' are important only if they were not isolated examples and they themselves led to further developments. That said, we should always be aware that new information might turn up, and thus be wary of claiming that anything is a definite first.

Another aspect of public sports history is the commissioned official history of a club or association. Here there is a major danger of history by omission, when unpalatable information is simply ignored. All the histories of Celtic Football Club note that it was founded to support local Catholic charities, but none goes on to say that within a decade it had become a limited-liability company, had begun to pay dividends of up to 10 per cent, and had virtually ceased to donate to charity! Such history with deliberate omissions may cater for the celebratory, nostalgia market but it is not 'good' history, sports or otherwise.

Film and television directors have made documentaries using archival footage and often, at least at the television level, involving critical sports historians. So far, film has been less mindful of academic credibility or historical accuracy, thus presenting the public with embroidered versions of actual sporting events. This difference in approach between the two media is unfortunate and perhaps confusing to the consumer of sports history, since more people watch television and films than read history books or visit specialized museums.

A highly readable genre has emerged in recent decades combining literature, history and personal reminiscence. Nick Hornby's best-selling *Fever Pitch* (1992), based on his reminiscences of life as an Arsenal fan, spawned a host of imitators of varying quality. Although weak on authority, these works are strong on authenticity and bring in the passion and emotion of sport, something that is sadly lacking in most academic writing on the topic. So, should fiction be incorporated into the historian's toolbox? Personally, I see a novel about boxing in the 1930s written in the 1930s as a more reliable historical source than one about boxing in the 1930s written in the 1990s.

AVOID NOSTALGIA

Sport is a significant part of the economic, social and political activity of most nations, and historians and sociologists should want to discover the origins and development of links between sport and the wider community. Unlike sports scientists, sports historians cannot experiment; they are rooted solidly in empirical data. They should be careful to specify whether the examples they use are the most representative or the most interesting. They must prevent myths from becoming conventional wisdom. They should ask the 'whys?' as well as the 'whats?' The great danger is that sports history becomes overwhelmed with nostalgia, a longing for an idealized past that has more to do with the perceived problems of the present than with the real past. If this happens, sports history becomes sentimental, reactionary and built on the implicit assumption that the sporting past was a better place in which to play games. It wasn't.

2

WALK THE WALK:
PRACTISING SPORTS HISTORY

History is an empirical, interpretive social science. Unless there is some evidence from the past, there can be no sports history. Yet historical data should not be accepted unconditionally. Researchers are always constrained by the quality of their source material, and sports historians must be aware of the context in which the material was produced. Historians should always ask three major questions of any primary source material: When was it produced? What was the authority of the person producing it? Why was it produced?

It is important to know when any material was produced. Sports have changed over time, and a description of a game or sporting event today might be almost incomprehensible to spectators of yesteryear; just consider bare-knuckle prizefighting and modern gloved boxing, folk football and the English Premier League, and floodlit T20 and traditional Test matches. Sport is not fixed in time, and neither is language. If we look at fielding positions in cricket, 'long stop' has long gone but the one-day game has taken 'sweeper' from soccer, while the latter now features strikers, midfielders and wingbacks, playing positions that were unknown before the 1970s. Tennis has introduced the tiebreak and lawn bowls the set. Ideas and philosophies can also change over time. A case in point is the perceived relationship between sport and alcohol. Today it is recognized that alcohol depresses the nervous system, impairs both motor ability and judgement, reduces endurance and, as a diuretic, can cause dehydration, none of which are conducive to sports performance.

In the past, however, the drinking of alcohol, particularly ales and porters, was positively encouraged as a perceived aid to strength and stamina. In the 1880s adverts professing the fitness-aiding qualities of alcohol were common, and even in the interwar years Bass advertised its beers as health- and fitness-promoting. And, of course, some readers may recall the 'Guinness is good for you' campaign from the middle decades of the twentieth century. Hence, when reading material on a particular sport it is essential to know the date at which the work was produced, otherwise misinterpretation can occur.

The second question to be asked of the evidence is about the authority of the person responsible for producing the material. Have they some expert knowledge or inside information? Are they encumbered with value judgements? When it comes to the performance-enhancing drugs debate, for instance, are they an official, an athlete, an athlete convicted of drugs offences, a chemist, a doctor, a member of the public or a member of the International Olympic Committee (IOC)? Whatever their position, it is likely that their point of view is not a neutral one, and historians must be aware of this when assessing the value of any statement.

Third, it must be asked why the document was produced. Was there a hidden agenda or was a political message being surreptitiously promoted? Consider the examples of invented tradition mentioned in the previous chapter. Both the reports of the Baseball Commission set up in the early twentieth century to decide when the game originated in America and of the investigation into the origins of rugby by Old Rugbeians in the 1890s had predetermined conclusions. The British Empire featured as a subtext in the Agenda Club's report on the conditions of boy golf caddies in pre-First World War England. The club was 'an organization of men in all parts of the country who realized that all is not well with England'. Although their overt focus was the blind-alley nature of caddying as an occupation, their proffered solution was to persuade the youths involved either to join the Navy or to emigrate to the Dominions.

After all this comes the matter of cracking the code in which the material was written. Take just five minutes to look at a racecard as laid out in the sports pages of most newspapers. Unless you are a regular visitor to the bookmakers, you will probably find it incomprehensible. What on earth does the combination of figures and letters convey? Unless you know the language or communication code, a message may

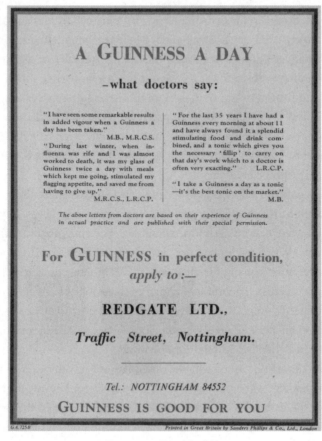

Guinness is Good for You.

be meaningless. How many Americans understand what 'lbw' is? And how many Europeans a baseball box score? Every sport has its own concepts and language, impenetrable except to those within the sporting fraternity, which acts as a barrier to keep out the uninitiated (and unwanted). In this, sport is no different from the law, academe and other areas where language is used to enhance mystique. If you want to do sports history research, you must know the code, that is, the language/terminology of the particular sport under review.

Moreover, as suggested above, language can change over time. Read this fight description by Pierce Egan, an early nineteenth-century sports journalist: 'The champion took on a Johnny Raw and used his bunch of fives to tap the claret and give the young bruiser several nobblers resulting in a suit of mourning and broken ivories. Although dished, he showed bottom in the milling and groceries were thrown in the ring at the end of the fight.' It is understandable, but must be mentally translated for the sense to be fully apparent.

Part of the code to be cracked involves understanding the definitions writers have employed. What exactly did they mean when they wrote of 'fair play', 'Olympism' or even 'sport' itself? Certainly in the nineteenth century 'amateur' and 'professional' were social, not economic, concepts. You were not labelled as a professional if you were a gentleman who rode (or rowed) against other gentlemen for high-stakes wagers. Wages were another matter, and the Amateur Rowing Association did not mince its words when it defined an amateur as not including anyone 'who was or ever had been by trade or employment for wages a mechanic, artisan or labourer'. When historians and sociologists investigated football hooliganism before 1914, what definition of 'hooliganism' did they employ to ensure that like was being compared with like, not apples with oranges? Riot and gang warfare are not the same as spitting and swearing; a fist fight between a couple of spectators is not the same as a mass fan battle; and verbal misconduct by a few spectators is not the same as mass racist or obscene chanting.

Finally, there is the issue of interpreting the data. Historians make great use of archives for retrieving knowledge about the sporting past. These are vital sites of information, but care must be taken in their use, since they can also be sites of power that privilege some information above others. What evidence is collected and what is saved can be functions of power in past and present societies. Hence subordinate groups – usually people who do not keep diaries, are not interviewed and are too often nameless – do not always have their voice 'heard' in historical documents. It is essential to check the means by which the materials were originally produced and have come into the archives, and whether items have been lost, destroyed or altered. For example, in the archives of the Australian Swimming Union all documents relating to Dawn Fraser's ban from the Australian team have been mutilated and all references to her behaviour in Tokyo deleted. Decisions about what is important enough to be recorded and archived are often discriminatory, and exclude the voices of subordinate groups. To take two examples from golf: club minutes show the decisions of the committees (albeit democratically elected ones) rather than of the membership; and the previously mentioned Agenda Club inquiry into the welfare of golf caddies interviewed golf club secretaries but not a single caddie. This criticism does not mean that the archive should not be used, but rather that the user must be aware that the documentary evidence is partial. History written on the basis of archived material is not fiction, but the past that it uncovers may not be the whole truth. That said, we must remember that there is no absolute truth, just versions of it.

TYPES OF EVIDENCE

Since the 1970s the nature and diversity of the evidence used by sports historians has evolved tremendously. Traditionally, in keeping with the practices of other sub-disciplines in history, scholars relied on written sources such as diaries, minute books, letters and official reports. Over time researchers began to make use of oral and email interviews, visual sources such as film, photographs and works of art, and material culture such as playing equipment and sports spaces.

Oral history can provide personal perceptions of events and what they meant to particular people. It can literally give a voice to those not represented in archival sources. There is a danger that such testimony, if unmediated, can become anecdotal and contribute little to any wider picture, although postmodernists would argue that the recollections of even one individual can show lived experience and give life to dry, conventional historical evidence. However, verbal evidence should not be accepted uncritically and collaboration should be sought from other witnesses and sources. There are inherent problems, such as the risk of false and selective memory, the subconscious interjection of hindsight, the silences on taboo subjects and the random survival of those interviewed. It is a time-consuming process with several legal and ethical challenges to be faced.

Art historians have long recognized the link between the visual and sport, but sports historians have been slower to come to terms with art as a source material. However, as part of the visual turn, some sports historians have begun to use artworks as sources, most significantly the American sports historian Allen Guttmann, who, in his book *Sports and American Art: From Benjamin West to Andy Warhol* (2011), describes how artists have portrayed some four centuries of American sport. Additionally, material such as photographs and film allows us to appreciate how the past looked (but bear in mind that both can be doctored). Indeed, both film and photographs confirm the very existence of the past, and film has the added dimension of movement, the body in action being a central feature of sport. A collection of stereo photographs in the Amsterdam City Archives shot in quick succession in 1890 has enabled the reconstruction of an entire skating movement, something that was not available on film at the time.

Yet, like newspaper text, visual works must be interpreted. Sports historians should be aware that the 'visual gaze' often needs to be explained. Why are some items foregrounded, but others left to the margins? Is the picture an artist's interpretation or a realistic scene? Moreover, like photographs, artworks can be manipulated and edited, as in the painting of the Roses rugby match in 1893 by William Barnes Wollen, which hangs at Twickenham Stadium, home of the (English) Rugby Football Union (RFU). Clearly he applied artistic licence since, although it was raining on match day, both the players and the pitch appear dry. Moreover, at least two of the players depicted did not participate in the game, and the faces of several spectators were replaced by those of RFU officials. The painting was lost to public view for some sixty years, and after its discovery in a second-hand shop in Newcastle in 1957 a myth developed that players who had defected to the breakaway Northern Union in 1895 had been painted out of the picture. Historians who have traced the men taking part reckon that if that were the case there would have been only two players left on the pitch. In fact, the picture was completed before

Skating in Amsterdam in the 1880s.

William Wollen's depiction of the Roses rugby match of 1893.

the split occurred. There is certainly a 'ghost' player who came to light when the RFU had the painting cleaned, but the most likely explanation is that Wollen had forgotten to include the match referee and hence had to remove a player to put in George Rowland Hill – who, incidentally, did not actually referee the game, but *was* RFU Secretary.

Other visual evidence includes inn signs that often reflect the way of life, both past and present, and thus may offer clues to the sporting connections of the public house in a particular area. Yet care must be taken in their interpretation, since not all are what they might seem, the animal ones especially. Many bears, boars, bulls, falcons, greyhounds and hawks are representative of the coats of arms of local nobility rather than animals of sport. Cock Inns might indicate fighting cocks or the provision of cockshying, in which tethered birds had sticks thrown at them, but could also refer to the spigot on a barrel of ale or even have religious connotations. Geographical semantics mean that bull is sometimes indicative of Boulogne – as in Bull and Mouth (Boulogne Mouth) for the entry to the French harbour – rather than the animal subjected to baiting.

It has been suggested that fiction could be a valuable source, since it is a cultural force that has shaped how people understand the world around them. Yet sports historians have been reluctant to use such sources, viewing them as unreliable and subjective. Nevertheless, works of fiction, particularly those written in the period being studied, can cast light on the context in which sport took place. Literary texts can moreover add colour and give insights into matters on which conventional sources are opaque, in particular the role of sport in everyday life. They can also communicate the passion and emotion of sport, something that is lacking in most academic histories.

With the exception of scholars examining preliterate and classical societies, to whom history by artefact is almost a default position, sports historians have generally been ambivalent about using material culture as exploratory or explanatory devices. Sports museums, in contrast, make material culture the basis of their exhibitions and communication with the public. Sports historians generally need to appreciate the validity as evidence of artefacts of all sorts, including costumes and equipment, sporting venues and landscapes, and trophies and prizes. That said, Cait Murphy has recently written a history of American sports based on objects including statues, medals, equipment and costume, bricks, soil and even a brain scan, titled *A History of American Sports in 100 Objects* (2016).

USING EVIDENCE

Two further points can be made about evidence and its use. First, sports historians should bear in mind the files they did not track down in the archives and the memories that oral testimony did not reveal. By default, existing evidence is generally prioritized over missing evidence; one is seen as factual, the other as fictional. Reasoned and plausible speculation based on fragmentary evidence is one thing; assertion when there is no evidence is quite another. Nevertheless, I stress that reasoned speculation is not a historical truth, but a hypothesis awaiting testing by further evidence. This, of course, is the nature of much historical revisionism. Second, I have a strong aversion to the approach of those sports historians who practise what I call 'reverse research', in which they know what they want to conclude and so search solely for evidence that will support it. The data may be sound, but not the methodology. Contrary evidence must be explained, not ignored. There are also those who fall into the fallacy of writing history backwards, assuming that there must be a link between present-day sport and that in the period they are examining.

Evidence should also be contextualized. One of my favourite football scores is Hibernian 3, Rangers 2. That Scottish FA Cup final result in 2016 is sports history, or at least an uncontested sports history fact.

Sports journalists might add life to the score by noting that trams – the main mode of public transport when Hibs had last won the cup, in 1902 – had just returned to the capital; and that Rangers, smarting from being declared insolvent and as a consequence relegated to the lower divisions of the Scottish Football League, were seeking the first major trophy of their new existence. Yet sports historians could contextualize it even further. They might note that Hibernian was founded as a Catholic club, whereas for over a century until the 1980s Rangers had never knowingly selected a Catholic player. They might compare the crowd invasion at the end of the match with that of 1909, when Rangers and Celtic fans fought each other, destroyed the goalposts, set fire to parts of the ground and attacked police and fire officers.

Another example where context can illuminate an argument concerns the golfer Harry Vardon, the Tiger Woods of his day. His biography contributes to the understanding of an early champion golfer troubled by tuberculosis and marital difficulties. Although interesting, it is more useful as sports history if it is contextualized into asking if tuberculosis was an industrial disease of professional golfers and whether the marriage problems emanated from the time he spent away from home making a living as an elite professional, designing courses and playing in championships. These queries could be followed up statistically: how many other golfers had that illness, and how did this relate to the general population?; How much time did top professional golfers spend on the road? Good sports history looks at more than the ludic; it contextualizes events by placing them in a wider social, political, economic or cultural environment. Sports historians should not focus too much on events within sport but rather look for the wider implications of their studies beyond the boundaries of sporting practices. The idea of historical context requires historians to understand and consider the broader dimensions in which events occur, and not only to ponder how contemporary observers saw the world but to develop an appreciation for the way in which past cultures made sense of their realities.

APPROACHES TO SPORTS HISTORY

The world of sports history is one of plurality, reflecting the fact that history is contested terrain. It has increasingly been recognized that we can have sports history from different perspectives, involving diverse interrogations and interpretations of the source material. Evidence can be seen from different viewpoints and approached using different techniques. There are dichotomies between those who opt for quantification and those who prefer a qualitative approach; between those who seek information at the aggregate level (often the quantifiers) and those who look at the individual (mainly the non-statistical historians); between those who apply theory and theoretical concepts and those who are more empirically focused; and between those who pose modern questions in a historical setting and those who try to understand what mattered to people in the past, bearing in mind that what we call history or the past was once the present. No topic in sports history will ever be exhaustively researched, partly because, as the cultural and academic climate changes, new ways of looking at historical issues are formulated and new concepts are developed. Historical knowledge is always provisional.

Despite my emphasis on evidence, there is certainly a role for theory in sports history. Indeed, I believe theory is central to understanding the social science and history of sport. Some sports historians, particularly those from a social history background, have applied theory explicitly in their work, notably the theory of the European philosophers Antonio Gramsci, Michel Foucault and Pierre Bourdieu, joining those who earlier had implicitly used the ideas of Karl Marx. Economic historians of sport have always worked in an economically theoretical framework. Nevertheless it is true that few sports historians explicitly discuss theoretical issues, although many of them are aware of theoretical concepts and theories such as modernization, materialism, hegemony, structuration, feminism, discourse and textualism, which they use to inform their work and help them to make their explanations and arguments. Class, status and power have featured in sports history for a long time, and as new conceptual issues have emerged on the socio-political agenda they have been taken up by some sports historians. One problem with attempting to apply theory is that there is sometimes an unwillingness to challenge that theory when it does not align with the information in the archives. No theory is immutable. Sports historians must be prepared not only to use theory, but to adapt and modify it. Until substantiated by evidence, theories are just competing hypotheses; they might aid our understanding, but they do not explain a situation completely. Empirical support is a necessary concomitant for accepting any hypothesis. I see no place in sports history for anyone who accepts a theory in its entirety and then slavishly and uncritically applies it with a 'one theory fits all situations' mentality.

LIES, DAMN LIES AND BATTING AVERAGES

There are many ways to conduct sports history. Personally, I am a numbers man (although innumerate readers need not panic – statistics will be used sparingly in this volume). There are two situations where the use of numbers is almost inevitable. One is financial information, which must involve figures. The other is that the establishment of growth or decline in any variable requires figures to justify the direction of change. I also believe that statistics can be important more generally. Argument by example is no substitute for the use of hard, quantified data; statistics provide a sounder basis for historical assertion, and measurement can allow historians to be more precise in their answers. Statistics can be used descriptively, to set the historical scene and show the (relative) importance of the particular incident, event or theme being studied; for example, studying the environmental impact of golf will be enhanced by a preliminary discussion in statistical terms of the number of golfers, the growth rate in participation and the consequent rise in demand for golf facilities. Unfortunately, non-quantifying sports historians sometimes implicitly use statistics, often in a cavalier manner. Every time historians make a claim of 'many' or 'most', they are implying (usually erroneously) that they have done some counting. Too often a few examples have shown something that is seized on as being typical without the additional spadework necessary to justify such a statement. Isolated examples can offer support, but no reputable scientist or social scientist would accept results based on one or two tests, so, similarly, sports historians should not use a handful of examples to make sweeping claims. Ultimately, the calculations may back up the initial idea . . . but they may not. Numbers enable us to get beyond impressions.

However, any quantified data, like other source material, must pass the authenticity and validity tests, and users should not offer spurious precision to several decimal places. Less numerate readers should be cautioned that small numerical differences may not be significant to the conclusion of any debate. Numbers are the essence of that history that looks at collective experiences, such as sports crowds or groups of professional players, but this quantification might be seen as less necessary by those researchers more concerned with the experience of the individual. In seeking to generalize, aggregation can marginalize those who do not fit the standard pattern, those who are in effect statistical outliers. Clearly, pioneers in any area of sport are likely to be such outliers.

The early use of computers by historians was for number-crunching. My own involvement in the 1970s was to recalculate the price of English corn to show that the 'official' price, used to determine the sliding scale of import duties in the nineteenth century, had a statistical flaw. This necessitated inputting about two hundred weekly market prices for three different grains over a period of thirty years. Government policy based on dubious statistics: it couldn't happen today! The new digital world promises much more. It is clear that the digitization of the archive (widely defined to include newspapers and magazines as well as conventional sources such as correspondence and diaries) offers sports historians access to unprecedented amounts of research material. Of course this material did exist before, but now it can be imported to the researchers' desks via their computers. There, keywords can be typed and years of issues searched much more quickly than in the past, when archives had to be physically visited and pages turned by gloved hand. On the downside, today the researcher can miss the serendipity that this sometimes yielded as the eye caught an unexpected headline. One thing to be careful about is the choice of keyword, since the artificial intelligence of the digital system is not yet able to read minds and cannot distinguish ethnic 'race' from horse 'race' or foot 'race'. And, as with all historical evidence, computerized information is only as good as the data inputted. What demographic historian in the future will discover that my middle name is actually 'Nil', since it was only by rechristening myself that I could persuade Her Majesty's Revenue and Customs to accept the electronic form I was submitting!

WHERE NEXT?

Digitization can go beyond the static cache of archived documents and become part of the archive itself, often a dynamic one that reveals the complex range of possible arguments by inviting the digital audience to engage with the evidence. Social media in the form of fan sites, blogs,

Twitter and so on provides a voice to many who might not have been heard a generation ago. Whether they are all worth listening to is another matter. Allowing anyone and everyone to have their say may satisfy equity expectations, but it is not the way to advance historical knowledge. Too much of what purports to be open-access sports history is assertion and opinion unsubstantiated by evidence. This is not to decry non-academic amateur historians, many of whom offer solid empirical sports history studies. My real issue is with those who allow personal and political prejudice to outweigh historical evidence, or who ignore evidence altogether. Others, probably the majority, generalize from a single historical example, unaware that it might not be representative. Nevertheless, social media creates true public history by providing a dynamic site of discussion, constituting a communication tool that can engage communities. Wikipedia, for example, claims to harness the wisdom of the crowd. Yet, as with any source, academic historians must use it with caution, because the production of knowledge can in fact be dominated by special-interest groups or by one or two individuals.

Despite my best endeavours, the statistical approach to sports history has fallen into disfavour. In a host of academic areas, including sports history, there has been a shift away from quantification to the qualitative. Developments in historical methodology, particularly those methods referred to in epistemological shorthand as the 'cultural turn', have influenced sports historians to a greater or lesser extent. The cultural turn embraces a host of sports history approaches, including the use of literature, high art, radio broadcasts, cinematic representations and aspects of popular culture. This 'new' approach contends that the past contains a variety of discourses, competing truths and power dynamics that scholars must sort out.

Cultural history, which currently dominates academic sports history, has strong links with social history, out of which sports history emerged in the 1960s as part of the 'history from below' movement. It tends to focus on why people believe themselves to be doing what they do, and looks at feelings, emotions and attitudes. Sport can excite the senses and invoke the memory: the smell of liniment in the changing room; the sound of bat hitting ball; the taste of the half-time orange; the touch of the ritual handshake before competition; and the sight of the flag fluttering on the golf green. Emotion is a central element of sporting experience.

What happens in sport can engage the individual psyche or inflame the psychological urges of millions. Unfortunately for the historian, emotions do not come neatly organized in archival form, ready to be downloaded to show what it was like to be a passionate baseball supporter in the 1890s or a bare-knuckle fighter in the 1820s. Historians must somehow develop strategies for reading the emotional parameters of sports. They must search for new source material, perhaps in match programmes, the local press, diaries and novels, to excavate the sporting sensibilities of past generations. What we have to bear in mind is that what is history to us was life to them.

PART TWO

SPORT THROUGH
THE AGES

This section will discuss broad sweeps of sport practice and development over two millennia or more. The first chapter takes us from antiquity through the medieval period, the Renaissance and the Enlightenment, arriving at the beginnings of industrialization. It demonstrates that sport was not invented in modern times, although sports historians have tended to focus on that period to the relative neglect of both the classical and pre-modern eras. Ironically classicists, who study ancient Greece and Rome, actually come from one branch of history that has embraced sport as a subject. What we must note is that we are less aware of the extent of sport, especially for the lower classes, the further back in time we go, simply because earlier sports are less well documented than later ones.

Then comes a chapter dealing with the period when the Western world industrialized. It examines, and dismisses, the idea that modern sport was invented in Britain and then exported elsewhere. Nevertheless, it sees modernization as the underlying force behind the emergence of workplace participatory sport, mass spectator sport, the expansion of commercialism and professionalism, and the creation of amateurism in reaction to modernization in sport and in society.

The final chapter in this section looks at major changes in the sporting landscape since the First World War. During this period cultural shifts influenced change in the format and character of many sports. Who in 1920 would have believed that one day the United

States would win the Women's World Soccer Championship, or indeed that such a tournament would even exist? What cricket fan would have envisaged switching on an electronic device to watch one-day games in India and Afghanistan, or that the headquarters of that sport would now be in Dubai? Who would have imagined that the Olympic Games would have been hosted in Rio de Janeiro and would have featured golf, synchronized swimming, mountain biking, taekwondo and the triathlon?

It is acknowledged that the time frame adopted is essentially a Westernized one, charting the development of sport in Europe and its dissemination from there to other regions. However, I hope due recognition is made to indigenous sports in the non-Western world, something that will be returned to at the close of the book.

3

SPORT BEFORE THE
INDUSTRIAL AGE

S port may well pre-date literacy. We simply do not know. Even when
societies became literate, given the paucity of surviving written
information, we have to rely on relief sculptures and painted wall
art in ancient Egypt and urn decoration and sculptures in classical
Greece for depictions of sporting activities about whose function we can
only speculate.

When cultures disappear their sports go with them, and we are left
with only fragmented evidence; we no longer know how these sports
were played or what the motivation was for participation. Were the youths
vaulting over bulls in ancient Crete performing acrobatics for amusement, or as an initiation rite, or as part of a religious ceremony? Similarly,
we rarely know if the footballer sacrificed on the temple altar in pre-
conquistador Mexico was on the winning or the losing side, or why anyone
had to die after a sporting event. A major difficulty when studying antiquity is distinguishing myth and belief from historical evidence, since the
two were closely intertwined in Greek and Roman life.

What we can say with more certainty is that at times in ancient Egypt
the pharaoh had to perform a physical sporting act to demonstrate his
continued ability to rule as protector of his people. He had to run between
two semicircles about 55 m (180 ft) apart, a feat that also served to renew
his divine power. Whether this was strictly sport is arguable, but it was
physical activity, albeit not too taxing, involving a challenge. Other sports
in ancient Egypt, the ancient Levant and later in ancient Greece and

imperial Rome had distinct martial functions. In the period immediately before the 18th Dynasty (*c.* 1539–1292 BCE) Egypt was ruled by foreign conquerors, the Hyksos, who had used chariots and longbows to gain victory. Once they had been driven out, succeeding pharaohs, aware of the military application, encouraged archery and chariot racing.

We know little about Greek sport before the eighth century BCE, although frescoes in two different regions at two different times during the Bronze Age (3200–1050 BCE) depict bull-leaping (although we do not know its rationale) and boxing. Then, for three centuries or so, we have no extant evidence on any sport until the poems of Homer (although of course no one is sure when he lived), which mention chariot racing, running, wrestling, boxing, throwing weights and throwing the discus. The eighth century BCE brought the first Olympic Games, which – perhaps surprisingly – can be dated specifically to 776 BCE and was held at Elis in the Peloponnese, about 190 km (120 mi.) from Mount Olympus. For the first 48 years the only event was the stadion, a short foot race. However, by 468 BCE the Games were lasting five days and included three running events (but no marathon, which is a modern invention), boxing, wrestling, pankration (a combination of wrestling and boxing in which only biting, gouging and attacking the genitals were barred), chariot racing, horse racing and the pentathlon, consisting of javelin, discus, long jump, running and wrestling.

Other athletic festivals also developed, and by the sixth century BCE a sequence of four major events had been established. The Olympics and the Pythian Games (at Delphi) were held every four years and the Nemean Games (at Nemea) and the Isthmian Games (at Isthmia) every two years. There were many less prestigious events, as well, and when ancient Greek athletics reached its peak in the second century BCE, there were hundreds of athletic festivals, many with stadia specifically built to accommodate them, around the Mediterranean and Near Eastern world. It should be noted that Greeks lived in perhaps a thousand autonomous communities stretching from what is now the east coast of Spain to what is now southern Ukraine.

These games were primarily religious events, each presided over by a god. Olympia was a walled sanctuary (the Altis) in honour of Zeus, with a stadium attached. The Altis was dominated by a huge temple housing a statue of Zeus surrounded by statues erected by athletes in thanks for

Panathenaic prize amphora featuring runners, 332–333 BCE.
Artist's impression of ancient Olympia, 1891.

their victories, as well as gymnasia, baths and hotels. Athletes accepted that victory was divinely ordained, and successful ones offered gifts to the deities for their perceived help. In contrast to the modern Olympic creed, in which the emphasis is on taking part – on the struggle, rather than the triumph – the ancient Greeks only liked winners. Only victors counted; the gods did not support losers. To the winners went olive leaves, oil, occasionally even money, and kudos; the losers got nothing, no fame, no fortune and no record of their performance.

The prevailing view today is that all Greek elite performers were professional, not in the sense of sport being their full-time occupation on which they relied for income, but in that they competed for prizes, some of which could be valuable. Using assumptions that minimized the value (such as the lowest price of oil and the highest wage), the historian David Young calculated that the one hundred amphoras awarded to the victor in the foot race at the Panathenaic Games in classical Greece represented 847 days' wages for a skilled craftsman of the time, and could have bought half a dozen slaves or possibly a house. Not all prizes were at that level. Lesser ones might be an oxhide or an animal that could be sacrificed. Yet, especially when we move forward into the Hellenistic period (after the death of Alexander the Great in 323 BCE), some were even more valuable and all were tax-free.

Some professionals could be full-time. There were enough festivals for freelance professionals to undertake tours in which they combined a number of local games with one of the more significant, and possibly highly lucrative, events. Evidence indicates that both individuals and, especially, states sponsored or subsidized talented athletes and – in the case of the more successful, who brought renown to their city – offered public pensions after they retired from competitive sport. Additionally, so keen were some states to gain victories that they persuaded star performers

Not in the Greek lexicon

'I can find no evidence of amateurism in Greek sources, no reference to amateur athletes – no evidence that the concept "amateurism" was even known in antiquity. The truth is that "amateur" is one thing for which the Greeks never even had a word.'

David Young, *The Olympic Myth of Greek Amateur Athletes* (Chicago, IL, 1984), p. 7

to change their citizenship with offers too good to refuse except by the most loyal.

The Olympic Games gave Greeks from across the Hellenic diaspora an opportunity to reinforce their cultural identity by coming to the motherland. So many attended that in the fifth century BCE a new stadium was constructed to hold more than 40,000 spectators, in a relatively isolated spot in the northwestern corner of the Peloponnese. Participants, too – provided they could establish their Hellenic credentials – travelled from afar. Although the records are incomplete, they show that between 480 and 324 BCE winning athletes came from 65 different communities not just in the Greek homeland but also in southern Italy, Sicily, north Africa and Asia Minor.

Following its defeat at the Battle of Corinth in 146 BCE, Greece became part of the Roman Empire. Yet, despite being ruled by Rome, much of Greek culture remained the same and the Olympic Games continued to be held. Some later Roman emperors, who admired Greek culture, revived the splendour of the Games and restored the site and buildings, but by the third century CE the lists of victors are increasingly uncertain and incomplete, and by the end of that century they stop altogether. When the Roman emperors adopted Christianity they discouraged and, eventually, outlawed old 'pagan' religious practices, including the Olympic Games. Under Christianity, sporting time and sacred time were no longer allowed to coincide. The emperor Theodosius I formally abolished the Games in 393 or 394 CE.

At grass-roots level, from the sixth century BCE Greeks used gymnasia and *palaistrai* (smaller, privately owned facilities) for daily exercises and for the physical education of young male citizens, most of whom would never compete at major athletic contests. They exercised and trained for personal enjoyment, not to secure sporting victories. In the Roman world, of which more will follow, the bathhouses with their exercise yards (*palaestrae*) performed a similar function. By the fourth century BCE sport was part of civic life in the *polis*, the city-state that was the characteristic Greek political form. Cities built gymnasia, which became places not just for physical recreation and exercise but for intellectual pursuits including reading, writing, music and philosophy.

This has led to a serious misconception in our interpretation of Greek culture. Many people know – at least, they did before Latin was downgraded in the curriculum – the phrase *mens sana in corpore sano*, a sound mind in a healthy body. It allegedly highlighted the ancient Greeks' attitude to sport, one in which the intellect was cultivated as well as the body. Such an idea is epitomized in the athletic career of the famous philosopher Plato, who was credited with winning wrestling tournaments at the Pythian, Nemean and Isthmian games, where competition was restricted to a dozen or so of the best wrestlers in Greece. The phrase later became a slogan for those who idealized the athletic system of ancient Greece: for Pierre de Coubertin when promoting the idea of a modern Olympic Games; for Avery Brundage when cementing his long-time presidency of the IOC; and for countless others who extolled amateur sport in the nineteenth and twentieth centuries, but who – ironically – were probably unaware of the extent of professionalism among classical Greek sportsmen.

David Young has explored how the phrase came to be associated with ancient Greek athletes, considering that there is no contemporary evidence whatsoever that they ever cultivated both mind and body. His research has exposed the false notions behind what has become conventional wisdom. He shows that scholars who developed these ideas relied on dubious sources, often written long after the events in question (including one written in medieval times), and then embellished their 'findings'. Young found the concept of an ancient Greek intellectual scholar to be pure myth. There is not a single word in any ancient Greek text to support the idea. Not one of the thousand or so victors at the Olympic or Pythian games was ever noted for any intellectual achievement. No Greek prominent in the intellectual world ever won a major athletic event; Plato wrestled solely at his local gymnasium. Young argues that the archaic and early classical Greeks admired both physical and mental excellence, but that the two were not expected in the same individual. His work demonstrates the importance of consulting reliable sources and the difficulty in eradicating an invented tradition.

The phrase *mens sana in corpore sano* acquired its modern usage only in the mid-Victorian era. It was originally a call neither for academic excellence nor for sporting prowess, but simply for health. It appears in the work of the Roman satirist Juvenal, who denounced those who prayed for power, fame or longevity and suggested instead that they should pray for general good health, for a sound mind in a sound body.

Perhaps someone should have noticed that the phrase was in Latin – not a language the ancient Greeks were conversant with!

This brings us to the topic of sport in imperial Rome. By the beginning of the Common Era, the city-state of Rome had become the centre of an empire, one that encompassed the entire ancient Mediterranean and the diverse sporting cultures within its boundaries. Rome itself had early on developed particular sporting practices that merged and changed when they met other cultures, so that by the first century CE a peculiarly Roman sporting practice had been established. Whereas participation in athletics was a component of Greek identity, it was sports spectatorship that identified the Roman. What stands out were two major spectator sports, gladiatorial combat and chariot racing, the former especially a mass cultural phenomenon in the ancient Roman world.

The thousands of spectators who flocked to the Colosseum in Rome in the first century CE to watch a day of gladiatorial combat – in the morning men hunting and slaughtering wild animals, and in the afternoon men with sword and shield against opponents perhaps with net and trident, the two sessions punctuated by the midday execution of criminals – were not paying for their pleasure. This day of thrills and deaths would have been funded by a patron. Roman sporting events, like the Greek ones that had preceded them, were virtually always communal occasions with funding often provided by priests, who were required or expected to present gladiatorial performances, or by a wealthy donor hoping to build goodwill with the community, so charging for entry was contrary to purpose. Indeed, in many cases sporting events were combined with 'giveaways' of various kinds, such as feasts for all comers. The men who vied for consulships and other elected offices had to win the favour of voters, and accepted ways of doing so included the sponsorship of games. Given that there was no pricing system, segregation was maintained by law, with sections of amphitheatres reserved for different categories of socio-economic status. Senators and other high-ranking individuals received preferential seating at the front of the stands, thus not only gaining an unimpeded view of the action but being put on display before the rest of the crowd. When power became more centralized in the emperor, sponsorship became his prerogative (at least in Rome itself), and, set apart in a special box in the Colosseum, he presented himself to his subjects while also demonstrating his power over life and death by granting or denying life to defeated gladiators.

The profit-makers in all this were gladiatorial managers who ran establishments of fighters and hired them out to promoters organizing combat. They paid a hiring fee of between 10 and 20 per cent of the gladiator's value, but had to pay the full cost if he were killed or seriously wounded. The gladiatorial managers insisted on sureties for this eventuality, and a system developed of the promoters using financial middlemen who, presumably for a fee, would offer credit sufficient to cover such mishaps. Thanks to the imperial imposition of price control in 177 CE, we know that gladiators were valued at between 3,000 and 15,000 sesterces, depending on rank. The hierarchy was determined by the gladiator managers, who had an obvious incentive to inflate the grades, but against that, if the fighters did not perform at the expected level the reputation of the stable would suffer, with consequent deleterious market effects. Additionally, by law, the promotions required gladiators from all ranks to be supplied, so it was in each manager's interest to have a portfolio of combatants of varying skill and qualities.

The gladiators were highly trained, skilled, professional sportsmen. With few exceptions, they were not free citizens, but rather condemned criminals, prisoners of war, slaves or freeborn men who had sold themselves to pay debts. There was a career structure based on a system of ranking, and a new entrant, if successful, could work up four ranked grades to become valued at 15,000 sesterces. As well as being housed and fed by the stable manager, win or lose they were entitled to 20 per cent of their hiring fee as a wage, often obtained a share of any prize money awarded, and could also receive presents from fans or gamblers; the ultimate gift was their freedom. Some freed gladiators continued to fight, negotiating their terms directly with the promoters. On the basis of sweeping assumptions and a conflation of gladiatorial experiences from 177 CE with wage information for 301 CE, a middle-ranked gladiator earned perhaps 2,000 sesterces for a bout, equating to roughly fourteen days' wages for an unskilled labourer – although, as far as we are aware, the gladiator had few living costs to cover.

Contrary to popular assumption, gladiators did not normally fight to the death. Gladiatorial bouts were stylized fights that, although real and with violent consequences, were as much performances as competitions, rather like the present-day World Wrestling Entertainment (WWE) fights. Combat was controlled by referees and conventions of fighting, and losers did not necessarily die. Death was certainly a possibility in a fight between trained combatants with real weaponry, but a gladiator could submit and ask for mercy, a request that was often granted by the wealthy Roman citizen who had organized and paid for the rented fighters, since it saved them money. Fewer gladiators were therefore killed than has been commonly supposed, and a few exceptional characters fought more than fifty times, although most top-ranked gladiators participated in fewer than twenty combats. Taking twenty bouts as a norm and applying the highest hiring rate available, career earnings come to just 60,000 sesterces, less than two years' wages for an unskilled worker: scant reward for risking life and limb, but sufficient perhaps to buy his freedom if that was an objective.

Chariot races were associated with regularly occurring religious festivals and, where possible, were held in purpose-built facilities known as circuses, hence Juvenal's famous phrase that the population could be kept happy by the provision of 'bread and circuses'. The circuses themselves were huge arenas with seating for thousands of spectators, and there were dozens of them throughout the Roman Empire. The most famous, the Circus Maximus in Rome, was both a sporting facility and a political showpiece, especially after being reconstructed in monumental fashion during the ascendancy of Julius Caesar, in 49–44 BCE, when large sections of stone seating were added and the line that separated the two sections of the track – the *spina* – was decorated with treasures from Rome's imperial conquests.

The race meetings could last for several days, offering excitement, danger and the opportunity to gamble. Staging the chariot races was the responsibility of four racing teams, factions identified by their colours of blue, green, red and white. They began as independent contractors but became controlled by the emperor himself in the later years of the empire. From the faction leader and team manager to charioteers, apprentices, veterinarians, farriers, grooms, cobblers and more, the factions were self-contained entities that dealt with every aspect of preparing a team of horses for the track; they procured the horses, maintained the stables, trained the drivers and provided the chariots. In the Greek world the horses, charioteers and jockeys were a symbol of the owner's prestige; in the Roman world the charioteers and their horses were the public face of a sports business. Charioteers and their horses became celebrities in their own right, commemorated with monuments and epigrams. They were almost exclusively low-born, but, as with gladiators, those who were slaves could earn their freedom by their success as performers, and all drivers who survived the dangers of the racetrack could do well financially out of the prize money they won. A prime example was the charioteer Diocles, who was born in a Roman province of the Iberian Peninsula, and, during a 24-year career, won 1,462 of his 4,257 races and accumulated over 35 million sesterces.

AWAY FROM EUROPE

Much Western scholarship relating to sport in the ancient world has focused on Europe and the Near East, but as far as we can surmise, games were played everywhere. Let us briefly turn to a couple of areas, pre-Columbian Mesoamerica (present-day Mexico and Central America) and ancient China.

More than 1,300 stone stadia, from central Mexico to El Salvador and western Honduras, discovered by archaeologists show that the Olmec civilization of Mesoamerica played games with balls made of rubber (an indigenous product), either with sticks or using various parts of the body, depending on regional custom. The earliest evidence of the Mesoamerican rubber-ball game comes from the Mexican highlands in the period 1500–1200 BCE. The nature of the game has been surmised from ceramic figures, low-relief sculptures, wall paintings and remnants of markers and rings in the playing areas. Succeeding civilizations, foremost among them the Maya, Toltec, Mixtec, Zapotec and Aztec, continued the ancient tradition and made the game into a powerful religious ritual with severe consequences for the players. For its participants this Mesoamerican ball game could be a matter of life and death, since human sacrifice sometimes accompanied the games, although patterns of execution varied from culture to culture. Mayan accounts describe death penalties carried out immediately after the games, sometimes for the captain of the losing side, sometimes for the entire losing squad, sometimes for the captain of the winning side, and on rare occasions for the entire winning team. Sacrifice was important in all religions of Mesoamerica. It was believed that human blood was necessary for the continuity of the universe, sustaining the sun and warding off the forces of darkness.

The ball court at Chichén Itzá, Mexico, the largest in ancient Mesoamerica.
A goal in the Chichén Itzá ball court.

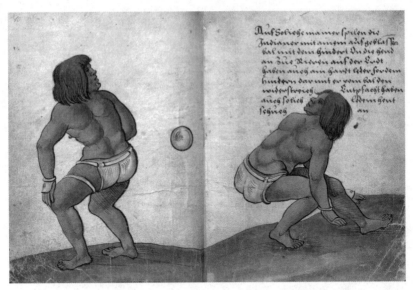

Aztec ball players performing for Charles v in Spain.

Documents from the period of the conquest indicate that the game was played by nearly all adolescent and adult males, both commoners and nobles. The latter often played on monumental courts in ceremonial centres. Such was the extent of the game that in Aztec times some 16,000 balls were imported annually from the rubber-tree growing areas in the lowlands to the Aztec capital of Tenochtitlán.

The size of the arenas that held the ball courts indicates that the ball games were not mass spectator sports, but provided both in the game and the accompanying pageantry a symbolic re-enactment of the myth of the Maya Hero Twins, often seen as complementary forces such as day and night, moon and sun, or sky and earth. They also presented an opportunity for gambling. The games, like many other indigenous sports, failed to survive the Columbian exchange – the widespread transfer of plants, culture, human populations, technology and ideas between the Americas, West Africa and the Old World in the fifteenth and sixteenth centuries – which brought Spanish rule and Christianity to Mesoamerica.

Other sports on which we have more than minimal information include *pelota mixteca* (which resembled European real tennis), in which teams wearing padded gloves propelled a ball back and forth; and *los voladores* (the flyers), in which four participants climbed to the top of a tall pole and then, tied to ropes coiled around the pole, leapt from the top

Figure of a *pelota* player.
Nineteenth-century game of chinlone, also known as caneball.

and spun around the pole, flying outwards from it until they reached the ground. There were also running sports as practised by the Tarahumara people from the state of Chihuahua, who traditionally ran long distances in hunting deer or delivering messages. Men often ran team races that could last all day and even overnight, in which they had to kick a hand-carved wooden ball without using their hands, while women participated in races propelling a handmade ring using sticks.

Archaeological excavation in Asia has suggested that chinlone, a traditional caneball sport in Myanmar, dates back to the second century BCE. How it was played at that time is, however, unknown. Documents from the tenth century CE present it as a non-competitive game in which the players had to keep the ball up in the air using only their legs and feet. There is a significant problem in ascertaining the nature of sport in Asia two or more millennia ago. We do know that many 'traditional' Asian sports were reinvented in the nineteenth and twentieth centuries to promote cultural nationalism and, more recently, to attract tourists. They were simulations rather than authentic products. Whether others were passed on unchanged through the generations via oral testimony is debatable. From the experiences of European countries that have been researched more thoroughly in the West, it is unlikely that there was a long, unchanging history with an unbroken lineage over such a long period. So what we think we know about early Asian sport is mainly conjectural and, to a degree, based on evidence from later times. The existence of early Asian sport can be established, less so its practice.

Another problem we face is that we do not know the extent to which ideas about sport or even the sports themselves were transmitted across Asia. Murals from the Koguryǒ dynasty (37 BCE–668 CE) in Korea depict wrestling and striking poses, but they seem to mimic earlier Chinese murals, suggesting a Chinese origin for these physical activities.

In the period 700–300 BCE China was characterized by the rise of city-states that, although ultimately incorporated into a larger empire, developed political relationships with each other. Confucius noted that among the essential diplomatic skills for the educated elites at this time were two sports, archery and chariot driving. The dominance of Confucian culture (in which exercise was seen as an educative tool) led to Chinese sport shedding any earlier competitiveness in favour of an emphasis on harmony of movement. Under Confucianists physical culture was designed to reinforce moral values and serve as a cohesive ritual to help maintain the status quo, and so most sports became recreational, non-competitive physical activities. Archery, for example, had been competitively organized at first, but it began to emphasize social status

Wushu at the 2005 National Games of China.

rather than the shooting performance of the participants, with distinctive equipment allocated strictly according to the social quality of the shooters.

Other ancient Chinese sports about which we have information include racing on stilts, which has been traced to two and a half millennia ago, dragon-boat racing, first recorded in 400 BCE, kite flying, a form of football called *cuju*, wrestling and *wushu*, covering a variety of martial arts. Cuju dates back to the thirteenth century BCE and began as an aggressively competitive game, often used by military mandarins to develop the fighting spirit of their troops and improve their physical condition. Two thousand years later vigorous competition had declined and the game had become gentler, its prime objectives now grace and harmony of movement. Wrestling had a long history, too, with one early version (*jiao li* or *juedixi*) imitating the way bulls butted their horns. The sport achieved its greatest popularity during the Song Dynasty (960–1279 CE) with the development of professional wrestling tournaments. There were even female wrestlers, although they were entertainers rather than competitors, sometimes wrestling naked to attract spectators. Criticism from orthodox Confucianists eventually led to women wrestlers being banned. Wushu, still practised today, covered a wide spectrum of martially inspired practices based on the fighting methods of particular animals. Feudal China had many tribes, each of which appears to have had its own version, rules and styles.

One interesting suggestion that requires more research is that ancient China did not demonstrate insular exceptionalism but was influenced by contact with central Asians who had been Hellenized in the easternmost part of the former Macedonian empire. These Asian rulers trained in gymnastics and employed wrestling coaches who had learned their craft in Hellenistic gymnasia. There is support for the hypothesis of Greek/Chinese contact in recent theories about the production of the Chinese warrior sculptures in the Xian tombs, where Hellenic design influences have been noted. Given the Greek emphasis on winning, if the theory of sporting contact holds it may have implications for the view of Chinese sport being non-competitive.

MORE THAN TILTING AT WINDMILLS

One of the most prevalent images of medieval sport is the armoured knight on horseback ready to engage in jousting. Knights also took part

Depiction of jousting, 1568.

in mock battles (melées and tournaments) in which horses, equipment and men could be captured by the winning side. Indeed, knights can be considered professional sportsmen who participated in tournaments not only to maintain their martial skills but also to make material gains. By the early fourteenth century the tournament was an established sporting fixture, and one estimate is that a knight might tourney once a fortnight or so. Some events were large spectacles; that at Lagny-sur-Marne near Paris in 1179 involved about 10,000 participants – some 3,000 knights and their retinues, and the rest fighting mercenaries.

Sport occasionally interrupted war. During the medieval period in Europe the culture of the truce at battles and protracted sieges was often an occasion for sporting or martial contests between besiegers and besieged, as a means of alleviating the tedium and abject misery that plagued (often literally as well as metaphorically) both sides. The most famous examples are the foot combats between the English and French garrisons stationed at Josselin and Ploërmel in Brittany in 1351 and the jousts between the English and French at Saint-Inglevert in 1390, during a year-long truce between the two nations.

Jousting emerged as a separate sport from tournaments. Views on jousting have been revised in recent years, and it is now accepted that, although violent, it was less dangerous than has been previously supposed. Deaths were relatively uncommon but were highlighted by contemporary chroniclers, and the knights involved emphasized the dangers of the sport so as to glamorize their bravery. Indeed, the aim was not to kill or maim one's opponent but to shatter one's lance (made of soft wood designed to splinter on impact, adding to the spectacle) on his shield or armour. The sport varied across Europe, both in eligibility to participate and in objective. Whereas in northern Europe the knightly classes restricted jousting to men who could prove their noble lineage, in Italy, where there was less of a landed feudal hierarchy, jousting was popular among the merchant bourgeoisie and city-dwellers; and in Germanic areas the objective was not to shatter one's lance but to knock an opponent out of a purpose-built, low-canted saddle.

With the spread of projectile warfare (longbow volleys, armour-piercing crossbows and, later, firearms), knightly skills became less useful in battle and tournaments became exhibitions more of horsemanship than of martial ability. Over time the knight was transformed into an elegant courtier. Jousting continued in England until the third decade of the seventeenth century, but had been abandoned on the continent following the death of Henri II in a joust in 1559. It was replaced by other displays of equestrian skill, such as cane-throwing on horseback, which featured on the Iberian Peninsula.

Illuminated manuscripts, other pictorial sources and literary texts all show that medieval people of all classes practised a wide range of ludic physical activities. For example, William Fitzstephen's description

Fourteenth-century female archer shooting at a rabbit.

of London at the end of the twelfth century documented a number of games and activities in which citizens participated, including archery, bear-baiting, cockfighting, football, hunting, ice skating, leaping competitions, stone-throwing and wrestling.

SPORT IN THE PRE-MODERN ERA

The three or four centuries before 1800 are often referred to as the pre-modern era, a time before Western society became industrialized, when agriculture was the dominant economic sector and industry was composed of unmechanized craft activities, and when rural recreation and rural demographics predominated. Sport was linked to agricultural cycles and religious festivals; the limitations of the transport system usually forced sporting encounters to be highly localized; and often there were no precise boundaries to where sporting contests could be played and how long they would last.

Throughout pre-modern Europe a host of sports were pursued, although most Europeans would have labelled them games rather than using the British nomenclature. The Flemish sports historian Roland Renson has categorized them into ball games, bowl and pin games, throwing games, shooting games, fighting games, animal games, locomotion games and acrobatics. Let us look at a few in a little more detail.

Ball games could be played using the hand or foot, or even a batting device. Traditional European team handball games included *pärkspel* on the Swedish island of Gotland, *kaatsen* or *balle pelote* in the Dutch province of Frisia and in Belgium and France, *pallone elastico* in Italy and *pelota* in Spanish Valencia and the Basque country. Football includes the traditional *calcio fiorentino* still played in Florence, although this is today more a tourist attraction than a true competitive sport. Varieties of batting devices were used, including the racquets of the French tennis-style *longue paume* and the sticks of *crosse*, a version of golf played in France and Belgium. Among the bowl and pin games were *ruzzola*, a form of cheese-rolling played in central Italy, in which heavy wooden discs are rolled for distance in a number of throws; *pendelkugeln*, from Germany and Hungary, in which a bowl hanging on a wire is swung at pins; and *beugelen* from the Dutch province of Limburg, in which a shovel-shaped bat is used to roll a heavy, round bowl through an iron ring set into the ground.

Throwing games featured the heavy projectiles of Swedish *varpa*, the quoits of *malha* in Portugal, the logs of *jogo do panco*, also in Portugal, and the *tiro de bola* road bowling of Aragon, Spain. Shooting encompassed among many others the popinjay targets still popular in Flanders and the crossbow festivals of the Italian *balestrieri*. Wrestling, one of the oldest fighting sports, had variations all over Europe, including Icelandic *glima*, Scottish *backhold*, Breton *gouren* and *lucha canaria* from the Canary Islands. French practitioners of *savate* employed both fists, and feet and sticks were used in *la canne*, another French sport, and in *jogo do pau* from Portugal. Jousts held on water featured as *joutes girondines* in the Gironde area of France and *Fischerstechen* in Ulm, Germany. Many animal sports were brutal (to modern eyes) and involved cruelty towards and the death of the designated victim. In Catholic areas geese, ducks or hens were often decapitated, either by having missiles thrown at them or as a result of their necks being grabbed at speed. However, in France and Spain bull-running could also be dangerous, sometimes fatally so, for the human participants. Locomotion sports featured *fierljeppen* (jumping for distance with a fen-pole) in the Dutch province of Frisia and the *salto del pastor* (shepherd's jump) practised in the Canary Islands. Acrobatics included *salto del caballo* (vaulting the horse) in the Aragon region of Spain and *castells* (human pyramids) in Catalonia.

Even these limited examples are illustrative of a general point that differences between countries were more common than similarities. Moreover, the type of skill required varied. Renson has examined four regions in detail, and finds that physical strength was of great importance in the Basque region and in Scotland, but of less importance in Gotland, and never seemed to have a role in Flanders, where precision and agility were emphasized. Clearly, pre-modern Europe exhibited considerable ludodiversity.

All the traditional sports mentioned above were still being practised in the early years of the twenty-first century. A plethora of others, however, had fallen by the wayside, particularly as agriculture declined and, along with it, many rural traditions, especially regional ones. If we look just at Britain, how many readers know much, if anything, about the following half-a-dozen sports that were once popular in particular areas: crimogiant, doddart, schrush, troap, trunket and wallops? Let me enlighten you. Crimogiant was a Welsh version of kick-shins, practised by Pembrokeshire men wearing thick shoes with nails projecting from the sides. Such was their renown at this pursuit that the nickname *crommogwr* (kick-shinner) became used for the county's male inhabitants. Doddart was an early northern version of bandy or hockey played by two teams, employing the doddart, a curved stick, to propel a wooden ball. Schrush was another variant of hockey, played in Dorset using scrushes, sticks with curved ends, to hit a round stone. Troap was for two players; the striker hit a piece of wood called a nacket and the other threw it back as near to the striker as he could, the distance from the striker determining the scoring. Trunket was similar to cricket, but using a short stick as a bat and two holes in the ground instead of wickets; the batsman was out if caught on the full or if the ball was placed in the hole while the batter was running. Finally, wallops was a form of skittles played in northwest Yorkshire, in which a 1.2-metre (4 ft) walloping stick was thrown at nine skittles arranged in a square.

Nevertheless, historians must be careful to find evidence that sports actually existed and were not invented traditions. In 1967 the ancient Suffolk sport of dwile flonking was revived using the Waveney Rules of 1585, by which one team danced to music around an opponent who attempted to throw a beer-soaked cloth at them when the music stopped. In fact, this was a totally fabricated sport whose inventor had exploited imagery and terminology resonant of 'merrie England' as a publicity stunt for a village fete.

Peace was a scarce commodity throughout the pre-modern period, and nations, cities and communities constantly had to be prepared for military action. In mainland Europe sport for defence of the nation was promoted by the state in Prussia, France, Denmark and Sweden, whereas Italians relied on local communes for their defence. Learning to use the crossbow was seen everywhere as a patriotic duty, an obligation transferred to rifle-shooting from the late seventeenth century. On the other side of the Channel, in Scotland the northern burghs regularly held military gatherings for inspection and training purposes. Known as *wappenschaws*, they involved several sports, such as archery, fencing, swimming, jumping, riding, running, wrestling and throwing the bar, all designed to acculturate young men into a form of military masculinity and keep the adult male population physically fit and ready for the king's service. The Scottish kings themselves had Parliamentary legislation passed to keep the Scots war-ready by banning football and encouraging archery, practising with arms and armour, and other martial pursuits.

Some sports remained exclusive to particular social strata. All European elites enjoyed hunting, usually on horseback, but their quarry were animals forbidden to the lower orders, who, in any case, could hunt only on foot on common land. Other sports were the sole province of the lower classes precisely because of their class connotation. Swimming and rowing were skills associated with sailors and watermen, and foot races were for messengers; all these were thus generally not considered appropriate for those of a higher social status. The lower orders might want to imitate their social superiors (indeed, such emulation stimulated the demand for mass production during industrialization), but the reverse was never true. Even when the upper classes shared the pursuits of the lower, it was often temporary, as at festivals and carnival, and always on their own terms. They might watch the same event, but from the grandstand or a private carriage at race meetings or the ringside during prizefights.

The growth of sport in the pre-modern world raised the spectre of disorder, disruption and debauchery, and during the Renaissance occasionally national, more commonly local, civic action was taken against some sports, especially those of the lower classes. Nevertheless, playing sporting games at which skill counted and utilitarian gains could be made in health and military preparations was generally tolerated more than was gaming at dice or cards. What were frowned on were sports where body contact could erupt into mass violence, and those associated with the festive and carnivalesque culture of the time. At carnival societal norms were set aside and authority could be challenged and ridiculed, albeit only briefly. What was feared was not the nature of the sports themselves but the consequences of the emotions they aroused. There was a gradual shift throughout Britain and Europe from a 'festival' culture to a 'leisure' culture, but formal carnival retained its hold in the more Catholic countries, such as Italy, with those held in Genoa, Milan and Rome sometimes including horse racing and that in Venice being associated with a regatta. Additionally, with a rise in sports in urban areas, restrictions began to be placed on facilities, including the licensing of tennis courts and bowling alleys and the prohibition of some street games, as civic authorities aimed to prevent commerce from being impeded and property damaged. Then there was the question of time, particularly involving the honouring of religious obligations on the Sabbath, a concern in England and Scotland especially.

In the eighteenth century three major themes can be identified in the development of sport. First there was the increased role of gambling in the promotion of sport. Of course, any activity in which the result is uncertain could tempt people to wager, but sport had an edge in that it was not usually chance alone that determined victory. Backers would make their own assessments of the relative merits of the participants, and stake their wagers accordingly. Certainly wealthy gamblers in Britain and colonial America promoted matches for betting purposes between horses, cocks, pugilists, wrestlers, runners and cricket teams. The second outstanding feature was the emergence on a larger scale of commercialized sports. This was especially true in Britain, where economic development increased spending power earlier than was the case in Europe. Two groups were prominent here: those in the drink trade, who offered venues for a range of sports, sold alcohol to the spectators and began to charge admission fees; and those in the printing industry, whose expansion enabled sporting events to be advertised, marketed and publicized.

Finally, there were sports clubs, those voluntary associations that helped to construct relationships of rivalry and bonding between males. In Britain in the early eighteenth century a movement began that involved the formation of clubs for many purposes, not least for sports such as cricket, golf, pugilism and horse racing. One view is that modern British sport emerged from this new form of associativity, which developed autonomously in Britain following the state's retreat from the control of associative activities. This was in contrast, it is argued, to the situation in countries such as France and Germany, where the formation of a club continued to require the explicit or implicit approval of the state. There, modern sports developed in ways consistent with the objectives of the state, most notably the need to maintain military preparedness.

To vastly simplify what was a complex scenario that varied across Europe, by the end of the eighteenth century the promotion of health and fitness, the enjoyment of carnival and the preparation for war, while still of some consequence, had lessened in relative significance as reasons for pursuing sport. In contrast, gambling, commercialism and associativity had grown in importance, and were in the vanguard of what was to dominate sport in the next century.

Many traits of modern sport are evident from as early as 1450, and the succeeding two centuries brought many written rulebooks and instruction manuals (important to the standardization and diffusion of sports), the building of dedicated sport spaces, a European-wide trade in sports equipment, and the emergence of a professional class of athletes, coaches and officials. What is not yet clear is whether the examples we know of are precursors rather than initiators, or atypical rather than commonplace, and further research is needed before full support can be given to moving the threshold for the beginnings of modern sport back to before 1800. What can be accepted is that some of the pre-conditions for the emergence of modern sport originated before widespread industrialization, but that its actual take-off may have required further stimuli. Mass spectator sport existed before the end of the eighteenth century, although it was intermittent, often annual at best, since mass markets for paying spectators required not only money and the leisure time in which to spend it, but also a concentration of population and ease of access to venues. Income, even in the eighteenth century, was still low, and many sports events remained dependent on patronage (as they had been in classical Greece and Rome) rather than commercial entrepreneurs. Urbanization, industrialization and the ensuing revolutions in transportation and communications systems would soon produce the necessary conditions for the next step in the commodification of sport.

MEANWHILE, ACROSS THE ATLANTIC

In modern times Americans emphasize their exceptionalism in the types of sport they play and watch, and, despite the pre-modern colonies in America being founded by white British settlers, this was also true in the pre-modern period. Pugilism, which was held in high regard in Britain as a demonstration of courage, was considered unmanly by the American colonists, who also stayed aloof from fairs and festivals, both common in the Old World, and the sports associated with them. Nor did they play cricket (that came later) or participate in folk football (that never came). On the other hand, rifle-shooting and horse racing were highly regarded in the New World because of the immense importance of shooting and riding in everyday life; indeed, the very lives of settlers could depend on possessing these sporting skills. Horse racing, of course, was also popular in Britain, and the sport in America followed the British pattern until the mid-eighteenth century, when shorter and more oval tracks came into vogue (the nearest British equivalent would be the Roodee in Chester). The big difference between American and British racing was the jockeys, because American owners frequently put black slaves on their horses. Slaves were also employed in America as divers for salvaging shipwrecks and clearing waterways, and their talents were tested by the colonists, who promoted swimming and diving matches. Yet horse racing had also been practised by the indigenous population. Horses had been introduced to the New World by European settlers and transformed the lives of the native populace, who rode them to hunt buffalo, to fight against other tribes, and for some on the Great Plains, for sport. Horse racing was not just for recreational diversion, but was built into their culture as a means of asserting and enhancing the status and prestige of the riders – male ones, of course.

FOOTBALL, BUT NOT AS WE KNOW IT

Forms of football were played throughout medieval, Renaissance and Enlightenment Europe, although the manner of their playing varied widely. In France the game, called *soule,* was often a cross-county one that pitted one village against another. One version allowed the ball to

Calcio match in Florence's Piazza Santa Maria Novella,
based on a design by Giorgio Vasari (1511–1574).

La soule match in Normandy, 1852.

be struck by a stick, initially a shepherd's crook but later a specially constructed piece of equipment. In Italy *calcio*, still the name employed for soccer today, was not played with the foot at all, and the ball had to be projected by hand. In England the rules varied with locality. In some regions the ball was mainly kicked; in others it was primarily thrown or carried. Sedgefield (Northumberland) had two teams of unlimited numbers; Atherstone (Warwickshire) had no teams at all, the winner being the player 'holding the ball at 5 pm'. The Atherstone game had no goals; Ashbourne (Derbyshire) did, but they were nearly 5 km (3 mi.) apart, more than twelve times the distance that separated them at Alnwick (Northumberland). Hallaton's Easter Monday football match was called bottle-kicking but employed neither a ball nor a bottle, instead using a small wooden cask of ale. There was simply no need for standardization, since there was no likelihood that villages would want to challenge others, apart from those where inter-village rivalry was traditionally the focus of the game, such as Hallaton versus Medbourne in Leicestershire.

4

THE INDUSTRIAL AGE
(AND SLIGHTLY BEYOND)

S port is a dynamic product, and clearly by 1914 it was very different from that at the beginning of the nineteenth century. In 1800 sport was predominantly rural, as we have seen – as was the population. But in Britain by 1914 organized league matches had superseded folk football and were being played in urban stadia holding thousands of spectators, and a county cricket championship had replaced one-off gambling matches and friendly fixtures. In the United States baseball had emerged as the national sport, played in two major leagues with an annual play-off for the 'world' title. In Australia cricket, a sport inherited from the mother country, had developed into an interstate competition while Australian Rules football, a sport invented by Australians, had developed into league competitions within each state. More generally, new sports had been created by the application of technology, such as bicycle racing, which was very popular in continental Europe. In short, sport had been modernized.

The rise of industrial economies, extensive urbanization, and new communication and transport technologies were part of the transition from traditional to modern societies. Part of this transition involved the development of new leisure activities, including sport, which was subject to the same driving forces. Industrialization ultimately resulted in higher wages and more leisure time. Urbanization allowed the emergence of mass markets for spectator sport. The development of a cheap sporting press brought sport into the household, and the railway served as the fundamental infrastructure for the rise of national leagues. It also changed mindsets; before the advent of the railway network in Britain, for example, it was as quick (but still slow) to travel from Edinburgh to Amsterdam or Copenhagen as it was to visit London.

It would be remiss not to mention the pioneering theoretical work of Allen Guttmann, who in the early 1970s put forward a model postulating that sport became modern when it fulfilled seven major criteria. First, such sport was secular, with no religious reasons for participation. Second, it demonstrated equality; theoretically everyone should have an opportunity to compete, and conditions of competition should be the same for all contestants. Third, it introduced the idea of specialization both within a sport and between sports. Fourth came rationalization, in particular the invention of written rules, but also via the development of coaching and sports science. His fifth feature was bureaucratization, with every major modern sport having its national and international organization to establish universal rules and oversee their implementation. Sixth was quantification, by which modern sports transform every athletic feat into statistics. Following on from quantification is his seventh point, the modern emphasis on records. Like many models, Guttmann's was an ideal-type postulation that may never have all its conditions fully satisfied. However, it has stood the test of time, if not in its entirety then as a basis on which others have built, so that his work remains the starting point for any academic study of the modernization of sport.

INDUSTRY AND SPORT

Convention has it that modern sport originated in Britain in the nineteenth century as a direct consequence of the country's industrialization, and spread from there to the rest of the world. This is a very Anglocentric view, resulting partly from British hubris but also because much early sports history research did not transfer across the barrier of language. In fact, both aspects of the conventional wisdom on the subject have now been challenged.

Look what we invented

'Modern sport was born in England at the time of the industrial revolution.'
Jean-François Bourg and Jean-Jacques Gouguet, *Économie du Sport*
(Paris, 2005), p. 4

The role of industrialization as a driver of modern sport is too often taken as a chronological correlation without the causal relationship being fully specified. It is hard to see how early industrialization could have had an impact on sport, and it has now been recognized that the process of industrialization was a drawn-out one that accelerated significantly only in the second quarter of the nineteenth century. The first factories were little more than a bringing together of handicraft workers under one roof. Even when power was adopted for mechanization it was limited to areas where water flow was fast. The textile works on the hillsides of Lancashire and Yorkshire had neither a significant influence on national economic production nor any real impact on leisure patterns of workers generally or even in the counties themselves. Nationally, even by the mid-nineteenth century 5.5 million of the 7.25 million industrial workers were employed in non-mechanized industry, and agriculture was still the largest employment sector. Only when steam became the driving force for mass production did factories become less geographically determined and industry begin to change the environment in which sport took place as increased urbanization, concomitant on industrialization, began to lessen the open space available.

The major impact of industrialization on sport came in its later stages as the widespread application of steam power vastly increased productivity, thus enabling employers eventually to shorten the working week for their labour force and pay higher wages. This had two major consequences for sport. First, it helped to create a mass market for spectator sport by setting Saturday afternoons free of work and thus providing a time slot into which gate-money sport could fit. Second, for those who preferred being active to watching others play, the increase in disposable income allowed the purchase of bicycles and other sporting equipment.

NOT A BRITISH EXPORT

But did modern sport then spread from Britain to the rest of the world? Sport did accompany British settlers, soldiers, civil servants, missionaries and educators as they extended the empire across the globe. It served to bind together the white imperialists, but it also provided a mechanism by which they sought to 'civilize' the indigenous populations. Yet, although Britain incubated many athletic pursuits, others had no connection with that country and were a product of the diverse movement cultures extant in Europe. Two less hubristic British sports historians have examined 22 significant sports and suggest that only six or seven can be considered as having uniquely British origins. They actually identify four clusters of sport development within Europe alone: not just the British but also German, Soviet and Scandinavian versions. The British is characterized by an absence of state intervention, a reliance on private organizations and domination by an anti-commercial ethos through the ideology of amateurism. The German cluster originated in nineteenth-century militarized forms of physical culture and was marked by an emphasis on the collective, the individual body in harmony with the body politic, and a non-competitive ethos. Scandinavia had a variant on the German with an equal focus on improving national spirit and defence in the nineteenth century, but placed greater emphasis on individual movement, bodily harmony and aesthetics. Additionally, its notion of *idrott* (sports) proposed a recreational outdoor physical development in harmony with nature. In the Soviet/Eastern European cluster that emerged in the twentieth century, sport was an extension of the state apparatus, both in spheres of mass display and the cultivation of elite athletes. Moreover, in America, although British sports immigrated with the colonists and prizefighting and horse racing vied for precedence as early spectator sports, the sport that emerged as America's national one in the late nineteenth century was baseball, one that had British origins but no popularity in its homeland.

W. S. Hedges, *A Race Meeting at Jacksonville, Alabama,* 1841, oil on canvas.

Edward Trickett beats John Sadler for the world sculling championship in 1876.

The later developments of American football and basketball were clearly innovations from within the United States.

Then we have Australia, which began its Western existence as a set of British colonies at the other end of the world, although, in a way, the tyranny of distance helped it to develop its own sporting culture. It is one of a select group of industrialized countries that place a premium on sport. Any nation that recruited sportsmen's regiments in the First World War, that has turned out in thousands to pay homage at the funerals of sporting heroes, and that has declared public holidays for race meetings must have seen sport as a major ingredient in its culture. The Australian language – they speak English, but differently! – reflects the importance of sport in the life of the nation, since approximately one in every thirty words has a sporting context. The country has often measured itself in terms of international sporting success, one that has been out of all proportion to its population, beginning with Edward Trickett's world sculling championship in 1876, a title Australians held in an unbroken run until 1907, continuing through the cricket triumph over the mother country in 1882 and in the medal-winning performances at the first modern Olympics, in 1896.

No doubt the popularity of sport was aided by the gender ratio of the infant colonies. Throughout the nineteenth century males continued to outnumber females, and a bachelor subculture developed that emphasized the trinity of gambling, drinking and sport ('manly' ones only, of course). Moreover, as Australia developed its inhabitants clung to the seaboard in relatively few cities, whose sizes meant that there were sufficient teams to provide high-quality intracity competition. Additionally, Australia has always had a mixed economy in which the government invested in infrastructure; in sport, local authorities owned most of the sports grounds (a unique feature of Australian elite club sport is that most teams took electoral district names) and control of ocean beach space was vested in local government. The long economic boom resulting from the gold rushes from the 1850s to the 1890s provided the wherewithal for sport to be incorporated into the built environment, where civic pride and money combined to provide high-quality sports facilities across urban Australia.

WORKPLACE SPORT

One of the emerging areas of significant sports participation in the nineteenth century was that of workplace sport, in which employers provided sports facilities for their workers out of a desire to improve labour relations, promote loyalty to the firm and reduce labour turnover. Initially, many employers had seen sport as inimical to industrialization. The violent human and animal sports of rural Britain, the ploughing matches and hedge-laying contests that demonstrated agricultural skills, and the mob football matches played over extensive areas of land were seen as incompatible with industrial society, industrial locations or industrial work patterns. The demands of industrial employers for a disciplined workforce capable of working long and regular hours throughout the year undermined the leisure calendar of the agrarian economy, in which bursts of intense activity at planting, harvesting or shearing time were interspersed with long periods of irregular work. Not only did industry reduce the amount of leisure time available, but also industrialists joined religious evangelicals, political economists and other middle-class reformers in attempting to change workers' attitudes to both work and leisure. Sobriety, thrift, order and hard work were all part of a new morality of respectability that they intended to impose on the working class.

Slowly, however, industrialists came to accept that regulated sport, shed of its earlier associations with excessive brutality, alcohol consumption and gambling, could contribute positively to output, particularly by creating a loyal and dedicated workforce. A bowling green and cricket field were provided for the employees of Chadwick's Eagley Mills in Bolton as early as the 1830s. In Scotland there was a shinty match in February 1852 between two calico works owned by the brothers Alexander and John Orr Ewing. Sport was becoming viewed as rational recreation, to be encouraged in appropriate circumstances rather than criticized. For workers, urbanization replaced the community allegiance of the village with anomie and anonymity, but this was something that could be countered by sport and its emotional stimulation. This might be one reason why workplace sport was seized on by company labour forces: with the expansion of cities and the increased size of factories, men lost their 'neighbourhood' workmates, and the workplace might have been seen as the site for playing alongside people with whom there was daily contact.

These and other examples from the mid-nineteenth century came via the philanthropic, often authoritarian, paternalistic family firm, looking for deference and dependency from its workforce. Here the provision of sport was often independent of other benefits, unlike in the next stage, beginning in the 1880s, when joint stock company formation, more complex managerial structures and increased labour militancy paved the way for a switch from family-firm 'caring paternalism' to formal company welfare provision, offered to workers as part of long-term managerial policies beyond that of the market relationship of the wage contract. In this phase sport often came as part of a strategic welfare package, along with pension schemes, savings banks and other economic benefits. The demarcation line between the two phases is not hard and fast – no doubt there were still small-firm 'caring paternalists' in the 1890s – but corporate welfare was becoming the more significant form of welfare provision. As firms grew and the organization of production became more complex, the face-to-face contact between employer and worker was severed and, although conscientious management might offset this, generally the relationship between managers and staff became more impersonal. Loyalty to the enterprise became of increased importance as new technology led to interdependent continuous production processes in which stoppages and strikes in one department could close down a whole factory; indeed, 'loyalty' became the overarching ideology at Lever Brothers, the world-renowned soap manufacturer. By the early twentieth century workplace sport had spread across a range of industries and service sectors, and it became a significant part of working-class culture in the period before the First World War.

There may have been an element of altruism in some sports provision. The Dunbartonshire calico producer Alexander Wylie saw workers' sport as a means of self-improvement, maintaining that 'recreation of the proper sort, following moderate work, helps to make a man inasmuch as it brings into play and develops those faculties that would otherwise remain dormant'. He advocated muscular Christianity and the 'encouragement of that manly, brave, thoroughly fair and gentlemanly demeanour in games which has characterized the youth of so many of our public schools'. However, he may also have shared the views of William Lever, founder of the company town Port Sunlight on Merseyside, who was, according to his son, a 'humanitarian coupled with enlightened self-interest', who believed that a healthier and more educated labour force would also be a more productive one. The provision of sports facilities did not undermine capitalist profit orientation; good business and social responsibility went hand in hand.

For some employers, workplace sport served to offset increased labour militancy in the late nineteenth century. Although the extent of 'New Unionism' among the unskilled and semi-skilled workers should not be exaggerated, there is no doubt that a strike by their matchmakers in 1888 forced Bryant & May towards a welfare policy that included sports clubs. Other firms, such as the London gas suppliers the Gas Light & Coke Company and the South Metropolitan Gas Company, also moved into welfare provision to offset the growing influence of the unions. The Thames Ironworks Football Club (later West Ham United) was started by the foundry owner shortly after a major strike and was part of a programme to improve cooperation between workers and management. Certainly, despite their humanitarianism, even the Lever brothers saw welfare provision as a weapon in the fight against unionism. Companies offered their workers good-quality facilities, often more cheaply than those available elsewhere. Sometimes they controlled the sports clubs tightly; occasionally the workers were given freer rein to run their sports affairs. Yet the workers were entirely dependent on their employers for such sport. The team sheets were headed by the company name and the facilities bore that name; the employers owned workplace sport.

Such ideas about welfare, productivity and profits were transnational, and similar developments occurred in other countries. By 1916 at least 230 companies across the United States were providing some kind of recreation for their employees. Baseball, basketball and bowling helped to acculturate immigrant workers into American life and, more generally, the sports facilities provided promoted health and company loyalty, both of which were seen as good for business. Given that British capital and management dominated the Australian business scene before 1914, it is unsurprising that some firms transferred their welfare provision to their Antipodean enterprises. However, it has been shown that many workplace teams began at the white-collar level and were organized by the employees themselves, before spreading to workers in lower-status occupations under the aegis of their employers. Australian business proprietors, in common with those elsewhere, realized that modern sport fitted in well to the new urban, industrial environment because it emphasized the attributes employers wanted: discipline, loyalty, fitness and obedience. Moreover, in the Victorian tramways and railways, in contrast to the British experience, the respective trade unions took over what had begun as an employer initiative and created an identity of interest between workers and unions.

THE EMERGENCE OF MASS SPECTATOR SPORT

Mass spectator sport existed before the end of the nineteenth century, but it was intermittent, often annual at best. It was not until the economic benefits of industrialization filtered down to the mass of the population that a large and regular paying clientele could be relied on for sports events. Money, the free time to spend it, a concentration of population and easy access to venues all came with urbanization and the development of transport between towns but especially within towns. Earlier urbanization did not fulfil the latter requirement. The 'walking cities' of early America were not big enough to promote commercialized sport, but later those towns that were large enough required intra-urban transport for demand to become fully effective. Later, in all countries, industrialization and associated urbanization created the conditions in which organized, commercial, gate-money sport could flourish.

Essentially, demand for sport was stimulated in the developed world by rising real income and a concentration of population, aided by the development of the mass media. The response on the supply side was to enclose grounds (to ensure that gate money could be collected) and erect stadia (to offer better views, which could be charged for). Once such investment had taken place, regular events to attract paying customers were necessary to cover the overheads, and the employment of talented professionals to reinforce this attraction soon followed.

Many traditional sports had always been minority pursuits, and these disappeared with the lessening of agriculture's importance to the economy. Some traditional rural sports survived the transformation of society into an urban, industrial one, but only by changing themselves. Pugilism (or prizefighting) switched from bare-knuckle endurance events to gloved fights with a limited number of timed rounds and decisions on points if there had not been a knock-out. Cricket at the elite level in England eventually developed a formal county championship rather than 'friendly' challenge fixtures, and in the northern counties competitive leagues emerged. In horse racing – probably the first real national sport in both Britain and the United States – courses began to be enclosed and entry fees charged to spectators. It attracted larger crowds than other sports, but towards the end of the century it lost support in relative terms as the public began to identify with their local teams in soccer and baseball.

THE COMING OF LEAGUES

In both Britain and the United States the growing popularity of sport led some clubs to seize the commercial opportunity to charge admission fees and eventually pay their players. It is arguable that Americans had fewer qualms about seeing sport as a means of making money. Such developments led to the emergence of leagues, beginning in America with the National Association of Professional Base Ball Players, formed in 1871. It lasted only four years, but its immediate successor, the National League, survives and, with its territorial franchises, annual championship tournaments, revenue sharing and the reserve clause, has shaped the nature of American team sports for more than a century. In Britain major football leagues were established in both England and Scotland to provide weekly competitive fixtures in place of ad hoc friendly matches and cup competitions from which teams might make an early departure.

There was little experience for these organizations to draw on, so each developed its own way of working. The main decision to be made was the type of league system that would operate. In simple terms, leagues could be run in one of two ways: as a closed competition, where the number and names of teams generally remained static; or with an element of dynamism via promotion and relegation. The closed system was adopted in all the major American professional team sports, as well as in Australia, whereas most European team sports opted for the open system, although there were exceptions, such as the English County Cricket Championship, which adopted promotion and relegation only when it split into two divisions as late as 2000. Individual sports tended to have tournament competition rather than leagues, although at the non-elite level, leagues for the teams of tennis, golf or bowling clubs became commonplace.

THE CREATION OF THE AMATEUR

In the nineteenth century the Victorians created the concept of the amateur, the person who played solely for the love of their sport. What emerged alongside this concept was an ethos of how sport should be played. The pursuit of the chosen activity should be seen as an end in itself, done simply for the pleasure it afforded, with a consequent downgrading of achievement, training and specialization. Players should exercise self-restraint, masking exuberance in victory and disappointment in defeat. Moreover, not only should they comply voluntarily with the rules, but also they should adopt a chivalrous attitude towards their opponents. This does not mean, as some writers interpret it, that the Victorians did not care about winning. They did, but the way the game was played mattered more. There was no joy in winning if the moral code of fair play had not been adhered to.

The central tenet of amateurism was a class-based one of playing sport in an appropriate manner with the right sort of people. Initially, the amateur sporting bodies who legislated against professionalism defined it in social rather than economic terms. Put simply: to be a gentleman was to be an amateur; to be working class was to be a non-amateur. So it was quite all right for gentlemen riders or oarsmen to compete against each other for wagers or cash prizes. The entry qualification for the inaugural Henley Regatta in 1839 made it clear who was not wanted. Events were

Henley Regatta in the 1890s.

restricted to amateurs and, although no definition was supplied, it was implicit in the clause that considered as eligible 'any crew composed of members of a College of either of the Universities of Oxford, Cambridge or London, the schools of Eton and Westminster, the officers of the two brigades of the Household Troops, or of members of a club established at least one year previous to the time of entering'. A similar situation still pertained in the late 1870s, by which time many influential rowing men wanted the regulations tightened; in 1879 the Amateur Rowing Association declared that an amateur 'must never have taken money . . . nor ever taught, pursued, or assisted in the pursuit of athletic exercises of any kind as a means of livelihood, nor have ever been employed in or about boats, or in manual labour; nor be a mechanic, artisan or labourer'.

This was at the extreme end of the anti-professional class spectrum, but certainly to many middle-class sportsmen professionalism lowered sport to the standard of a trade. Merely to play alongside paid players was sufficient for some gentlemen, such as the amateur footballer N. L. Jackson, 'to hazard their self-respect'. Arguably Jackson himself was a professional sporting entrepreneur who made money from promoting the Corinthians, a football club that he founded and ran for 22 years ostensibly to improve the quality of the England international team. Under his management they played matches around the world (often asking for larger guarantees than professional clubs), claimed large expenses and published no accounts.

However, other entrepreneurs who promoted mass spectator commercialized sport saw paying talented men as a necessary cost of creating a good-quality product. When the tide of professionalism became irresistible, the reaction was to control the players rather than exclude them. In football, for example, maximum wage legislation was imposed and disciplinary sentences for on-field misbehaviour remained the prerogative of the Football Association, which governed all football, rather than the Football League, which ran the professional game.

There is a view that amateurism was more than a class-based concept designed to prevent the working class from playing with (and probably beating) middle-class participants; it was also a reinforcement of the work ethic, a vital cog in the wheels of capitalism. Behind the hostility to professionalism in sport exhibited by some members of the middle class was an underlying capitalist ideology that saw leisure as something that should be earned. Others felt that playing sport in the correct manner emphasized qualities that were of use to the industrialist – teamwork, discipline and obeying orders – but this should not be exaggerated. Such sport encompassed the idea of chivalry (fair play) rather than of industrial capitalism, and, as can be seen from Henry Newbolt's famous poem 'Vitaï Lampada', sport taught the virtues of war not commerce. True amateurs abhorred any professionalism, even when it came to coaches, who were either regarded as unnecessary or, if they could help performance, certainly should not be paid for their services.

The British may have invented amateurism; they certainly allowed hypocrisy to accompany it. The protocols of amateurship were breached by talented middle-class participants who wished to make their living from sport but did not want to be labelled 'professional', with its strong working-class connotations. The home of such shamateurism was county cricket, especially towards the end of the nineteenth century, when most counties lengthened their fixture lists and put increased pressure on the free time of their amateur players. To enable them to afford to play, excessive broken time payments were made or, more commonly, artificial posts such as assistant club secretary were created, which were in effect sinecures. This allowed them to continue to share the gentleman's changing room, travel first class to matches and dine separately from the paid players. The most blatant of these shamateurs was Dr W. G. Grace, the best cricketer of his generation (and that was not just his opinion), who made significant sums of money from exhibiting his prowess at the game. In 1873/4 he obtained £1,500 plus expenses for taking a team to Australia; the professionals who accompanied him received expenses and £170 each. Eighteen years later he demanded, and got, £3,000 plus expenses for a similar venture. Perhaps this money could be considered as reasonable compensation for the employment of a locum and loss of earnings as a doctor while overseas, but the ethics of an amateur pocketing nearly £1,500 from a testimonial in 1879 and over £9,000 from another in 1895 are questionable. The *Wisden Cricketers' Almanack* of 1897 acknowledged that 'Mr [*sic*] W. G. Grace's position has for years, as everyone knows, been an anomalous one, but *nice customs curtsey to great kings* and the work that he has done in popularizing cricket outweighs a hundredfold every

Dr W. G. Grace, shamateur par excellence.

other consideration.' Grace regularly captained the Gentlemen against the Players. Clearly caste rather than money was the real distinction between amateur and professional.

Other countries adopted the concept of amateurism, but not necessarily the British version with its attached middle-class, non-economic value system. Whereas for the British middle-class amateur the way the game was played was the most important factor, for his American counterpart the result mattered more. In Australia – where, it being a British colony, more sympathy might have been expected with the amateurism of the mother country – there was in many quarters a reaction to (and a rejection of) the class-based aspects of amateurism. This was particularly true of the Australian cricketers, one of whom explained in his tour diary that they felt the English custom of separating the amateurs from the professionals was 'priggish and out of place'.

ALL THOSE NOT IN FAVOUR SAY 'NAY'

We have already seen how employers changed their minds about the cost and benefit of sport, taking a more favourable line as the century progressed. Similar changes in attitude to sport can be found among religious bodies and educational institutions. However, medical opinion of the participation of women in sport remained almost implacably opposed.

Much religious opposition to sport focused on spectators and players desecrating the Christian Sabbath, designated as a holy day for worship rather than a holiday for play, although this was essentially relevant to Protestant-dominated nations and far less emotion surrounded the question in regions where the 'continental Sabbath' dominated leisure cultures. Generally the Sunday observance lobby in Britain was successful in keeping the day free from sporting activities. Indeed, any sports event that charged gate money was legally forbidden to be held on a Sunday. However, adherents of a growing secularism saw no harm in participating in sport on the seventh day. For such middle-class sportsmen tennis courts, croquet lawns, riverbanks and golf courses became sites of conflict between their progressive attitudes and those of a conservative, reactionary clergy. By 1913 some 40 per cent of English golf clubs had adopted Sunday play, although many of these accepted that caddies should not be employed or refreshments served on that day. Notwithstanding the

Sunday debate, some churchmen both Protestant and Catholic added the playing fields to their evangelical and social discipline armoury of rational recreations and encouraged sport, either directly by founding clubs or indirectly via physical activities within the Boys' Brigade, the Church Lads' Brigade or the Young Men's Christian Association. A search of the local press of eight northern towns has suggested that in 1914 some 38 per cent of football teams and 44 per cent of cricket teams were church-based, with participation often dependent on church attendance.

In the early nineteenth century educators generally held that sport was anti-intellectual and should not be encouraged, but by mid-century public-school headmasters were beginning to recognize that sport could prove a useful tool for social engineering. It was at this time that the Roman concept of *mens sana in corpore sano* was resurrected to form the basis of a new sporting ideology by proponents of muscular Christianity and amateurism. It made its reappearance as the motto of the Liverpool Athletic Club in the early 1860s and became widely adopted as a rallying cry of athleticism among English public schools. Although athleticism became the dominant public-school ethos, there were those who vainly objected to compulsory sports participation. At university sport was a voluntary activity for undergraduates, and there it was never as dominant as in the public schools. Nevertheless, there were Oxbridge critics who protested against the health risks involved in contests, to excessive competition, to taking sport too seriously, to training for what should be recreation, to too much attention being paid to record setting, and – a refrain familiar to modern academics – to the misuse of resources.

Although the views of the medical profession were based on the 'scientific' evidence of the time, they were also rooted in social and cultural prejudice. Nineteenth-century medical orthodoxy insisted that physically woman was inferior to man: she was frailer, her skull smaller, and her muscles more delicate. Physicians saw the body as a closed system possessing a limited amount of vital force; hence energy expended in one area reduced the amount available for use elsewhere. Most physicians consequently insisted that women's energy and strength be confined to motherhood, and girls were made to understand that from puberty onwards all bodily strength should be dedicated to maternity and caring for others. Gradually some physicians accepted that the small, frail and weak woman could (even should) be encouraged to become stronger, but within limits; too strong was unfeminine. Then there was the problem of menstruation. Doctors led public opinion in considering periods as regularly occurring handicaps to female sporting activity, a view that continued well into the twentieth century. Two points are worth noting. The first is that historians have often used selective quotations in their desire to make a case, and have not quantified the degree of medical opposition to female participation in sports. The other is that historians have discovered new sources, such as company sports archives, that suggest that more women ignored such medical strictures than was once thought.

CHARLOTTE DOD (1871–1960)

One of the most versatile sportswomen of all time, Charlotte 'Lottie' Dod excelled in tennis, golf, hockey and archery, and she participated in several winter sports. She was the youngest of four children, none of whom had to earn a living, because their father had made a fortune as a cotton broker. All of them spent much of their young adult lives playing sport at a high level.

In 1883, aged just eleven, Lottie entered her first tennis tournament, the Northern Championship held in Manchester, playing in the ladies' doubles with her sister Anne, who was eight years her senior. Although they lost in the second round, having received a bye in the first, the pair won the consolation trophy. This was a sign of Lottie's potential. In 1885 the sisters won the Northern doubles title, and that same year Lottie won her first singles title (at the Waterloo tournament in Liverpool). The next year she won the West of England championship, and in 1887, aged 15 years and 285 days, she became the youngest ever Wimbledon Ladies' champion, a title she retained the following year. She took advantage of her youth to wear a shorter skirt than other female players (but one still falling to her calf), which increased her mobility on the court. Through playing so much with her brothers, she had developed a style of play with strong ground strokes and smashes at the net, an innovative mode for women.

Dod did not bother entering Wimbledon in 1889, because she was on a sailing trip with friends, and in 1890 she did not play competitive tennis at all. However, she returned to the grass in 1891 to win Wimbledon again, a title she defended successfully for the next two years. She then gave up serious tennis with a record of having lost only five singles matches in all the tournaments she had played in, and having amassed 38 tournament titles in singles, ladies' doubles and mixed doubles, the last often with her siblings.

In 1895 Dod joined her brother Tony on a trip to St Moritz, Switzerland, where she passed the prestigious St Moritz skating test for women; the following year she successfully attempted the men's test, only the second female to have done so. She was the first woman to toboggan the famous Cresta Run, competed in curling, and, with her brother, climbed several mountains. Did I mention that she also cycled around Italy?!

Dod first played golf when she was fifteen, but she did not pursue it seriously until 1894, when she was eliminated in the third round of the British Ladies' Amateur Championship. In 1898 and 1900 she reached the semi-finals, and in 1904 she won the title, becoming the only player to have won British titles in both tennis and golf. In 1905, in the week before the Amateur Championship, she represented Britain in a match against the United States and in the same year played for England in two home internationals against Scotland and Ireland. In the tournament itself she lost in the fourth round, and she never played golf competitively again.

Having taken up hockey in 1897, Dod was one of the founding members and captain of a club in Spital, Merseyside. In 1899 she became captain of the Cheshire county side and was selected to play for England in their loss against Ireland. The next year she scored both goals when England beat Ireland in a rematch. A bout of sciatica prevented her from playing against Wales, and she gave up hockey following her mother's death in August 1901, apart from an occasional game for her club.

After golf, the next sport Dod participated in seriously was archery. After the family home was sold she moved with her brothers to Newbury in Berkshire, where she joined the Welford Park Archers. She won her first competition in 1906 and finished fifth in the Grand National Archery Meetings (toxophily's equivalent of Wimbledon) in three successive years to 1908, the latter achievement gaining her

selection for the London Olympics. She led the field after the first
day, but eventually finished in silver medal place with 642 points, 46
behind the winner. Two years later she almost became national champion in a third sport when she was narrowly beaten at the Grand
National meeting.

The Welford Park Archers disbanded in 1911, and Dod lost
interest in archery and in participatory sport generally. However, until
her late eighties she continued to attend Wimbledon regularly. She
died in 1960, fittingly while listening to a radio broadcast of the tennis
championships in which she had made sporting history.

Charlotte 'Lottie' Dod, the youngest ever Wimbledon champion.

This is reflective of the point that the ambivalence towards sport and outright opposition in some quarters was by a minority and was generally unsuccessful. The culture of sport was too strong to be overcome. Much more of the population responded positively to the exhilaration of playing and watching sport than decried it on moral and medical grounds.

THE FIRST WORLD WAR (AND THE SPANISH FLU)

Our period ends with the tragedy of the First World War, a devastating conflict that toppled old empires, redrew the national maps of the world and reconfigured the economic, social and political trajectories of most of the world's nations. It may seem crass to talk about sport in a scenario that cost millions of lives, but the war plunged modern sports into the war effort, as propaganda, morale-booster and even training regimen. Yet, as elsewhere, truth must be separated from myth.

Two sporting images of British troops have become part of Britain's collective memory of the First World War: a Christmas Day football match in 1914 between British and German troops and, more generally, men advancing into battle kicking a football ahead of them. There is an element of truth to each, but neither holds up fully to scrutiny. Certainly British and German troops fraternized at Christmas 1914 over about 30 km (20 mi.) of the British lines, but a detailed search for (and of) evidence suggests that it is improbable that a 'proper' football match occurred. Moreover, the 'football charges' were limited to ten months between late September 1915 and early July 1916, involved few military units, and indeed possibly occurred only twice. Neither story is totally false, and that is the danger with myths: the element of truth on which they are based offers a degree of protection from common-sense rejection. The 'Christmas football match' and the 'football charge' are what might be termed micro-level 'myths'. However, there is a possible myth at the macro-level that must also be investigated, principally the tenet that sport had for some time been a way of preparing soldiers for war and that public schoolboys in England were conditioned to believe that the values, skills and abilities that permitted them to excel in sport were analogous to those that were required to prevail in warfare.

The nub of the argument is that Britain's educational institutions for the upper and middle classes used sport in a way that its practitioners could easily and effectively adopt for military purposes. The logical chain runs as follows. Public schools played sport in a particular way; this way of playing encouraged certain characteristics that could be transferable into warfare; many military officers attended public school; ergo public school sport was helpful to the war effort. However, I would argue that this view has become conventional wisdom without being appropriately tested. It has been recycled not researched. Where is the real evidence that this occurred? That many army officers attended public school and that games were played at those schools is a correlation but not proof. Statistically we do not know what proportion of public schools adopted an educational policy formally encouraging the development of athleticism with its compulsory games and associated character-building, or what proportion of military officers were educated at public school. The answers may be 'the vast majority', but this must be shown, not assumed. Even if we look less quantitatively, there are still unanswered questions. As partially closed communities, public schools were in a position to impose athleticism on their pupils, but we do not know whether the boys actually accepted the ramifications of code. To what extent did they merely pay lip service and then get on with trying to win however they could? Was it compliance rather than commitment? Were they indoctrinated by osmosis? Did playing sport automatically endow the boys with military capabilities? Did they accept the tenets of athleticism at all? What I am asking is whether there were more Flashmans than Tom Browns. We just do not know.

Some of the team games played at public schools featured in officer sport. Certainly football and the army had long-standing connections. In January 1851 a team representing the 93rd Sutherland Highlanders beat one from Edinburgh University in a football match. The Royal Engineers won the FA cup in 1875, and an Army Football Association was formed in 1881. Yet the skills of football and cricket were not in themselves military assets. Other sports, however, offered techniques that could be readily transferred to martial requirements. There was a public-schools shooting tournament, but, even though it was a team competition, it does not appear to be highlighted as character-building in the literature.

It would seem that at officer level in the forces the emphasis was not on games but on equestrianism. Officers spent a large proportion of their time hunting, and, although the glory days of the military steeplechase had passed by the end of the nineteenth century, racing too remained a popular officer activity. Add to these sports the polo and pig-sticking practised abroad, and equestrian sport can be seen as central to an officer's sporting life. All were considered by some military men to assist the human capital formation of the army officer. Indeed, as late as 1911 the Army Council declared that hunting had 'special military value' and polo possessed 'distinct military advantages'. Hunting, steeplechasing, polo and pig-sticking accustomed men to the taking of physical risks. These activities certainly required horsemanship and courage on horseback (rather than on the playing field). Yet none was part of the public schools' extracurricular programme. The necessity of owning horses for their equestrian activities forced officers to have substantial private incomes, and restricted entry to the regiments to those who could afford an officer lifestyle. They may well thus have been class-based activities, since field sports largely defined the rural upper classes in Britain. Many of the younger members of this group would have attended public school, but the equestrian link is with their social class not their school life.

Of course, the mechanism of sport aiding war was not necessarily the sports in themselves. It was the way they were played that was regarded as teaching the psychological and physical tools necessary for war. In the words of Professor Tony Mangan, the major proponent of the concept of athleticism in the public schools, 'physical exercise, taken considerably and compulsorily, was a highly effective means of inculcating valuable instrumental and impressive educational goals: physical and moral courage, loyalty and co-operation, the capacity to act fairly and take defeat well, the ability to command and obey.' There is no doubt that some public-school-educated officers accepted that sport made the warrior, and some certainly took into the services the belief that war was only another form of sport, the 'greater game'. There is, however, some incoherence in such links. If the ideas were inculcated, were they all suitable for military purposes? The 'athleticism' view that winning might be important but the manner of securing victory is even more so may not be good military policy. As in sport, so in war: playing fair is not always the best way to ensure victory.

At the end of the war came the 'Spanish Flu', a pandemic more devastating than the war itself in terms of lives lost. In late 1917 military pathologists reported the onset of a new disease with high mortality at a major troop staging and hospital camp in Étaples, France. Wartime censorship in France, Britain and the United States disguised the level of mortality, whereas in neutral Spain the press were free to report on what was happening, with the result that, in the public mind, Spain was the initiator of the pandemic. Yet, although some 3–5 per cent of the world's population died, we know little about how the disease affected leisure activities. When it comes to sport, all that has been commented on was the cancellation of the final National Hockey League play-off match for the Stanley Cup because five members of the Montreal Canadiens team and their manager were bedridden by the disease. One of them, Joe Hall, later died. It seems strange that the 1918 pandemic has, by and large, been omitted from most sports scholarship. Apart from reports about the 1919 Stanley Cup Finals and baseball legend Babe Ruth contracting the flu twice, there seems scant research into the impact of those years on sports. Perhaps the recent COVID-19 outbreak – which has led in the sporting world to the cancellation or suspension of individual matches, entire contests, tournaments and even the 2020 Olympics – might change their outlook.

5

THE PAST CENTURY
OR SO

A major feature of sport over the past century was an expansion in the numbers playing. This came from demographic expansion coupled with rising incomes and leisure time, and was also influenced by greater provision of sports facilities.

One special area of sports provision that became significant for some time was workplace sport. It became a major way in which young adults, both male and female, were introduced to post-school sport in the inter-war years. For example, works-based teams, leagues and cup competitions expanded throughout Britain for both men and women in this period. There was a significant development of inter-business sporting rivalry, with the establishment of competitions and events solely for company teams. By 1939 more than a quarter of football clubs and nearly a fifth of cricket clubs in some northern towns had originated in a workplace, and the Industrial Welfare Society suggested that in the 1930s at least 25 per cent of workers were members of company sports clubs. Employers saw this provision as an addition to company welfare schemes that could create loyalty to their firms and undermine the growth of trade unionism, while workers felt the quality of the provision was better and often cheaper than that available elsewhere.

Workplace sport expanded throughout the developed world. In the 1920s hundreds of American businesses sponsored sports programmes and some unions, such as the International Ladies' Garment Workers' Union, countered management with their own sports sessions. Factory girls at the Western Electric plant in suburban Chicago had first-class facilities, including a 4-hectare (10 ac) athletic field for the firm's 28,000-member athletic association, allegedly the world's largest. Their employees organized a lunch-hour programme that included baseball, basketball, bowling, cycling, golf, gymnastics, swimming, tennis and athletics. And, of course, in the newly created Soviet Union in the 1920s the influence of the Proletkultists (from 'proletarian culture') led to labour exercises in factory yards and farm meadows with men and women swinging hammers or scythes, simulating work movements in time to music. The Soviet system also involved the sponsorship of sports clubs (labelled Dinamo) by the security and armed forces and, later, via trade unions such as those for white-collar workers (Spartak), railway workers (Locomotiv) and car workers (Torpedo).

Interwar Europe was characterized by massive construction of publicly funded, local participatory sports venues based on an imperative to improve public health. Germany led the way, taking advantage of the prohibition on military education imposed by the Treaty of Versailles to adapt army training facilities for public use. Even in Britain, where there was a reluctance for state intervention in the sporting area, national governments saw a need for improved public health, although the onus for provision was left to local authorities. In the United States, as part of its New Deal building programme, the government invested in public parks and sports facilities. In some countries, notably within the Communist Bloc, state provision of sports facilities continued throughout the second decade of the twentieth century, although this was not a monopoly of the left, since Australia and Scandinavian nations did likewise.

Another area in which sports provision increased significantly was school sport. In the nineteenth century the British public schools had been at the forefront of pursuing sport for the purposes of socialization. In the twentieth, throughout the parts of the world that could afford to provide state education, children were encouraged to play sport for health, friendship and enjoyment.

Not possessing the means to purchase equipment or not having sufficient time free from work have always kept some people out of sport, but for much of the history of sport, as we will see later, social and cultural barriers were deliberately raised to keep people out by virtue of their social class, race and ethnicity, and gender. Fortunately, during the last

One hundred metres heat at the 2014 Invictus Games.

century many such obstacles to sports participation were eroded and even destroyed.

Looking at the Olympics as a barometer, no events for women were scheduled at the first modern Games, in Athens in 1896, but tennis, golf, swimming and diving were introduced before 1914. Athletics was another matter, and no women competed in track and field until Amsterdam in 1928. When several women collapsed exhausted after the 800 metres, no middle-distance events for women were held until the resurrection of that race in Rome in 1960 and of the 1,500 metres at Munich in 1972 (rather than assuming that the 1928 women competitors had been pushing their bodies to the limits to try to win an Olympic medal, as is widely accepted to be the norm among all athletes today, the Games administrators then saw such an occurrence as unbecoming). The marathon first appeared in 1984 in Los Angeles. At the 1996 Atlanta Olympics, 26 teams had no women, but at Beijing, twelve years later, only three teams were all male; under pressure from the IOC, those teams – Brunei, Saudi Arabia and Qatar – sent women to the London Olympics in 2012. Parity of sports has been almost achieved with the introduction of boxing in 2012, ski jumping in 2014 and rugby in 2016.

The twentieth century also brought an acceptance of sport for athletes with a disability. This began in the late nineteenth century with sport for the deaf and has gradually, although with some acceleration in recent decades, expanded to include sportspeople with all kinds and levels of disability. Now we have the Invictus Games for mentally and physically wounded service personnel, the Special Olympics for those with intellectual disabilities and, of course, the elite-level Paralympics for athletes with a disability, which joined the mainstream in 2012 at the London Games.

STADIUM SPORT

The increased leisure time and greater disposable incomes that enabled more people to play sport also meant that others increasingly watched sportspeople who were more proficient than themselves. For much of the twentieth century this often took place in vast stadia holding tens of thousands of spectators. In medieval times cathedrals dominated the landscape; now, thanks to developments in construction technology, it was edifices to the religion of sport that were the most visible structure in many communities. Here fans come to worship their teams. These buildings, even the smaller (but still large) indoor sports complexes, held more people than factories, office blocks, residential complexes or, of course, cathedrals themselves.

In the United States in the interwar years steel-reinforced concrete stadia with car parks enabled clubs to cope with the increased use of private cars. Many of these were for college football, not just professional teams. Elsewhere there was a focus on national stadia, something alien to America despite its focus on sporting patriotism. England built Wembley Stadium in 1923, initially to host an exhibition but to continue for major sporting events including international football matches. In Uruguay the architecturally leading Estadio Centenario in Montevideo hosted the first FIFA World Cup, in 1930, in which the hosts beat Argentina before a crowd of 100,000 people. Home football games in Scotland against the auld enemy were played at Hampden Park, where 149,415 spectators saw Scotland win 3-1 in 1937. A year earlier Berlin had hosted the Olympics, for which the Nazi government had created a city within the city. The Reichssportfeld included police and fire stations, shops, post offices, arenas, playing and practice fields, schools, offices, car parks and subway stations, as well as the stadium itself.

Post-war stadia, although often smaller than the interwar ones, became symbols of modernity. They were climate-controlled, and many had retractable roofs and artificial turf. In this way they took the role of the weather out of the sporting equation, be it for spectators or players. What they did not change was the basic rule of economic pricing with more expensive boxes and private suites for wealthier spectators. Such socio-economic differentiation has existed in sport since the first grandstands were erected. Yet it can be argued that in some sports traditional local support is being priced out by what one English Premier League player scathingly labelled the 'prawn sandwich brigade'.

In Australia many sports stadia had been owned by local authorities, which leased them to electorate-based Australian Rules football teams in the winter and cricket clubs in the summer. Such ownership by the city became standard practice in the United States for reasons of city boosterism, initially for amateur sport but eventually also for professional teams. Unlike most conventional businesses, which must pay local authorities for the right to run a business, sports franchises in the United States often exert pressure on local and regional government to have a stadium built for their use and for other operations to be subsidized. There is a willingness on the part of the local authorities to do this in order to gain status as a 'Big League' city and, more debatably, because of the assumed positive economic impact of having a major sports team in the community. It is not just in America that the financial burden of stadia has been shouldered by taxpayers. The Stade de France, the national stadium built in Paris in the 1990s, had half its construction costs paid by French taxpayers, although profits went to the venue's private operators.

However, the most recent, and by far the most expensive, stadium to be built in America runs counter to this generalization about public subsidy. The Los Angeles Stadium and Entertainment District (now known as the SoFi Stadium) being built at the time of writing at Hollywood Park in Inglewood, California, is estimated to cost over $5 billion, all of it private money. Investors were attracted by plans to make it more than a stand-alone building to be used only for twenty National Football League (NFL) home games a year. This is in itself double the normal amount, since the stadium will host both the LA Rams (relocated from St Louis in 2016) and the LA Chargers (relocated from San Diego in 2017). The project includes a 70,240-seat stadium and a 6,000-seat performance

centre under one roof, and will anchor a 120-hectare (298 ac) complex
of office buildings, shops, restaurants, residential units, hotels and parks.
Given its proximity to the airport, the stadium has had to be sunk 30 m
(100 ft) into the ground to comply with the height limits aviation imposes
on buildings.

YOU DON'T HAVE TO BE THERE

The media and sport have had a long-standing, symbiotic relationship,
one offering promotional publicity and second- and third-hand spectatorship, the other source material for copy and a ready market for its
consumption. During the last century a revolution in communications
technology transformed the way sport was presented and experienced,
and spectator sport has increasingly become about those who watch on
television or online rather than venture out to the venue itself. Initially,
however, it was listening not watching that first attracted the stay-at-home
sports fan. Radio brought the sound of sport into millions of homes.
When the African American Joe Louis beat 'Nazi' Max Schmeling for
the heavyweight boxing title in 1938, some 60 million people tuned in to
listen. Such was the popularity of sports broadcasting that in the same
year, when the Australian cricket team was playing a Test series in England
but no direct broadcast was available, a synthetic one was arranged. After
each over, a cable was sent with brief details of proceedings. In the studio
back in Australia four commentators improvised by tapping a pencil
on the desk in front of them to simulate the sound of bat hitting ball,
or using the eraser end if the ball went through to the wicketkeeper. A
gramophone recreated the cheers and jeers of a faraway crowd. Not quite
fake sports news!

Boxing was the first sport to be widely televised (in the 1940s), since
the action in the limited-size ring was easy for the static cameras to cover.
As television technology improved, other sports became attractive to
fireside fans. Of course, gone are the days when you had to guess the
colour of the snooker balls on black-and-white television. Yet some sports
organizations resisted the new technology. Many English football clubs
felt live screening would affect their gate revenue, and, although baseball
was America's first national team spectator sport and dominated the
market well into the 1950s with extensive press coverage and live radio

Joe Louis, world heavyweight boxing champion 1937–49.

broadcasts, the conservatism of Major League Baseball owners, who resisted overtures from television companies, allowed the NFL, College Football and, slightly later, the National Basketball Association to become the viewers' choice sports.

In the early twentieth century physical attendance at the venue was essential to elite club revenues, but more recently the importance of local markets has decreased as income from broadcasting rights has become the dominant item in their accounts. Most of the profits of the Super Bowl, for example, emanate from media contracts. In fact, the money from television contracts now appears to be the driving force in many sports. The previous arrangement of mutual benefit has become dominated by the media, in terms not only of the ownership of sports clubs and sporting events but of defining and shaping what sport is. This leads to the danger that the sports industry becomes too reliant on one source of revenue. Competition between broadcasters is currently keeping income high for sports organizations, but it can go wrong. When the Irish broadcaster Setanta Sports' contract with the Scottish Football League collapsed in 2009, several clubs were placed in financial jeopardy.

The media tail may now be wagging the sporting dog. Sport has compromised itself by changing its playing and organization rules to suit broadcasting companies. The tiebreak in tennis and similar devices in other sports were introduced to enable schedules to be met. Moreover, contracted television stations increasingly determine the starting times of events. One kick-off time for the twice-a-year 'El Clásico' football match between Barcelona and Real Madrid is now under consideration for 10 am, to suit television audiences in Asia, with the other at 10 pm for the North American market. In many countries media companies now own sports clubs and teams, as with Sky Broadcasting's professional road-cycling team, and they also sponsor events, again as with Sky, which began funding the British Masters golf championship in 2015. Both these arrangements have now ended, so perhaps another change is on the way.

NOT MORE OF THE SAME

From the 1960s onwards commercialism in sport began to reach new levels. Media developments helped to bring huge new audiences, making sport an attractive proposition for advertisers. We have now reached a stage that some commentators have labelled hyper-commodification, when sport has in their view been penetrated by market forces to an unprecedented extent. Three key features are usually identified. First, elite clubs have become organized as corporate bodies, in which profits are given higher priority within the (sporting) enterprise than social and cultural considerations. Associated with this is the fact that they have become transnational identities, with fans (or are they now consumers?) drawn from a world market; power resides with large investors; franchises can be shifted; and in some countries sports clubs can be bought by media interests who may have agendas not congruent with that of the fans. Second, players have become totally professionalized, with greater geographical mobility and no longer representing their local community. Third, there has been a proliferation of advertising and merchandising, the latter often purchased by global supporters, who may never attend a game in person but who still seek to identify with a team. Merchandising has been a way for clubs to capture the utility of their fans further. Replica shirts have become a ubiquitous component of global fashion, as the Manchester United jerseys that adorn bodies in every region of the globe today testify. They have been joined by products with only a tenuous connection to the sport played by the team – own-label wines, fragrances and children's toys – as merchandise sales have soared to rival revenue from gate receipts for the largest clubs. Indeed, some teams have become brands more than sports clubs.

Clubs exploit fashion within sport, but there is also fashion emanating from sport. Whereas sports clothing is for participants, sportswear, although often inspired by sports clothes, is for anyone. Today modern sportswear can be as much about leisurewear style as practical advantage in the arena; football shirts can send signals about a player's biometrics to the coaching staff, but they also serve as replica products (in a cross-generational market) that can be worn on non-match days. This cross-fertilization began in the 1930s, when for some consumers sportswear was becoming leisurewear. In both North America and Europe, the staple look of sports fashions were mix-and-match separates, often in toning colours, or contrasting bright mixes of wool blend or cotton. These designs incorporated sports shirts and jumpers for men and women, to be worn for urban leisure as well as for active pursuits, and gradually a coordinated look of smart-casual separates in easy-wash materials became promoted as an 'assemblage' or 'ensemble'. Worldwide, this became an international and cosmopolitan way of dressing, elegant and androgynous, with tennis and basketball shoes pre-dating trainers as the leading leisure footwear.

THE DECLINE OF AMATEURISM

In 1913 the Native American athlete Jim Thorpe was stripped of the decathlon and pentathlon gold medals he had won at the Stockholm

Olympics the year before, when it was discovered that he had played baseball as a part-time, minor-league professional earlier in his sporting career. Today top professionals battle it out in almost every Olympic sport. Indeed, a major feature of twentieth-century sport was the decline of amateurism at the elite level. At least, this was a feature of the Western world; the Eastern bloc conspicuously disregarded any regulations with their use of both military and student 'amateurs'.

In the 1960s the restrictive regulations began to crumble. In 1963 cricket abolished any distinction between 'gentlemen' amateurs and professional 'players'; all participants henceforth were known simply as cricketers. Tennis went open in 1968. In 1992 the IOC, for many decades a hard-line advocate of amateurism, caved in, and in 1995 rugby union became the last major mainstream sport to allow professionalism, finally recognizing what had been a de facto position in the southern hemisphere for some time.

One major bastion remains: American college sport. Universities and colleges of further and higher education worldwide are dedicated to teaching, learning and research, but in the United States, uniquely, they also host a sports enterprise that has become part of the mass entertainment industry. In 2017 it generated $13 billion, which compared more than favourably with the NFL ($14 billion), Major League Baseball ($10 billion) and the National Basketball Association ($7.4 billion). College football brings in mega-bucks; the post-season Bowl games, for example, brings in over $32 million for the Peach Bowl and nearly $20 million for the Citrus game in Florida. So where does this money go? Well, not to any extent to the athletes involved. But there are others who do very well financially out of college sport. The head coaches of the four football teams who opened the 2019 season in a double header had taken home a combined $26.4 million in pay the previous season, and the coach of the University of Alabama football team was the highest-paid public employee in the state that year, with earnings of $8.3 million. Despite being the drawcards for spectators and television audiences, the athletes receive little direct financial reward. Until 2014 no allowances at all were provided for living expenses; all the athletes obtained were fee scholarships, training and the lure of future major-league contracts. This changed after a report in 2013 by the National College Players Association showed that 86 per cent of full-scholarship football players lived below the poverty line, despite often being committed to training and playing for more than forty hours a week.

As might be anticipated in the land of the mighty dollar, there is plenty of evidence of illegal payments and other inducements to the athletes. Among the more recent transgressions of National Collegiate Athletic Association rules, the University of North Carolina was exposed for giving athletes grades without them ever doing any work, and the University of Louisville coach Rick Pitino's basketball programme was found to have provided prostitutes for prospective players and financial inducements to attract the athletes to the university. This is nothing new. Back in 1929 the Carnegie Foundation surveyed 112 colleges and universities and found that only 28 were running 'ethical' sports programmes. As yet, such transactions have been insufficient to create a free market for these talented athletes. Eventually I suspect the lid will blow off the volcano and the college athletes will be recognized for what they are: skilled professionals worthy of reward.

Despite the media emphasis on elite sport, most sport today is still played by amateurs at recreational level. By amateur today we mean someone who does not receive any economic benefit from playing; indeed, the reverse is often the case and the amateur more often than not actually has to lay out money in order to play, be it a club subscription or the cost of travel to the match or of replacing damaged equipment. The majority of sportspeople thus remain amateur by the financial definition. Whether they still adhere to the Victorian amateur ethos is another matter.

TECHNOLOGY

The application of technology in sport has had a massive impact during the last century. Let's compare some items of sporting equipment in the 1920s with their later equivalents. Wooden-shafted golf clubs have been superseded by graphite and titanium versions, and the stiff bamboo vaulting pole has given way to the flexible carbon-fibre one. Some modern equipment could not even have been envisaged a century ago; athletes with physical disabilities could rarely play sport at all, but today 'cyborg technology' has allowed some even to challenge able-bodied competitors.

Sportspeople with apparently perfect bodies (well, much better than I ever possessed, at least) have accepted that technology can offer improvements. The eyes have become regarded as another piece of equipment to be changed by technology. Golfers, baseballers, basketballers and others have had laser surgery to improve on normal eyesight. While normal vision is 20/20, the golfer Tiger Woods had an operation to give him 20/15 vision, which means in essence that he can see in detail at 15 ft (4.5 m) what a normal-sighted person would see at 20 ft (6 m). The rules of golf do not allow the use of a device to measure distance or gauge the slope of the green, but now players can become the device themselves. The baseball big-hitter Mark McGwire used contact lenses to improve his vision to 20/10, which helped him to smash the season home-run record in 1998. This was accepted by the baseball authorities, but his use of steroids to enhance his muscles was not. Technology in sport has its dark side.

Scientific knowledge and technology have helped athletes to break records by improving not just their bodies but also the environment in which they perform. Modern swimming pools for international events have wave-reducing lane ropes to absorb the splash from nearby swimmers, and running-track surfaces have slip-resistant lanes that return energy to the legs rather than drain it as did the old, uneven cinder circuits. One estimate is that Jesse Owens, winning Olympian in the 100 metres in 1936, who had a best time of 10.2 seconds, would have been only a stride behind Usain Bolt's 2013 World Championship winning time of

Golf club designed by superstar golfer Tiger Woods for Nike.

9.77 seconds had he had the benefit of modern track, running-shoe and starting-block technology.

The growing economic importance of making the correct decision has led rule-enforcers to improve their decision-making by using technology to determine if a rugby ball was grounded correctly or whether a tennis ball landed in or out of court, and generally to improve communication between referees and their assistants. These are merely the culmination (so far) of previous technological applications such as the introduction of goal nets to football in the 1890s and the photo-finish camera brought to the racetrack in the 1940s. The process is ongoing. Many sports, but not yet all, allow players or coaches to appeal against an umpire's decision, a process pioneered in American football. Video centres well away from the action, often in another city altogether, now intervene to determine rulings. As I write this in October 2019, I am watching Tottenham Hotspur being awarded a penalty against Bayern Munich after a foul was checked by the Video Assistant Referee based in Paris. For the record, Harry Kane scored, but Bayern won the match 7-2.

SPREADING THE WORD: INTERNATIONALIZATION, COLONIALISM AND GLOBALIZATION

International sports events expanded in the twentieth century thanks to improvements in transport and, of course, public interest in their outcomes. The modern Olympics had been cancelled during the First World War but were revived in Antwerp in 1920 (less representation for the losing nations in the war, which were banned until 1928). In 1930 the first FIFA World Cup was held, in Uruguay. Both have achieved mega status, although this was never envisaged when they began. The early Olympics were not even stand-alone affairs but rather accompaniments to international expositions (from which they borrowed the idea of a dizzying scale of spectacle and a kaleidoscopic range of activities), and the first World Cup had but thirteen entrants and needed no qualifying competitions. Yet both increasingly gripped the public imagination, and ultimately, aided by the reach of television, they achieved quadrennial international cultural significance. Europe-wide sporting competitions did not really develop until after the Second World War, and can be seen as part of the consolidation of Europe into what has become the European

Union. There are still few teams that represent Europe as a whole; the major exception is in the Ryder Cup, a competition between professional golfers from Europe and the United States. Most major sports now have their own world championships, save American football.

Globalization involves the process of international integration arising from social, economic and cultural interchange that promotes universality. It is often seen by contemporary critics as harming local cultures by the superimposition of an international one, usually that of the United States or another Western nation. One might think from the television images beamed in from across the world that sport has become a globalized product, but the degree to which this has occurred has not been assessed.

Certainly, betting on sport has become globalized, but what of sport itself? In the previous chapter it was argued that national cultures produced and popularized different sports in different areas of the world. It is sometimes alleged that these models of sports development have now been undermined by globalization, but really soccer is still the only truly global sport. It is association football that attracts a worldwide television audience, not baseball, cricket or Formula One motor racing. The World Cup was the first single-sport global team event, but it was also unique for being the first global competition to allow professionals to participate. It began the expansion of the international market for football talent that cemented soccer as the world game. As befits the world game, the supply line for balls has become multinational. Footballs that once required stitching in local cobblers' workshops were later obtained from South and East Asia, where labour was plentiful and cheap. In turn mechanized production in China has undercut the low productivity of the hand-sewers of Pakistan and Thailand. Yet this is more an international division of labour based on comparative advantage than true globalization.

In the nineteenth century British imperialists painted the world atlas pink, and its military forces and civil administrators carried British sport to the furthest reaches of the empire as part of their cultural cargo. This continued into the twentieth century, but by this time the United States was also in the globalization game. Apart from basketball, however – which has had a place in the Olympics since 1936 – American sports have not grabbed the imagination of non-American audiences. But perhaps globalization should be considered more subtly than simply as the domination of a type of sport. As members of the major superpower emerging from the First World War, Americans thought they could use sport to spread American culture and ideology throughout the world, much as Britain had done in the previous century. However, while other countries accepted the American idea of defining nationhood through sport, they rejected Americanization in favour of their own nationalism. Globally, the role of American sports has been much less dominant than American films, television shows, pop music and fast-food restaurants. Some scholars argue that, no matter what the sport, Americans taught the world how to sell it, how to package and promote sporting events as a commercial enterprise. Nevertheless, although globalization might be seen in attitudes to the promotion of sport, here too the American pursuit of profit has not been fully replicated around the world, and investment in sport for national and individual kudos still occurs often enough.

Rarely were the indigenous populations forced by government decree to learn the sports of their imperial masters. Any pressure to play the imported sports came from individuals, not rulers or governments. America, itself once a British colony, has never sought to become a formal imperial power, but it has created a major informal empire via trade and investment, with the greenback as the dominant currency. Yet it is a similar story, with non-government envoys and others trying to persuade indigenous populations to play American sports rather than making this a condition of trade or political negotiations. A prime example might be the Young Men's Christian Association (YMCA) and its associated sporting ideology. In this version of muscular Christianity, young men were encouraged to seek God in the gymnasium. Sport was considered a useful agency for religious conversion and the propagation of Western culture and civilization. Hence the early years of the twentieth century brought a proliferation of YMCA gymnasia across North America and a growing demand (with a response on the supply side) for physical educators to train and take the YMCA philosophy abroad, especially to developing countries. Yet research has shown that the Americans working for the YMCA did not always follow the party line in the way they taught sports to Indian and Chinese participants; rather, in order for the sports to be accepted they had to acquire local cultural characteristics. It was the same story when the colonies adopted British sport, in that they also adapted it, sometimes the rules but also the manner in which it was played.

Contrary to conventional wisdom, globalization might prove beneficial to non-Western nations as they increasingly assert themselves in the
decision-making and economics of international sporting events. This
could reshape the power structures within international sporting bodies,
which traditionally have been dominated by Western nations. Satellite
television and the associated specialized sporting networks have created
a new imperative for international audiences. These include the markets
of non-Western nations, cricket with its huge Indian following being
an exemplar. In turn India has used its economic bargaining power to
change its position in international cricket politics, although cricket is still
a multinational sport, not a global one. Indications of potential change
can be seen in the hosting of recurring international sporting events by
non-Western nations and the growing investment of non-Western funds
in Western sports clubs.

Elite sports can expose – for good or bad – a country to the world.
In the twenty-first century what were labelled the BRICS nations (Brazil,
Russia, India, China and South Africa) have all hosted sporting mega-
events, reflecting the economic growth of these emerging economies.

AMERICANS ARE DIFFERENT

As a sweeping generalization, European sport has developed in a different
way from that in the United States. The major sports played have differed
between the continents, with America developing basketball, baseball, ice
hockey and its own version of football, whereas virtually all Europeans
have kicked a soccer ball and others have made tennis, gymnastics and
cycling significant participant and spectator sports. The development
of these sports was organized in different contexts. Again to generalize,
schools, colleges and universities were paramount in the United States,
while in Europe the major role was taken by voluntary clubs and associations. American sports were commercialized and professionalized earlier
and more thoroughly than those in Europe. Leagues at both amateur and
professional level in Europe were based on promotion and relegation, but,
in contrast to this open system, the United States, especially at professional level, operated closed leagues of competing franchises. These leagues,
established as profit-seeking businesses, remained national in orientation
and without any international regulatory bodies, a fact that often led to

competing leagues in the same sport, whereas European competitions had more international appeal and were set up and governed by international non-profit federations. The American government scarcely influenced the development of sporting organization, function or culture. Sports in the United States were market-driven and developed independently of the state, while in Europe, especially after the Second World War, governments increasingly intervened in the sporting realm.

A few caveats must be made. There will be exceptions to all these statements. Some sports are played everywhere; significant examples include tennis and golf. America does have voluntary clubs and non-profit-orientated sports bodies, but they don't have the significant influence that their equivalents have in Europe. Finally, Europe is a collection of nations, many of which, as we have seen, had their own sporting characteristics.

WHAT NEXT?

The modern age is one of fast food, immediate communication and instant gratification. This has had an impact on those sports where time seemed almost irrelevant. Throughout the cricketing world, Test matches lasting up to five days (with no win or loss guaranteed) have lost out to much faster versions – one-day cricket, with each side facing 50 overs (300 balls), and T20, with each side facing only 20 overs (120 balls) – and another is now being introduced with only 100 balls a side, which could be played in an evening or an afternoon. In the United States, Major League Baseball, a booming industry but with the oldest fan base of any major American sport, has looked to attract younger spectators by experimenting with new rules that could shorten games, such as a twenty-second pitch clock and limited time for pitching changes, although so far they have been tried out only in off-season games and in minor leagues. In golf, after years of complaints of slow play, from 2020 those golfers on the European Tour who exceed fifty seconds in preparing and executing a shot if they are first to play on a hole (only forty seconds if they are the second player) will have a stroke added to their score.

New sports continue to emerge. The twenty-first century has seen e-sports, now instituted in the 2022 Asian Games; drone racing, in which 'pilots' wear googles to get the view from the cockpit of their craft; world chase tag, a competitive form of parkour; and quidditch, a land-based take on the Harry Potter game that is both physically active and gender-neutral. Whether they will gain the popularity in participation and spectator numbers of some of the more 'traditional' sports, time will tell. Certainly, e-sports are attracting both players and spectators, many of whom had little time for conventional sports. When it comes to looking at the future, much sports journalism predicts solely on the basis of the here and now, seeing single events as possible tipping points in the history of a sport, but historians must be more cautious with predictions. History teaches us that there are trends as well as fluctuations, and it is the former more than the latter that show the way forward.

PART THREE

SPORTS

This section will focus on what the author considers important sports in historical terms, although of course that is a matter of personal preference. By necessity the histories will be brief, covering only key points and topics in the development of each sport and information that might be new and interesting to readers. It is assumed that readers will know something about sport, so generally little mention will be made of specific rules and practices. Except perhaps for basketball, which most sports historians accept began in 1891, it is impossible to be precise about the date of origin of any sport, and the ensuing chapters will not attempt such a task. Indeed, the author believes that firsts are relatively meaningless historically, and what is more important is typicality and when a sport achieved popularity. All sports perhaps owe their distant origin to man's instinct to fight, to hunt, to run, to throw, to kick and to travel, hence the groupings: combat sports, field sports, equestrian sports, locomotive sports, bat and ball sports, football codes, water sports and winter sports.

Combat sports exist worldwide, although historically individual nations have exhibited preferences for particular forms, such as bare-knuckle pugilism in Britain, sumo in Japan and various martial arts throughout Asia. We examine the development of these and other combat sports, their interaction with other cultures and their modification over time. Next come hunting, shooting and fishing, sports that take advantage of natural resources (of the animal kind). Animals also feature in – indeed are central to – equestrian sports. Historically, horses were the locomotive power of inland transport throughout Europe and the basis of military power worldwide, but today the horse exists primarily as an animal used for recreational purposes: showing, riding, jumping and racing. It is the last that is the main focus of our brief historical study. We then turn to human and mechanical power, looking first at the runners in sprints and endurance events before examining cycling, which became a major participant and spectator sport in Europe, and finishing with motorized power on two wheels and four. Like bicycling, both motor racing and motorbike racing stemmed from technological developments in the transport sector.

In the following chapter I took the liberty of labelling golf a bat and ball sport. The members of the Royal and Ancient Golf Club might not agree with this, but my golfing partners would concede that if I went round with a cricket bat it might be an improvement. We also look at tennis, cricket, hockey, lacrosse, shinty and hurling. Next we feature just balls, although of varying shapes. Everywhere in the world has had a version of football, but the main codes that have developed are soccer, rugby league, rugby union, Gaelic football, American football and Australian Rules. In looking for the origins of football, historians – by training so fixated on documented evidence – may have paid too much regard to its formal codification. Yet codes rarely appeared out of nowhere, and in many cases they may have been based partially on games that were being played without written rules. Travelling through and on water forms the basis of the next chapter, and then frozen water features as the underlying element of winter sports, which stemmed from an ability to use ice- and snow-covered land for recreation.

The final chapter groups a few sports not by character but by geography. Americans, by which I mean inhabitants of the United States, play their own sports: basketball, which they invented (although it was a Canadian who started it off); American football, which they devised but not totally independently of other codes; and baseball, which they claim to have invented but did not.

6

FIGHTING TALK:
COMBAT SPORTS

Cudgelling and singlestick were forms of duelling with wooden weapons that developed out of sword practice. By the mid-nineteenth century in Britain contests in both disciplines were common features of parish wakes, fairs and race meetings. In cudgelling, two weapons were used, one about 2 ft (0.6 m) long for defence, the other – a longer one with a wicker basket to protect the hand – for attack. In singlestick, as the name implies, only the latter implement was employed. Competitors stood a yard (1 m) apart and, although strikes were allowed to any part of the body, their objective was to cut the skin anywhere above the lower jaw, so that the blood ran an inch (2.5 cm). The decline of patronage for rural sports generally and the disappearance of specific events at which those sports were played ended public competition by about 1860. Singlestick continued for members of the London gymnasia until the 1890s, although with the use of protective masks, but thereafter the popularity of the sabre made singlestick redundant, except for training servicemen in swordplay up to the First World War.

Kickshins, crimogiant in Wales, and clogging in some northern English mining areas were (con)tests of masculinity in which men wearing heavy boots, often with protruding nails, kicked each other's shins until one cried 'Enough'. Hacking, as shin-kicking can be termed, was not unique to this sport; it featured in Devon wrestling and was integral to the dispute over what forms of violence could be used in early rugby.

FINGERS, FISTS AND GLOVES

'So I gathered all the little strength I had, and I socked my thumb
in his eye, and with my fingers took a twist on his snot box, and
with my other hand I grabbed him by the back of the head; I then
caught his ear in my mouth, gin his head a flirt, and out come his
ear by the roots! I then flopped his head over, and caught his other
ear in my mouth, and jerked that out in the same way, and it made
a hole in his head that I could have rammed my fist through, and I
was just goin' to when he hollered "Nuff".'

Thus did a Kentuckian describe the latter stages of a 'rough and tumble'
fight in which he emerged not unscathed himself but triumphant.

Among the common folk of the late eighteenth- and early nineteenth-
century American frontier, it was virtually unregulated brawling rituals
that shaped concepts of manhood and honour. Before a bout, the fighters
decided whether to 'fight fair' under Broughton's prizefighting rules (if
they had heard of them; see below) or 'rough and tumble', often also
known as gouging. Most opted for the version in which it was permissible
to tear and rend each other, with eye-gouging and castration not infrequent
occurrences. The emphasis on maximum disfigurement and severing
body parts made this style of fighting unique; except for a banning of
weapons, it was a no-holds-barred contest won only when one fighter gave
up or was incapacitated. Gouging out an opponent's eye was the ultimate
objective of most fighters, the most celebrated of whom hardened their

Francisco Goya's portrayal of cudgelling in the early 1820s.

fingernails and honed them sharp. There were no professional fighters as such, although money could be made from gambling on the result or first blood. Men fought for informal village and county titles, for the kudos of being local champion. More than this, in many cases it was the way disputes were settled and even minor slights avenged. To modern eyes the brutality seems barbarous, but perhaps it was less so to the inhabitants of the backwoods who saw daily danger and regular violence in a land frequented by wild animals, outlaws and indigenous tribes.

Pugilism, while perhaps less brutal than the frontier fights, was still a gory business. The bare-knuckle bouts ended not in a decision on points but by one of the combatants being unable to continue. A round ended when one of the protagonists was felled (or chose to go down), and then they had thirty seconds to get back on their feet in the centre of the ring. Fights could therefore last many rounds and take hours to complete. A set of named rules was issued in 1743 by the pugilist-turned-boxing promoter Jack Broughton to control the conduct of prizefights in his London amphitheatre. The rules were few, but they demonstrated the complexity of regulating a violent spectator sport involving gambling as they contained clauses to determine the result, outlaw crowd disorder, choose adjudicators, disallow certain practices by the fighters and prevent financial impropriety. Although formulated for Broughton's own amphitheatre, these rules were quickly accepted for all fights of any importance, possibly because, as he noted, they had been approved by 'the gentlemen' who sponsored the fighters. Despite competing codes, Broughton's rules continued to be the dominant form until Victorian times. The one major omission – the legitimacy of going down without being struck – began to be specified as foul play in the articles of agreement (which continued as explicit additions to rules to remove ambiguity for a particular contest). Over time this became unnecessary, and later articles often covered only basic details of any stakes.

In 1838 the London Prize Rules superseded those of Broughton. They outlawed headbutting, kicking and biting, and hitting below the belt, and defined the size and situation of the ring – 24 ft (7.3 m) square and on turf surrounded by ropes. Yet the sport was on the ropes itself. Increasingly, magistrates were deciding that prizefights were illegal, partly because men were being paid to assault each other but especially because the fights were held in the open air, with little means of controlling crowd access or behaviour.

The next major change was the coming of the Queensberry rules in 1867, which paved the way for the transformation of bare-knuckle fighting into modern gloved boxing. However, fighting under Queensberry rules did not replace bare-knuckle contests overnight. Boxing's legal position still required clarification. What had to be shown was that the sport demonstrated that the players had to utilize skill to earn points in order to win, rather than it being a contest to exhaustion. Fixing the number of rounds to be fought was a way around this, with a ten-second count being declared a knock-out rather than giving the downed fighter thirty seconds or a minute to get back to their feet, as in prizefighting.

In the 1890s the newly formed National Sporting Club, a group of primarily aristocratic supporters of boxing, specified the size of gloves to be used at each weight level (another innovation), although there was no formal institutional control of the sport until the establishment of the British Boxing Board of Control in 1929, the same year it met with its American and French equivalents to ratify amended Queensberry rules as the International Boxing Rules. Unfortunately, such a meeting of minds has been a rarity in professional boxing. Hence world titles abound at all

---

The Queensberry rules were not the idea of the Marquess of Queensberry

John Sholto Douglas, the 9th Marquess of Queensberry, has two major claims to fame. First, he was the nemesis of the writer Oscar Wilde, who sued Queensberry for libel after he publicly objected to Wilde's liaison with his son Lord Alfred Douglas. The suit was dropped, but it led to Wilde's conviction in 1895 and his imprisonment for homosexuality. Second, all boxing fans have heard of the Queensberry rules, which paved the way for the emergence of gloved boxing to replace bare-knuckle prizefighting. These were first published by the Amateur Athletic Club (AAC) in 1867 as a set of twelve rules for conducting boxing matches. Although Queensberry was a member of the AAC, it was not he who actually devised the code, but a friend of his from Cambridge University, John Graham Chambers. However, Chambers was no nobleman, and the AAC felt – rightly, as it turned out – that aristocratic backing might bestow some respectability on a sport that had fallen into disrepute. So Queensberry gets the credit. Chambers went on to rewrite the rules for billiards and devise the Putney rules for rowing that were adopted by the Henley Regatta.

John L. Sullivan, the first recognized world heavyweight champion of gloved boxing.

weights. Promoters see marketing value in attaching the label 'world title fight' to their bouts, so they find or organize a body to sanction it and there is no overall governing body to clarify the situation.

Unlike most sports, boxing developed a different set of constitutive rules for amateurs and professionals. This came first with the Queensberry rules, which, for what were labelled sparring competitions (for non-professionals), specified a fixed number of rounds with the result to be

Wrestlers in the United States, c. 1900s.

decided on points, whereas for a while the professional bouts remained endurance contests. Generally the history of amateur boxing is that the fighters have shorter bouts and are protected more than professionals. Another difference from professional boxing is that the amateur code does have an international controlling body: two, actually, but they don't fight each other. The IOC is responsible for boxing at the Olympics, but, more generally, the International Amateur Boxing Association, established in 1946, is in charge and runs an undisputed set of world championships.

Boxing exists in a precarious legal position, since it involves physical assault and the deliberate infliction of pain and injury. Some countries, notably Sweden – home in the 1960s to the world heavyweight champion Ingemar Johansson – have now banned it. In Britain medical opinion is firmly against the sport, but several private members' bills have failed to get a parliamentary majority. Essentially, it survives partly because participants consent to be assaulted, but mainly because society chooses to tolerate it.

CATCH-AS-CATCH-CAN

Heard of the Russian athlete Vladimer Khinchegashvili or Davor Štefanek from Serbia? No? What about two Americans, Helen Maroulis or Kyle Snyder? All these, it is suspected, will be unknown to fans of Hulk Hogan, the Undertaker or other WWE WrestleMania stars. Yet they were Olympic gold medal winners in wrestling at the Rio Games of 2016. They might well have been the last of their type, since in 2013 the IOC announced that all wrestling would be dropped from the Olympics after 2020, but sweeping reforms in organization, match rules and equality policies persuaded the Committee to review the situation, and the sport was reinstated, at least for the Games to be held in 2021 and 2024. The development of amateur wrestling has been aided by the setting of time limits for bouts and a system of determining the winner when neither wrestler has gained a fall. The sport has mainly been the province of Europe, although, as readers of John Irving's *The World According to Garp* will appreciate, it has become a significant high-school and college sport in the United States.

Wrestling has a long history. In the Book of Genesis, Jacob was said to have wrestled an opponent all night before he could become the patriarch Israel; for the non-believer, more acceptable evidence might be the depictions of the sport on 5,000-year-old Egyptian vases. That it allows full confrontation in a test of physical superiority with limited chances of serious injury may account for its wide diffusion, longevity and popularity. Injuries are common in wrestling, but they are generally not serious. Safety has been a key feature of modern amateur wrestling. Holds and tactics that jeopardized life or limb were always illegal, but more modern rules have banned virtually any hold that pressurizes a joint in a direction contrary to its normal movement.

A greased wrestling match (*Güres*) in the gardens of the sultan's palace, c. 1809.

When wrestling was dropped from the Olympic programmes in 2013, the successful effort to have it reinstated was headlined by the claim that some 30 million people worldwide participated in the Olympic versions of the sport, and countless millions more in other forms. One of the traditional versions is oil wrestling, a centuries-old sport in rural parts of Asia but now centred on a major festival held annually in the Turkish town of Edirne, in which more than 1,500 wrestlers participate, their bodies and leather trousers soaked in olive oil to make gripping difficult. There are some two hundred forms of wrestling worldwide, but the Olympics recognizes two major ones, freestyle and Graeco-Roman; the latter – surprisingly, in view of its name – bears little relation to the actuality of the sport in ancient times, but was invented in the nineteenth century by European wrestling aficionados, based on how they thought ancient wrestling might have looked. In freestyle wrestling competitors have more flexibility of moves and tactics than in Graeco-Roman. They can take a wide variety of holds on both the upper body and the legs, whereas no grappling below the waist is permissible in Graeco-Roman, nor any use of the legs to reinforce a hold. Most regional and national varieties of wrestling are versions of freestyle with particular rules that distinguish them from others. What might be termed 'folk-wrestling' helped to create regional sporting identities for Cumberland and Westmorland, and Devon and Cornwall in England and, across the Channel, Brittany.

Professional wrestling as entertainment developed from both branches of the sport. In the early twentieth century the Estonian Graeco-Roman star George Hackenschmidt also fought under freestyle rules. He won a series of widely watched bouts against the Turkish champion Ahmed Madrali, and in 1905 toured the United States, where he defeated Tom Jenkins for a self-styled world championship. Over a career of more than 2,000 contests, he lost only two fights. Such was his celebrity that he was recorded in early films, where his physique and wrestling style can still be admired. Professional freestyle wrestling has centred on the United States, where it developed out of the popularity of wrestling in postbellum America. Tournaments in the 1880s drew hundreds of participants and stimulated the emergence of a professional circuit, one not yet tainted by the theatrical performances of later years.

By the 1920s professional wrestling as sporting entertainment was becoming choreographed and losing its unpredictability – a vital feature of sport. However, while it abandoned its integrity as a sport, it gained success as a spectacle. One wrestling impresario of the time, Charles Cochran, claimed in his autobiography *The Secrets of a Showman* (1925) that 'the public did not want straight wrestling – they wanted a "show".' The major supplier of professional wrestling today is WWE, which began as the Capitol Wrestling Corporation in 1952 and now hosts more than three hundred live events each year as well as telecasting to some 150 countries. Although the bouts are scripted and follow a storyline, they have found a ready market among sports fans who prefer the spectacle to true competition. It used to be called the World Wrestling Federation, but the World Wide Fund for Nature did not appreciate its acronym being taken over and after a court battle – in which the outcome could not be fixed – WWF became WWE.

Another form of professional wrestling is sumo. Some in the West might deem it a freak show in which obese children and even more obese adults are paraded to an admiring audience, but is it any more freakish than 7-foot basketball players or 300-pound gridiron footballers who can run even time? It is one of the oldest martial arts, perhaps dating back to 23 BCE (if descriptions written eight centuries later can be so accurate!), but certainly it can be traced to 821 CE, when, with archery and equestrian archery, it formed one of the great annual tournaments at the Japanese imperial court.

Sumo involves significant preparatory ritual. The wrestlers enter the arena via a path of flowers; they cast salt and stamp their feet to drive away demons; and, depending on their ranking, they can spend up to four minutes crouching, stamping and glaring before the physical contest actually begins. Some of the traditions are ancient, but others are only a few centuries old, such as the design of the ring (a circle inscribed in a square). Rather than being modernized, sumo has been traditionalized by the introduction of religious elements into a previously secular sport and by linking it more closely to medieval Japanese culture. For example, the referee's hat resembles the headgear of a Shinto priest from the Heian period (794–1185 CE), but it was introduced in 1909, a form of invented tradition. All wrestlers belong to a training stable, the oldest of which date back to the late eighteenth century, and, similar to WWE wrestlers, are given new names when they begin their career. There is a hierarchy of rank based on each wrestler's success in the six annual fifteen-day tournaments.

Sumo wrestling in 1870.

The Japanese as a nation have been reluctant to give equality to foreigners and were shocked in January 1993 when Chad Rowan (wrestling
as Akebono Tarō), who had left his native Hawaii in 1988 to enter the
world of professional sumo, became a grand champion. It was something
they had to get used to. In 1999 another Hawaiian, Fiamalu Penitani
(wrestling name Musashimaru Kōyō), claimed the title, to be followed
by two Mongolians in 2003 and 2006 respectively. From the spring
tournament of 2006 there were 32 consecutive tournaments without a
Japanese winner. The foreign-born champions hailed from Mongolia

and Eastern Europe, where a tradition of wrestling of a different type provided them with new moves such as leg sweeps and lateral movement not employed in traditional sumo, in which brute strength had been the key to success in the past. The Japan Sumo Association implemented an unwritten rule to allow only one foreign wrestler per stable, and at the New Year tournament of 2017 they were able to celebrate their first home-grown grand champion for nineteen years when 175-kilogram (385 lb) Kisenosato took the title.

MARTIAL ARTS

There are probably as many martial arts as there are Asian countries. Some are well known to Westerners, such as judo, ju-jitsu, kendo, karate, kung fu, tai chi and tae kwon do. Others are less so, for example in the Malay-speaking world silat (and its many variations), which combines self-defence, athletic performance and dance with spiritual, aesthetic and ritual accompaniments; and naginata, taught mainly to girls in Japanese schools and colleges, which began as warfare using long single-bladed sticks to cut down horsemen, but became transmogrified into a non-violent discipline for personal development.

To most Asian participants, martial arts are not just sports for competition, recreation or health, but cerebral activities concerned with self-development, philosophical attributes and spiritual awareness. Tai chi, for example, is a Chinese martial art linked to Daoist meditation, philosophy and traditional medicine. Best known in the West as a health and longevity exercise for seniors (and practised as such by many Chinese), it can also be a serious and strenuous physical martial art. This latter aspect was developed in the nineteenth century by Yang 'the Invincible' Luchan, who had learned it in its indigenous home of Chenjiagou in Henan province. He was appointed martial-arts instructor to the imperial court and reputedly remained undefeated in many challenge matches against martial-arts masters in Beijing.

Tae kwon do, on the other hand, is not really for the elderly or invalid. It is a Korean martial art that involves kicks and hand blows. The basic techniques have been practised for 2,000 years, but it was developed in its modern form during the 1940s and became formally known as tae kwon do in 1955. It now has the most practitioners of any martial art

Kendo competition.

worldwide. Tae kwon do became an Olympic medal sport in 2000, but had been preceded by judo, which gained Olympic status in 1964, the first Asian sport to gain such recognition. Judo ('the gentle way') developed in Japan in the late nineteenth century. Its techniques originated in the ju-jitsu of the samurai, reformulated and codified by Kanō Jigorō, who stressed the avoidance of force and emphasized a character-building philosophy of educating the player physically, mentally and spiritually. The physical techniques themselves were based on scientific principles that used an opponent's force against them so that a skilful smaller person could throw a larger one. Older martial arts were considered rich in spiritual symbolism but unsuited to a modernizing society, which Japan aspired to be, whereas judo, as a 'new' martial art, was in the vanguard of the modernizing movement and was adopted by the police and the army as well as being introduced into schools and universities. It then spread steadily around the world, aided by Japanese emigrants and tours by Japanese judo experts. It has been transformed from a small, esoteric martial art into a modern, Westernized, international sport, and its rules have changed to bring in weight categories, time limits, floor dimensions and the wearing of blue *judogi* for television appeal. Although the sport is now practised with less regard to the underlying philosophy, even the most competitive players respect the tradition and etiquette.

Many martial arts are forms of unarmed combat, but not kendo, which is a form of two-handed fencing with bamboo poles. Traditional swordsmanship came under threat from the modernizing movement in Japan, but was saved in a modified form by the development of kendo, or kenjutso as it was then called. As with judo, it was adopted by the police. However, Japanese schools opted for Western gymnastics and did not really take up the sport until the interwar years, when the Japanese military began to influence education policy and demanded that it should emphasize patriotism and spiritual training. One result of this was that kendo became a compulsory school subject. It was around this time that the sport was officially called kendo. After the Second World War the Allied Pacific Command banned martial arts in Japan, but kendo was eventually allowed once more if it focused on its spiritual rather than combative aspects.

Although many martial arts have over the years borrowed ideas and techniques from others, in recent times a form of fighting termed mixed martial arts (MMA) has gained popularity in the West. In these contests, short of carrying weapons, participants can use any combat skills they wish to. The origin of contemporary MMA can be traced to Brazil in the early twentieth century, when the brothers Carlos and Hélio Gracie, sons of a Scottish immigrant, opened a ju-jitsu academy in Rio de Janeiro. For publicity, they advertised that they would challenge anyone who wished to fight them, and their *vale tudo* (anything goes) battles soon attracted crowds large enough to fill local soccer stadia. For the next five decades the Gracie brothers and their sons defeated martial-arts experts from around the globe and developed Gracie ju-jitsu, also known as Brazilian ju-jitsu. Brazil already possessed its own martial art, capoeira, which combined self-defence, acrobatics, dance, music and song. It was developed in the early sixteenth century by slaves who used it to disguise the fact that they were practising fight moves. After the abolition of slavery in Brazil in 1888, capoeira was declared illegal, but by the 1920s the authorities had begun to relax the enforcement of its prohibition, and martial artists began to incorporate capoeira technique into their practice. In 2014 UNESCO ruled that capoeira was part of Brazil's cultural heritage and granted it protected status. However, Gracie ju-jitsu was less cultural and more violent.

In the 1980s Hélio Gracie's son Rorion brought his Gracie challenge to the United States, offering $100,000 to anyone who could beat him or one of his brothers. This further popularized Brazilian ju-jitsu and led in 1993 to pay-per-view 'Ultimate Fighting Championship' tournaments, the first three of which were won by Royce Gracie. Rules were few, and fights could be ended by the referee, submission or knock-out. All styles were welcomed, including sumo, although the 270-plus-kilogram (595 lb) wrestler lost to a karate exponent half his size. It was bloody and dangerous and it appealed to the television viewer, although not to opponents of human blood sports. Several American states banned such competitions, but MMA was saved by the creation of a governing body, the International Fighting Championships, which gained legitimacy for the sport by imposing new rules, including weight divisions, time limits and a judging system. The largest MMA promotion company is the Ultimate Fighting Championship, whose title-holders as of November 2019 reflect the worldwide appeal of the sport: among them a Mexican American, an African American, a Croatian American, two fighters born in Nigeria, and competitors from China, Kyrgyzstan, Brazil and Hawaii.

7

THE KILLING FIELDS:
HUNTING, SHOOTING AND FISHING

Hunting is a general term used to denote the pursuit of wild animals, usually but not always with dogs. Falcons were used as hunting birds in two ways: being released to circle above prey that had been flushed out from cover using dogs; or pursuing their quarry, such as herons or cranes, on the wing. It was a spectator sport, although the latter version required them to be on horseback, since the chase could cover several miles. It was also a high-status sport from medieval times into the sixteenth century, something that gentlemen were expected to pursue. Heraldic designs drew on falconry to express power; hawks were exchanged between great families and given to the monarch when he or she visited; and most estates had an establishment of professional falconers. Yet by the end of the seventeenth century falconry had declined in importance and popularity. The monarchy no longer followed it and manpower on estates shifted towards gamekeeping, looking after hounds and servicing guns as shooting and fox hunting took falconry's place in the hunting hierarchy.

As with many aspects of sport, it was technology that changed the competitive balance. Falconry suffered from a static technology, since equipment, methods of training and ways of controlling disease remained virtually unchanged from the Middle Ages. In the meantime the development and continual improvement of firearms created a new sport of recreational shooting. The key factor is that shooting had a military purpose, whereas falconry did not. The quest for better military firearms had a spin-off effect on sporting guns and, especially after the development of the wheel lock and flintlock, eventually made them safer and more accurate. Moreover, guns were fired by their owners while falcons had generally been flown by trainers. With the coming of shooting, gentlemen began to compete against each other as marksmen, and their skill began to be gauged by the number of kills they made. Shooting had arrived as a competitive field sport. It also helped that shooting was less dependent on the weather than falconry and that guns did not have to be fed, trained and retrieved when they flew away.

Although falconers had supplied estates with some game, especially partridges, it was the thrill of the sport that had attracted its adherents, not the by-product of filling their pantries. In any event, changes in the

Traditional falconry in India, early 18th century.
Modern falconry in United Arab Emirates.

Medieval deer hunting, from *Le Livre de la Chasse* (Book of the Hunt)
of Gaston III Phoebus, Comte de Foix.

rural economy, especially animal husbandry, reduced the importance of
hunting as a source of meat. It is noteworthy that falconry survived much
longer in less developed and more thinly populated areas of the world,
especially among nomadic communities, as on the Russian steppes, in
northern India and China, and in the Arabian Desert.

Recreational hunting for deer was introduced into Britain by the
Romans but faded away, as did many Roman innovations, when the
empire collapsed in the fifth century CE. As a sport in Britain its revival can
be traced to the medieval period, when deer hunting was undertaken by
the nobility on horseback using hounds bred for the purpose. The growing
popularity of the sport led to the creation of specialized deer forests, where
men were employed to protect the animals from illicit hunting. Hunting
and its associated horsemanship provided powerful status symbols for
the nobility and in eighteenth-century France functioned as a rite of
passage in court culture. Across Europe royal forests exclusively reserved

for their hunting allowed rulers to display their wealth and power, and it became fashionable for the nobility to build hunting parks on their large estates. Followers of hunting attempted, usually successfully, to limit who could hunt such prey and when, so confining all such hunting to their own social group. Game laws from 1671 onwards restricted the hunting of game to those qualified by land ownership and birth, perhaps 1 per cent of the population, and the Black Act of 1723 in England applied the death penalty to deer theft.

Hunting was found all over Europe and colonial America, and in Britain, where first the deer and then the lowly fox was the focus. The shrinking of royal forests and deer parks through increased economic exploitation brought a drastic reduction of the deer population. In some areas deer hunting continued, and packs of specialist staghounds were maintained, but in areas such as Leicestershire, in order to continue to enjoy hunting, new cultural status was ascribed to the fox – previously considered vermin – and it became a highly respectable prey, worthy of being hunted by the nobility and gentry. It offered the mounted riders who took part the thrill and challenge of the chase. Open land was essential for such hunting, and the activity was always associated with the wealthy, most especially the landed classes; it became more popular in the eighteenth century as the economy grew and more men had the wealth to get involved.

Although ultimately hunting is goal-orientated, its supporters also focused on the process, particularly as agricultural enclosure reduced the

---

Do you know John Peel?

D'ye ken John Peel with his coat so gay?

D'ye ken John Peel at the break o' day?

D'ye ken John Peel when he's far, far a-way.

With his hounds and his horn in the morning?

For the sound of his horn brought me from my bed,

And the cry of his hounds which he oft time led,

Peel's 'View, Halloo!' could awaken the dead,

Or the fox from his lair in the morning.

Cumberland hunting song written c. 1824 by John Woodcock Graves (1795–1886) in celebration of his friend John Peel (1776–1854), an English fox hunter from the Lake District volume of open countryside and increased the importance of a rider's ability to leap their horse over gates, fences and walls. This led directly to the development of point-to-point racing and indirectly to the emergence of showjumping as an equestrian sport. Hunting was seen as a manly and healthy form of exercise. It is rarely a solitary pursuit, and it also provided a source of associativity. Hunt clubs and private packs, run by rich owners, often offered generous hospitality and heavy drinking during the evening after the hunt. More generally, hunting literature contains many claims that the sport unified rural society. Most were along the lines promulgated in 1808 by John Hawkes, a friend of the famous huntsman Hugo Meynell, that 'the field is a most agreeable coffee-house, and there is more real society to be met with there than in any other situation of life. It links all classes together, from the peer to the peasant.' The hunting field was open to all. Foxes were vermin, so there were no game-law qualifications to be met and land belonging to others could be traversed (with appropriate sporting compensation). However, although the farmer or tradesman was welcome to ride alongside the hunting gentry, fraternization – if it can be labelled as such – ended there. There were no invitations for such people to the hunt balls, dinners or races; there, social distinctions were emphasized and reinforced.

Conventional wisdom on the history of fox hunting was that the sport was taken up by the gentry only after the Restoration of the monarchy in 1660, and that before then the fox was controlled as befitted vermin by digging or forcing it out of its hole and killing it quickly with the aid of nets or terriers. However, research into medieval art and literature has demonstrated that huntsmen of the time practised fox hunting and employed similar methods to those used in the modern world. Fox hunting simply became more popular in the eighteenth century, rather than being a newly developed sport. The pioneering role given to Meynell, who hunted the Melton country in Leicestershire, has also been undermined by researchers. He was labelled 'the father of modern hunting' by the nineteenth-century writer Nimrod (the pseudonym of Charles James Apperley), who credited Meynell with developing new techniques of hunting such as breeding specialist hounds. However, the latter's reputation was based solely on the sycophantic narratives of Apperley, who, despite his claims to the contrary, neither knew nor hunted with Meynell.

Fox hunting in Victorian England.

Fox hunting in North America followed the English fashion with the exception, or so it is claimed, of the kill being a key feature of the chase, especially if the prey (red fox, grey fox, coyote or bobcat, depending on location) managed to go to ground. None of these animals was seen as vermin to be eradicated, and the hunts justified themselves as markers of social exclusivity, like the American country clubs, of which some early ones ran their own hunts.

BIRDS OF A FEATHER

Shooting now features as an Olympic target sport, but it made its debut in the Games in Paris in 1900 as a competition to shoot live pigeons. Indeed, shooting live birds was a common pastime in nineteenth-century Britain; sparrow shooting tended to be dominated by the working class, with pubs as venues, and pigeon shooting the province of the socially elite. The Hurlingham Club in southwest London, now more famous for polo matches, was a significant venue, and retains a pigeon motif in its logo.

These shooting sports have disappeared, but every year some 15 million pheasants are blasted out of Britain's autumnal and winter skies,

Men's skeet shooting at the 2008 Beijing Olympics.
Pheasant shooting, c. 1790.

although only about one-tenth of those have been born in the wild. In fact, between 35 and 50 million birds are released into the British countryside each year after being bred on game farms, about half coming from France (before Brexit, at least). Those that are not shot fall victim to predators, disease and motorists. This importation of farm-bred birds is the third stage in the development of bird shooting. The first was 'rough shooting', in which individuals or groups walked around the estates shooting birds that had taken flight. Next, to cater for those who wanted their sport less strenuous, came the battue, in which birds were driven by beaters towards waiting marksmen. In both cases the birds were generally bred in the wild, even those raised on estates. However, from the 1950s the intensification of farming led to a severe decline in wild birds, particularly partridges but also pheasants. The response of the estate owners and their gamekeepers was to breed birds on game farms and release them on to the estates. The shooting season lasts for only four months but sustains an industry that is estimated to be worth £2 billion. In itself, however, shooting is uneconomic and must be classed as conspicuous consumption. The overall cost of running a shoot is almost £40 per bird shot and typically game dealers pay 20–30 pence a bird, although some shoots give the carcasses away and others dispose of them in landfill and incinerators. It is killing for pleasure, not hunting for food or exterminating vermin: but that is the shooter's choice.

The Royal Lion Hunt of Ashurbanipal.

Such a pastime is reminiscent of Ashurbanipal, the ruler of Assyria in the seventh century BCE. Relief sculptures from his palace show him as a merciless hunter killing lion after lion from his chariot, on foot, with a bow and arrow or with a sword. Like all rulers of the time in the Near East, he was depicted as a chariot-riding archer-warrior, there to defend his people and their property from not only foreign enemies but marauding wild animals. Yet in a way this was fake history, since he did not hunt the lions; they were brought in cages to be released for him to slaughter. It was the killing that was important, not the hunting. So it is with trophy hunting, whose adherents kill big game without any risk to themselves. The act of hunting lions in Kenya had existed long before such overt displays of conspicuous sporting consumption as 'champagne safaris', but, as in much history written from an imperial perspective, the indigenous contribution has been ignored, thereby allowing the values of the nineteenth-century aristocratic hunts to create an image of African inferiority. Yet it was native hunters with their legacy of tracking skills and knowledge of animal behaviour that enabled the visitors to collect their trophies.

SPINNING A LINE

Angling is a major recreational sport. A survey of people over sixteen years old in the United States in 2001 estimated that more than 9 million of them were seawater anglers and just under 30 million freshwater ones. In Australia more than one-third of the population participate, especially in sea-fishing, since the population in that continent clings to the seaboard. In Britain there is a constant but unsuccessful lobby for a fisherman to be shortlisted for the Sports Personality of the Year award, to acknowledge the nation's most popular recreational sport. Although harpoon, spear and bow-and-arrow fishing are still practised, it is rod-and-line angling that dominates the sport.

Freshwater angling developed from subsistence fishing, but can be differentiated from that (and from commercial fishing) by the fact that its participants impose handicaps on themselves to make the sport more difficult. They essentially promulgated the idea that the fish should have a chance of not being caught and, if caught, would not necessarily be killed. Such recreational angling undermined subsistence fishing as riparian rights began to be commercialized. In Canada, for example, fishing clubs leased the Atlantic salmon rivers and excluded Native Americans who had fished there for generations.

The seventeenth and eighteenth centuries were a period of significant development for angling equipment with the invention of hooks with offset points (still used today), rods with guides for lines along their length, and the gaff for lifting hooked, heavy fish from the water. In the nineteenth century came the greased line that floated to aid fly-fishing and lighter, metallic turntable reels with governors that allowed smoother release of the line. In the next century split-bamboo rods were superseded by those made from fibreglass and carbon fibre; synthetic lines eliminated the need for greasing; and plastic became the dominant material for artificial lures.

In Britain wealthy fly fishermen would buy craftsman-made rods and reels from Hardy's of Alnwick in Northumberland, but thousands of working-class anglers went elsewhere, particularly to Allcocks of Redditch, Worcestershire, which had diversified from its chief industry of needle-making into fishhooks and other fishing equipment using methods of mass production. Whatever the method of production, centralization of output became the norm. Although Hardy's fishing-tackle production continued to be craft-dominated, the firm eventually operated in a four-storey factory producing more than 3,000 rods per annum but still employing local women as outworkers. Nevertheless, it remained in the small town of

Salmon fishing in the Fraser River, British Columbia.

Alnwick, and such was its reputation (and that of its workers) that other angling production companies also moved there.

Recreational sea fishing, usually requiring more stamina and physical exertion, developed later than freshwater angling because it was more dangerous and required more equipment, often including a boat. It is also different in that ocean fish are affected by tides and there is a greater variety of species to fish, many of them considerably larger than their freshwater cousins. There are essentially two types of sea fishing: inshore surf fishing, done from the shoreline, often from rocks; and offshore fishing. The former is more dangerous than many people realize, since waves can wash anglers out to sea or cut them off from a safe refuge. It is the latter, however, that has captured the headlines because it includes game fishing for the monsters of the fish world, tuna, shark, swordfish and marlin.

Most people fish for pleasure, relaxation and the personal challenge, but there is also a competitive side to the sport. There are casting competitions looking for accuracy over distances up to 100 m (330 ft); ironically, the first such competitions were held on lawns to ensure accurate measurement. Fishing generally focuses on two elements: total catch weight, as in the working-class fishing competitions that I participated in with my grandfather in the 1950s; or largest individual fish, which, if of substantial size, often ended up in glass cases in public houses or the manorial estates of the gentry, depending on who caught it. There were, however, no glass cases available for the 679-kilogram (1,496 lb) bluefin tuna caught off Nova Scotia in 1979, or the 692-kilogram (1,525 lb) black marlin hooked off Peru in 1954.

Modern technology has altered the balance (if there ever was one) between anglers and their intended catch. In particular, anglers no longer have to rely on experience and expertise to find fish; sonar equipment does that for them, and also identifies the species and size. Yet the greatest danger to freshwater fish comes not from anglers but from humankind more generally via pollution from insecticides, herbicides, industrial waste and discarded plastic.

SPORTS WITHOUT RULES

Most country sports did not require formal, written rules either because they were not competitive (in the sense of having acknowledged winners and losers) or because they were not associated with gambling. Where those factors were involved, written rules did emerge, as in coursing and cockfighting. The few written rules in hunting, shooting and fishing were essentially local ones, often concerned with financial matters, such as when hunting subscriptions or capping fees should be paid. As with all sports, field sports had their own language, terminology known primarily to the cognoscenti. (Only true hunters would know to count hounds in couples, including half couples when a pack had an odd number.) Yet, although such knowledge could be used to separate the informed from the parvenu, it was conventions of behaviour that really distinguished the true sportsmen. Some conventions, however, were there for safety, since field sports could be hazardous: anglers risked deep and fast water; hunting required riding at speed and the jumping of fences; and shooting involved dangerous weapons. In hunting, for example, it was emphasized that it was wrong to ride too close behind another hunter, particularly when jumping, because this could cause serious accident. Other conventions related to guaranteeing good sport by ensuring that there would be sufficient quarry either on the day or in the future, so, for example, an awareness was cultivated among anglers as to the size and number of fish that should be taken. Finally, other conventions governed the way in which the sport was conducted: in effect a form of fair play for the creatures involved. Recreational anglers used rods and lines, not the nets of professional fishermen; shooters used their guns for birds on the wing, not on the ground; and huntsmen chased the fox rather than trapping it. The penalty for breaking the convention was not a sending off but social disapproval and no further invitations to the shoot or the banks of a salmon river.

However, whereas most sports had rules of the game, in Britain hunting, shooting and fishing had game laws that set the parameters for field sports by determining who could participate, where they might occur, and even when they could take place. This contrasted with the situation in the United States, where restrictions on hunting, shooting and fishing were for many years regarded as incompatible with the freedom promised in the Constitution. The British game laws were blatant class legislation, set within the law of property, which awarded the aristocracy and landed gentry an exclusive privilege to kill certain birds and animals. Angling had its own legal regulations by which the riparian owners had exclusive rights to determine who could fish there. The very existence of much hunting, shooting and fishing was thus based on what the law did or did not allow.

Field sports were not a peculiarly British recreation, but they were perhaps ritualized to a far greater extent there than elsewhere. They had to be undertaken in an appropriate manner. This gave opportunities to ridicule the 'funny foreigner' who wore the wrong clothes and failed to understand the conventions. Dressing in the proper hunt uniform was seen as a matter of etiquette. If full dress was not affordable, a top hat, black coat, boots and tweed or cord breeches were acknowledged as a suitable alternative, although this immediately labelled the wearer as socially inferior. In shooting, many proprietors or tenants devised their own pattern of tweed to blend in with the local colours of the hill, and the wearing of this estate tweed or tartan became a cultural practice. In angling, social distinctions were often reflected in fishing methods and catch. Game fishing, like game shooting, was for wealthier participants and used artificial flies as lures for salmon and trout, whereas coarse fishermen – the name says a lot – used natural bait for other varieties of indigenous fish.

LAST RITES? ANIMAL RIGHTS

The morality of the interaction between sportspeople and animals has been questioned in the past in relation to 'brutal' animal sports such as bull-baiting and cockfighting, which were eventually made illegal in Western society. More recently in some countries the hunting of animals with dogs has also been prohibited, as urban sensitivity overrode rural tradition. The origins of the attack on animal sports lay with the Victorian anti-vivisection movement, which sensitized public opinion to the plight of animals, but the modern animal-rights activists are more direct, provocative and confrontational, such as the Hunt Saboteurs Association, an animals-rights organization whose protests at and disruption of fox hunts in Britain have achieved wide publicity.

All sports involving animals have been attacked. Rodeos, horse racing and greyhound racing have faced legal challenges and physical disruption, although the sports that involve the deliberate killing of animals have borne the brunt of the opposition. Several animal sports have been forced to change their character. Some hunts now either pursue a volunteer human

Rodeo competitor in saddle bronc riding.
Bull riding at the 2007 Calgary Stampede.

runner or follow a scented trail; some big-game safaris have shifted from the rifle to the camera, to the chagrin of the trophy hunters; and some fishing promoters have adopted a policy of catch and release, although they are still criticized for subjecting the fish to pain in the first place. Like animal circuses before them, hunting, shooting and fishing may be sliding down an inclined plane, if not towards extinction then certainly towards decreased participation.

8

HORSES FOR COURSES: EQUESTRIAN SPORTS

I n ancient Greece both horse and chariot racing were significant sports, although – as was the case in modern racing until well into the nine-teenth century – it was the winning owners who gained the kudos, not the jockeys (who rode bareback) or the charioteers. To ensure that they were celebrated, owners often spent large sums on statues or on epic poems to commemorate their victories. The Greek racecourses were ru-dimentary, often just clearings surrounded by spectators standing on flat terrain, unlike the banked rows of the Roman circus, where the favoured sport was chariot racing, the oldest and longest-lived mass spectator sport in the Roman world.

Byzantium was the continuation of the Roman Empire in its eastern provinces during late antiquity and the Middle Ages, when its capital city was Constantinople (present-day Istanbul). It survived the frag-mentation and fall of the Western Roman Empire in the fifth century CE and continued to exist for another thousand years until it fell to the Ottoman Turks in 1453. Chariot racing continued to hold sway, but it came under increasing government control. The sport had largely been financed by individual cities in the earlier Roman period, but by the late fifth century it came to be funded entirely by the imperial government. As the imperial budgets tightened following the Arab conquests in the seventh century, racing became restricted to Constantinople. There the Hippodrome, which could seat 100,000 spectators, was directly next to the imperial palace. As in eighteenth-century Britain, the sporting venue also functioned as a political one, and race day became an important opportunity for the emperor to engage with the people.

ACROSS EUROPE ON HORSEBACK

Although equestrianism was a dominant aspect of late medieval Spanish culture, horse racing did not play a major role. Unlike horse racing, which is traditionally laid out as a competitive contest with regard to speed and skill, the Iberian equestrian spectacles focused on riding skill and equine swiftness within the general social framework of *gallardía*, a mixture of elegance, nobility and gracefulness. This equestrian *gallardía* – especially in its most noble form of *juego de cañas* – served in the sixteenth century as a distinctive signature of Spanishness even far beyond the borders of the Iberian peninsula. These medieval equestrian spectacles differed in their social function. Whereas *juegos de cañas* were almost exclusively used by grandees and noblemen to display skilful, athletic and intricately orchestrated equestrianism in specific, often clearly defined public settings, *bohordos* and similar artful martial games were not restricted to high nobility and took place in various public places.

On both sides of the Alps the heyday of urban horse racing came in the later fifteenth and early sixteenth centuries, although the scenarios in Italy and Germany were very different. The German races had a shorter tradition and generally attracted only local interest. In Italy, palio races dating back to the thirteenth century were held in nearly every town and city across the northern and central parts of the peninsula. They formed a racing calendar running from February to November, and gained a high level of public attention. The major cities, such as Rome, Bologna, Siena and Ferrara, all held several such events annually. Between June and October, Florence alone hosted no fewer than seven differently awarded main races, from the Palio di San Giovanni, the most prestigious event in the whole of Italy, to the Palio di Sant'Onofrio of the Florentine dyers' guild.

Tourists, and indeed locals, still enjoy the biannual Palio di Siena in which ten horses and riders, dressed in the appropriate colours, represent ten of the seventeen *contrade*, or city wards. The race circles the Piazza del Campo, on which a thick layer of earth has been laid. Preceded by a pageant, the race covers three laps of the piazza, each taking around thirty seconds. There are two races, one in July (begun in 1633) in honour of

Greek chariot racing.
Roman chariot racing in the Circus Maximus.

the Madonna of Provenzano, and one in August (from 1701) to coincide with the Feast of the Assumption. The race was (and still is) dangerous, and the saddle-less jockeys frequently fall off on the tight turns. From 1729, for reasons of safety, the number of horses was restricted to ten; the seven contrada missing out compete in the next race, with a lottery determining the three remaining places.

Then we have Britain, central to the development of modern horse racing. There are references to racing horses in the epic Anglo-Saxon

Palio de Siena, 2011.

poem *Beowulf* and to horse sales and races at Smithfield in London in the twelfth century, and there are claims of racing in the Scottish town of Lanark in 1160. In the sixteenth and seventeenth centuries there is more tangible proof of the sport. Trophies were given by wealthy families or town councils; the oldest extant are the tiny Carlisle Bells, dating from 1599, which were fastened to the bridle of the winning horse. A silver bell was presented to winners at Chester, where the oldest surviving racecourse in Britain was laid out at the Roodee, just outside the town walls, in 1540. A course was mapped out on the Town Moor at Doncaster in 1595, and the earliest known rules of racing were also drawn up in Yorkshire, at Kiplingcotes in 1619. The county became the centre of racing and breeding for two centuries, until it was eclipsed by the vast expanses of Newmarket Heath, where the Stuart kings had popularized horse racing. Throughout Britain the Restoration led to the creation of new race meetings and the revival of old ones. The sport became a fashionable pastime for the aristocracy and gentry, who engaged in match racing between two horses, on which large sums were wagered. Races also took place at local fairs dating back to pre-Reformation times. These were frequently held on public holidays and were filled out with contests for farmers' half-breeds, hunters and occasionally even carthorses and ponies, often competing for simple prizes such as a saddle or a pair of spurs. Others continued to be sponsored by the local burgh or magnate, but the trophies, once a simple bell, had now become a drinking cup or punch bowl, an early mark of racing's association with alcohol. Early races were long by modern standards, 4 mi. (6.4 km) being a common distance, and many were run in heats (to get more racing out of a limited number of horses), the overall victor having to win two heats to gain the prize. It could not always have been easy when spectators on horseback frequently followed and sometimes overtook the runners. Horses carried heavy weights of 140–96 lb (63–90 kg) and were sometimes ridden by their owners.

ON THE HOME STRAIGHT: THE MODERNIZATION OF RACING

During the latter half of the eighteenth century racing began to adopt more familiar features. Grandstands were built at major racecourses to accommodate wealthier patrons. Some of them, as at York and Doncaster, were substantial constructions, often among the largest buildings in the town. Races for three-year-olds, first tried out in the 1730s, increased in popularity, and three of the Classics for such horses – the St Leger, the Oaks and the Derby – were inaugurated before the end of the century, the first at Doncaster in 1776 and the other two at Epsom in 1779 and 1780. These less mature animals had to be raced over shorter distances and under smaller weights than in earlier times. This led to races of 1–2 mi. (1.6–3.2 km) and the use of lightweight professional jockeys. Sprints of less than a mile were introduced for yearlings – although these were later banned – and for two-year-olds. By the 1820s nearly half of the recorded races were for animals under the age of four, and traditional heats and match racing were declining.

By the 1830s racing was a major British sport, organized at local level the length and breadth of the country; the Classics and other major races had been established, and large crowds were attracted, reputedly more than 100,000 at Doncaster, Epsom and a few other venues. However, using Guttmann's criteria (see Chapter Four), racing did not appear to be modernized at this time. While it undoubtedly operated in a *secular* environment and was highly *specialized*, it was only partly *rationalized* and *bureaucratized* and failed almost entirely to meet Guttmann's conditions of *quantification* and *records.* There was also little *equality* in terms of gender or ownership, but it could be argued that full equality can never be attained in the sport because of the financial cost of participation. Guttmann's model failed to give sufficient attention to the roles of gambling, professionalization and commercialization, all of which might change the view of how modernized racing was before Victoria became monarch in 1837. Whatever the semantics of the situation, during the nineteenth-century internationalization of the sport Britain led the way in exporting horses, race names, racing models and the style of governance to much of the racing world. It is arguable that it was the national sport up to the 1880s, since it attracted more spectators in aggregate than did any other sport.

RACING TODAY

In many respects horse racing is a unique sport. It is full of paradoxes. How can medieval systems of measurement coexist with the modern

----

Colour me confused

As early as 1762, the Jockey Club had recommended that owners furnish their jockeys with coloured racing garments – shirts and waistcoats or jackets, with caps – in order to make identification on the racetrack easier for both spectators and judges. By 1833 there were 150 colours (from roughly 700 owners) listed in the Racing Calendar. Even in 1870, when the strong arm of the Jockey Club was felt throughout racing in Britain, only 870 racing colours were registered out of an estimated 1,250 owners, about 70 per cent of the whole; compulsory registration was eventually introduced in 1890. Yet the benefits of coloured clothing as an aid to recognition were probably limited in the early nineteenth century because numerous owners chose the same pattern and hue – there were six sets of all black in 1808. The proliferation of colour combinations by 1870 must have made the judges' task even harder without the benefits of modern technology. It seems unlikely that officials or spectators could differentiate Scotch plaid, shepherd's plaid, tartan or Rob Roy tartan at speed and distance, or distinguish at the winning post between sky blue, light blue, Mexican blue, mazarine blue, Eton blue, Oxford blue, peacock blue, blue bird's eye and plain ordinary blue. It is little wonder that the results of races with fields of seven or eight sometimes end lamely with the phrase 'the Judge could place only the first three.'

technology of artificial surfaces and computerized handicapping, and images of fashion and high society with those of corruption and seediness? It is highly professionalized, with little room for the amateur. It has no grass roots, and while many spectators at football and cricket games will have played those sports, few racegoers will have mounted a horse, let alone ridden one in a race. Another unusual aspect of racing is that it has large attendances but no real fan base. Spectators seldom follow particular horses or jockeys as they might a local team, and there is little shared, communal experience associated with winning or losing; racing is largely for individuals, both at participant and spectator level. Nor is it for the sedentary viewer. In most other sports you take your seat and the event unfolds before you. In racing, to get the most from the spectacle, you have to follow proceedings from stand to paddock, from paddock to rails, and from rails to winner's enclosure.

Horse racing has declined in importance even in countries such as Great Britain and the United States where once it was the national pastime. It is striving to keep its economic balance while heading steadily on an inclined plane towards sporting obscurity as it faces challenges from an ageing spectatorship and from the expansion of Internet gambling that offers betting on virtually any sport. Yet it should be stressed that racing has never been a viable industry and has always been dependent on 'voluntary' contributions from owners and trainers to keep it going.

BETTING

More than anything else, racing is associated with gambling. Racing and betting have always gone hand in hand, from the simple wager on a match race in the eighteenth century to the millions spent on the Internet today. Other sports have betting but, Dubai apart, racing *needs* betting. Betting on horses was initially a matter of individuals wagering between themselves as to the likely outcome of a match between two thoroughbreds. Bookmakers then emerged, willing to accept bets from all comers, but for years they made little contribution to the sport on which their livelihood depended. Not until a betting levy was introduced in 1961 (following the legalization of off-course betting shops in 1960) did bookmakers and their clients contribute directly to the funding of racing in Britain. Elsewhere, legal betting was primarily based on the totalizator (introduced in Britain in 1929 but less significant than other forms of betting on the horses), in which all bets – less a percentage – were divided among those with winning tickets rather than the negotiated odds of the bookmaker and the starting prices of the betting shop. It was the deduction of the percentage that allowed racing to take a greater slice of betting turnover.

It is this relationship with gambling that leads to allegations of corruption in racing. One of the most famous instances was the 1844 Derby, in which the 'winner', Running Rein, was disqualified after it was demonstrated that the horse carrying his name was actually an animal called Maccabeus and, worse still, was a four-year-old, somewhat of an advantage in a race supposedly restricted to three-year-olds. Later that century the state of New York, particularly its metropolitan area and the resort of Saratoga Springs, became the centre of American racing after the Civil War, but much of this was attributable to the involvement of corrupt politicians and organized crime that protected and promoted horse racing, often because it was the gambling sport par excellence. Racecourses connected the underworld with Tammany Hall, allowing illegal off-track betting to develop on a significant scale. Yet an assessment must be made as to whether the problems of other sports with drugs, bribery and gambling scams were greater or lesser than those of the turf, and whether the racing stables were as dirty as some areas of business life, notably the financial services sector.

THE ORIGINS OF THE RACING THOROUGHBRED: AND BEYOND

In the century from 1650 more than two hundred horses were imported into Britain from the Ottoman Empire and the Barbary States of North Africa. These eastern imports, conventionally referred to as Arabian, radically changed Britain's equestrian culture. British breeders took the smaller foreign animal with its pace, appropriated it as English and used it to develop the thoroughbred. In this they were following the tenets of agricultural improvement but also pursuing miscegenation, something less tolerated in society than in the stud, where race mixing occurred for the sake of English bloodstock. Tradition has it that the modern racing thoroughbred is descended from three stallions brought to England between 1690 and 1730, the Byerley Turk, the Darley Arabian and the

Godolphin Arabian, all identified by their English owners' surnames. It is ironic that none of these is recorded as ever having raced! These Arab stallions have been given all the credit for thoroughbred development, with little regard paid to the mares with which they and their male descendants were mated; this, of course, is no different from the anonymity of the mare in any studbook analysis before the emergence of genetic theory. Recent research, however, has drawn attention to the significance of other eastern horses and also emphasized the contribution of mares to the genetic make-up of the breed.

Much of the detail on the pedigree and racing performance of horses over two centuries or more can be garnered from the *General Stud Book* and the *Racing Calendar*. First published in 1791, the former is still the registry for British thoroughbreds. The latter has been published annually since 1773 by the Weatherby family. Originally a private venture whose main purpose was to provide an accurate list of race results, together with advertisements of future meetings, it gradually developed in the first half of the nineteenth century into the unofficial mouthpiece of the Jockey Club, the ruling body of the turf. Although recent research has cast doubt on the accuracy of both publications in their early years, they are still useful: and for more than their intended purpose. A search of the *Racing Calendar* enables an analysis to be made of the changing geography, extent and concentration of racing, as well as giving glimpses into social aspects such as the role of women, while both publications allow us to see changing taste in the naming of horses. Ironically, the allegedly straight-laced Victorians witnessed races won by Pudenda, Little Yid and Sweetest When Naked, none of whose names would make the starting stalls in today's more permissive but more politically correct society.

GALLOPING AHEAD: THE AMERICAN JOCKEY INVASION

Another international transfer with significant implications came in the late nineteenth century, when a solitary American jockey, the African-American Willie Simms, rode in British racing in 1895. His unusual riding style – virtually crouching along the horse's neck, with short stirrups, high knees and a tight rein – was in contrast to that of the English jockeys, who sat more erect with a comparatively straight knee and a good length of rein. Simms secured only four wins, insufficient to rank him in the top fifty in the jockeys' championship. Yet these wins were the product of merely nineteen mounts, a winning percentage of 21.5, among the highest in the land. Although he never returned, his visit was a precursor of an American invasion of the British turf that was to have a significant effect on the practice and performance of horsemanship throughout world racing.

How the American riding style originated is not clear. In his auto-biography, Tod Sloan – to whom British turf historians often attribute the American seat – claimed that he discovered the advantages of the forward seat one day when trying to stop a horse that had bolted with him in the saddle. On another occasion he said he lit on the style when larking about in the training yard. In the 1890s, however, his riding caused no comment in the American racing press, which suggests that such a style was already commonplace. A reasoned view is that it was devised by poorer stable hands in the southern states, who often had to ride workouts without saddles, forcing them to grip the mane and lie along the horse's neck for balance.

Simms had first shown the American seat to British racegoers in 1895, but its real effectiveness was demonstrated in the next five years. Lester Reiff came over for a spell in 1896 and had sixteen winners. Next to arrive was Sloan. On his first short visit, in autumn 1897, he had 53 mounts and won on twenty of them. He returned the following autumn, again as the punter's friend, with 43 winners out of 98 mounts, a phenomenally high percentage of 43.9. At the first October meeting at Newmarket, the headquarters of the English turf, he rode twelve winners out of sixteen mounts. In 1900 four of the top ten riders in the British championship were from the United States. Reiff was champion, with Sloan in close attendance, followed by Johnny Reiff (Lester's lightweight brother) and John Henry 'Skeets' Martin. In addition, nineteen-year-old Danny Maher arrived late that season and secured 27 wins from 128 rides, a sign of the talent that was to bring him the jockeys' championship in 1908 and again in 1913.

Although the style was derided at first, racing experts eventually conceded that, by cutting wind resistance and giving a better weight distribution on the horse, the monkey-on-a-stick form of riding could be worth a 4.5–6.5-kilogram (10–14 lb) advantage. Although not every American jockey had the ability of Sloan and Reiff, their results led to the engagement by British owners of lesser-ranked American riders. They enjoyed less success, but each mount they took was one less for British jockeys, who became convinced that redundancy beckoned unless they too took up the American style.

JUMP RACING

Racing over fences and hurdles is essentially a British sport and has secured little following elsewhere, apart from the famous Velká pardubická, a cross-country steeplechase run on the second Sunday in October in Pardubice, Czech Republic, since 1874. The course is almost 7 km (4⅓ mi.) long with 31 obstacles, the most famous of which is the dangerous Taxis Ditch, a 2-metre-deep (6½ ft) and 5-metre-long (16⅓ ft) ditch hidden behind a 1.5-metre-high (5 ft) hedge.

Said to have originated in Ireland in the 1750s, the idea of racing horses across country from one church steeple to another, jumping obstacles on the way, derived from the hunting field. However, it was not commercialized until 1830 with the inauguration of the St Albans Steeplechase. Although this event lasted only a few years, the idea caught on, and by the early 1840s there were more than sixty races, the most famous of which became the Grand National run at Aintree. This has evolved into a national institution, and one-third of the adult population is said to have a flutter on the race, which is a listed event for terrestrial television. Despite its popularity, many people do not realize that it is not a high-class race but a handicap event that does not necessarily attract the best jumpers. For these, there is the Cheltenham Festival, held for three days every March, at which almost half of Britain's grade-one jump and hurdle races are scheduled. It has a long Irish connection, with spectators, horses and jockeys all crossing from the Republic to contribute to the atmosphere.

Hurdling is at the bottom of the horse-racing hierarchy. Most books about horse racing fail to mention it at all, except for the Champion Hurdle run, part of the Cheltenham Festival. The first recorded hurdle race was at Durdham Down, near Bristol, in 1821. It has evolved into an intermediate type of racing that simultaneously offers a training ground for horses that will become steeplechasers and an opportunity for extending the careers of mature flat-racers. At the elite level the sport can be exhilarating, but at most meetings hurdles are little more than fillers

St Albans Steeplechase, 1837.

in the racecard, a chance for apprentice chasers or mediocre flat-racers to try and earn their keep – an unlikely proposition, given the relatively low level of prize money at the lower end of the sport.

HARNESS RACING

The old trotting track at Goshen in New York state was the first sporting site in the United States to be designated a National Historic Landmark. It commemorated the emergence of what some claim to be the nation's first modernized sport, which began in the United States in the early nineteenth century with farmers using their workhorses, usually the Morgan, a distinctive American breed. At that time the sport was generally called trotting, a misnomer that was amended to harness racing towards the end of the century, reflecting the fact that the sport encompassed both trotting and pacing. In the former the horse's legs move together diagonally (front right at the same time as rear left), whereas in pacing front and rear right are synchronized. Originally both trotters and pacers were ridden to saddle, but they soon became attached to a sulky, a light two-wheeled carriage built to hold a single driver.

A revolution in the sport occurred in the 1940s following the creation of the United States Trotting [*sic*] Association from three existing bodies. Night racing was introduced, and within two decades most major cities had at least one track: the sport now stretched from coast to coast. New mobile starting gates reduced the number of recalls, common under the barrier starts, and a cause of frustration to spectators, bettors and the drivers themselves. The sport also established itself in Sweden and Australia, and in both countries it has Americanized, adopting the mobile starting barrier, larger tracks, more sprint races and handicapping by classification rather than distance.

OLYMPIC RIDING SPORTS

Equestrianism is a rare sport in that it allows men and women to compete against each other, although this equality took time to develop at the Olympics. Dressage, showjumping and eventing all began their unbroken runs at the Stockholm Games of 1912, but women were not permitted until 1952, 1956 and 1964 respectively.

Dressage, which takes its name from the French word for training, is the most artistic of all horse sports. The French developed it during the Renaissance, and because sixteenth-century courtiers emphasized the importance of the artistic over martial skills, it featured in courtier activities as a non-competitive form of demonstration and display of the mastery of an art, despite being based on military horse manoeuvres. Dressage tests the development of the horse's natural gaits of walk, trot and canter, and at the elite level involves a prescribed set of movements plus a freestyle section choreographed to music. All the movements of the Olympic dressage can be seen in the demonstrations at the Spanish Riding School in Vienna, an institution dedicated to the preservation of classical dressage. It has existed since 1572 and is named after the Spanish horses that are used exclusively there. Its performances were originally presented only to guests of the Habsburg court, and even when they were opened to the public at the end of the nineteenth century, it was only for special occasions, but after the fall of the Austro-Hungarian empire in 1918, the school opened regular performances to the general public to help pay for its upkeep.

In showjumping, a sport that developed in Western Europe and the United States, riders guide their mounts around a course of obstacles

Show jumping at the 2009 Dublin Horse Show.
Polo played by Indian princesses.

within a time limit. Eventing began in the United States as a test of cavalry horses and their riders. It combined galloping long distances, negotiating obstacles and performing parade movements. In the Olympics it takes place over three days. Dressage takes place on the first day, although with lower standards than for the elite version. Day two involves cross-country riding designed to test jumping ability and endurance. The final day is for stadium jumping, with lower obstacles than in showjumping proper.

POLO

Polo was played in ancient times in several parts of the world, including Central Asia, the Persian Empire, China and India. Its importance to Near Eastern and Arabian societies can be seen in the remains of old polo grounds, descriptions in ancient texts, and artistic representations. Polo players decorate the pages of a fourteenth-century edition of the *Shahnama* (Book of Kings), the national epic of Iran; in Arifi's fifteenth-century *Book of Ecstasy* the ball and polo stick symbolize imperial power and mystic love; and in ancient legend the Prince Siyavush played polo against the Turanians, hitting the ball to the moon and defeating the steppe people. However, polo was culturally appropriated by British army officers in northern India in the mid-nineteenth century, and was brought back to their homeland as an ideal training sport for mounted troops, honing both the horse's and the rider's skill at charging, manoeuvring and defending. Ex-officers formed civilian polo clubs in the late nineteenth century, a time coincident with its spread to the United States, and British ranchers took the sport to Argentina, a nation that consistently tops the world rankings of the modern sport.

9

TAKING SPEED:
FROM FOOT POWER
TO WHEEL POWER

Until the mid-Victorian era athletics (labelled 'pedestrianism') was generally the province of professionals and took two major forms. One was endurance events against the clock, most notably Captain Barclay's successful challenge to run or walk a mile (1.6 km) every hour for 1,000 hours at Newmarket in 1809. Although not a professional, Barclay won a wager of 1,000 guineas for his feat and allegedly tens of thousands more in other side bets. As the nineteenth century progressed, distance and sprint races between runners became more common. They took place all over England but had two major centres: Manchester – where mile races became the mode – and Sheffield, where sprinting was the forte; in all areas, the races were usually handicapped to provide more excitement to spectators. The pedestrian meetings became popular spectator sports and were often held in arenas constructed by publicans as adjuncts to their drinking premises. As well as running, they often also involved walking races, jumping, throwing and hurdling events, elements of which had been traditional rural sports.

Two events of traditional professional sprint racing continue to this day, the Stawell Gift in Victoria, Australia, and the Powderhall (New Year) Sprint in Edinburgh, Scotland. Both take place in traditional heartlands of competitive running for money prizes. The Stawell race began as the 1878 'Easter Gift' of the local athletics club, and has been run annually since, except for four years during the Second World War. It was first organized as part of what Aussies call 'the Show', an annual rural exhibition (like the Highland Show in Scotland) but with fairground attractions, and within a short time was attracting visitors from around the state. It has become the most prestigious foot race in the Antipodes, and is televised around Australia. Despite economic problems in the twentieth century, attempts to move the race to more populous places were resisted thanks mainly to state government subsidy. It was run over 130 yd (changed to 120 m in 1973), with participants receiving handicaps of up to 10 m (33 ft). In 2010 times in the heats were slower than expected, and the track was discovered to be 3 m (10 ft) too long.

Some 10 m shorter than the Stawell event, the Edinburgh race was held at the Powderhall Stadium, created specifically for athletics although later incorporating a greyhound track, for more than a century (by a year) from its inception in 1870, when it attracted more than 25,000 spectators over the two days of heats and finals. In 1971 the race was transferred to the city's Meadowbank Stadium, built to host the previous year's Commonwealth Games, and in 1998 to the racecourse at Musselburgh, slightly to the east of Edinburgh. It was there in 2016 that Jazmine Tomlinson became the first female winner, a feat not yet possible at Stawell, where women have had their own race since 1989 but one now with prize money equal to the men's event. Gambling has been the mainstay of both the Stawell and Edinburgh events. Stawell has a dedicated bookmakers' compound, and the Scottish New Year race takes place concurrent with a race meeting and all the associated betting facilities.

Amateur athletics (track and field for Americans) were an 'invention' of mid-Victorian Britain, and focused on the athletics club rather than the individualism of the professional pedestrians, or 'peds'. They were first organized in Britain in 1868 by the Amateur Athletic Club, which was superseded by the Amateur Athletic Association (the 'Three As', as it became known) in 1880. The focus of these organizations was the gentleman amateur, and this gave British athletics a distinctly middle-class feel; in the United States, on the other hand, athletics was influenced by emigrant Scots and their Highland Games and became more egalitarian and meritocratic, hence that nation's greater success in track and field at the Olympics. The amateur and professional side of athletics were kept separate until the late twentieth century, but now, at the elite level, there are no amateurs on the track except in the American colleges, and those who make the Olympic teams usually turn professional.

MARATHON MEN (AND WOMEN)

Endurance racing has continued. Today there are races through waterless deserts and frozen tundra, and from one end of a country to the other. However, it is the marathon (26.22 mi./42.2 km) that has become the gold-standard long-distance event. It was introduced at the reinstituted Olympic Games in Athens in 1896 and has been on the programme ever since. It was created to commemorate the Greek soldier Pheidippides, who – it is said – ran to Athens with news of the victory over the Persians at the Battle of Marathon. He then dropped dead. Since five centuries elapsed before any account of this was published, scholars are wary of the story's historical accuracy. A definite myth is that the marathon distance was determined by Queen Alexandra's desire in 1908 to watch the start of the Olympic marathon from Windsor Castle, thus causing the route to be extended from the planned 26 mi. (41.8 km). The reality was that the proposed entrance into the White City stadium could not be used, which necessitated some extra yardage. Moreover, 26.22 mi. was not the distance used in 1912 (24.98 mi./40.2 km) or 1920 (26.56 mi./42.7 km); it became the standard distance only when ratified by the International Amateur Athletics Association in 1921.

Marathon running is more than the Olympics. There are some thousand or so run each year worldwide, the oldest being the Boston Marathon, inspired by the Athens race and inaugurated in 1897. It is held on Patriots' Day, a holiday celebrating the start of the American War of Independence, deliberately linking the event with Athens, which is often cited as the home of democracy. Many marathons cater for elite runners and offer significant prize money, but the majority of the participants, thousands in some cases, are recreational runners taking part for fun and, these days, often for charity. They start after the elite performers, who, in turn, are preceded by wheelchair participants.

The first woman to be recorded as completing a marathon was Violet Piercy, who in 1926 ran the Polytechnic route from Windsor to London (reminiscent of the 1908 Olympic race, but a slightly different course). However, this was not an official race. Women were excluded from official marathon races until the 1970s. In the United States the right to participate in distance running became an aspect of the women's movement; some women ran unofficially in leading events such as the Boston Marathon,

Wheelchair participant in the 2017 Chicago Marathon.

but faced opposition from the athletics authorities. In Europe there was less resistance, and many private athletics clubs encouraged women to run long distances, including marathons. By 1984 there were sufficient women running marathons for it to become an Olympic event, and that year the American Joan Benoit won the Los Angeles race.

Saturday 12 October 2019 was a remarkable day in marathon history. As the Nike-sponsored Kenyan runner Eliud Kipchoge crossed the finishing line in Vienna, the clock read 1 hour 59 minutes and 40.2 seconds. The two-hour barrier had been smashed. It was not an official world record, because teams of runners were employed to reduce Kipchoge's wind resistance, but it has changed thinking about what can be achieved. The last great barrier to be overcome was the four-minute mile, first achieved by Roger Bannister in 1954 but now commonplace (at least where the mile is run, rather than the 1,500 metres). Whether Kipchoge's epic feat will lead to similar regular occurrences must await the test of time. A day after Kipchoge's epic run, another Kenyan, Brigid Kosgei, smashed the women's Chicago Marathon record by 81 seconds, a time that had stood for sixteen years. She, like Kipchoge, was wearing Nike's Vaporfly trainers (albeit a version not yet available to the public), which are designed to absorb energy when the feet hit the ground and return some of it to the stride. Perhaps the next barrier to be overcome is a two-hour time for female marathon runners; but that is unlikely in my lifetime, at least. No matter what time they record, I will always feel sorry for the fourth-placed finisher in the marathon: 26 miles 385 yards and no bloody medal!

6 MAY 1954: IFFLEY ROAD, OXFORD

After the athletes had completed three laps of the Iffley Road running track, the handbell was rung to signal one circuit to go. The spectators who glanced at their watches realized that something special was taking place. The three laps had taken just 3 minutes 0.7 seconds; the four-minute mile was on. The stocky Christopher Chataway took the lead halfway through the third lap and led until the far straight of the last lap, with the taller Roger Bannister behind him until Bannister lengthened his stride, accelerated past Chataway round the final bend and, with head back and arms splayed out, broke the tape. After watches were checked, the race announcer gave out the formal finishing positions of competitors in the race and then said 'Time', but waited a fraction to heighten the tension before continuing 'Three minutes . . .' No one heard the rest of the announcement in the cheering, although he did add 'fifty-nine point four seconds'.

Breaking four minutes for the mile had been an obsession among middle-distance runners, but the world record of 4.01.3 by the Swede Gunder Hägg had stood since 1945. Three athletes were knocking at the door: John Landy from Australia; Wes Santee, a student at the University of Kansas; and Bannister himself. Bannister had been favourite for the 1,500-metre title at the 1952 Helsinki Olympics, but he finished fourth, out of the medals. This forced him to rethink his running and training strategies with the ultimate aim of smashing the four-minute barrier. Although often regarded as the consummate amateur, Bannister took a professional approach to breaking the record. As a medical scientist he knew the value of laboratory experiments, and this was how he treated his attempt at the four-minute mile. It was a scientific experiment, planned out in detail. He enrolled Chataway, and later also the athlete Chris Brasher, to assist him in a more systematic and rigorous training regime, taking advice from the renowned

Austrian-born Franz Stampfl, one of the leading athletics coaches of the 1950s and '60s, who developed his own interval-training system.

In May 1953, at the annual athletics match between Oxford University and the Amateur Athletic Association in which he was to feature so spectacularly the following year, Bannister set a new British record of 4 minutes 3.6 seconds. The next month he ran just two seconds above the four-minute barrier at a special race inserted into the Surrey Schools Championship programme, but so obvious was the pacemaking (Bannister almost lapped Brasher) that the British Amateur Athletics Board refused to ratify the time as a British record. Pacemaking was regarded as illicit. A lesson was learned. When the next attempt was made Bannister chose the Oxford/AAA match again and, to ensure that his time would be ratified, both Brasher and Chataway made sure they finished the race, second and fourth respectively, to score points in the match and be classed as bona fide runners. The race itself was organized meticulously. The bespectacled Brasher was to set a pace for the first two laps of about two minutes before dropping back and letting Chataway take over. All the other

Roger Bannister breaks the four-minute mile barrier.

runners were told to keep out of the way, although whether they could have matched Bannister's pace is debatable.

Bannister's world record did not last long. On 21 June 1954 Landy ran 3.57.9 in a race at Turku in Finland. The showdown between the two four-minute milers came at the Empire Games in Vancouver on 7 August. Bannister won after an epic race in which Landy led almost all the way, with Bannister overhauling him at the end to triumph. They both broke four minutes, Bannister coming home in 3.58.8 to Landy's 3.59.6. This was Bannister's response to those critics, many from within the sport, who claimed that he was not a real runner and had never won a race against a rated opponent.

Although the distance is rarely run in these metric days, the current world mile record is 3:43.13, held by the Moroccan Hicham El Guerrouj. Bannister would not have even entered the home straight in that race had he been on his 1954 schedule, but then he achieved his record on a cinder track wearing conventional spikes. What might he have done with the benefit of technological developments in running footwear and track composition? It is such technology that has made running a mile in less than four minutes almost commonplace. Still, Bannister enjoyed more than his four minutes of fame. He retired from athletics at the end of the 1954 season to concentrate on his career in medicine, and he was knighted in 1975.

PEDAL POWER

In 1868 business and civic leaders in Paris sponsored a 1,200-metre (3,940 ft) race around a Paris park with the idea of showcasing not just the city but also French ingenuity in the form of the bicycle. To their chagrin, the race went to an English rider, James Moore, who demonstrated his proficiency at longer distances when he also won the 133-kilometre (82½ mi.) race from Paris to Rouen the following year, beating more than three hundred local riders. His average speed was around 13 kph (8 mph), despite having to dismount at each incline. This event, the world's first long-distance cycle race, was promoted by the newspaper *Le Vélocipède Illustré* (Bicycle Illustrated). The race was purportedly held to demonstrate the efficiency of the bicycle, but it also helped the paper's circulation.

Few people had travelled such a distance, at least not often, and the idea of doing it on a bicycle and at as high a speed as possible when the roads were potholed and bicycles had wooden wheels and metal tyres was exciting. Unusually for nineteenth-century sport, the race was also open to women, although they competed in a separate category from the men. That race went to a foreign rider, too, the American Margaret Taylor.

Despite these races, track cycling was the early stimulant to bicycling as a spectator sport. Until the 1880s most races were held in velodromes, where, unlike with road races, spectators could be charged entry fees. Over time long-distance races faded from the indoor agenda to be replaced by a variety of races including two-competitor sprints with their tactical aspects, pursuits that are out-and-out speed trials for both individuals and teams, and paced racing, where several riders are led around the velodrome by motorcycles for several laps before an all-out race takes place.

From the 1890s, newspapers started organizing races on public roads, partly to show that bicycles could cover great distances but mainly to

Charles Terront, winner of the first Paris–Brest–Paris cycle race, 1891.

boost their sales and their advertisement revenue. Roadside spectators could view races only briefly as the riders passed by, and there came a demand for more information, which the hosting newspapers could supply. Most of the French, Belgian and Italian annual races from one city to another, now called classics, were run on distances ranging from 250 to 400 km (155–250 mi.), which means that the best riders often had to race for more than ten hours to complete the course.

It was in France that the most famous bicycle race in the world emerged. In 1891 another newspaper, *Le Petit Journal*, hosted the Paris–Brest–Paris race over a distance of 1,200 km (746 mi.). But that was topped after a meeting of the editorial staff of *L'Auto*, at which the journalist Géo Lefèvre suggested a race around France. Thus the Tour de France was born. There are two other members of the elite Grand Tour club, both of which were established by newspapers. The Giro d'Italia was sponsored by *La Gazzetta dello Sport* in 1909, and in 1935 *Informaciones* created the Vuelta a España. As the names suggest, cycle racing was a major mainland European sport. Today road cycling has three major categories: the stage race, which can incorporate an individual time trial, diverse surfaces and changes in weather; the criterium, in which cyclists race laps around a street circuit; and the single-route race between two towns.

Bicycle racing emerged from the newly popular activity of cycling. This popularity was not because people wanted to race against each other or the clock, but because it offered a new, faster form of transport and opened the way to riding for recreation, to venture into the countryside and, like tennis and golf, to allow men and women to participate together.

The Italian job

At times the Italian organizers of the Giro d'Italia, one of the three Grand Tour cycle races, have attempted to ensure that an Italian national won the race. When the star Italian rider was a climber, as was Gino Bartali in 1937, they increased the importance of mountain stages and decreased that of the individual time trials. They did the reverse for Francesco Moser in 1977 and Giuseppe Saronni in 1981, who preferred riding on the flat. Moser won again in 1984, when the French cyclist Laurent Fignon had been favourite (but not of the Italians). They cancelled a hard mountain stage that would have suited the Frenchman and then used the draught of a helicopter to slow him down in the final time trial.

It was a symbol of modernity. It was also recreational riding that produced a revolution in cycle design in the mid-twentieth century, when off-road bikes came into demand. However, both the BMX and the mountain bike then became instruments for competitive cycling and now feature at the Olympics, although not yet at the World Cycling Championships.

CIRCUITS OF DEATH AND GLORY

Motor sport is dangerous. Eight motorcycle world champions have died while practising or racing in Grand Prix events. And it is not just the riders and drivers who suffer fatalities. At Le Mans in 1955, a total of 83 spectators were killed when Pierre Levegh's Mercedes rear-ended another car and jumped the safety fence. In motor-car racing up to 2019, some 24 drivers were killed at Daytona, 27 at Le Mans, 30 at Monza, 48 at the Nürburgring and 57 at Indianapolis. However, the most dangerous racing circuit in the world is one for motorbike racing, the Snaefell Mountain course, a road circuit complete with street furniture where the Isle of Man Tourist Trophy is held annually. Between its inception in 1907 and 2019, official practice sessions and the races themselves claimed 260 lives.

Yet these are also racetracks where fame and glory can be achieved. Some have become synonymous with their sport and established themselves as cultural sporting institutions. The first Isle of Man TT race was held on a 15-mile-long (24 km) course, but in 1911 it was transferred to the Snaefell circuit, which is longer by some 23 mi. (37 km). It is a sports Mecca for bike riders the world over, many of whom take advantage of an informal tradition, dating from the 1920s, that on the Sunday between practice week and race week spectators can ride around the circuit themselves.

One of the world's most prestigious motor races – and the oldest active endurance race for sports cars – is the Le Mans 24-hour, held annually since 1923 on the Circuit de la Sarthe, a mix of public roads and dedicated sections of racing track near the town of Le Mans in northwestern France. The winner is the car that covers the longest distance over the 24 hours of the race. It was started as a deliberate contrast to Grand Prix racing (in which speed is of the essence) by emphasizing reliability. One of its traditions was the start, in which the competing cars were lined up

Jacky Ickx, Belgian racing driver, 1971.

along the length of the pits. Until 1962 that was done in order of engine capacity, but beginning in 1963 qualifying times determined the line-up. The starting drivers stood on the opposite side of the front stretch. When the starting flag dropped, they ran across the track, entered and started their cars without assistance, and drove away. Feeling that this type of start was unsafe, in 1969 the Belgian driver Jacky Ickx opposed it by walking across the track while his competitors ran, although he was nearly hit by a competitor's car. Ickx and his fellow driver (driving is shared between two or three drivers) went on to win the race. The start was changed in 1970. Cars were still lined up along the pit wall, but the drivers were already inside and strapped in. The following year a rolling start was adopted. Other traditions include using the French tricolour to start the race, and a waving of safety flags on the last lap by track marshals as a means of congratulating the finishers.

In the United States two motor-racing venues stand out, Indianapolis and Daytona. The Indianapolis 500-mile Race is the world's oldest major automobile race and the fastest of its kind. Better known as the Indy 500 or the Indianapolis 500, it is held annually at the Indianapolis Motor Speedway over Memorial Day weekend, in late May. It is contested as part of the IndyCar Series, the top level of American Championship Car racing, an open-wheel open-cockpit formula. The speedway complex was

Indianapolis 500 in 1913.

built in 1909 as a tar and gravel track, but after two long-distance events attracted 15,000 paying customers, it was rebuilt in 1910 with more than 3 million bricks – hence the nickname 'brickyard' – and drew 60,000 attendees. This stimulated the owners to do even more, and they decided to organize a 500-mile (805 km) race with a prize of $25,000, which was first run in 1911. Most drivers in the early years at the Speedway were assisted by a mechanic, who rode along with them during the race, monitoring gauges, making repairs to the car, advising them of approaching cars from behind and communicating with the pits using hand signals. From 1930 to 1937 drivers were required to have a riding mechanic; otherwise it was voluntary. It was dangerous, and the mechanic could easily be thrown from the car. Six have died during a race and a further six during practice. The event is steeped in tradition, in pre-race ceremonies, post-race celebrations and race procedure. The most noteworthy and most popular traditions are the 33 cars (a larger field than at the other IndyCar races) lining up three-wide for the start, the annual singing of 'Back Home Again in Indiana' (begun in 1946) and the victory lane bottle of milk (Indiana is a dairy state). Although attendances are not officially disclosed, the permanent seating is now 250,000 and infield patrons raise the race-day attendance to approximately 300,000, surely the largest sports crowd in the world.

The green flag signals the start of a new NASCAR season at Daytona.

The Daytona International Speedway racetrack in Daytona Beach, Florida, has been the home of the Daytona 500, the most prestigious race in NASCAR (the National Association for Stock Car Auto Racing), since it opened in 1959. It was built with high banking to permit higher speeds and give fans – more than 125,000 of them – a better view. Over a million cubic metres of earth were used, and the excavated hole became a lake because of the high water table. The race is held in winter, meaning that most of it is run at night, and although lights were installed around the track in 1998 they are dimmed so that the drivers must rely on their own headlights. The aerial view of the track from planes at the nearby airport is spectacular.

When I lived in Australia, one Sunday each year would be devoted to sitting in front of the television watching Peter Brock dominate the Hardie-Ferodo (as it was then called) 1000, an endurance event on the picturesque Mount Panorama circuit in Bathurst, New South Wales. This road course of just 6 km (3¾ mi.) has been used for both car and motorbike racing since its construction in 1938 as an unemployment relief project. Its distinguishing feature is its hillside location, which provides steep climbs, a twisting, precipitous descent, a variety of corners and excellent viewing. Its Easter motorcycle racing weekend attracted riders and spectators from all over Australia, but regular and violent

Inaugural Monte Carlo Rally, 1911: Henri Rougier and
his mechanic. No prize for guessing who is who!
Monte Carlo Rally 1977.

confrontations between bikers ('bikies' in Australia) and the police put paid to the meetings in 1988. The circuit was then devoted to motor racing, especially the Bathurst 1000, inaugurated in 1963. Concern for safety now precludes open-car racing, and the race has become the province of closed-body cars.

Although it is no longer of major significance in the motorsport calendar, for years the Monte Carlo Rally (officially the Rallye Automobile Monte-Carlo) was a highlight as cars converged on Monaco from starting points all over Europe. It began in January 1911, when 23 cars set out from eleven different locations to rally together in Monte Carlo, where the winner was judged not just on speed but on a combination of the elegance of the car, passenger comfort and the condition in which it arrived in the principality. Time later became the deciding factor, but as late as 1991 competitors were able to choose their starting points from approximately five venues roughly equidistant from Monte Carlo. The race was seen as an important means of demonstrating improvements and innovations to automobiles, and in 1966 five of the first six finishers were disqualified for not being publicly available production models. It has become a four-day event held along the French Riviera, and is now but one rally in the World Rally Championship.

10

OUT CLUBBING:
BAT AND BALL SPORTS

Cricket developed in agricultural areas in southern England during the eighteenth century. The arable farming of that area meant the workforce had long periods of relatively low-intensity labour, maintaining crops as they grew and preparing for the next round of planting, followed by intense bouts of harvesting over a few weeks of each year. In such a work setting – unlike livestock-based farming, where working cycles were both annual and daily – cycles of recreation also allowed consecutive days of play. Cricket initially developed through the patronage of gamblers, whose need for clarity in their betting led to the emergence of written rules, which were first published in 1744, although the game was not truly codified until the formation of Marylebone Cricket Club (MCC) in 1787. Like the other gambling sports of the time, it had upper-class support, because aristocrats saw the game as providing an opportunity to socialize with their peers, act out political and social rivalries in the sporting arena and maintain a relationship with their tenants, and, perhaps above all, as a means to gamble. Yet, unlike in horse racing and pugilism, they played in the same teams as their tenants and labourers. This willingness to play alongside their inferiors in cross-class teams was formalized in the nineteenth century in the distinction between gentlemen and players.

As a sport that was widely understood by all classes and in most regions, cricket became one that travelled with the military, with missionaries and with schoolteachers as they made an empire. It became a sport in which manliness, courage and obeying orders were seen as important, especially in the British public schools (which are actually private institutions), whose pupils often went out to administer the empire and took the sport with them as part of their cultural baggage. Although it is now played in many parts of the world, its strength is in the ex-dominions and colonies of the British Empire, with the notable exception of Canada. By the later stages of the nineteenth century the game had set down roots not only in Britain's colonies of white settlement but also in other key parts of empire, such as the British West Indies and what was then widely known as the Indian Subcontinent.

By 1835, when a new set of rules was instituted, the MCC had become recognized as the sole authority for drawing up cricket's laws and for all subsequent alterations. In the nineteenth century it drove gambling out of the game, instigated a championship between English counties and began playing international matches against Australia, although the inaugural officially recognized Test match between Australian and English cricket teams took place in as late as March 1877 at the Melbourne Cricket Ground, where Australia beat a professional team led by James Lillywhite by 45 runs. Reciprocal tours then created a pattern of international cricket. The Ashes was established as an ongoing competition during the Australian tour of England in 1882, when a surprise victory by the Australians led to a mock obituary of English cricket being published in the *Sporting Times*, containing the phrase 'the body shall be cremated and the ashes taken to Australia'.

When pitch standards improved and gave a decided advantage to batters, international Test matches could be drawn-out contests. In March 1939 the fifth Test between South Africa and England was played at Durban. The teams had agreed that it would be timeless, because England were one up in the series and a definite result was required. This had been commonplace in Test series outside England, and indeed was the

---

That's not cricket

The inaugural first-class international cricket match between teams representing their countries was, perhaps surprisingly, not between England and Australia but featured sides representing the United States and the British Empire's Canadian Province. It was played in New York in September 1844, and the Canadians won by 23 runs.

The MCG: Melbourne Cricket Ground, 1877.

case for all Test matches in Australia. However, after twelve scheduled days, two of which were rest days and one affected by rain, the match was called off with England just 42 runs short of their target and with five wickets in hand. They had to get back to Cape Town to catch their boat home! Nearly 2,000 runs had been scored, and each wicket to fall had cost over 55 runs. No wonder this became the last timeless match to be played internationally.

Home-based timeless Tests doubtless assisted Donald Bradman, Australia's (indeed the game's) greatest batsman of all time, to maintain a Test batting average of 99.94, equating to almost a century every time he went out to bat. The scale of this achievement is such that his nearest rival, current Australian player Steve Smith, trails in at 63.14. No wonder an Australian songwriter composed 'Our Don Bradman' in his honour. His average could have topped a century. In his last Test innings, against England in 1948, a mere four runs would have assured this, but he was bowled for a duck on only the second ball. Since England lost by an innings, he did not have the opportunity to make amends in a second time at the crease.

Test matches still took up to five days and could end without a positive result, as could four-day county matches in England and interstate games in the Australian Sheffield Shield competition. Eventually, in reaction to this, a more spectator-friendly form of the game was introduced that guaranteed a result (possibly even if the weather intervened) with a one-day version that had a limited number of overs, usually fifty a side but now in the fastest form of the game only twenty for each team (the '20/20'). The most popular form of the game in Australia – a country that idolized the timeless Test – has become the Big Bash, in which sides representing the capital cities, ostensibly the state teams with imported guest stars, play each other, often under lights, in matches limited to twenty overs batting for each side, thus fitting in with the recent zeitgeist, that of instant gratification, fast food and fast communication.

31 JULY 1956:
OLD TRAFFORD, MANCHESTER

The cricket ground at Old Trafford, home of Lancashire County Cricket Club, has a deserved reputation for having matches affected by rain. Only two Test matches in England have been abandoned without a ball being bowled because of precipitation; both were at Old Trafford. In July 1956 the touring Australian cricket team would have welcomed a third instance.

However, the weather for this fourth Test of the series between England and Australia, which began on 26 July, was fine for the first two days. England won the toss, chose to bat and made 459. In reply Australia reached 62-2 at tea on the second day, both wickets falling to off-spinner Jim Laker, a Yorkshireman who played for Surrey. However, in the last session of the day Laker took 7 wickets for 8 runs in only 22 balls and the visitors collapsed to be all out for 84. They were asked to follow on, but it looked as though rain would come to their assistance; only 45 minutes' play were possible on the third day and just an hour on the fourth. Heavy overnight rain saturated the pitch, but the start to the final day was delayed by only ten minutes.

At lunch Australia had reached 112-2 (both victims of Laker), and with just four hours to survive there was a chance that the Australians could escape with a draw, but then the sun came out and its warmth turned the pitch into a spin bowler's delight and a batsman's nightmare. Laker became unplayable, the ferocity of his spin a contrast to his quiet personality. He took wicket after wicket until Australia were 205-9. Laker had already taken all ten wickets in an innings against Australia that season when they had played Surrey. Could he do it again and become the first bowler to achieve the feat in a Test match? He could. At 5.30 p.m. Len Maddocks, the Australian wicketkeeper and number eleven batsman, padded up to a delivery that was on target to hit the stumps, and was adjudged out leg before wicket. England had won by an innings and 170 runs. Laker had taken nineteen wickets in the match; his Surrey and England bowling partner, Tony Lock, had just one, but between them the two spinners had bowled out Australia twice. A popular couplet after the match ran 'Ashes to ashes, dust to dust; if Lock don't get you Laker must.' But there wasn't much dust to be seen on that final day. The Australians had complained about the state of the pitch, claiming it had been tailored to suit England's spin attack, but, as might be expected, the Lancastrian authorities strongly denied the charge.

When Laker returned home that night his Austrian wife, Lilly, who knew little about cricket but had fielded several congratulatory phone calls, allegedly asked him, 'Jim, did you do something good today?' He certainly had. Laker's 10 wickets for 53 remains the best bowling figure in test cricket worldwide, and his 9 for 37 in the first innings still ranks fourth in all-time performances. His overall 19 for 90 is unlikely to be beaten, because he had the advantage of a pitch that had remained uncovered during the rain. Nowadays pitches are more protected against the elements, and the phrase 'a sticky wicket' has become a colloquial anachronism.

The saint soon became a sinner, at least in the eyes of the cricket establishment. In 1960 Laker published his autobiography, *Over to Me*, in which he roundly criticized his Surrey captain, Peter May, for poor people-management. He also went on a diatribe about middle-class amateurs who did not want to play as professionals because of the social status implications, but who often earned more from the game via 'expenses' and sinecure positions in the county administration than did the paid players. The establishment was not pleased. The Surrey authorities withdrew Laker's free pass to the facilities at the Oval, the county's headquarters, which they had given him on his retirement in

1959, and Marylebone Cricket Club, the ruling body of English cricket, cancelled his honorary membership. There was a later rapprochement, however, and Laker's ashes were scattered on the Oval playing surface after his death in 1984.

Donald Bradman (left) goes out to bat in 1932.

The dominant 20/20 competition is the Indian Premier League, which began in 2008, partly (although the Indian cricket authorities deny it) as a reaction to the Indian Cricket League, founded the year before by a private promoter and quickly folding in face of the new, officially sanctioned tournament. It is run as an eight-team, city-based franchise valued as a brand in 2019 at $6.9 billion. Attendances are the highest of any cricket league, as is the television audience, which has attracted massive sponsorship for the competition, currently from a Chinese smartphone manufacturer. There is an annual player auction, plus three trading windows in which players can be transferred, although only with their consent. The average salary for two months' work equates to $4.3 million a year, the second highest in any sports league. Two costume innovations, reminiscent of the Tour de France, are that the top scorer at any time during the competition wears an orange cap and the leading wicket-taker a purple one.

Whereas cricket has become radical in its format, it has been conservative in restricting technological change. The present maximum width of the bat was set at 4¼ in. (10.8 cm) back in 1771 after one player defended his wicket with a blade as wide as his stumps. A length limit of 38 in. (96.5 cm) was added in 1831. There have been no restrictions on the shape or weight of the bat, which has given bat-makers the freedom to experiment with hollow-backed bats, bats with shoulders and the like. However, attempts to change the composition of the blade from wood to aluminium were blocked, although protective coverings of thin plastic have been allowed, provided they do not cause 'unacceptable damage' to the ball. The 1744 code laid down that the ball must weigh between 5 and 6 oz (142–70 g). This was narrowed to between 5½ and 5¾ oz (156–63 g) in 1774, and it still stands. There was no specification on circumference until 1838, when between 9 and 9¼ in. (22.9–23.5 cm) became the rule, a figure that was reduced slightly in 1927 to accommodate the official makers, who had been producing a technically illegal ball for some years. Generally, apart from some mechanization in production, technology left the ball alone until the introduction of floodlit matches, when a suitable white ball had to be devised for greater visibility. Strangely, there is no rule about the composition of the ball, which by tradition remains leather.

STICKS AND STONES

Standing on the first tee of the Old Course at St Andrews, with the expanse of the links in front and the imposing clubhouse behind, the wind picking up from the sea and the pot bunkers waiting to trap the unwary, unskilled or just unlucky, can prompt the golfer to muse on where all this began. The answer – unexpected to some, including the Scottish tourist industry – is: probably not in Scotland! Scottish folklore has it that a shepherd used the hook on his crook to knock a stone into a rabbit hole, and thus golf was invented. Yet, contrary to the underlying premise of Visit Scotland's campaign to encourage tourists to visit the 'home of golf', the sport was not Scottish in origin. Indeed, representations of balls and striking implements have been discovered in many nations far from Scotland, including China. When you think about it, this is not surprising. The world is full of sticks and stones, and there is a limited number of things that can be done with them.

Current thinking is that a version of golf was brought to Scotland as part of trade that developed between the ports on its eastern coast and the Netherlands. How it came to Holland or how it developed there is still unknown. Maybe it was from China. Scholars there claim that the ancient Chinese game of *chui wan* (literally hitting a ball with a little stick) resembled golf in that the objective was to use a club to hit the ball into holes in the ground. Evidence has been found that it existed during the Song, Yuan and Ming dynasties (960–1644 CE), before disappearing during the succeeding Qing Dynasty. These scholars suggest that the game may have been transferred from China to Europe in the cultural exchanges that we know occurred during the Middle Ages.

Golf was popularized in Scotland from the seventeenth century onwards, primarily as a short game – little more than putting – played in churchyards and other limited areas by a broad spectrum of the population using minimal and often basic equipment. However, as it developed into the longer game that we now recognize, it required more land and became less democratic. The club, with its ability to raise funds collectively, became the instrument of golf expansion, much of which took place south of the border, in England, first as Scottish golfing outposts but later in clubs dominated by English players. Golf became one of the fastest-growing recreational activities of late nineteenth- and early twentieth-century Britain, and at one stage in the 1890s a new golf club was being established every two or three days. From only a few thousand playing the game at the beginning of the 1880s, by 1914 some 350,000 golfers were 'spoiling good walks' around the country. Most of these players were members of a club, that traditional British organizational institution in sport and other activities. While golf was not a sport of courage and overt masculinity like cricket and the football codes, it was still framed as a male-dominant activity, although it would appear that by 1914 some 60,000 women were members of golf clubs, perhaps one-sixth of all registered players.

Golf was also seen as a 'rational' recreation, justifiable for its health benefits. Ethically sound, physically demanding (although to a limited extent) and out in the open air, it improved mind, body and health, both physical and mental. It afforded sufficient exercise for all without being too energetic for the older or less robust, and concentrating on the ball allowed players to forget their worldly cares, at least for a while.

The basic elements of golf have not altered since the game began, and hitting a ball with a stick into a hole in the fewest strokes possible is still central. There are a few other constants, such as the use of the sport to cement business relationships and the general layout of a course, apart from increased length. Yet aspects of the golf product have changed, some of them significantly, not least the rules, which are essential for the creation of golf in its game form. The first published rules, the thirteen clauses of the Leith Rules issued by the Honourable Company of Edinburgh in 1744, have swelled to a near two-hundred-page document covering almost anything that might occur on the course. Some of the rule changes have been necessitated by developments in equipment technology. A step change occurred in the early twentieth century, when the rubber-cored ball rendered the gutta-percha version (which itself had replaced the feather-filled ball) obsolete almost overnight. Similarly, the coming of metal-shafted clubs in the 1920s made hickory clubs a heritage object. The tautologically named 'metal woods' have entered the golfer's bag, and large-headed drivers have become popular, although currently there are set limits to the length of the shaft, the area of the club face and the overall volume of the head.

Golf costume switched from being a uniform to identify players from a particular club to a fashion item for women in the interwar years.

Edwardian golfers had caddies to carry their clubs, and those labelled first-class also offered advice on how to play the course. The raising of the school-leaving age coupled with the development of the personal golf trolley has meant that this scenario has practically disappeared, except for the elite professional. The teaching professional remains, but has been supplemented by electronic coaching aids for the club golfer and an array of personal trainers, psychologists and injury therapists at elite level. In terms of facilities, courses have become longer in response to ball and club technology, but otherwise haven't changed much. Most golf clubs worldwide remain private institutions and have lagged behind society in the adoption of non-discriminatory membership policies. Pay-and-play courses, which have proliferated in recent years, are more commercially operated and less exclusive. Golf is unlike many sports in that spectators cannot see the whole event. They have the choice of following one set of players around the whole course or staying in one place and watching each set of golfers pass through. Television has revolutionized the sport/spectator relationship in golf by allowing viewers to see the event more holistically.

Golf varied from most other early sports in being slow to develop a central organization. Until 1888 the rules emanating from the Royal & Ancient Golf Club (R&A) – first issued in 1754, when the club was known as the Society of St Andrews Golfers – specified that they related to the game as played on the St Andrews links; but then they became titled Rules of Golf by the Royal & Ancient Club of St Andrews, with the local rules included as a separate item. Although many clubs adopted these rules or, more precisely, adapted them to suit their own circumstances, there was no single recognized rule-maker in golf until the 1890s, when the R&A responded to calls from within the sport, first to consolidate existing rules and then, in 1897, to establish itself as the ultimate rule-making authority. However, Americans adopted the Scottish game so enthusiastically that they sought to have a say in its rule-making, and in 1922 the United States Golf Association set up its own Rules of Golf Committee. Almost immediately it went its own way by approving steel-shafted clubs, something not acceded to by the R&A until 1929. There have been major disputes between the two organizations, in the 1950s over the size of the ball and in the 1960s over penalties for unplayable balls, but now there is an agreed power-sharing arrangement, with quadrennial meetings to revise the rules.

ANYONE FOR TENNIS?

Lawn tennis (as distinct from royal or real tennis, with its Renaissance origins) was invented in the late nineteenth century for the English suburban middle class with their expansive lawns, although its method of scoring was based on older traditions. The origin is generally attributed to Major Walter Clopton Wingfield's invention of a game called *Sphairistikè*, which was transmogrified and popularized as lawn tennis. Its great appeal was that men and women could play it together.

The first open tennis championship (although all the competitors were British) was organized by the All-England Lawn Tennis and Croquet Club in 1877, when Spencer Gore won the only title on offer, the gentlemen's singles. The ladies' singles, won by Maud Watson, was added to the programme in 1884, the same year as the men's doubles. There were some long runs of consecutive title wins by individuals and doubles pairings, such as William Renshaw, who won the men's singles from 1881 to 1886, Reggie Doherty (1897–1900) and Laurence Doherty (1902–6), with the Doherty brothers taking the doubles title in 1897–1901 and 1903–5. One reason for this, in addition to their talent, was the challenge system whereby the title-holder did not have to compete until the final itself. This was dropped in 1922. The Wimbledon Championships, as they became known because of their location, was followed as an elite major event by the United States Open (1881), the French Open (1891), and the Australian Open (1905). These events became collectively known as Grand Slam tournaments in 1924. Tennis featured in the Olympics before the First World War, but was dropped in 1924 because of disputes over amateurism in the game, only to return as a fully professional sport in Seoul in 1988.

At the amateur club level, tennis was a team game played by individuals representing their clubs, and these turn out not to have been the class-ridden stereotyped institutions that some suggest. The sport was widely played across all classes and regions, and a substantial proportion of tennis clubs in the mid-twentieth century were works-based.

This team form of tennis was replicated at the higher echelons in the Davis Cup for male teams representing their nation. It was founded in 1900 for competition between teams representing the United States and Great Britain. Perhaps too much credit has gone to Dwight Davis, a young (only 21 at the time), wealthy, self-publicizing American player, who presented the cup named after himself to the United States Lawn Tennis Association (USLTA) in 1900. In reality he usurped the glory from those whose efforts had developed the international relationships necessary for this to occur. By 1905 the tournament had expanded to include Belgium, Austria, France and Australasia, a combined team from Australia and New Zealand that competed together until 1914. Initially it was played as a challenge cup in which teams competed against one another for the right to face the previous year's champion in the final round. Beginning in 1923, the world's teams were split into two zones: American and European. The winners of the two zones then met to decide which national team would challenge the defending champion for the cup. In 1955 a third zone, the 'Eastern Zone', was added, and eleven years later the European zone was split into A and B groups.

Beginning in 1972, the format was changed to a knock-out tournament, so that the defending champion was required to compete in all rounds, and the Davis Cup was awarded to the tournament champion. In 1981 a tiered system of competition was introduced, in which the sixteen best national teams competed in the World Group and all other national teams competed in one of four groups in one of three regional zones. In 2018 the International Tennis Federation (ITF) voted to change the format of the competition to an eighteen-team event at the end of the season, with the intention of becoming more attractive to sponsors and broadcasters. There is promotion and relegation to this elite group, and more than one hundred teams enter the competition annually. The first winner of the new-format competition, played in Madrid, was Spain. The female equivalent of the men's international tournament used to be the Wightman Cup, instigated in 1923 for competition solely between Great Britain and the United States, but in 1963 the ITF agreed to organize a women's team championship, now known as the Billie Jean King Cup.

Despite its often-perceived aura of conservatism, the All England Lawn Tennis Club (croquet was dropped from the title in 1882) was to the fore in lobbying for the open game and finally got its wish in 1968, when amateurs and professionals were allowed to play against each other competitively. However, the move to open tournaments did not go smoothly, partly because of the continuing resistance by traditionalists among tennis administrators who insisted that players be categorized into three groups:

amateurs, contracted (to one of the commercial circuits) professionals, and registered players, who were freelance but able to earn prize money. They then refused to allow the contracted professionals to represent their country in the Davis Cup. An immediate impact of open tennis was that the commercial promoters of tournaments now had to compete with traditional events to attract the leading players. Indeed, as a price for allowing the players they had under contract for their own circuits to participate elsewhere, such promoters demanded a share of the profits and of sponsorship money, as well as a say in tournament regulations such as the type of ball to be used. Ultimately, however, these promoters lost out, but not to the traditional authorities. Instead, their nemesis was the emergence of associations to look after the interests of the professional players, and eventually the Association of Tennis Professionals (ATP) and the Women's Tennis Association (WTA) took over the organization of elite tennis tournaments, apart from the Slam events.

JOLLY HOCKEY STICKS AND MORE

Hockey, or something resembling it using a ball and stick, can be found in Egyptian tomb paintings of four millennia ago, but the modern version began in England in the second half of the nineteenth century. It was built on the previous century's more violent, localized versions, which centred on the Royal Military College at Sandhurst and various public schools. The first documented rules were by the Blackheath Hockey Club in 1861, from which hockey developed as a game for the middle classes, many of whom disliked the growth of mass spectator sport and the coming of pro-fessionalism. Its players were all amateurs and there were no leagues, only friendly fixtures. Men's hockey spread around the world, but, significantly, Britain's military presence brought the game to India, which became a powerhouse in the sport, winning gold at consecutive Olympics from 1928 to 1956. The Moseley Ladies' Hockey Club is credited with adapting the men's rules to make the sport more suitable for women. Although women held the same ethical attitudes, the two games had separate and often fractious developments, with women gaining Olympic status only in 1980, partly because of opposition from the men's international body. Originally called hockey, the term 'field hockey' is often used now to distinguish the sport from ice hockey.

Ball game of the Choctaw: the original lacrosse.

Lacrosse was a Native American game pre-dating European contact, and the conquest and colonization of North America, but which was later appropriated into Western culture by the invaders. European fur-traders in the mid-seventeenth century described contests in which up to a thousand male warriors would participate, using wooden sticks with small animal-skin nets attached to pass around a 'ball' of stone or skin wrapped in fur. Over the next two centuries indigenous lacrosse fell away as Western colonization extinguished Native American cultures. By the mid-nineteenth century, after the vast majority of tribes had been exterminated, pacified or Westernized, lacrosse stood on the verge of extinction. At that point, with indigenous tribes no longer a threat, white settler societies began to romanticize vestiges of the lifestyles of what they now called the 'noble savages', and to incorporate some of them into Western culture. The Canadian William George Beers 'invented' modern lacrosse in the 1850s and '60s to honour North American indigenous traditions, but ironically, as the modern version of the game spread from Beers's home town of Montreal to the rest of Canada and the United States, Native American players who tried to join in were frequently excluded owing to the excuse that they did not fit its 'gentlemen amateur' ethos. Since the 1860s the modern version of lacrosse has spread throughout North America, becoming a popular intercollegiate and professional sport, and the rest of the world. It featured at the Olympics of 1904 and 1908, but failed to sustain its place in later Games.

Hurling and shinty, two highly physical contact sports played on vast areas with a minimum of rules, and both with thousands of years' history, have a strong resemblance to each other in methods of play and scoring, but no evidence of a common origin has been unearthed. They are perhaps simply two of the many ball-and-stick games played across Europe since early times. There are differences in the number of players – (fifteen per team in hurling and twelve per team in shinty) and the length of the game – 60 or 80 minutes in hurling, depending on the competition; 90 in shinty.

Celebrated in Gaelic myth and legend, shinty is a minority Scottish sport played mainly in the Highlands and Islands. The modern game is governed by the Camanachd Association, founded in 1893. Its first meeting was at the Highland town of Kingussie, home to the team that won twenty consecutive league titles (1986–2005) and went undefeated for four seasons in the early 1990s.

Penalty shot in hurling.

Shinty player in the Kinlochshiel versus Strathglass
Balliemore Cup Final 2009, a Scottish knock-out competition.

Hurling is one of Ireland's national games, and is played throughout the Republic and Northern Ireland, but with its strength in the south. It developed its modern form under the aegis of the Gaelic Athletic Association (GAA), which was formed in 1884 partly to preserve Irish sport and cultivate its popularity for future generations in the face of outside cultural influence. At that time hurling was a local, customary and non-standardized game traversing rough country with goals often miles apart, akin to the way much folk football was played elsewhere in Europe. The ball may be caught in the hand (unlike in shinty, where playing the ball with the hand, whether intentionally or not, is deemed a foul), kicked, or struck with the hurling stick, but it cannot be lifted by hand from the ground. A major skill is the ability to carry the ball by bouncing it on the stick while running at speed. Perhaps uniquely among elite team sports, players' names are not on their jerseys. Both shinty and hurling are tough and spectacular, but they have never achieved the status of major spectator sports outside their homelands, and in shinty's case not even there. Hurling was an unofficial sport at the 1904 St Louis Olympics, where in the final Fenian Football Club (Chicago) beat Innisfails (St Louis).

11

MOVING THE GOALPOSTS:
THE FOOTBALL CODES

Australian Rules football has not received due credit for being the world's first football code played beyond the confines of one locale (unlike the many versions of public-school football in Britain). The game is specific to Australia. Although, to a modern observer, it resembles an amalgam of all other codes of football, it actually owes nothing to any of them. When Thomas Wentworth Wills and his Melbourne cricketing colleagues developed the game in 1858 as a means of keeping fit during the winter, they could not draw on the experiences of the Football Association (not formed until 1863) or the Rugby Football Union (1871). What Wills could do was incorporate ideas from his time as a schoolboy at Rugby, but the new game was not based on the Rugby school version to any significant extent. What eventually developed was a unique combination of rules that owed little to other codes, but has not influenced them, either.

It has several distinctive features, some of which reflect Australian cultural heritage, particularly the concept of everyone getting a 'fair go' and the 'larrikin' anti-authority attitude. On the field it has a unique closed-fist method of passing the ball, and features spectacularly high marks, when a player often clambers on an opponent's shoulders to catch the ball. There are 22 players in a team, although only 18 can be on the ground at any time; players are interchanged rather than substituted. Points are awarded for near misses at goal, and not only is there no offside, but players cannot be sent off for foul play, although any reported offenders are ineligible for the end-of-season award as 'best and fairest' player.

Australian Rules was organized into a state-based competition in 1877. In 1990 the competition became the Australian Football League (AFL), confirming that it was by then, at the elite level, a nationwide competition, although state leagues continued to function. At state level it has been organized around electorate districts within the major cities. Unlike many other football codes, there are no knock-out cup competitions, and instead the top of the league at the end of the season is declared 'minor' champion before an elaborate play-off system to determine the 'major' champion. Essentially, Australian Rules football has existed as a game in isolation from the rest of the football world, although occasionally adapting its rules for international matches against Gaelic football teams from Ireland.

There is controversy over whether Australian football owes anything to indigenous games played by Aboriginal communities. In mid-2019 the AFL declared that the sport was 'undoubtedly' influenced by marngrook, a high-marking game played before European settlement in the western districts of Victoria – an area where Wills had lived from the age of four until he left for school in England at fourteen. This runs counter to the view expressed in an official history commissioned by the AFL in 2008 in which the author, Gillian Hibbins, maintained that the idea that Australian Rules originated from Aboriginal games was 'a seductive myth'. It is accepted by all historians of the sport that Aboriginal people played many different forms of football, but there is no written or visual evidence that these had any influence on the official Australian game. Wills never mentioned having seen Aboriginals playing football, and the rules he and his contemporaries drew up were clearly based on those of English public schools. However, the AFL now claims that it has been privy to oral history from some Aboriginal elders, and has consequently revised its views.

It is suspicious that the revision coincides with an apology issued by the AFL to the indigenous player Adam Goodes for its failure to support him during the last months of his career (1999–2015), when the Sydney Swans star was hounded by racist abuse from opposing fans. It would seem that in order to atone for its past attitude and behaviour towards indigenous players, the AFL has opted to rewrite sports history. Most probably, the connection between Aboriginal people and Australian football is the reverse of the AFL claim. The writer Roy Hay has demonstrated that those indigenous people who survived the ethnic cleansing of the Europeans and finished up working on cattle stations or living in religious missions played Australian Rules almost from its inception. They saw white men playing, liked what they saw and forced themselves into the game, first as individuals but later forming their own teams and becoming good enough to win local leagues.

Ironically, one of the men who took a leading role in the development of Gaelic football was once a good enough rugby player to feature for Phoenix against Dublin University in the first Leinster Senior Cup final in 1882. However, Michael Cusack then dropped rugby (and cricket) in favour of promoting traditional Irish sports, and joined with six colleagues to form the GAA. At a time when an increasing number of Irish people were rejecting both British politics and British cultural domination, Cusack and his colleagues saw themselves as the sporting equivalent of those seeking to preserve Irish language, literature and culture.

But what was traditional Irish sport? Hurling was certainly uniquely Irish, but various forms of football had been played in Ireland since the fourteenth century, and, even though in some areas it had its own name, *caid*, there was nothing distinctively Irish about any of the versions. If it wanted to promote Irish football, the GAA would have to invent it. The first rulebook was devised in 1884 by Maurice Davin, one of the founders of the GAA and a prominent Irish sportsman. It said little about how the game should be played, especially in terms of handling or not handling the ball. The sport differentiated itself from rugby in the fact that a goal was scored by the ball going *under* the crossbar, and in the size of the teams (between 14 and 21 players), the dimensions of the pitch (120 × 80 yd/110 × 73 m) and the length of the match (60 minutes). However, there was too much variation in the way matches were played, a situation ameliorated by three major rule changes before 1888 that gave the game distinctive features. First, the handling of the ball was restricted to catching and hitting, with carrying and throwing prohibited. Second, bodily tackling was outlawed. Third, point posts 7 yd (6.4 m) to the side of each goalpost were introduced, and in the event of a draw on goals (0-0 was becoming too common) the match was to be decided on points scored. The game seems never to have had an offside rule as distinctive as those in soccer and rugby.

Once these distinctive features of the Irish game were determined, further rule changes tended to be for entertainment value only. To open up the game, teams were reduced to seventeen-a-side in 1892 and fifteen-a-side in 1913. Goals became worth three points, and matches were won by the team scoring most points in total. The point posts themselves were abandoned in 1910 and replaced by uprights on the goalposts; kicks over the crossbar and between these posts scored a point.

Gaelic football was almost immediately successful as a spectator sport. Team structures were based on locality, principally the Catholic parish and, at a wider representational level, the county. Spectator identity with teams was virtually guaranteed. The creation of an All-Ireland championship, the first in any team sport in Ireland, offered the chance of national glory. More than that, attending matches became a convivial family affair. Unlike other codes of football in Britain, matches were played on a Sunday, with the blessing of the Catholic Church and a reminder that mass should be attended first.

Supporters of the game felt that the GAA articulated a popular nationalism, both political and sporting. Moreover, the latter was not dependent on victories over other nations, a rarity in Irish soccer and rugby, where humiliating defeats were common. As a sporting organization it promoted Ireland first. In 1886, just two years after its establishment, the Association committed itself, through its rulebook, to supporting Irish industry. The rule stated that all equipment used on the field of play, from footballs to jerseys and boots, should be of Irish manufacture. However, it remained a relatively unprogressive organization in terms of commercial activity, relying mainly on gate revenue for its income, until the 1990s, when it restructured and brought in major sponsors. Yet the sports it controls, including football, remain entirely amateur, as they have been since its foundation. The GAA remains an unusual organization in the world of contemporary sport in that the bulk of its surpluses are spent on the grass roots of its clubs across the country, to the benefit of the local communities that are the bedrock of the sport.

THE REAL FOOTBALL

All countries have had games in which a ball has been kicked around. Yet soccer, as most of the world knows it, was a British invention. It

Shrove Tuesday football in Kingston upon Thames, 1865.

came from three distinct (so far as we know) strands of development. First was folk ('mob' to some) football, which can be traced back several centuries and some details of which appeared in Chapters One and Three. Second, recent research has shown that football matches (as opposed to folk football games) played under defined, printed rules were more prevalent by the 1830s than previously thought. Nevertheless, although there were common features among these rules, they were still local and regulated only the match for which they were proposed. Throughout Britain in the next three decades there were clubs playing under rules of various levels of sophistication, with differences in the amount of handling allowed, the size of the pitch, the type of goal and the level of violence permitted. Despite this popularity, it is unlikely that football could have developed any further without standardized rules, a matter of importance as transport improvements made possible matches outside a team's immediate locality. Here the third strand appears, public-school football. These schools developed their own brands of the game, and pupils could find sufficient competition within their own school via the house system. However, when former students wished to play at university and elsewhere, problems arose. In London, teams of Old Boys each followed their own distinct rules, leading either to agreements on composite rules for a specific fixture or to home-and-away matches under each side's conventions. The Football Association (FA) was founded in 1863 in an attempt to bring some order.

The history of soccer and its spread around the world could take a volume of its own – indeed, several authors have done just that – so here I will just look at two aspects that I feel merit special attention. First is the role of Glasgow in the early development of the game; second is the emergence of the English Premier League as one of the game's major modern institutions.

Soccer historians have paid too little attention to Glasgow, which I argue was actually the centre of the soccer universe before 1914. In the first international match between Scotland and England, in November 1872, all of the Scottish side came from Queen's Park, a Glasgow team not to be confused (as did the FA in its trophy room) with the English side Queens Park Rangers. Looking at Glasgow within Scottish football, between 1873 and 1914 Glasgow clubs won the Scottish Cup 25 times and were runners-up on nineteen occasions. Twenty of the 23 League titles before 1914 also went to Glasgow. Queen's Park was an amateur club, but in 1914 owned Hampden Park, then the largest football stadium in the world, with a capacity of over 100,000; in 1912 an alleged 127,303 spectators crammed in to witness Scotland's football team draw 1-1 with England. When Ibrox, home to Rangers, and Celtic Park are added, three Glasgow stadia had an aggregate capacity of more than 250,000.

Turning to Glasgow's relationship with English football, if we look at performances south of the border, Rangers reached the semi-final of the FA Cup in 1887 and Queen's Park the final on two occasions. Fergus Suter played for Partick, another Glasgow club, against Darwen in January 1878, and later that year joined that Lancashire club along with his teammate James (Jimmy) Love. This stimulated an exodus, and by 1884 there were 58 Scottish players in English football. The Glasgow Charity Cup was established in 1875 and became the model for major tournaments in England, including those in London, Birmingham and Sheffield. No other city could rival Glasgow. London had Crystal Palace but nothing to rival Hampden Park; it hosted the FA but not the Football League, whereas both the Scottish League and the Scottish Football Association (SFA) were based in Glasgow; and in 1913/14 only two of the twenty Football League First Division teams came from the metropolis, and that season they finished nineteenth and twentieth!

One of the most significant developments in soccer in recent decades is the creation of the English Premier League (EPL), which was founded in 1992, when the existing First Division of the four-division Football League split away to become an independent organization. Economically, the elite clubs were attracted by the prospect of more television income, and this was obtained by signing with BSkyB (Sky), a subscription channel offering sport via satellite, a new phenomenon in the British media. Elsewhere the EPL was less innovative. Its size was inherited, in that there were 22 teams in the existing Football League First Division when the breakaway took place. In 1995, at the insistence of the International Federation of Association Football (FIFA), the size was reduced to twenty teams by relegating four and promoting only two that season, although that was the end of turkeys voting for Christmas. The EPL also had the legacy of being an open league with quality control operated via promotion and relegation. Another inherited feature was club ownership, which at the time was predominately by non-quoted joint-stock companies, although in reality it was the fiefdom of individuals, often local businessmen. There was a brief flirtation with the stock market until city institutions accepted that football clubs were not attractive investments for those seeking financial returns. This was less of a concern to those individuals in a wave of change that began with the Russian billionaire Roman Abramovich's purchase of Chelsea Football Club in 2003. This heralded the development of a 'benefactor' model of foreign ownership in which the motive of short-term playing success outweighed financial considerations. In effect, EPL clubs became executive toys.

The EPL clubs face a dual business objective, involving both success on the field and raising sufficient revenue to ensure that this would happen. They have four major revenue streams to draw on: sponsorship, merchandising, gate receipts and the sale of broadcasting rights, the last being the undoubted financial milch cow that has underwritten the development of the league. The sale of these rights is the only revenue stream negotiated collectively by the league. This is a prime example of a monopolistic situation with one seller and several potential buyers, a situation ripe for exploitation and profiteering. Undoubtedly it is satellite television that has made the EPL a global brand, with claimed viewing figures of 3 billion across 225 countries.

The EPL has transformed the commercial behaviour of elite English football. Between 1991 and 2008 the aggregate income of EPL clubs grew at a compound rate of more than 16 per cent. Yet stated profits were not reflective of the increased commercial activity; only four clubs reported making a gross profit, and the debts of EPL clubs totalled £484 million by 2008. The reason for this was straightforward: profit-maximization was not at the heart of the business strategy of EPL clubs. The potential surpluses did not materialize because the drive for playing success (or avoidance of relegation) led to much of the revenue being spent on the wages of (and transfer payments for) players; unlike many sports leagues, the EPL did not opt for either a team or a player salary cap. One consequence has been an enormous rise in player reward. When the EPL was formed, the average annual wage was £75,000, but by 2008 this had risen to £1.1 million.

Such wages have attracted the best. In the first squads of the EPL only eleven players did not come from the United Kingdom or Ireland, but line-ups now resemble a league of nations. Aston Villa was the last team to feature an all-English side in the Premier League when it lost 4-1 to Coventry in February 1999. Once foreign players became so important, it made sense to appoint foreign managers who had both experience in handling such players and the contacts for their recruitment; not one English manager has ever won the premiership title (remember, Sir Alex Ferguson is a proud Scot). Moreover, some 60 per cent of EPL clubs now have a majority foreign ownership. The only truly English quality of the EPL now is its location. The inflow of foreign funds and human capital has had some negative consequences. Clubs in the lower levels of English football no longer receive the volume of transfer fees they used to. There has been a refusal by the EPL clubs to accept any responsibility for the performance of the England team; they reneged on their initial promise to reduce the league to eighteen clubs, and they have reduced the opportunities for young English players to play at the top level. The national game has moved beyond national control, at least economically.

THE OVAL BALL

Rugby emerged as yet another variant of kicking and running with a ball, although the ball itself was oval rather than spheroid to assist in passing the ball by hand. It became formalized as rugby union when it was codified by the Rugby Football Union (RFU) in 1871.

Two major features stand out in the history of rugby. One is the emergence of rugby as the national sport of New Zealand, a country that has come to dominate the game internationally. The first recorded match was in 1870, but it kicked on, with the sport gaining impetus from 1876, when New Zealand's national government abolished the autonomous provincial ones. Rugby seems to have stepped in as a source of provincial sporting rivalry to replace the previous political one. The sport also took advantage of an emergent national rail system with a standardized gauge, which facilitated inter-provincial matches. The first provincial Rugby Union was established in Canterbury in 1879, followed by Otago in 1881 and Auckland in 1883, although there was no national Union until 1892. By 1893 there were eighteen such associations and some seven hundred clubs.

Yet in 1888–9 a New Zealand team had already become the first overseas side to tour Britain, although this was a commercial venture, not an official side. This New Zealand Native Football Team, as it was called, was to have been all-Maori, but non-Maori players were added to make it more competitive. They were the first New Zealand sports side to wear an all-black outfit; they also performed a haka before the start of each match. The tour lasted fourteen months and involved 107 rugby matches, nine of Australian Rules and two of soccer, the latter played in Australia at the end of the tour. The first official tour to Britain came in 1905–6, one in which the All Blacks won every match except the last, against Wales, a loss attributed to a controversial disallowed try by the visitors. The tourists returned home as heroes, having cemented rugby as the most significant cultural symbol of the nation.

The second significant occurrence was the schism that occurred in 1895 over broken-time payments to working-class players, who lost earnings if they missed work in order to play. In 1895 22 northern English

Too many in the scrum

For many years historians accepted that in 1882, according to a New Zealand newspaper, the country had an estimated 50,000 rugby players, a number that gave substantial clout to the claim that the game was already the country's national sport. Nobody went to the newspaper archives to check the veracity of the figure, which had been cited in a university dissertation. Eventually one sports historian noted that, since there were only three hundred known teams in the early 1880s, the number must have been erroneous. He then worked out that the typist preparing the thesis had hit one key too many, multiplying the original 5,000 players tenfold.

The All Blacks performing the haka prior to playing Australia in 2017.

clubs left the RFU to form their own Northern Union, where such payments would be permitted, something the RFU would not countenance. It
would eventually lead to full professionalism, but that was not the initial
objective. In fact, the Northern Union set tight regulations to maintain
an air of respectability about the new institution, including one that said
men were eligible to play on a Saturday afternoon only if they could
demonstrate that they had worked full-time during the preceding week;
and some jobs, such as working for a bookmaker or in a public house,
were proscribed. The Lancashire club Broughton Rangers, who won the
Challenge Cup in 1902, were actually fined because their players had not
worked on the morning of the final.

Initially, the Northern Union played the same game as before, but
piecemeal by 1906 it had reduced teams to thirteen-a-side, cut the value
of goals and increased that of tries, abolished the lineout, and introduced
the play-the-ball rule after a tackle. All these were designed to open up
the game and render it more entertaining for a paying public. Essentially,
they switched from rugby union's emphasis on forward play to a more
free-flowing style featuring skilled and speedy backs. However, it proved
difficult to expand in Britain outside the northern industrial areas, because soccer had already gained the working-class audience elsewhere.
When expansion came it was overseas in Australia and New Zealand.
The Antipodean influence was reversed in 1922, when the Northern
Union changed its name to the Rugby Football League, adopting the

nomenclature of the Australians and Kiwis, who had used the term 'rugby league' in 1907 and 1908 respectively.

Although rugby union holds a world cup tournament, the early results in the finals tend to be predictable, because rugby has less strength across nations than soccer. Seven, sometimes all eight of the quarter-finalists can be identified before the tournaments start. At the international level, rugby union has not followed the example of FIFA and pushed resources into developing the sport worldwide. Its policy has been essentially to give more to those who already have a lot. This was borne out by a recent plan – fortunately now defunct – by World Rugby (formerly the International Rugby Board) to form a twelve-nation world league comprising the existing six nations of the northern hemisphere, the four teams from the southern hemisphere competition, and the addition of Japan and the United States. It was to be a closed competition, with no prospect of promotion to existing second-tier nations who, unlike Japan and the United States, could not bring money in with them. A television deal was to guarantee each participating union some £7 million a season. Short-term profits were to be prioritized over longer-term development. The argument of World Rugby was essentially the 'trickle-down' effect forwarded by right-wing development economists (not a total oxymoron), which postulates that if the rich get richer there will be more to give away to the poor. Pull the other one!

12

. . . NOR ANY DROP TO DRINK: WATER SPORTS

Swimming and bathing have a very long history. The earliest visual representations of swimmers are more than 11,000 years old. In ancient Greece a person was considered ignorant if they could not read or swim; and in classical Rome swimming was part of military training, although in later years a bathing rather than a swimming culture became dominant. Swimming was one of the knightly attributes, but it fell out of favour in medieval times; let us not forget that it was the ability to swim – or at least float – that could determine if a woman was deemed a witch or not. More generally, it was the danger of entering water that was stressed, no matter the competence of the swimmer. A change of attitude came in the sixteenth century with the publication of swimming manuals analysing the scientific side of the activity. Nevertheless, swimming did not catch on as a popular pastime until the nineteenth century, which also brought the emergence of competitive rather than merely recreational swimming. By 1837 England was holding a national championship for professional swimmers.

Before the mid-nineteenth century swimming was chiefly a masculine activity, undertaken both for exercise and for recreation, while women were restricted to bathing, which implied simply immersion in water, often in the hope of curing an ailment. Gradually, however, swimming became more acceptable for women, because it had a lifesaving aspect and could offer mild but beneficial exercise. Indeed, unlike many other forms of sporting activity, swimming broke through the barrier of medical opposition to female participation. Female doctors especially advocated swimming as an exercise that could prepare women to bear healthy children. By the end of the century swimming rather than merely bathing was being promoted to women as conducive to their physical health.

The issue became one of morality rather than medicine. Should women be allowed to swim where men could watch them? When this was solved in the affirmative, it was then a question of how revealing their costumes should be. Restrictive and heavy clothing could in fact be life-threatening to swimmers. Men had always bathed naked, except when the presence of women necessitated the wearing of 'drawers'. In 1890, when the Amateur Swimming Association (ASA; now Swim England) instigated a regulation, one-piece bathing suit for men, such drawers still had to be worn under the costume itself. All this passed unchallenged, but swimming attire for women was a much more contested area. There was a constant clash between respectability and functionality, although it was the latter that eventually gained precedence for most female swimmers. Interestingly, when a regulation costume for women was brought in by the ASA, it was an all-male committee that made the decision on its design.

Swimming provided an avenue for professional swimmers. Many 'professors', as Victorian professional swimmers often entitled themselves,

Women in swimming attire, Collaroy Beach, Sydney, 1908.

advertised their personal successes in competitive swimming as a way to attract clients to employ them as instructors and coaches. Some who taught swimming also gained positions as baths superintendents, and others made money from performing in aquatic displays. One of the most famous was Captain Matthew Webb, who in 1875 became the first person to swim the English Channel. The London Stock Exchange closed to welcome him on his return and, lower down the social scale, his image appeared on Bryant & May matchboxes. A slow but strong swimmer who once won an endurance match against a paddling dog, he was awarded the first Stanhope Medal by the Royal Humane Society when, while serving as second mate on the Cunard Line ship *Russia*, he dived into the waters while in the middle of the Atlantic Ocean in a forlorn attempt to rescue a sailor who had fallen overboard. In 1883 swimming cost him his own life when, in an effort to raise money for his family, he drowned trying to conquer the rapids at the foot of Niagara Falls.

There were also female professional swimmers. Most were teachers, but quite a few were in the public eye, whether in the pool or on the stage, displaying their diving skill, swimming in endurance events, performing aquatic entertainments and even racing for money. It was these women who became the most prominent and most admired of nineteenth-century professional sportswomen, and it was these women too who pushed the boundaries of acceptability before the male gaze. They de-manded a tighter costume than was worn by conventional swimmers, both for functionality (given the feats they were performing) and to titillate the male spectator whose admission fees provided a significant source of income.

Making it on the sports channel

Brave Captain Webb has made his fame,
He's England's pride and glory;
And many will repeat his name,
And tell the wondrous story
Of how he fought against the sea,
And battled with the billows;
For twenty-two long hours swam he
To gain the Calais pillows.
Play the Game: Victorian and Edwardian Sporting Songs (Tadworth, 2001), p. 27.

Captain Matthew Webb, the first person to swim the Channel,
which he did from Dover to Calais.

As in athletics and other sports, the IOC was initially reluctant to allow
women to compete in strenuous swimming events over distances. When
female swimming was introduced to the Olympic Games in Stockholm in
1912, women were restricted to the 100 metres freestyle and the 4 × 100
metres relay, this despite the endurance displays of female swimmers in
the nineteenth century. Today the men's and women's programmes are
almost identical, and contain the same number of events, the only difference being that the freestyle distance is 800 metres for women and 1,500
metres for men. Women also have synchronized swimming, a competitive
version of what had begun as entertainment in the 1920s.

DUCKING AND DIVING

The most spectacular form of diving today is that from the cliff divers of
Acapulco, Mexico, which began as a commercial enterprise in the 1930s.
Each day the La Quebrada divers plunge up to 41 m (135 ft) headfirst into
the sea below. Yet they were not the first to make money from exhibiting

their high-diving skills. Back in the early days of the Industrial Revolution in Britain, Sam Scott dove from the roof of a five-storey warehouse in Manchester into the River Irwell. Even more dangerous than the dive itself was the water, made toxic by industrial waste. However, he survived both and went on to repeat the feat at another industrial site in Bolton. High diving as a sport was officially recognized only in 2013, when it was introduced at the World Aquatics Championships in Barcelona. Men dive from a height of between 22 and 27 m (72–89 ft) and women from 18–23 m (59–76 ft). Practice is not easy, since there are few high towers, so the divers train for each component of their dive separately and hope to put it all together successfully on the big day. For safety reasons, these divers generally enter the water feet first.

Conventional diving seems to have had two origins: one based on the plunge as a swimmers started a race, and the other developed by gymnasts, who found diving a less risky way of practising their moves. National plunging championships, in which the objective was to travel

Wu Yiwen and Huang Xuechen, synchronized swimmers, 2013.

underwater as far as possible without using a stroke, began in England in 1883 and continued until 1937. My school still held its own championship in the late 1950s, hiring the local colliery baths for the purpose. 'Plain' diving, as it was called, also featured at the 1904 Olympics, but in London in 1908 'fancy' diving was added to the programme and came to dominate the sport. Synchronized diving for pairs was adopted as an Olympic event in 2000.

Diving has suffered organizationally from always being linked with swimming, despite having more in common with gymnastics. Divers often feel that swimming officials do not understand the needs and concerns of the diving community. However, swimming governing bodies have been reluctant to allow diving to become independently governed.

INTO THE SURF

The accepted history of surfing is that it was a traditional practice in Hawaii that came close to extinction in the nineteenth century under the missionaries, only to be revived as part of Hawaii's tourist industry in the 1890s and exported to the Pacific coasts of the United States and Australia. Credit for spreading the knowledge of surfing is usually attributed to Duke Paoa Kahanamoku, an indigenous Hawaiian who won swimming medals at the Stockholm Olympics of 1912 and used his celebrity status to advance the cause of surfing. There are significant problems with this narrative, not least that it assumes that indigenous surfing existed nowhere else; there is evidence of surfing from the 1640s in what is now Ghana. To be fair, we know little about indigenous surfing around the Pacific, but it did exist. Second, it did not almost die out, and there was at most merely a waning of the practice. The story of its decline was one pushed by the missionaries themselves as a fundraising exercise.

A major technological breakthrough that helped to popularize surfing after the Second World War was the use of fibreglass to seal the light balsa-wood core of the surfboard. These lightweight boards gave surfers greater flexibility and control (as much as they are ever in control of the sea, anyway), and required less physical strength to undertake manoeuvres. For the vast majority of surfers the contest is between them and nature. Recreational surfing has etiquette regarding precedence on waves, but no rules or scoring.

Duke Kahanamoku representing the United States in an Olympic parade.

Competitive surfing began in Australia as part of lifesaving carnivals in the interwar years, at the same time as the Pacific Coast Surf Riding Championships developed in California. In both countries, competitive surfing really established itself in the 1960s, and during the next decade a world professional surf tour emerged. The main problem with surfing as a spectator sport is that few people really understand the scoring mechanism. At one time it was based on distance covered, but then it became more subjective, so that judges looked at degree of difficulty, combination and variety of manoeuvres, and speed and flow of the ride. As in diving and gymnastics, efforts are made to reduce the influence of individual judges by discounting the highest and lowest scores and averaging the others.

Although the occasional shark attack and fatalities from wiping out on a big wave make the headlines, surfing is a relatively safe sport. Estimates are that the average surfer incurs an injury once every 250 days of riding waves, a price most are willing to accept for pursuing the waves. In the mid-1990s tow-in surfing began in Hawaii, using jet skis to drop surfers where they could catch a large wave. It was popular for a while, but became regarded as elitist and environmentally damaging. However, it has now been revived, particularly at Nazaré on the Portuguese coast, where monster waves of 20–25 m (66–82 ft) are a regular occurrence.

In contrast to the hedonistic, free-and-easy surfing culture that emerged on the recreational side of board-riding, surf lifesaving developed around a military style of discipline and drills, with the lifesavers strictly regimented by their clubs and associations. Yet here again there is a traditional narrative that does not bear scrutiny. The perceived wisdom, one promulgated by the official bodies, is that it began for humanitarian reasons and later developed a sporting offshoot based on lifesaving techniques. Yet the initial objective of the lifesaving movement was simply to get sea bathing accepted in the face of repressive laws and a disapproving establishment morality. At the beginning of the twentieth century beachgoers in Australia – a country in which, despite its vast territory, the bulk of the populace clings to the seaboard – faced opposition over their costumes, over sunbathing, and over mixed-gender sea bathing. Surf bathers took a proactive response by forming lifesaving beach patrols to demonstrate their respectability, and in 1907 twelve Sydney lifesaving clubs came together to form the Surf Bathing Association of New South Wales (to become the Surf Life Saving Association of Australia in 1920), with the objectives of providing better facilities for bathers, instituting improved lifesaving methods and providing rules for proper conduct by surf bathers. Despite their initial opposition, local councils realized that this volunteer force would supply humanitarian aid on the cheap, and accepted its services. However, many if not most of the volunteer lifesavers joined the movement primarily for its camaraderie and sporting activities, rather than out of humanitarian convictions. For them, saving bathers who ran into difficulties became an offshoot of the sport, rather than the reverse. The sporting events later morphed into 'ironman' endurance competitions in which the competitors ran, swam and paddled boards, all basic lifesaving skills. These events caught the public imagination, and in the 1980s rival ironman circuits were established geared to a television audience and bringing significant personal sponsorships to the elite participants.

WE ARE SAILING

Most societies developed some form of sailing as part of their transport system, but as a sport it may have originated in the Netherlands. Whatever its source and wherever it took place, sailing was until the late nineteenth century the province of the wealthy. Cheaper boats then became available for recreation and racing, although yacht clubs retain a reputation – whether justified or not – of being class-bound.

Yachts come in all sizes, from ocean-going cruisers (often for recreational sailing rather than racing) to single-sailor dinghies. These days races are often held for a standardized class of boat, but historically, before mass production, each yacht was unique and a form of handicapping had to be devised. The first internationally recognized version came in 1886, based on waterline length and sail area, but in 1907 boat length was given more weight. In fleet races, boats of the same type race against each other. In handicap races, boats generally cross the starting line together and officials calculate who has won once all boats have finished. Some of these races award both the handicap winner and the boat that took line honours. A perennial complaint about race results, especially at the elite level, is that too often they are determined off the water, not so much by pre-race strategy meetings but by decisions of the stewards in the protest room. Competitors are honour bound to sail by the rules, but, in the absence of an all-seeing referee, protests are common; indeed, boats carry a protest flag on board to hoist when they feel they have been fouled or cheated. At the protest hearing, a committee attempts to establish the facts – not an easy task without video evidence or independent observation.

Yachts starting in a regatta during Cowes Week, 1827.

Outside the Olympics, the America's Cup has become the major international yachting competition. It is one of the oldest sporting trophies to be awarded in regular international competition. Its origins lie in an 85-kilometre (53 mi.) race around the Isle of Wight, held in conjunction with the Great Exhibition of 1851. The race was won by *America*, a schooner that had been sailed from the United States specifically to compete in the event. The winning owner then offered the trophy in perpetuity for 'friendly competition between foreign countries', as represented by a recognized yacht club in a head-to-head series of races. Since the holder determined both the venue and the regulations for the event, it was un-surprising that the Americans retained the trophy until 1983, fending off some 24 challenges before Alan Bond's *Australia II* brought the trophy down under, to the delight of the Australian prime minister Bob Hawke, who declared that 'any boss who doesn't allow his workers time off to celebrate is a bum.' My reaction as a naturalized Aussie was to send messages to my American friends that our millionaire beat your millionaire; ours was later jailed for fraud. Coincidentally, I lived in a seaside suburb where all the streets were named after America's Cup yachts, my residence being on Shamrock Road, commemorating the losing challenger in 1899. Since Australia's victory, both New Zealand and landlocked Switzerland have added their names as holders, and in the seven events so far in the twenty-first century the United States has not featured as either holder or challenger in four of them: changed days!

In the twentieth century the Sydney to Hobart, a 1,000-kilometre (621 mi.) race between the capitals of New South Wales and Tasmania, became an iconic event in the southern hemisphere. It was established in 1945 and always begins on Boxing Day. In recent decades media interest has focused on the several around-the-world races, both fully crewed and single-handed.

Sailing can be dangerous. Drownings through ignorance, ineptitude and inexperience are an ever-present possibility, but even the saltiest of sailors can fall prey to bad luck, especially where the weather is concerned. After the 1998 Sydney to Hobart race there were no celebrations, just thanks for survival. The boats were caught in a savage storm in the Bass Strait, with hurricane-force winds and waves topping 9 m (30 ft). Six people died.

TALES FROM THE RIVERBANK

The history of rowing has two distinct strands, one professional and the other very decidedly amateur. In the days when rivers and coastal waters were the major avenues of commerce, watermen played a vital role in keeping the economy moving. We can only speculate that rivalry between these skilled, muscular men led to challenges and informal races. As far as can be ascertained, this was the origin of the first organized races in Italy, where they were termed 'regattas', a label that is still used throughout the world. At such events held in Venice, races between women who transported goods to market by boat were widespread from the late fifteenth century until the late eighteenth century. Certainly the first competitive rowers in Britain were professional, in that they earned their living rowing the boats that either carried passengers across rivers or were used to break bulk on cargo ships come to port. One of the first recorded trophies for such rowers was Doggett's Coat and Badge, originated in 1716 by the actor Thomas Doggett. In acknowledgement of the years that he had been ferried across the River Thames, he donated a perpetual prize

Charles Courtney (United States) and Ned Hanlan (Canada),
professional scullers in the 1870s.

The annual Boat Race between the universities of Oxford and Cambridge.

for the local ferrymen, who raced for it over a course between London Bridge and Chelsea, a distance of roughly 8 km (5 mi.).

In the second half of the nineteenth century professional rowing competitions and the associated gambling became popular, drawing large crowds and attracting substantial press coverage. For the participants, the rewards offered were more lucrative than the money earned from ferrying passengers or shifting cargo. Elite professional rowers from Britain, North America and Australia competed in challenge matches for world titles with large prize money and substantial side bets; between 1876 and 1907 seven Australians held the title for an aggregate of 22 years. In truth it was a peculiar form of spectator sport, since for much of the race the competitors would be just two dots in the distance. Clearly some spectators came because of the carnival atmosphere, with sideshows, brass bands, and food and drink – especially drink – stalls. Professional sculling fell away as the sport reeled from allegations of corruption, but also from the decline of river-borne passengers and freight, and the emergence of new mass spectator sports that offered better viewing and more excitement. Amateur rowing then reigned pre-eminent in the rowing world, not that the two had ever connected, since the former was a sport with a strict definition of amateurism.

The first amateurs were university college crews and public schools. The focus was on crews of eight, six or four, rather than individual rowers as with the professionals. One of the most durable – if now somewhat meaningless to most spectators – rowing races is the annual Boat Race between Oxford and Cambridge, which has been held on the Thames since 1829. First organized at Henley, it switched in 1849 to the course that is still rowed today, 6.8 km (4¼ mi.) between Putney and Mortlake, a distance three times longer than a modern championship course. One of the world's oldest surviving sporting events, it became an annual event in 1856, marking the start of the social season for England's upper classes. Participants must be students at the relevant university, although the enrolment of international racing stars on one-year diploma courses is not unknown.

The crowds drawn to the Boat Race at Henley tempted leading local residents, keen to attract commerce to the area, to establish a regatta there in 1839. It continues today as a social spectacle for the spectators and an international class event for the participants. However, it is the Olympics and World Championships that are now the real targets for elite rowers. There they race in multi-laned, specially designed courses, unlike at Henley, where only two lanes are used on a river course in single-elimination style. Henley took one of the strictest definitions of

Dragon boat racing in Aberdeen Harbour, Hong Kong, 2011.

amateurism in any sport with, among other clauses stating who could not qualify as an amateur, the class-based anyone 'who is or has been by trade or employment for wages a mechanic, artisan or labourer, or engaged in any menial duty'. In 1920 the American Jack Kelly was allegedly refused entry to Henley's Diamond Sculls, the Regatta's most prestigious event, because he had once been a bricklayer. He gained double revenge: first, by winning the gold medal at that year's Antwerp Olympics and, later, by his daughter Grace moving up the social ladder somewhat by marrying Prince Rainier of Monaco.

By the twentieth century European rowing, even in Britain, began to be focused on rowing clubs rather than schools and colleges. In the United States, on the other hand, it lost its appeal on campus but nothing emerged to take over, until two events in the early 1970s prompted a renaissance. First was the Alden Ocean Shell, designed by the naval architect Arthur Martin, which provided a cheap, easily transported boat for recreational use that could be rowed in rough water. It proved a hit and encouraged thousands to take up rowing, many of whom moved on to the more formal, competitive version of the sport. Its impact rivalled that of technological change a century before in the coming of the sliding seat and swivel oarlock. The other major catalyst to rowing expansion was Title IX, a law requiring colleges that received federal aid to provide equal funding for men's and women's sports. This led to dramatic growth in female participation, especially after women's rowing was introduced at the 1976 Olympics.

Meanwhile, in Asia, the dragon boats paddled on.

Irving Brokaw, who represented the United States in skating at the
1908 Summer (!) Olympics, with his wife on Central Park Lake.

13

SLIPPING AND SLIDING: WINTER SPORTS

S peed skating, a recreational extension of the movement of people along the frozen canals of the Netherlands carrying goods to market, is the more natural form of skating. It was the domain of the labouring classes, whereas figure skating, which emphasizes elegance, belonged to the higher classes. The first type to develop was long-distance skating, initially between towns in ice-bound parts of Europe – particularly the Netherlands, where one such event, the Elfstedentocht, involved skating through the eleven towns of Friesland in a day – but later on circuits of some 500 m (547 yd) in outdoor ice rinks. These rinks were also the first sites for organized short-distance racing, but the real home of such sprints was the indoor rink, which could accommodate the tight tracks of some 110 m (120 yd) on which several skaters raced each other in what often became – by accident rather than design – a collision sport. In contrast, the longer-distance circuit races generally featured just two skaters at a time, racing against the clock rather than each other. Fittingly, the inaugural meeting of the International Skating Union (ISU), in 1892, was held at Scheveningen in the Netherlands, but ironically in midsummer. An early decision was to establish the speed-skating distances at 500 m, 1,500 m, 5,000 m and 10,000 m; to become an overall combination winner, skaters had to win at three of these distances.

Figure skating crosses the borders between sport, art and entertainment. In the late eighteenth and early nineteenth century it was an elegant art form, practised primarily by upper-class men in cold climates on frozen ponds and lakes, usually in urban parks and estates. Today it is a middle-class sport undertaken at indoor rinks, in which girls outnumber boys except at the elite level. The jumps and spins of modern figure skating were initially frowned on when it became a competitive sport, because the emphasis was still on aesthetics and grace. The subjective nature of judging in figure skating means that it is not as easy to identify a winner as in speed skating, where, unless a rule has been infringed, the result is determined objectively. This has led to much controversy, usually when judges from different countries have come to an agreement to aid each other's nationals; in the pairs competition at the Salt Lake City Olympics in 2002, for example, collusion between the French and Russians led to the unprecedented award of a second gold medal to the Canadian couple who had finished second. This led ultimately to a revision of judging criteria, with more emphasis being laid on measurable technical ability than on subjective creative artistry: an about-turn from the early days of figure skating.

At the beginning of the twentieth century the ISU was hoist by its patriarchal assumption that because women would not be capable of competing against men there was no need for a rule to exclude them. It was unable to prevent the English skater Madge Syers from competing for the world title in 1902 and gaining the silver medal. She went on to win the first ISU Women's Championship in 1906, and took the women's gold at the London Olympics in 1908.

ROUGH AND TUMBLE

As did many sports, ice hockey, one of the world's fastest, emerged out of a melange of folk versions with varying rules and equipment. It was played in cold countries where learning to skate was part of growing up. Nevertheless, again like many sports, it is still a cultural rather than a natural creation, and has developed over the decades primarily as a white male sport in which the projection of manliness on to the game has led to the incorporation of significant sanctioned violence, fusing science with savagery.

The first formally organized game of ice hockey was in the Canadian city of Montreal in 1875, and it was in Quebec that what had been a recreational pastime became a sport. From Montreal a speedy, skilful and unruly game emerged to spread across Canada and elsewhere, and ice hockey became a world sport. Its home remains North America, but it is also strong in Sweden, Finland, the Czech Republic, Russia and the former Soviet states.

The first North American league, the International Hockey League, was short-lived (1903–7), but two others emerged, the National Hockey Association (NHA) in 1910 and the Pacific Coast Hockey Association (PCHA) a year later. The NHA folded in 1917 but reformed as the National Hockey League (NHL), and after 1926, when the PCHA went under, it became the sole major professional hockey league in North America. It began as six teams, but expanded from the late 1960s onwards and currently has 31 teams, seven from Canada and the rest from the United States. The major trophy in professional ice hockey is the Stanley Cup, instigated in 1893 by Lord Stanley, who became an avid fan of the game while serving as Governor General of Canada. It is claimed to be the oldest trophy for professional sport in North America, but not everyone realizes that initially it was given to amateur hockey teams. Not until the formation of the NHA and the PCHA did it become a professional trophy.

In 1908 the International Ice Hockey Federation (IIHF) was established in Paris with the aim of governing and developing ice hockey throughout the world, although all the founding members were European and neither the Canadians nor the Americans joined until after the 1920 Olympic tournament. Canada won gold medals at that Olympics and the following ones, until 1936 in Berlin, when Great Britain, fielding a team with British-born recruits from Canada and other hockey-playing nations, gained a surprise victory. Another Olympic shock result came at the 1980 Winter Olympics held in Lake Placid, New York, when a fully amateur United States team, the youngest in the competition, won the gold medal. To do this they beat a Soviet team in what became known as the 'Miracle on Ice' match. The Russians were almost fully professional, had won gold in five of the previous six Olympics and had thrashed the Americans 10-3 in an exhibition match earlier in the year. Finishing the first period tied at 2-2, and with the Soviets leading 3-2 after the second, the Americans scored two more goals to take the lead during the third and final period and then held out for ten minutes against Soviet pressure to win the game. This did not guarantee them the gold (or even a medal), since the finals were played as a round-robin series and the Americans had still to beat Finland – which, of course, they did.

For many years Canada dominated international ice hockey, but it resigned from the IIHF in 1970 when that body refused to allow professional players in international competitions. Seeking to demonstrate that it was still the best team in the world, Canada agreed to what became known as the 'Summit Series', matches between Team Canada (with all the players drawn from the NHL) and the Soviet Union, regarded as the best international 'amateur' side. The series was an eight-game affair held in September 1972, during the Cold War, a fact that heightened tension beyond that of hockey itself. The first four games were held in Canada, with the Soviets taking a surprise (to Canadian pundits) two games to one lead with them to Moscow for the second set of games. The Russians won game five to take a 3-1 series lead, but the Canadians won the final three games to take the series. The final game was won in dramatic fashion, with the Canadians overcoming a two-goal Soviet lead after two periods and scoring the winning goal with only 34 seconds left on the clock.

SKIING

Skiing as a sport has four main divisions: cross-country, alpine, jumping and freestyle, all with origins in the Nordic countries of Norway, Sweden or Finland. Although skiing for utilitarian purposes had existed for a long time, skiing for pleasure on any scale was really begun by wealthy European tourists in the late nineteenth century. Exclusive clubs were formed, and they devised for their members tests that eventually morphed into races.

Until the interwar years cross-country, which had begun in Norway, was the dominant form of recreation skiing. Races were generally either 15 or 50 km (9½ or 31 mi.), the latter being known as the 'winter marathon'. An offshoot (pun intended) was the biathlon, which includes target shooting and originated in international military ski patrols. In the interwar years the thrill of speed took over and alpine skiing spread throughout the world – the snow-covered bits, at least. This has two forms: downhill as fast as you can go; and slalom, where you do the same but swerve between obstacles on the route. Freestyle skiing dates from the 1930s and includes mogul, aerial and acrobatic. It appears to have begun as a sport in Norway, spinning off from skiers using acrobatics to liven up their training, but it was in the United States that competitive freestyle events began in the 1960s.

Peter Prevc (Slovenia) winning the 2016 World Cup
Ski-jumping title in Titisee-Neustadt, Germany.

Ski jumping is the most graceful of the ski disciplines, with participants apparently floating through the air before landing in the 'telemark' position with knees bent, one foot in front of the other. Again, it seems to have been Norwegian in origin, and there is evidence that it was popular among Norwegian military personnel around the turn of the eighteenth century. Initially the jumps were integrated into cross-country races or at the termination of an alpine run, but eventually jumping became a sport in its own right. Jumps are judged on style and distance, although the aesthetic mark has diminished in importance as modern equipment has resulted in longer distances from higher hills. The recognized style of jumping was revolutionized in the 1980s with the innovation of having the skis spread in a V shape.

Perhaps the major controversy in the sport has been the long refusal to recognize ski jumping for women. This finally happened in 2004, but the flames of the struggle for recognition were reignited when the IOC rejected pleas to allow a women's event at the Vancouver Winter Olympics of 2010. So outraged were some of the athletes that they took the local organizing committee to the Supreme Court of British Columbia, claiming that not to allow a women's event breached the Canadian Charter of Rights and Freedoms. They wanted the court to rule that if there were to be no women's ski jumping, then, on grounds of equality, there should be no ski jumping at all. However, the court decided that the subject was the responsibility of the IOC, not the hosting committee. The IOC's response was that it had refused to allow a women's event not because of discrimination but because there were insufficient technically qualified female ski jumpers, which would make gaining a medal easier than in other sports. In vain the protesters listed 135 top-level female ski jumpers from sixteen countries. Women did get to jump in Sochi in 2014, where the German Carina Vogt took gold.

DOWNHILL ALL THE WAY

Sledding in its forms of tobogganing, bobsled and that ultimate laxative, the luge, developed as a sport in the Alpine regions of Europe, where it emerged from the search of wealthy, thrill-seeking tourists for new forms of activity in the snow and ice. Initially it used the frozen banks of local roads, but this became impractical as sledding became more popular, and the first purpose-built run, 1,600 m (5,250 ft) at St Moritz, was built in 1903, followed in 1907 by one at Davos with 51 bends. Yet even in the late twentieth century there were still only nineteen officially sanctioned runs worldwide, and all but three were in the European Alpine area. The relative lack of venues compared to skiing and rink sports has restricted sledding as a spectator sport, although with its inherent danger it is often a highlight for the television audience viewing the Winter Olympics.

DOGGING YOUR FOOTSTEPS

The most famous sled dog race is the Iditarod, an Alaskan event run in early March from Anchorage to Nome, a distance of about 1,600 km (just under 1,000 mi.). Teams often race through blizzards and sub-zero temperatures that can go down to -73 degrees Celsius (-99°F) with the wind chill of the gales encountered en route. It began in 1973 as a test of the best mushers and teams, and was won that year by Dick Wilmarth in 20 days, 49 minutes and 41 seconds. In contrast, the course record, achieved by Mitch Seavey in 2017, is 8 days, 3 hours, 40 minutes and 13 seconds. In 1985 Libby Riddles became the first female musher to triumph in the race.

Each year around fifty mushers and a thousand dogs enter the event. There are currently 26 or 27 checkpoints, depending on whether the northern or southern route is taken (they alternate year by year), at which

Start of the Iditarod, Anchorage, Alaska, 2017.

supplies prepared by each musher are flown in ready for their arrival. There are three mandatory rests at which the health of the mushers and especially of their dogs is checked: one of 24 hours at any checkpoint; one of eight hours at any checkpoint on the Yukon River; and one of eight hours at White Mountain, about 130 km (80 mi.) from the finish.

There is, however, another race that is arguably tougher than the Iditarod. This is the Yukon Quest International, which like the Iditarod covers about 1,600 km, this race beginning in Whitehorse, the capital of Canada's Yukon territory, and ending in Fairbanks, the hub of Alaska's interior. It is tougher because mushers can use only one sled (they are allowed up to three in the Iditarod) and there are only nine checkpoints, which means sleds have to be packed for longer runs and mushers have to endure more camping.

SLIP-SLIDING AWAY

As with golf, the Scots often claim that they invented curling, although there is evidence from paintings and surviving artefacts to suggest that, again like golf, it originated in continental Europe. It was certainly popularized in Scotland, where, from the sixteenth to the early nineteenth century, curlers across the nation played under a variety of local rules

Curlers playing on a frozen-over lake, 1885.

with stones of different shapes and weights, and ice sheets of varying dimensions. Some time in the seventeenth century handles were added to the stones, improving accuracy. Then, in 1838, the Grand Caledonian Curling Club (now the Royal Caledonian Curling Club) was established and began to impose uniformity on the game. It was probably emigrant Scots who took curling to Canada, where it became a national game with the highest participation in the world. Its major home was on the prairies, where the harsh winters gave both relief from agricultural tasks and ready surfaces on which the game could be played.

The majority of nineteenth- and early twentieth-century curling took place outdoors, most spectacularly in the tournaments known as bonspiels, where hundreds of curlers would play on frozen lakes and lochs. There were instances of temporary sheds being erected over frozen natural ice, but significant indoor curling on artificial ice did not come until after the Second World War, when increasing prosperity provided a financial base for curling to use indoor rinks – which, of course, were available irrespective of the weather and time of year.

An unofficial men's world championship began in 1959, sponsored by the Scotch Whisky Association, but formal championships began after the formation of the International Curling Federation (now the World Curling Federation) in 1966. The nation with the best record in these is Canada, which has more than a million curlers to draw from. Yet Scotland can still claim to dominate the sport in one way: the raw material from which the curling stones are made. Until the standardization imposed on the sport in the 1880s, curling stones had been made from many materials, including iron, but then granite became the only approved format. Almost two-thirds of all the curling stones used in the world today were carved from the granite that occurs on the island of Ailsa Craig in southwestern Scotland, and since 2006 all the stones used at the Winter Olympics have been made from the Ailsa granite. This granite is quarried on the island by Kays of Scotland, a company that has exclusive rights to the island's primary resource but is permitted to quarry it only once every ten years, to ensure that nesting birds are disturbed as little as possible. This last occurred in 2013, when 2,000 tons of granite was harvested.

WINTER OLYMPICS

There was no clear distinction between the Summer and Winter Olympics until 1924. The London Games of 1908 had included ice skating, which appeared again in Antwerp in 1920 with the addition of ice hockey, although the two were held five months before the rest of the Olympic events. Given the Scandinavian penchant for skiing, the IOC had discussed including a winter sports week in the Olympic programme for the Stockholm Games of 1912, but the hosts turned the idea down because they were also hosting the Nordic Games in 1913 and did not want to disrupt those arrangements. In 1921 the IOC again considered the issue and approved a winter sports week, which was allocated to Chamonix by the Parisian authorities, who were hosting the 1924 Games. For reasons unknown, delegates from Sweden, Norway and Finland initially voted against the idea, but they later relented and sent athletes to participate, along with thirteen other nations. The pattern of the same nation hosting both the summer and the winter games was broken when London took

---

A snowy perspective

'My favourite sport in the Olympics is the one in which you make your way through the snow, you stop, you shoot a gun, and then you continue on. In most of the world it is known as biathlon, except in New York City, where it is known as winter.'

Michael Ventre, *Los Angeles Daily News*

on the 1948 Summer Games. The previous system had economies of scale, but the Scottish Highlands could not have coped, and the Winter Games instead went to St Moritz. From 1994 in Lillehammer the Winter and Summer Games began to be alternated at two-year intervals.

As the range of sports with different requirements expanded, the necessity for many different venues became a problem. Denver, which later withdrew its bid for the 1976 Winter Games, had suggested that the bobsled be held at Lake Placid, some 3,220 km (2,000 mi.) away. When Albertville, France, became the host city (really just a small town) for the 1992 Games, it actually staged only eighteen of the 57 events, the rest being spread over thirteen other venues and 2,230 sq. km (650 sq. mi.).

ICE YACHTING

One sport that is unlikely to make it into the Winter Olympics is ice yachting, which uses a boat resembling a yacht but with runners on its flat-bottomed hull, enabling it to glide at over 50 kph (30 mph) and accelerate to four times that in a strong wind. Early boats were basic, but, as in yachting proper, wealthy participants opted for larger and more complex designs, some of which were among the fastest vehicles in the nineteenth century. The sport gained wider popularity with a reverse trend towards smaller vessels that were cheap and portable. The skill is to control the boat, which does not have much forward resistance to overcome but can create a supplementary wind of its own, rendering spinning out and heeling over typical accidents. The Netherlands is often cited as the birthplace of modern ice yachting, but the sport is also practised elsewhere in Europe, in Canada and in the northern United States.

14

ACROSS THE POND: AMERICAN SPORTS

We do not know when baseball was first played in the United States, although the first written rules were probably those devised by Alexander Cartwright in 1845 for the New York Knickerbockers, who played intra-club matches in Hoboken, New Jersey. We do know that baseball was also being played in Massachusetts around the same time, but a rougher version in which striking the batter with the ball gained an 'out'. Cartwright's rules resembled later baseball, significantly establishing the foul line, which became a distinguishing feature of the sport. What did not survive was the absence of a strike zone; the batter being able to request a high or low pitch, which was delivered underhand; catches counting even after one bounce; and the requirement for the winning team to score 21 runs. Certainly, many Americans latched on to the idea of developing an indigenous sport to replace cricket, which had been imported from England as part of the cultural baggage of imperialism. So had baseball, ironically, but its new form was very different from the game played in rural England in the eighteenth century and the cultural fiction developed that it was a uniquely American game, a national pastime that represented the American identity of individualism combined with teamwork.

By 1858 the National Association of Base Ball Players (NABBP) was codifying rules and charging admission to games, and eleven years later the Cincinnati Red Stockings were the first professional baseball team with salaried players. As in other sports in other nations, however, the emergence of professionalism led to allegations of gambling and corruption that the NABBP and its successor, the National Association of Professional Base Ball Players, struggled to deal with. The solution hit on in 1876 by William Hulbert was to set up his own league, the National League of Professional Baseball Clubs. For the first time anywhere in the world, a sports league had been created, this one with a fixed number of teams, each with its own exclusive territory. The title of the league was significant. It meant that control of the game had been wrested from the players, who became employees rather than entrepreneurs. Unsuccessful efforts to challenge the league's position were made by two player-focused organizations, the Union Association (1884) and the Players League (1890), although a private-enterprise rival, the American Association, survived for ten seasons from 1882. The real competition came when the Western League (begun in 1885) was renamed the American League in 1899, sought major league status and established teams in some of the same cities as the National League. After three years a truce was negotiated and the two-league system, generally referred to as Major League Baseball (MLB), became the basis of modern baseball. By 1910 aggregate MLB attendances topped 7 million.

The MLB rekindled the idea of an end-of-season play-off (which had occurred occasionally in the late nineteenth century), but with the world championship at stake between the champion teams of each league in a seven-match competition. Before 1969, the team with the best regular season win-loss record in each league automatically advanced to the World Series, but since then each league has conducted its own championship series to determine which teams will advance to the World Series. As of 2018, the World Series had been contested 114 times, with the American League winning 66 and the National League 48.

The MLB monopoly flourished in the first half of the twentieth century, and the freedom from competition generated large profits for the club owners. For fifty years from 1903 MLB consisted of sixteen franchises at fixed localities, but in 1953 the Boston Braves relocated to Milwaukee, signifying the start of a new era. Competition developed between municipalities to attract an MLB team, a trend that was intensified by the American population shifting away from the northeast – the traditional homeland of MLB – towards the west and south. To preserve its monopoly, MLB needed both to move teams into new markets and

Major league baseball match, 2015, at Coors Field, Denver, home of the Colorado Rockies.

to maintain coverage in its existing ones. Relocation was only a partial solution; what was required was expansion. This began in 1961 with the creation of new franchises in the American League (Washington Senators and Los Angeles Angels), followed a year later by two in the National League (Houston Colt .45s and New York Mets). These were to head off a threat from a proposed new major league, the Continental League. Further expansion occurred in 1969, 1977, 1993 and 1998 to bring the total number of MLB clubs to thirty.

The last decades of the twentieth century were boom years for baseball, with attendance rising from 43 million in 1980 to more than 68 million in 2003. MLB income rose even more, from $320 million to $3.9 billion. In the twenty-first century MLB revenue has risen at double-digit rates; profits are now nearly $8 billion, and in consequence franchise values have soared, some to nearly $1 billion. Much of this money came from television deals. Once screen resolution became good enough to capture the flight of the ball, television companies competed to air what they felt was the national sport. To them it was cheap production; to MLB it was valuable income, reaching one-third of its revenue by the turn of the century. Unlike other leagues, which tend to negotiate television deals collectively, MLB has permitted local television deals. This has allowed some clubs to do better financially than others. In 2001, for example, the Yankees generated local New York television income of $57 million, while in Montreal the Expos garnered only $500,000, one reason why the franchise was transferred to Washington, DC, in 2004.

Yet there is concern within the sport that it faces difficulties in establishing an audience with a new generation of sports consumers. Essentially, baseball trades on tradition and community loyalty. Its player outfits are retro (some would say old-fashioned) and its games are too many and too long for an audience seeking instant gratification.

FOOTBALL, BUT NOT AS WE KNOW IT II

Although some cold water has been poured on the theory that educational institutions in Britain pioneered association football, this is less true of the development of American football, which was very much a product of the college system. Muscular Christianity found a ready home in the United States – it was at a YMCA in Springfield that basketball originated, as we shall see – and was an underlying theme behind the willingness of colleges there to take up football. At first the elite colleges played their own versions of football – some like soccer, others more like rugby, but none the same – and the desire to challenge each other led Yale, Princeton, Columbia, Rutgers and (later) Harvard to come together to agree on a set of rules, ultimately resulting in the formation of the Intercollegiate Football Association in 1876. The rapid expansion of higher education in the United States in the late nineteenth and early twentieth century boosted the popularity of American football, which in turn offered the institutions an athletic measuring stick against each other and a source of revenue as college football became the winter spectator sport of the populace.

By 1888, with the development of the scrimmage line, American football had become a game of tackling and blocking, with a clear distinction between offence and defence. Inevitably the violence inherent in what was fundamentally a collision sport led to deaths and serious injuries, and in 1905, after eighteen deaths in a single season, President Theodore Roosevelt felt compelled to intervene and met the football leaders of Harvard, Yale and Princeton at the White House in an endeavour to reduce fatalities. His intervention has often been credited with lessening the violence in the game, but in fact it was the death of a player a month later that compelled the heads of New York and Columbia universities to bring about a series of meetings that culminated in the legalization of the forward pass, a step that radically changed the way the sport was played. Nevertheless, it remained violent and death rates rose again, leading to further rule changes that removed most restrictions on the forward pass.

Because the colleges saw football as a form of character building and a force for moral instruction, they frowned on professionalism, and under their cultural influence the sport remained an amateur one well into the twentieth century. Even today the colleges proclaim that their players are amateurs, although they willingly act as feeders to the professional leagues via the draft system.

Professional football grew out of amateur clubs, generally dominated by college alumni. Some teams eventually began to pay their players, but, as in baseball, players switched allegiance during the season to such an extent that clubs came together in 1920 to prevent it. Ultimately what emerged was the National Football League, although it took almost a generation for the enterprise to stabilize and a further one for it to become profitable. Much of the structure was copied from baseball. Like MLB, it moved to create both monopolistic and monopsonistic control, the former by forbidding new or existing teams from moving into the territory of an established team, and the latter by prohibiting teams from bidding for each other's players. It also installed a commissioner to oversee the sport, and it was this willingness of the individual teams to accept strong central authority that paid huge dividends in the 1960s.

Although today the NFL is the financial and cultural colossus of American sport, until the 1950s football to the general public meant the college game. No one outside the few cities that had NFL franchises cared about the professional version. However, in the 1960s NFL matches began to be televised, and by 1965, according to one poll, professional football was America's favourite spectator sport. College football and the NFL then ran in parallel, each drawing huge numbers of spectators at the stadia and especially in front of television sets.

Football is the most profitable sport in America. In 2005 the average operating income of clubs in the NFL was almost $32.5 million, and all the teams made a profit. (Contrast this with the experiences of the English Premier League, where most teams are in the red.) These profits come from three major sources: gate revenue, television contracts and venue income.

Currently NFL clubs retain 60 per cent of their home gate, with the rest being pooled equally among all the other teams. Football has always shared more of its gate revenue than the other major-league sports, a decision that emerged out of attempts to stabilize a league that did not field the same set of clubs in consecutive seasons for sixteen years. More than any other factor, the NFL was made by television. The relationship was symbiotic; with its frequent stoppages, the game is ideal for commercial breaks, and on average television contracts account for more than half of each club's revenues. In the late 1940s and early 1950s teams negotiated individually with local or regional broadcasters. However, in the 1960s the incoming commissioner, Pete Rozelle, opted to sell NFL games as a single product over which the NFL had monopoly power. Moreover, all teams shared the fee equally, thus underwriting those with smaller spectator catchment areas. This was illegal under existing anti-trust legislation, but Rozelle successfully lobbied to secure a specific exemption for the NFL to negotiate media contracts. Where teams can make money as individual clubs is in venue revenue, which covers such things as pouring rights, parking, signage and luxury boxes. Several teams have relocated specifically because they were promised more of the venue revenues by stadium owners. These were often city governments who had built the venue to attract a major league team in the hope of creating employment and raising tax income, an intention rarely realized because teams generally play fewer than a dozen home games a year.

Television also became used as a barrier to entry for competing leagues. In the 1960s the American Football League (AFL) had challenged the NFL by securing television contracts, first with the ABC network and later with the NBC. This enabled the fledgling league to survive even though its franchises were in small cities with small crowds. The continued viability of the AFL eventually led the NFL to merge with it. A lesson had been learned, and henceforth the NFL spread broadcasts over all three major networks. That cut off a vital source of funds for potential rival leagues, such as the World Football League in the 1970s and the United States Football League in the following decade, both of which failed primarily because of a lack of television exposure.

HOOPLA

Most sports evolve until they reach a stage when codification occurs. Not basketball, which was invented in Springfield, Massachusetts, in 1891 by a Canadian, James Naismith, who had been charged with creating a game that could be played by men in a YMCA gymnasium. After failed efforts with indoor lacrosse, rugby and soccer, he hit on the idea of a passing game in which the ball had to be landed in a net 3 m (10 ft) above the ground. He wrote a set of thirteen rules and basketball was born. It was envisaged as a non-violent sport that fostered discipline, rationality and teamwork, all well suited to YMCA philosophy. There have been claims that the idea for the game actually originated with a friend of Naismith's, George Gabler, but these have never been substantiated and Gabler himself never challenged what has become conventional wisdom.

In basketball's early years the rules were ironed out to improve the playing of the game. Most significantly, although Naismith felt that nine-a-side was the optimal team size (he had initially believed that up to forty a side could play), it became standardized at five players each on the court. Dribbling, at first outlawed, was later allowed, and the speed of the game was improved by the development of open-bottomed nets, rather than having to retrieve the ball from on high after each score.

Basketball became a college game, and in 1910 about two hundred colleges fielded teams, but there was no national tournament until a couple of decades later. It was at high-school level that the game took off, and by the 1920s basketball outranked both football and baseball in terms of participation. In the 1930s there was a new wave of interest in men's collegiate basketball. Private entrepreneurs found a lucrative market in organizing matches between leading college teams. In particular the National Invitation Tournament (NIT), run by enthusiastic basketball journalists, drew large crowds. In reaction, the National Collegiate Athletic Association (NCAA) started its own end-of-season championship in 1939, which, thanks to relentless promotion, had by the 1960s eclipsed the popularity of privately organized tournaments. Yet it was the NIT that secured the first national television contracts in the 1960s, with the NCAA not doing so until 1970. However, by the 1990s the annual multi-week series (commonly known as 'March Madness') had become one of the most highly rated television events in American popular culture. What had begun as an eight-team tournament played on one site had grown to a 68-team extravaganza in numerous locations, culminating in a 'Final Four' play-off.

Most basketball historians accept that a team from Trenton, New Jersey, was the first professional side. In 1896 they toured Pennsylvania, New Jersey, New York and Connecticut, and after their victories they proclaimed themselves national champion. Two years later a professional league was formed, although, despite its name, the National Basketball League only had teams from Philadelphia and New Jersey. It fended off challenges from an Interstate League and an American League, but lasted only six seasons. Nevertheless, until the First World War there was always at least one professional league in the eastern states. These teams played a rough, crowd-pleasing game in courts surrounded by chicken-wire cages (supposedly to protect the players from spectators), which kept the ball continuously in play.

In 1946 owners of major ice-hockey arenas in the northeastern and Midwestern United States and Canada created the Basketball Association of America (BAA), specifically to play in large arenas in major cities, a different strategy from its rivals the American Basketball League and the National Basketball League (NBL). By 1948 it had become the league of choice for college players looking to turn professional. The following season it took over the NBL, and the new league was renamed the National Basketball Association (NBA). It had seventeen clubs, but consolidated to eight by 1953 by discarding the smaller franchises. The NBA does not recognize any of the achievements of the NBL, seeing the merger more as an expansion of the BAA than as a joining of equals. In 1967 the NBA was threatened by the formation of the American Basketball Association, which initiated a bidding war for star players and allowed the recruitment of college undergraduates. The reaction of the NBA was to expand to eighteen franchises with the intention of tying up the major cities. Its rival folded in 1976 and its major clubs joined the NBA.

Two factors that are less applicable to football and baseball help to account for the popularity of basketball. One is that it was taken up in significant numbers by women, especially those attending college, where they had their first opportunity to play a modern team game. The other is that from the street pick-up game through to college and professional level, basketball has increasingly come to be regarded as a

All-time basketball great Wilt 'the Stilt' Chamberlain
in his Harlem Globetrotters outfit.

game belonging primarily to and which has been most popularized in
black communities – an idea promoted in the early 1990s with the film
White Men Can't Jump, for example. From the 1960s onwards, possibly
associated with the emergence of civil rights and desegregation as a federal
policy, talented black players began to be recruited for traditionally white
teams. A watershed moment was the NCAA final of 1966, when an entirely
African-American starting line-up from the University of Western Texas
beat the all-white squad from the University of Kentucky. Yet it should
not be forgotten that black players had a long history in the game. African
Americans had flocked to the game in the early twentieth century, and

several prominent teams emerged during the next few decades, including the Harlem Globetrotters, who, as well as holding barnstorming tours, also had a home court – ironically, considering their name, in Chicago.

Two innovations that have reshaped the game and helped to make it more popular with spectators are the shot clock and the three-point shot. The former was introduced into the NBA in 1954 to ensure that a shot was taken after a team had had possession for 24 seconds. Scoring three points for a successful long-distance shot became NBA policy in 1979; other professional leagues had tried it earlier and the NCAA adopted it in 1980.

EXCEPTIONAL OR JUST DIFFERENT?

Americans often claim – sometimes boastfully, at other times just stating the facts – that they are exceptional in many things: military might, film and television production, and, of relevance to this book, sport, in which they created the games of American football, baseball and basketball. More than that, these sports remain different from those developed elsewhere, because they do not countenance drawn games. To quote the *Sports Illustrated* writer Frank Deford: 'Politicians love to boast about American exceptionalism: how special we are from all the merely ordinary, everyday, run-of-the mill countries around the globe. However I would say that what sets us apart, more all the time, is that we Americans don't like ties.' Sport to most Americans is about winners and losers, and that is something that ties do not allow to be clarified.

Americans don't like ties

The baseball game between Pawtucket Red Sox and Rochester Red Wings began on 18 April 1981. It finished on 23 June. Although the league in which the match was being played had a curfew rule of 12.50 a.m. (when the score was 2-2), the umpire's rulebook did not contain the relevant clause and the game continued until 4.07 a.m., when, with the score still 2-2 after 32 innings, it was suspended on the directive of the league director, who had been awakened by an early-morning phone call. Of the 1,740 spectators who witnessed the start of the match, just nineteen stuck it out to the end. But it wasn't really the end. It continued as a precursor to a regular season game when the teams met again in June. This time just one extra innings was required, and Pawtucket winning 3-2 after 8 hours and 25 minutes of playing time.

The concept of forbidding ties dates back to the earliest days of baseball, when extra innings were the rule until one side had a lead after an equal number of innings had been played. Technically, ties can still occur in Major League Baseball if a team runs out of pitchers; or if lightning storms threaten the players and fans; or if the time reaches one o'clock in the morning, when a curfew is called. In the past, too, before all teams had floodlights, darkness could end a game. These events were, and are, extremely rare, and in any case the game is often replayed so that a definite result can be obtained.

Basketball has high scores, which lessens the chances of a drawn game, unlike in soccer, for example, where low scores – even no scores – and draws are more commonplace. In any case, if the score is level at the end of regulation time, the NBA sanctions as many extra periods as are necessary until one team has a higher score than the other.

In contrast, for most of its history ties were common in the NFL, because until 1974 there was no such thing as overtime in regular season games. When the match was over it was over. Overtime was allowed in play-off games, however, and eventually the pressure of American fans' desire for a winner led to its introduction to the scheduled league games. Sudden-death overtime was introduced, in which the first team to score won the game, but it would still end in a tie if no one scored in the fifteen minutes allowed, unlike in the play-off games, which continued until someone did score. That is exactly what happened in the first regular season game played under the new rule, between the Denver Broncos and the Pittsburgh Steelers. Such drawn matches have become increasingly rare, even though a modified sudden-death rule was implemented in 2012, giving a side losing by a field goal an opportunity to gain a field goal themselves to equalize the game, or even a touchdown to win it.

Americans play their sport differently, but do other nations want to play American sports at all? Let us look at globalization in sport, which is often conflated, especially by those on the political left, with Americanization. Yet sport has not become McDonaldized, even with the global reach of American televised sport. Basketball is the one American sport that has travelled well, and it has featured in the Olympics since 1936. It first came to Europe via YMCA connections before the First World War, and garnered further interest through American troops stationed there during that war. In 1932 eight European nations formed the Fédération Internationale de Basketball, although the United States remained aloof from an organization that wanted to run a game invented in America. The sport boomed as a television-friendly game from the 1990s onwards, and all significant European nations now have national professional leagues from which stars have moved to play in the NBA. Today the NBA scouts every continent and has established elite coaching academies in several countries.

Turning to the history of baseball's development beyond America's borders, in 1888–9 the sports entrepreneur Albert Goodwill Spalding organized a global professional baseball tour, staging exhibition games to promote the sport and consequently sales of his company's baseball equipment. At the time he pronounced that baseball was the peer of cricket and rugby, and expected to see it become the universal athletic sport of the world. However, the success of the promotional tour was limited, partly because British sport had got there first but also because of the overtly racist attitudes of the players and, at the time, Spalding himself. Over the next century baseball developed significantly in only two parts of the world outside the United States – the Caribbean and the Pacific Rim – and in neither case was the game taken up simply because it was American.

The epicentre of the game in the Caribbean was Cuba, an island nation about 160 km (100 mi.) from Key West, at the southernmost tip of Florida. For much of its modern existence Cuba had been a Spanish colony, although its sugar-based economy became linked to that of the United States from the 1870s. Many Cubans went to work and study on the mainland, and those who returned brought baseball with them. A domestic league was formed in 1878. By the 1890s there were more than two hundred Cuban baseball teams, mostly self-organized, non-commercial ventures. The game caught on not because it was American, but because it was not Spanish. The more the Spanish denounced the sport, the more it attracted those seeking independence, and playing the game became an act of defiance against Spanish rule. Moreover, unlike in the United States, baseball in Cuba was racially integrated.

The Spanish–American War resulted in the Spanish withdrawing from Cuba in 1898, and after three years under American military occupancy, Cuba gained formal independence in 1902. Cubans controlled the island's nascent baseball industry and relationships were forged with their counterparts in the United States. The game flourished because it was played mainly in the off-seasons of the MLB and Negro leagues, so that both American players and clubs could spend time on the island, the former to earn money playing for Cuban teams and the latter making money from exhibition matches. However, after too many defeats by integrated Cuban teams, the American League (ABL) president banned its teams from going to Havana.

Despite its frequent occupation of Caribbean basin countries, the United States was not the cause of the spread of baseball in the region. That role went to Cuba, whose apostles spread the faith in the Dominican Republic, Venezuela, Puerto Rico and the Yucatán Peninsula. Cuba remained at the heart of Caribbean baseball until the colour line was breached in the United States with the employment of the black player Jackie Robinson by the Brooklyn Dodgers in 1947. This coincided with an attempt by the Mexican sports promoter Jorge Pasquel to challenge the MLB by operating a summer season and outbidding the Americans for skilled players. The MLB reaction was to blacklist any player who was tempted across the border, and to impose a secondary ban on anyone who played anywhere with or against the renegades. Because the breaking of the colour line had given dark-skinned Cubans the possibility of playing in the MLB, the Cuban League reached an agreement with the Americans that effectively rendered it a minor league for player development; the emphasis in Cuba was to prepare players for a career in the United States. This lasted until 1959, when Fidel Castro seized political power and broke all ties with America. Cuban baseball became a state-supported, amateur game whose players were good enough to win gold in the Olympics of 1992, 1996 and 2004. Elsewhere in the Caribbean, the Dominican Republic took over the role Cuba had relinquished, now supplying a tenth of all major-league players and a third of those in minor leagues. Overall a quarter of MLB players are Latino, as are two-fifths of minor-league players.

Baseball also gained a foothold in the Pacific Rim, where the Japanese League has become the second strongest in the world. Influenced by some American educationalists, Japan adopted baseball as part of its modernization strategy in the late nineteenth century, although the game was Japanized in that the government prohibited the use of (American) English terminology. Over time it became a major sport, with teams representing industrial and commercial companies rather than simply private, profit-seeking ownership, as in the United States. Japanese set-tlers and government officials took baseball to Taiwan and Korea, and Japan has become the hub of a trans-Pacific baseball world that operates independently of the sport in the United States.

Although a version of American football is played in Canada, generally the sport has not transferred to countries where different football codes have become established. However, in the late twentieth century the NFL made a determined effort to establish the game in Europe. Backed by the NFL as a means of developing young players by giving them more game experience, the World League of American Football operated in Europe between 1991 and 2007. It was formed to serve as a spring league, with seven of the ten teams actually based in North America. That format lasted for two seasons before, after a one-season hiatus, it was re-established in 1995 with six teams, all in Europe. In 1998 it was rebranded NFL Europe and in 2007 it became NFL Europa, in deference to the dominant spelling in Dutch and German. There was a lack of stability in the franchises, and ultimately five of the six teams were based in Germany. While attendances held up, this lost them television contracts outside Germany, and in June 2007, one week after the World Bowl XV, the league was disbanded. It had reportedly been losing about $30 million a season, and had become an expensive exercise in amassing exemption for NFL summer training camps. Today the NFL contents itself with playing two regular league games a year in London, although there is talk of a franchise transfer to the United Kingdom.

In sport America has exhibited exceptionalism, if not isolationism, and the one real world sport – soccer – was accepted as a mainstream sport relatively late there. Although basketball became an Olympic sport, baseball has appeared only intermittently and American football not at all, suggesting that some major American team sports have not transferred sufficiently across the world to justify their inclusion in one of the truly global sports festivals.

PART FOUR

SPORTING LIFE: SOCIAL AND CULTURAL ASPECTS

Three socio-cultural aspects of sport have been selected for examination: emotion, widely defined to include euphoria, pain and erotic arousal; discrimination and its erosion over time as societies have sought to make sport accessible to those previously denied entry; and finally the sports club, that association of players often more concerned with its social than its sporting significance.

Emotion is a central element of the sporting experience. What happens in sport can engage the individual psyche or inflame the psychological urges of millions. There is a tension between danger, violence and artistry in a context where the outcome of a contest is uncertain. Spectators do not merely watch sport from the terraces or the stands; they experience it, especially football, and they do so alongside others who identify with the same team. Moreover, sport allows spectators to participate in the game, not by actually playing but by seeking to influence the result with their partisan support. The theatre, and later the cinema, also affect the emotions of their audience, but those viewing never feel they can influence the outcome of the play or film since, unlike in sport, this is predetermined. Sport can incite passion, antagonism and violence; it can be sexually stimulating, involving both the male and the female gaze; and it can be painful, bringing physical injury and mental depression. Indeed, one downside of sport is the violence that is often associated with it, among both players and spectators. Can any reader imagine the pain of fighting backwoods' 'rough and tumble' in early nineteenth-century America, where testicles and ears could be pulled off and eyes gouged out? I had a very brief, undefeated career in amateur boxing (one fight), and that was enough for me. Rather than being health-giving, much sport is dangerous and, in an era of 'no pain, no gain', training for it is often injurious.

Discrimination is part and parcel of life, and it has existed in sport from the earliest days. Participation in Greek competitive sport was often restricted to males of higher social status. Indeed, given the propensity of the athletes to oil their bodies, access to participation has been described as being governed by the 'oily trinity' of being Greek, free and male. This continued, but over time a wider cross-section of Greek men began to be allowed to compete. This led the elite to shift to equestrian sports, which demanded ostentatious outlay – an example of conspicuous participation, but one limited to those who could afford it. Indeed, in many sports the inability to purchase equipment or pay fees has been a constant means of excluding those from lower socio-economic groups. Over time, playing sport became a way to cement, delineate or advance one's social position. In late nineteenth-century Britain the same city often had two or three golf clubs, each catering to a different stratum of society. The evidence is that people preferred to play with like-minded individuals, creating what is referred to as *bonding* social capital rather than the *bridging* social capital that crosses the boundaries created by religion, ethnicity, gender, politics, class or race. However, including only some inevitably necessitates excluding others, and this chapter will explore two main avenues of exclusion: race and gender.

Rules for joining clubs were a means by which 'undesirables' could be excluded and discrimination practised. Clubs existed not just for the playing of sport, and we will explore the social side of such associativity. Sporting activities combined conviviality, bodily prowess and ludic competition, which appealed to small peer groups. Sports clubs benefit individuals, communities and society. By facilitating access to sport they can contribute to health and fitness (including reducing obesity) – lifelong, depending on the sport – as well as to happiness and well-being; by providing a means for people to meet they can assist the formation of social capital, both bonding and bridging, and promote community cohesion; and by encouraging volunteers to assist in club affairs they help individuals take a positive social role from which they, the club and the community can gain. The club has become the basic unit of grass-roots sport, a key and ubiquitous institution in the development of sport. It enables people with a common purpose to come together, provides a basis for agreeing rules and regulations, creates a framework for competitive interaction, and secures a location for participation and sociability. It has a distinctive role in sports history, being one of the long residuals in sport encompassing behaviour and beliefs that tie the sporting present to the past, but it is also an example of transnational history, the spread of an ideology and institution across national boundaries.

15

PUSHING THE MIND AND BODY: EMOTION, PAIN AND VIOLENCE

Some modern sports fans are obsessive in the intensity of their support for a team. Yet this is nothing new. The second-century Alexandrian crowd at the Hippodrome chariot racing were described as being under the influence of some maniacal drug that prevented them from watching in a civilized fashion. Late nineteenth-century newspapers demonstrate the emotion of excitement among the 'barrackers' of Australian Rules football, the 'cranks' of American baseball and the sufferers of 'football fever' in English soccer. These were people, not always men, who were more than just spectators; they were obsessives noted by the contemporary press for the intensity of the emotions that coalesced around them. They included the Boston baseball fan seemingly 'under the influence of some mesmeric power . . . paralyzed by excitement', the Nottingham football supporters 'on the rack for the greater part of last Saturday afternoon, for, from their point of view, the contest must have been too close to be pleasant', and the Aussie Rules barracker in Melbourne who unleashed 'a frenzied howl of mingled rage and pain, spiced with wounded pride and dire apprehension'. If we can begin to understand the spectator culture, with its attendant passion and frustration, we might comprehend the instances of violence that sometimes accompany spectator sport.

It is important to emphasize that non-violent behaviour has always been the most typical spectator experience, even among the fervent club supporters. But occasionally the emotion of events has led to riots and disorder. Media commentators and sports officialdom far too frequently dismiss hooligan behaviour as being by mindless idiots and not real fans, but I have devised a typology of crowd disorder to suggest that such a view is simplistic. Admittedly, most cases of spectator violence have no instrumental purpose in that they cannot change the decision that has been made, be it the award of a goal or the disciplining of a player. Nevertheless, I would suggest that – with the exception of *outlawry* disorder, in which violence-prone spectators use sports events for antisocial activities by attacking officials, fighting and destroying property – most crowd disorder has an explanatory logic.

'Confrontational disorder' stems from the emotional attachment of fans to their team. I live in Scotland, where, in Glasgow, such attachment brings an edge to sporting contests beyond geography. Intracity rivalry in Glasgow between fans of Celtic and Rangers football clubs has overtones of sectarianism and ethnic hostility outwith the immediate catchment area of Parkhead and Ibrox, the sites of their respective stadia. There were (and still are) two distinct and polarized identities: Celtic has drawn its support predominantly from Irish-heritage Catholics, while Rangers was seen as a pro-Union, staunchly Protestant (read anti-Catholic) club. Given the appropriate circumstances, smouldering resentment between rival religious, geographic, ethnic or national groups can easily spark into open hostility, as it has all too frequently in Glasgow. In one such riot in 1967, supporters of the Turkish soccer club Kayseri clashed with those from Sivas, and 42 fans died before the army restored order. The animosity between rival fans in Indonesia is such that players in Liga 1 matches are often transported to games in armoured personnel carriers for their safety. Indonesia's football-hooligan culture has led to the death of 74 fans since 1994, including seven in the past seven years in incidents between Jakarta's Persija fans and those from neighbouring Bandung's Persib. In 2019 the bus carrying the Boca Juniors soccer team to the Argentinian cup final was attacked by opposing fans from River Plate. This resulted in the final being transferred thousands of miles away to Madrid in Spain. Can you imagine the English FA Cup final being played in Mexico City, or the Super Bowl being hosted at the Melbourne Cricket Ground?

What I term 'frustration disorder' occurs when spectators' expectations of access to the game, or the way it will be played and adjudicated, are thwarted. A prime example is the Scottish Cup final at Hampden

Park in 1909, when after ninety minutes the referee ended the game with the score level. Most of the crowd then anticipated that extra time would be played, but the teams were told to leave the pitch. The response was a riot that left 138 people hospitalized. Four years later French rugby fans, incensed by the decisions of the referee in a match against Scotland, stormed the pitch to attack him. Some of the rioters went on to block a Parisian street for several hours before being dispersed by mounted police and soldiers with fixed bayonets.

Then there is 'expressive disorder', caused by the intense emotional arousal that accompanies victory or defeat, especially if unexpected. When Brazil won the FIFA World Cup in 1970, allegedly 2 million people took to the streets to welcome the team home, but the celebrations left 44 dead and more than 1,800 injured.

My fourth category is 'remonstrance disorder', when sports events are used as an arena for political protest. The anti-apartheid demonstrations against the South African rugby team in the 1970s and '80s come to mind, but another example of political riot occurred earlier, in 1955 in Montreal, Canada. After the Canadiens' ice-hockey enforcer, Maurice Richard, was suspended for the remainder of the season following a violent altercation, fans protested that he was being victimized because of his minority status as a French Canadian. Public outrage erupted when the NHL president, Clarence Campbell, the man who had suspended Richard, attended the Canadiens' next home game. The ensuing riot lasted until three the next morning, with windows smashed, cars overturned and shops looted. The riot reflected rising ethnic tension in Quebec, and those with nationalistic feelings did not appreciate the anglophone president of an anglophone league suspending a French-Canadian hockey hero.

LUSTY BODIES

Some spectators are more interested in the bodies on display than the result of the game. One emotion associated with sport goes under a variety of labels, be it sexual attraction, erotic arousal or plain lust, although there is sometimes a difficulty in distinguishing aesthetic admiration from sexual attraction. Sports historians have tended to ignore the sexual connotations of the male/female gaze on the male/female athletic body. They have failed to come to terms with the erotic in sport, in part because of concerns about sexual politics and allegations that scholars who study the topic have contributed to the sexualization of athletes, especially female ones. However, we know enough to be aware that overt eroticism in sport is time- and culture-specific.

Sport and the erotic became institutionalized in classical Greece. In the sixth century BCE the city-states of Crete and Sparta introduced nudity into athletics, and literary sources and artistic depictions suggest that this became the conventional way to compete and practise. Indeed, the word *gymnos* (naked) evolved to mean naked for athletic pursuits. Athletic nudity set Greek sport apart from sport as practised elsewhere. Some see this as having connotations of eroticism, but it also served to reinforce social status, which became apparent in bodily appearance. Regular exercising in the nude produced an all-over tan, thus distinguishing those who had the time and means to do this from those with partial tans, such as farm workers, or with pale skins from working indoors, such as the most skilled craftsmen. It is not clear why nudity was the norm, but certainly for some participants and spectators it would have had (homo)erotic undertones.

Some medieval sports were part of fertility rites, and some commentators have seen sexual symbolism in the lance of the jousting knight. In the eighteenth century female pugilists fought stripped to the waist, foot races were held for scantily clad prostitutes, and near-naked female bodies were used to advertise sporting events in the press. However, we find less overt eroticism in nineteenth-century sport. A few artworks contain an erotic element associated with sport, although – apart from in high culture, such as art (which rarely included popular sport in its portfolio) – Eros tended to be taboo in any contemporary comment on sport. This was a period when respectable society feared that sports spectators might face the dangerous stimulus of sexual thoughts. Contemporary morality dictated that the female sporting body should be hidden from the male gaze under long skirts, which, of course, often concealed their naked private parts. However, the move of women into what can be termed 'movement' sports such as netball and cycling led to a demand for less restrictive dress by some participants, although change was considered less necessary by those involved in 'stationary' sports such as croquet, golf, archery and tennis (as it was played by most women at the time). Long skirts, numerous petticoats, high heels and above all tightly laced corsets therefore long remained the sporting costume of Victorian women. All that being

Eugen Sandow posing.

said, there is evidence of the erotic being exploited for branding purposes by the turn-of-the-century bodybuilder Eugen Sandow. Displaying his nearly nude body on stage differentiated him from other strong men who merely lifted weights, as did the private exhibitions he offered as part of his after-show routine to women (and men) who donated to charity for the privilege.

In Weimar Germany in the 1930s tennis developed a reputation for sexual impropriety, both hetero and same-sex, so, whereas most sports of the time cultivated sexual self-control, tennis attracted those who sought a release from moral restraint. In the late twentieth century it was accepted that power and eroticism meet most compellingly in the athletic body.

Sports costumes became more revealing, especially in athletics and beach sports, as they became ergonomically more efficient. Modern sports-people, both men and women, have sold their sexuality in fundraising 'pin-up' calendars. However, there may be a pushback, given recent highly publicized sexual scandals in sport and the world of entertainment. *Sports Illustrated*, which has published an annual swimsuit edition since 1964, now allows subscribers who do not wish to receive that particular issue an extra month's subscription in lieu.

Many athletes in mainstream sports still feel compelled to hide their sexual orientation when it does not fit the stereotypical view of the sportswoman and, perhaps especially, the sportsman. They fear that public or even official reaction could harm their careers. Others, however, have competed openly as gay athletes either within conventional sport or, particularly at grass-roots level, in clubs specifically catering for those who identify as LGBTQ+. Although the examples of star performers 'coming out' has had a role-model effect, more generally the visibility of LGBTQ+ athletes has been encouraged by the organization of the Gay Games, first held in San Francisco in 1982. There is less emphasis on medals and more on cultivating friendships than in mainstream sport, and the

Gay Games closing ceremony, Chicago, 2006.

Games celebrate gender and sexual diversity, and encourage achievement in a supportive environment. The organizers have had to contend with opposition from some areas of mainstream society, as well as political differences within the LGBTQ+ communities, although the spending power of the 'pink dollar' has persuaded cities to compete to host the Games.

DEATH, PAIN AND INJURY

Many dangerous or extreme sports expose the participant to the risk of life-changing injury or death. Fifty-one Formula One drivers have been killed since 1952, 32 competitors or spectators have been killed in the Tour de France since 1903, and, in the United States, it is estimated that one hundred competitors are killed each year while taking part in equestrian sports. Then there are the motorcycle enthusiasts who put their bodies at risk around the Isle of Man TT road circuit, complete with street furniture and an average of more than two deaths a year for the past century.

These fatalities are at one end of the injury spectrum, but all sports carry an element of health risk, some more than others. Can we imagine the pain of having one's face cut and cut again by the brine-hardened fists of a bare-knuckle pugilist? The gory descriptions of prizefighters by Pierce Egan and others show that they felt obliged to carry on through the pain barrier. Fights were not determined on points over a number of pre-determined, time-limited rounds, but by exhaustion, by a failure to come up to the scratch line. It was a bruising and bloody business in which irreparable damage could be done to the eyes and internal organs of tired fighters incapable of defending themselves properly.

Horse racing was and still is an especially dangerous sport. For jockeys, serious injury at work is not a possibility or even a probability; it is inevitable. Trying to control half a ton of horseflesh travelling at 40–55 kph (25–35 mph) while sometimes also attempting to jump obstacles is not an activity for the faint-hearted. National Hunt riders are always just one fall away from paralysis. Every leading jockey, whether flat or National Hunt, has suffered serious injury during their career. Terry Biddlecombe, champion jump jockey on three occasions in the 1960s, broke his shoulder blade six times, his wrists five times, bones in his left hand five times, his left collarbone, elbow, forearm and ankle once each, as well as cracking two vertebrae, dislocating his right ankle, breaking a rib and chipping a bone in his shin; not to mention more than a hundred cases of concussion.

Jockeys, especially on the flat, also face a more insidious danger, that of making the weight allocated to their horse. In 1850 the minimum weight set by the Jockey Club was a mere 4 st. (25.4 kg); it rose to 5 st. 7 lb (35 kg) in 1875 and remained at that level until after the First World War. Few riders raced at these weights – between 7 and 8 st. (45–50 kg) was more common – but they are an indicator that weights carried by runners on the flat could be artificially low, forcing the riders to 'waste' below their natural body weight. Long periods of inadequate nutrition reduced the ability to concentrate, affected the body's thermostatic ability

___

There is no such person as a fat jockey

The basic result of the 1886 Cambridgeshire horse race shows that St Mirin was beaten by a neck by Sailor Prince and that the losing horse carried 1 lb (0.5 kg) overweight. The jockey Fred Archer, rider of St Mirin, blamed himself for the defeat because he had failed to make the weight. While riding in Ireland Archer had received a telegram from the Duchess of Montrose, owner of St Mirin: 'My horse runs in the Cambridgeshire. I count on you to ride it.' Archer needed little persuasion. He had been a champion jockey for thirteen consecutive seasons but had never won a Cambridgeshire, a major non-classic race. He had been racing in Ireland at 9 st. 4 lb (59 kg), but so keen was he to break this drought that he undertook to ride at 8 st. 6 lb (53.5 kg), a reduction of 12 lb (nearly 5.5 kg) in less than a week. He attempted to achieve this by not eating at all on three days, counteracting the intake at other times by doses of a purgative devised for him specially by Dr Winter, a Newmarket physician, and, when not riding, making use of the Turkish bath attached to his Falmouth House residence. This left him so weak that, when riding on Wednesday 3 November at Brighton, eight days after the Cambridgeshire defeat, he contracted a chill, which he aggravated by insisting on fulfilling his engagement at Lewes the following day. He left that course in an extremely weakened state and was diagnosed on the morning of Monday 8 November as suffering from typhoid fever. The date was the second anniversary of his wife's death in childbirth. That afternoon his sister, who was taking care of him, heard a noise in his bedroom and found Archer armed with a revolver. She attempted to disarm him, but he placed the muzzle in his mouth and fired. He died a victim of illness, depression and wasting.

Caricature of Fred Archer, who starved himself to be
champion jockey for thirteen consecutive seasons.

and blood flow, and depleted liver glycogen – all of which could lead to accidents and serious illness. Wasting certainly contributed to the early deaths of the Victorian riders Tom French, John Charlton and Tom Chaloner, all of them Classic winners; John Wells, twice champion jockey; and Fred Archer, who held the title for thirteen consecutive seasons. Boxing, weightlifting and other sports with weight divisions also often necessitated sudden (and often drastic) weight reduction, although in modern times a gap of several days is permitted between weighing in and performing, except for jockeys, who must be weighed directly before each race. Bulimia has been a common illness of jockeys and also of female gymnasts, who participate in a sport in which body size is a major determinant of performance and where judges make subjective decisions.

Whereas spectators can feel emotional pain when their team performs badly, everyone who participates in sport is bound to suffer physical pain. Simply pushing the body to its limits – which are reached more quickly in some cases than in others – can bring suffering, but there are also accidents where limbs get broken, ankles twisted and teeth loosened. Grass-roots participants can opt out for a recovery period, but elite performers often continue even when injured and play through pain, thus risking turning minor injuries into major ones. This has often been required by coaches, managers and employers. A survey of English professional footballers in 1995 found that 70 per cent had been asked to play when not fully fit. Covert pressure is exerted on the injured players, such as segregating them at team functions, offering them fewer free tickets and placing many minor inconveniences in the way of these 'slackers'. The prevalent view from management is that the team is more important than the long-term health of the sportsperson. The sports workplace is simultaneously a site of medical expertise and extraordinary medical neglect. Professional athletes receive 'official' recognition from significant others for playing through pain, and the social support they get normalizes the experience of pain and carrying injuries. It enhances their status and legitimates 'playing while hurt', and it rationalizes away the health risks associated with this course of action. Let us not forget that these athletes are worried that, if someone takes their place and performs well, their spot may be in jeopardy.

Sport can leave a deadly or disabling legacy after the end of the sportsperson's career. The recent NFL concussion cases in the United States and the rate of dementia among British soccer players from heading the ball are now accompanied by a wider global awareness of the issue, and many question marks remain over the long-term impact on the body of playing rugby, soccer and many other sports. As well as head injuries, there are the long-standing problems associated with joint damage and mobility that are a legacy of playing contact sports.

STRESS

Most professional sports involve stress and anxiety associated with the pressure of performance, constant job insecurity and retirement at an early age. There is no place to hide on the sports field. Every time they play, sportspeople are subject to public and professional appraisal; and often their performance depends not just on themselves but on their teammates and the opposition. Cricket, for example, is a team game within which the individual is often isolated, worrying about his own form even in the midst of team success; this is clear from one study of cricketing suicides, some of whom first turned to drink because they could not handle the pressure of perpetual uncertainty. Indeed, insecurity is the hallmark of a career in professional sport. It stems from many sources, including fear of injury, loss of form, threats to jobs from newcomers, and the inevitable short shelf-life of professional sportsmen. Every day the professional faces the possibility of no work tomorrow, since losing in a tight finish, dropping an important catch or being injured in a tackle can all lead to non-selection. Moreover, being dropped for the next game or omitted from the squad is a public statement that a player is regarded as not good enough.

How professional sportsmen have coped with this constant pressure has not been fully researched, but there is no doubt that some resorted to alcohol. Although medical opinion in the nineteenth century often recommended alcohol as an aid to performance, for some drink became a performance-enabling mechanism. Within one sport, horse racing, we know that the low body weights required caused problems because the effect of alcohol is often aggravated by the lack of food; indeed, the nutrition expert Michael Lean suggests that alcoholism is a probable effect of being starved. It is thus no surprise to learn that in Victorian horse racing Bill Scott (winner of nine St Legers), George Fordham (fourteen times champion jockey) and Tommy Loates (champion in three seasons towards the end of the century) were all alcoholics.

VIOLENCE AMONG PLAYERS

Clearly many early sports, such as bare-knuckle fighting, cudgelling and kickshins, were inherently violent, but so was the traditional English sport of cricket. Indeed, in his famous poem 'Vitaï Lampada' (1892), the imperialist poet Henry Newbolt praised the courageous schoolboy batting as last man in on a bumping pitch in a blinding light. Today cricket is recognized as a dangerous sport, one in which one player hurls a hard missile at speeds in excess of 120 kph (75 mph) at another player less than 20 m (65 ft) away, armed only with a stick to defend himself. Indeed, it is ranked fifth in terms of injuries sustained while playing. Two longitudinal studies of cricket fatalities, one covering England and the other Australia, found an average of more than one death a year for at least a century. Yet even in the era of underarm bowling cricket was hazardous, partly because pitches were often unrolled and uncovered, which rendered unpredictable the bounce of a ball that had to be played by batsmen with unprotected hands. The danger was aggravated by the rules of the early game, which allowed batters to charge at fielders or hit the ball twice to prevent them from catching the ball; determined a run out by whether a fielder physically placed the ball into a 'popping hole' before the batsman slid his bat there; and gave the wicketkeeper liberty to take the ball in front of the stumps to effect a dismissal.

Some violence in contact sports is inevitable, and is accepted as such by all concerned: the hard tackle in rugby, the shoulder charge in soccer (but now outlawed in rugby) or the physical blocking of an opponent in American football. In more brutal sports such as boxing and mixed martial arts, violence is central to the contest. Yet on the field or in the arena, the rules of the game specify what violence is legitimate and what is 'foul play'. Unfortunately, the difference between the two is often a subjective one – not helped, as I found out in my study of violence in Australian sport, by a woeful ignorance of the rules by many players in many sports – dependent on the view of a particular referee at a particular time and not always agreed with by either players or fans. Before the First World War Scottish football authorities repeatedly had to ask referees to try to distinguish between rough and robust play. Where there is less disagreement (except between lawyers) is in the nature of criminal violence, when players transgress not just the rules of their sport but also the law of the land. When the Scottish international footballer Duncan Ferguson of Rangers headbutted Raith Rovers' Jock McStay in 1994 – a tactic not in the SFA's coaching manual – he was jailed for three months.

Sport is often seen as character-building, although the assumption is that it is *good* character that emerges. Turning a boy into a man via the sporting (public) school of hard knocks was an admired trait in Victorian England, but manliness can easily spill over into brutality, as can be seen in sport at either end of the social spectrum in the United States. Among the common folk of the late eighteenth- and early nineteenth-century American frontier it was virtually unregulated brawling rituals that shaped concepts of manhood and honour. Disputes were settled and even minor slights avenged by no-holds-barred contests in which mutilation and disfigurement were emphasized and eye-gouging and castration not in-frequent occurrences. Further up the social scale, participants in American college football at the turn of the century also used violence to demonstrate their manliness in a game that was extremely dangerous and at times brutal. Players wore little protection and there were many injuries and even fatalities – 24 in 1905 alone – from the vicious antagonism that was encouraged. Proponents believed that its violence and danger made it a manly sport, developing strength, courage and virility and countering what they feared was a growing effeminacy in society. The football field was one of the few spaces left in the public sphere that could be designated truly male. Unleashing the primal energy of young men in simulated battle could have a character-building effect, and any deaths of players were collateral damage. Proponents of American football claimed that violence was incidental to the game; opponents felt it was inherent. Surviving rule-books show the regular changes that were brought in to reduce brutality, but too many coaches turned a blind eye to what was occurring on the pitch. They argued that they promoted a game that was hard but fair; the number of fatalities and serious injuries suggests otherwise. Although deaths have declined, a survey of ex-professional players in the 1990s suggested that mild or severely crippled bodies were the norm rather than the exception, although most players said the cost was worth it and they did not regret having played. More recently, however, revelations that football damages not just the limbs and joints but also the brain has forced a rethink in the rules of play to make the game safer, at least lower down the playing pyramid.

Professional boxing is often cited as one of the most dangerous of modern sports, but in reality, in absolute terms, it is less likely to produce fatalities and serious injuries than mountaineering, horse racing, skydiving or motorcycling. The problem is its image and rationale. Other sports have accidents, but injury in boxing is deliberate, and pain and violence are sanctioned in the name of sport. Hitting below the belt has long been outlawed to protect the genitals, but protective headgear is allowed only for amateur fighters, despite the fact that brain damage is usually irreversible. The evidence is incontrovertible that repeated pummelling to the head can cause cumulative damage to the brain, and here time is no great healer. Occasionally acute brain damage occurs during the fight, particularly towards the end of a contest when a tired fighter with a loose neck can have his head flipped back rapidly by a punch. Fighters now train harder, but although their bodies are fitter, their brains are no more resilient than in the past.

Allowing brutality to beat skill undermines the very essence of sport, but violence in sport also has consequences for society. Injury via foul play inflates a nation's health bill and economically disadvantages those who are injured. Recent research into sport, violence and masculinity suggests that collectively these can lead to homophobia, disrespect for women, indifference to pain and an inability to form intimate relationships. The socialization process associated with many sports teaches athletes from an early age that hitting and being hit is acceptable on the sports field. Coaches have a central role in this legitimization of aggression and the teaching of violent practices. These views become exaggerated in elite commercialized sport, where physical dominance, a win-at-all-costs mentality and that oxymoron 'controlled aggression' are to the fore. One growing concern is whether female sport might be becoming more violent, particularly as access for women and girls to traditionally 'male' sporting preserves has increased. The fear in some quarters is that sport socialization might outweigh gender socialization.

VIOLENCE AGAINST ANIMALS

The bloodlust of brutal animal sports excited spectators, especially when they had bet on the outcome. Few in the seventeenth and eighteenth centuries had moral qualms about watching dogs attack bulls, bears, badgers and other dogs, or spurred cocks fighting to the death. As society supposedly civilized, such brutal sports became outlawed, although dogfighting still continues as an underground sport. The moral argument against the use of animals in sport – and in entertainment more generally, such as circuses – is that for humans (some Roman gladiators and schoolchildren excepted) sport is a voluntary activity, but animals have no say in whether they wish to participate. No one asked the bull whether it wanted to be challenged by a matador, or the cocks whether they really wanted to rip each other apart.

Today horse and greyhound racing are the only major sports (except shooting) that involve animals, and both are coming under increasing pressure from animal-rights activists and other groups opposed to cruelty to animals. Public revulsion over the mistreatment of elephants ended the Ringling brothers' circuses, and SeaWorld is in decline because people now regard keeping orcas in captivity as cruel. Horse and greyhound racing may be the next victims of change in public attitudes towards animals used for entertainment.

Greyhound racing in Florida.

Greyhounds were bred to run, hunt and kill any form of animal, but found their sporting niche in hare-coursing, in which pairs of dogs would challenge each other to hunt down a hare released in an open area for them to chase and kill. This sport was transferred to the United States in the 1840s and, in turn, the Americans exported a new version back to Britain in the 1920s, a decade after it had developed there. In this new form of greyhound racing, a mechanical lure was substituted for the live bait, with a small number of dogs (usually six) in the chasing pack over a set distance in a stadium setting. It was marketed in America as a humane version of traditional coursing. Certainly, no hares were ripped to pieces in races, although some were used illegally in the training of the dogs. Yet it has been questioned whether the back areas of the sport have been so humane. Overtly greyhounds appear to have been treated well, especially at the major tracks, but anecdotally there are tales of cramped and infected housing and poor diet, and evidence of over-racing with consequent injuries. These seem to be isolated occurrences, rather than systemic within the sport. However, those animals who show little aptitude for the sport chosen for them are culled at an early age, and the same fate befalls those who can no longer perform effectively. In present-day North American greyhound racing some 5,000–7,000 puppies (about one in ten of those bred for the industry) and 30,000 dogs are destroyed each year.

The situation is replicated in British horse racing, with more than 1,000 horses sent to the abattoir each year. Historically, most opposition to horse racing centred on its association with gambling and crowd misbehaviour, but as gambling became more socially acceptable – and approved by the government – and racecourses dampened the worst of social excess, objections to racing switched from concern about the misdeeds of humans to that about the welfare of horses. Some argued that even forcing a horse to race, especially over fences, was cruel in itself; others pointed to the injuries and deaths that occurred; and a third strand objected to the use of the whip. Whipping doesn't seriously injure horses, but it can cause pain and fright. A whip is the only artificial aid a jockey is allowed to use to balance a horse, to steer it, to keep it concentrated and, some would argue, to give it a necessary adrenaline rush of terror. The response of the authorities has been, first, to define areas of the body where the horse cannot be hit; second, to limit the number of legitimate strokes; and third, to develop air-cushioned and foam-covered carbon-fibre whips that can be used for balancing, straightening or reminding the horse without causing real pain.

Proponents of racing believe that horses are herd animals and that running alongside each other is a natural inclination; jumping, however, is less instinctive and horses have to be schooled in how to do it. Thoroughbred racehorses are fragile creatures and suffer many injuries, including musculoskeletal damage and exercise-induced pulmonary hae-morrhage. On average, over the past few decades, the famous Melbourne Cup meeting held every November at Flemington has resulted in one horse bleeding through its nostrils, one or two limping, and another suffering from heart or respiratory issues. Fatalities in horse racing are not uncommon: roughly one death for every 500 horse runs in jump racing, usually as a result of a broken neck, back or leg; and about 220 horses a year in flat-racing as a result of accidents on the gallops or at the track. In 2018 in the United States, 817 horses are known to have died while training or racing, although one knowledgeable commentator suggests that the real figure is closer to 2,000. But it is the events at which a cluster of horses die or have to be destroyed that make the headlines, as when four horses were killed on the opening day of the Aintree Grand National Meeting in 2000, or the Cheltenham Festival in 1996, at which ten horses died. Racing at Santa Anita Park in Arcadia, southern California, was suspended in 2019 after two dozen horses died in just over three months.

SPORT-RELATED VIOLENCE

Although sports violence is conventionally regarded as player misconduct and crowd disorder, academic commentators in Canada have brought in the concept of sports-related violence, which covers clearly intentional abusive or potentially harmful acts that cannot be easily separated from the sports process. This includes hazing and initiation in American college sports, sexual assault by players and coaches, abuse of partners by players or spectators after a bad result, parental abuse of their children and of match officials, participation in risky sporting activities and body manipulation sports, race- and gender-related verbal abuse, and the coaching of aggressive behaviour.

It is not clear whether male athletes commit more or less sexual assault than the male population at large, but much of what does occur is bound up with the acting out of masculinity and sexism. In the 2010s there has been a disturbing amount of sexual grooming and assault by predatory coaches who have used their power to sexually exploit the children supposedly in their care. We don't know whether this is a new phenomenon or merely more publicized than in the past, or to what extent it is a function of the increased number of children participating in sport.

Then there is what I term 'self-inflicted violence'. This is of two types. One is associated with risk sports in which the participant knows they have more than an outside chance of being injured or even killed, such as those people who choose to climb mountains, swim oceans or run across deserts. A little way north of where I used to live in Dunblane, Scotland, lies a sporting venue with literally one of the highest sports death rates in the world. Every year about forty people die on the Scottish hills and mountains, and the annual toll of the tired, the unwary, the unfortunate and the just plain stupid is greatest on the forbidding walls flanking the 8 km (5 mi.) or so of Glencoe. The second type occurs in sports in which body manipulation is required or considered desirable, so sportspeople ingest drugs to affect their body shape or bulk themselves up, as with American footballers and bodybuilders of any gender.

16

OPEN AND CLOSED DOORS: DISCRIMINATION IN SPORT

Ultimately, whenever they got the opportunity, sport has provided a means for indigenous populations to challenge social Darwinism's support of the idea of racial superiority and inferiority. But racism has been a major feature of sport in several countries, especially the United States, South Africa and, to my shame as one of its citizens, Australia. Until very recently the Australian attitude towards its indigenous population was a disgrace. Aboriginal people were not even counted as Australians in the Census of Population until 1966. Even now their rates of unemployment, incarceration and mortality (both from disease and from suicide) are considerably worse than those of white Australians.

The first Australian cricket team to tour England, in 1868, was an Aboriginal one, although the captain and coach was the former Surrey player Charles Lawrence, at the time a publican in Sydney. In the 1850s and '60s Australian Aboriginal people participated perhaps more freely in mainstream sport, particularly cricket, than at any other time in the nineteenth century; Christian missions sought to 'civilize' them via muscular Christianity, while country sheep and cattle stations brought them into their teams because of a shortage of white players. Some became more than competent at the game, giving rise to an exploitative commercial venture in which black Australians toured England to play cricket in front of paying audiences. Although none of their matches was at first-class level, the tourists performed creditably, winning 14 of their 47 matches and drawing 19 others. However, to encourage spectator turnout, many games featured the additional novelty of demonstrations of Aboriginal skills such as spear and boomerang throwing. Their standout player was Johnny Mullagh, who during the tour scored 1,698 runs and captured 245 wickets.

The visitors found it difficult to adjust to life in England; two players were sent home because of sickness and another actually died in Britain. This may have triggered action by the Victorian Control Board for Aborigines, which ruled in 1869 that it would be illegal to remove any Aboriginal person from the colony without ministerial approval, thus seriously restricting indigenous involvement in cricket and other sports. Indeed, from the 1870s sporting interaction became restricted as Australian colonial governments – influenced by theories of social Darwinism, which argued that the 'weaker' race could survive only if kept away from the 'stronger' – began to impose laws by which to distance Aboriginal people from white society, including the idea of 'protectionism', which prohibited them from leaving their reserves without permission from the authorities. Those who were allowed to participate in 'white' sports faced discriminatory practices. Jack Marsh, a fast bowler who played cricket for New South Wales at the turn of the century, was no-balled out of the game by cricketing officials, allegedly on account of his race.

A small number of Aboriginal men were enticed into professional sport, where their athletic talent was exploited by white promoters for financial gain. This was most apparent in boxing and pedestrianism.

Aboriginal cricket team, 1868.

Boxers were encouraged to adopt a non-defensive style of fighting, which was appreciated by spectators but proved damaging to the proponent. In pedestrianism, because of supposedly natural advantages, black professional runners were labelled in the programmes 'a' for Aboriginal, 'h.c.' for 'half-caste' (people of mixed ethnicity) or 'c.p.' for 'coloured person', usually meaning Asian.

In the twenty-first century Aboriginal participation on any scale in mainstream sports is still restricted to just three: boxing (where 2 per cent of the population has produced 15 per cent of national champions), rugby league and Australian Rules football. Much of this can be explained historically. A generally racist attitude in Australia has led to little appreciation by the white population of Aboriginal art, tracking or culture. What white Australians have always understood is sport, and it is in this field that Aboriginal skill and talent have been recognized. However, in the days leading up to the 1960s, when assimilation was the official policy, boxing, rugby league and Aussie Rules were the white working-class sports to which Aboriginal people were encouraged to aspire. Poverty kept them out of other sports, since Aboriginal reserves did not have swimming pools or gymnasia, or often even grass. 'Footy', rugby and boxing did not require much equipment, and eventually sufficient role models emerged in these sports to create a critical mass of participation.

The histories of several sports in the United States are replete with formal and informal segregation and widespread racism. A handful of talented African Americans played baseball at the elite level before 1885, when the American Association made a gentlemen's (!!) agreement not to sign black players. Soon afterwards, the manager of the Chicago White Stockings threatened not to field his team (with a consequent loss of revenue) against the Newark Little Giants if the latter selected a black player. This marked a systematic exclusion of black people from playing with or against white people. By the beginning of the twentieth century there were no black people in the white-run major or minor leagues. Baseball, of course, reflected wider American society at the time, since black people were excluded from virtually all white-controlled social institutions. Professional baseball clubs had little incentive to integrate, since most teams were in the north and most black people lived in the south. Team owners did not want to offend either their white players or their white customers.

Reintegration did not come until 1947, when Jackie Robinson was selected to play for the Brooklyn Dodgers, but even then an informal quota system was in operation by those teams who signed black players. Moreover, it took a further twelve years for all MLB teams to have at least one black player on their roster. While the colour line in professional football was more fluid, there were no black players in the NFL from 1934 to 1945. Many black players believed there was an unwritten agreement among white owners not to employ them; for their part, white owners and coaches argued that they did not field black players for their own safety, because those in the league before 1934 had been subjected to verbal and physical abuse.

The integration of African-American players into sports did not end discrimination. White managers and coaches still held to stereotypes about the mental and physical capabilities of African Americans, and refused to place them in leadership positions such as quarterback or middle line-backer, or even on the offensive line. It was not until 1968 that the Denver Bronco Marlin Briscoe became the first black starting NFL quarterback. In 1976 black people made up about 50 per cent of MLB outfielders and first basemen, but less than 10 per cent of pitchers, catchers and shortstops – the positions seen as more influential in the game. African Americans were not hired as coaches or managers until Bill Russell became the first black coach in the NBA at the Boston Celtics in 1966, and Frank Robinson became MLB's first black manager when he was appointed to the Cleveland Indians in 1975.

Black Americans fared better in two sports. In the immediate aftermath of emancipation black jockeys became sports celebrities, and a recently created database of 4,794 jockeys has shown that in 1880 African-American riders were over-represented in the jockey profession (22 per cent) relative to the proportion they occupied in the general population (13 per cent), and that the decline in African-American jockeys over time was less precipitous than had been conventionally assumed. Thirteen of the fifteen riders in the first Kentucky Derby, in 1875, were black, and Isaac Burns Murphy, the 'Colored Archer', won that race three times, earned around $20,000 in his best seasons, and had a winning percentage of 34 over his career.

In the boxing ring a black man could hit a white man without fear of arrest or lynching. Indeed, two black Americans, Jack Johnson and Joe

Jack Johnson, the first African-American world heavyweight boxing champion.

Louis, became heavyweight champions long before other sports accepted black people. Johnson was the first African-American heavyweight champion, reigning as world champion from 1908 to 1915, although he was a controversial figure because of his penchant for fancy clothes, fast cars and white women. Louis, who came a generation later, was far more acceptable to both black and white people, although early in his career he was subject to racial sniping. His rise corresponded with that of Fascism in Europe, and his defeat of the Italian Primo Carnera in 1935 and the German Max Schmeling in 1936 and 1938 brought him hero status.

Boxing was the only sport in eighteenth-century Britain in which athletes from minorities played a prominent role. The fact that early black pugilists such as the two formerly enslaved African Americans Bill Richmond and Tom Molineaux were allowed to fight in the British prize ring owed less to equality of opportunity in the sport than to racism as a promotional attraction. Yet once boxing replaced prizefighting and a controlling body was established, only British subjects born of white parents and resident in the British Isles for at least two years could compete for British championships. Non-white boxers could contest British Empire titles, but these were not as prestigious as British ones. The regulation was supported by the Home Office, which intervened to ban prominent black versus white fights in 1911 and 1923, and in the 1920s and early 1930s frequently advised promoters not to stage such contests. It feared that interracial title fights could provoke agitation and discontent among the racially mixed populations of the Dominions. Much later the Home Office became concerned that the colour bar was out of line with public opinion, but it was not until 1947 that increased government and popular pressure led to its removal.

Bare-knuckle fight between Tom Molineaux and Tom Cribb, 1811.
The spectator numbers were much larger than depicted.

INCOMERS

As a nation whose demographic history has been dominated by immigration, Australia also provides a case study on the (non)integration of migrants into mainstream sports. Until the Second World War, migration to Australia was essentially white and Anglo-Saxon in composition, but then the need for labour led to a massive influx from southern Europe, especially Yugoslavia, Italy and Greece. Official policy was to assimilate them into mainstream Australia, presumably including the nation's sporting activities, but this did not happen. The new immigrants did not play Australian Rules football; they did not play cricket; they did not play rugby of either code; in fact, the list of what they did not play is almost endless. What they did have knowledge of was soccer, and they brought the skills of that game with them; moreover, they did not have to speak English to play it. Since soccer was not the most popular football code in any state, there was no one to defend its takeover by the invading Europeans. Excluded from Australian sport by racism and lack of knowledge, the 'new Australians' played the game they had brought with them. So strongly did soccer become identified with them that by the 1960s it was referred to by other Australians in derogatory fashion as 'wogball'. These immigrant communities had turned to sport in the same way that British immigrants had done a century or more before them: they were using something familiar as a crutch in a new country.

THE OTHER 50 PER CENT

As a site of much male voluntary activity, sport has been a major method of gender fixing. For most of the nineteenth century, and well beyond in many countries, half the population faced restrictions on playing sport simply because they were female. Depending on the sport and the nation involved, mechanisms to enforce this included social disapproval from men *and* women, 'expert' scientific and medical opinion, and the ancillary and regulatory rules imposed by clubs, organizations and competitions.

A great sportsperson
'Who was the Australian cricketer who took 7-7 and made a century in the same match?' [Betty Wilson against England in 1958.]

Research is now showing that – thanks in particular to works-based activities – more women played sport in the late nineteenth century than was formerly believed, although still a meagre number compared to men. What we still do not know is the extent of female sporting involvement in the eighteenth century, and consequently whether those women playing sport in the late nineteenth century were attempting to return to previous levels of participation or breaking new ground.

It remains true that women were often prohibited or discouraged from playing sport, but such exclusion was never absolute. In ancient Greece, Spartan women participated regularly, and, more generally, there were a small number of athletic competitions for unmarried women, as well as sporting activities as part of coming-of-age rituals. Some scholars have seen the two victories of a Spartan noblewoman, Kyniska, in Olympian chariot races as an early feminist assault on masculine hegemony, but in fact it was not proto-modern feminist sentiment that led her to purchase a chariot team in order to win the most significant athletic contests. Instead, her male relatives manufactured the entire affair to discredit chariot racing as a dishonourable pastime that 'even a woman' could master if she merely had enough wealth to buy Olympic victories. Most Grecian women found it almost impossible to participate in sport. Such has been the case throughout the ages; and, when women were allowed to play, gendered rules were sometimes enforced, such as a limit of three sets in tennis, 'ladies' tees in golf and, more recently, lower nets in volleyball.

Exclusion is a cultural creation specific to sports in a certain domain at a particular time. Consider women's football. Women can play soccer in Britain at both amateur and semi-professional level, but in many Muslim countries they cannot play at all. However, even in Britain, from the 1920s until the 1970s they could not kick a ball on any ground registered with the FA, because its executive committee had decided to take a firm stance against female participation. Yet, before this exclusory decision, women's teams – such as the Dick, Kerr Ladies from 1917 – had been major charity fundraisers. At any point in time it is social mores that determine who is allowed to participate. Despite the prevalence of masculine terminology – ungentlemanly behaviour, batsmen and the like – there is nothing in the constitutive rules of sports to exclude women. Such decisions are made by sport governing bodies, event promoters and occasionally, as in some Muslim states, the government.

Some governments have actively encouraged women to play sport. For women in Russia in the early twentieth century, and later those within the Soviet sphere of influence, certain types of sport and physical activity were encouraged, although they were still governed by the cultural and gender norms of the nation. Under Soviet leadership sport was linked primarily with military preparedness, productivity and the avoidance of negative social influences, including religion. Throughout the twentieth century Russian leadership felt perpetually at risk of war and/or invasion. From the conflicts with Japan early in the century, through the horrors of the First World War and the October Revolution, to the international crisis of the 1930s and the Second World War, Russians looking both to the east and to the west believed an attack could come at any time. Preparing for absolute war meant that all citizens – men and women alike – must be physically, mentally and emotionally ready for combat. Thus, sport in the Soviet sphere was an avenue for gender equality, and Soviet women took to sports with an enthusiasm equal to that of men. By getting in first, the Soviets were able to win more medals in women's events, as well as demonstrating that socialism had overcome the gender inequality inherent in capitalism. The emphasis on military preparedness led women in these areas to participate in different sports from women in the West, such as sharpshooting, parachuting and aviation. Western critics, of course, might argue that the Russians offered equality by treating men and women equally badly.

Times change, and – at least in the Western world – women are now allowed to compete in most sports, even boxing, which for centuries has been the epitome of overt masculinity, a demonstration of manliness and its embodied characteristics of courage, tolerance of pain, and self-discipline. Social pressure has accounted for some changes, but in other instances the law was brought to bear. The Jockey Club was defeated in the 1960s, when Florence Nagle challenged its right to refuse training licences to women. The Club had a poor comprehension of social change, and clung stubbornly to its nineteenth-century view of what was a fit and proper role for women in racing, so female trainers such as Nagle had to allow their head lad to hold the licence in his name. After two decades of fruitless campaigning Nagle decided to take the Jockey Club to court to gain the right to train under her own name. At 72 she had no career to look forward to but pursued the issue as a matter of principle. Lord Justice

Denning did not agree with the views of the Jockey Club and, at the Court of Appeal in July 1966, pointed out that 'if she is to carry on her trade without stooping to subterfuge she has to have a training licence.' The Club went on to allow women to race on the flat as amateurs from 1972 and compete against male amateurs from 1974, but it resisted calls for female professional jockeys until 1976, when it was forced to concede this right by the Sex Discrimination Act 1975. Who would have imagined that at Windsor in August 2020 Hollie Doyle would become the first woman in the history of British racing to ride five winners in a day?

At the elite level, the first IOC set its face firmly against allowing women to compete as athletes, and they were not allowed to participate until the London Games of 1908, where the first woman to win a gold medal was Charlotte Cooper of Great Britain, in tennis. However, there were no track events for females until 1928. Things have changed. In 1991 it was decided that any new sport seeking to be included had to include events for women, and so by the time of the Sydney Games in 2000 women competed in 25 out of 28 sports, and in 132 events (44 per cent of the total).

Once women's sport became established and international kudos became attached to winning medals, it was men who had to be kept out. During the Cold War some in the West cast doubt on the true sex of Russian women, particularly the muscular Press sisters, Tamara and Irina. Gender verification testing (initially labelled 'femininity testing') was introduced in sport in 1966 at the Commonwealth Games in Kingston, Jamaica, and the European Athletic Championships in Budapest because it was suspected that a few men were masquerading as women. Risk assessment might have suggested that the problem was a minor one but, until the development of less intrusive tests, thousands of women were forced to undergo the humiliation and embarrassment of body examination. Yet the real gender problem has been not men deliberately trying to compete as women, but intersexuality and transsexuality. Although science recognizes androgyny and acknowledges that gender can be a continuum, sport administrators have had difficulty in coming to terms with the fact that gender is not a simple binary concept and that the tests cannot account for anomalies in genital development, internal organs, chromosomes or testosterone levels. They still prefer like competing with like.

Under guidelines introduced in 2016, the IOC allowed athletes transitioning from female to male to participate without restriction. Those intending to transition from male to female, however, are required to have kept their testosterone – a hormone that increases muscle mass – below a certain level for at least twelve months. The most recent gender-related issue in sport, athletics in particular, is that of women with higher testosterone than most other sportswomen because of differences in sexual development. World Athletics has argued that they should be allowed to race over distances of between 400 m (1,310 ft) and 1,600 m (1 mi.), distances where it is reckoned the advantage is greatest, only if they take testosterone blockers. Much of the debate has centred on the South African athlete Caster Semenya, who has won gold in the women's 800 metres at both the Olympics and the World Championships. There is politics involved, and many black South Africans claim the issue is not gender but race, in that Semenya does not conform to white Western versions of how a woman should look. What should be noted among all the furore is that although she won her races comfortably, her times would not have qualified her for the men's event.

In very few sports are women and men allowed to compete on equal terms. These now include most equestrian sports and some skill sports, such as darts and snooker. However, too often – even where no obvious gender advantage exists, as in lawn bowls and shooting – the sexes are separated. Golf has faced a challenge from female players who wish to enter events restricted to men. The organizers of the Open Championship have decided to lift the ban, but no places have been reserved for women – unlike for ranking male players – and they have to participate in the qualifying tournament. Yet some tournaments have opened up to women, particularly those for club professionals, since being employed by a golf club is the qualification, not gender. However, when Heather MacRae qualified for the Scottish Professional Golfers' Association championship in June 2009, even the reasonably high-quality Glasgow *Herald* headlined her venture as 'Pretty in Pink'. It also pointed out that she was allowed to play 5,556 m (6,076 yd) compared to the men's 6,092 m (6,662 yd).

DISABILITY

The Paralympic Movement originated in the wheelchair sports used as therapy at the Spinal Injuries Centre at a British hospital for those injured in war, Stoke Mandeville in Buckinghamshire. The first Stoke

Mandeville Games were held in 1948; the competitors, all in wheelchairs, were war veterans with spinal-cord injuries. In 1952 the second edition of the Games also included competitors from Israel and the Netherlands. The first official Paralympics were held in Rome in 1960 with some four hundred competitors from 23 countries, although the events were limited to disabled athletes who used wheelchairs, a restriction that was not eased until 1976, when athletes with different disabilities were included for the first time.

The first Stoke Mandeville Games had been timed to coincide with the London Olympic Games, but they were totally independent of the IOC. These days the Games' organizer, the neurologist Ludwig Guttmann, might be sued for ambush marketing! However, for many years the IOC, the group that chooses the host cities and determines eligibility for partic- ipation, ignored athletes with a disability. In the absence of any lead from the IOC, what became known as the Paralympic Movement developed independently of the official Olympic authorities. It was in its infancy in 1964, when Tokyo, host city for the Olympics that year, also took on the task of organizing the Paralympics, only the third to be held. It is now acknowledged that it was the Tokyo event that helped to standardize the use of the word 'Paralympics', although the importance attached to the Games in Japan was less about what it did for athletes with a disability and more to do with raising the nation's international standing. Not until Seoul in 1988 were the Paralympics held directly after the Summer Games in the same host city, using the same venues as the Olympic athletes. This precedent was followed in the next three Games, until it was formalized by the IOC in 2001. The Winter Paralympics were first held in 1976 in Örnsköldsvik, Sweden, but since 1992 they have used the same venues as the official Olympics.

As the Paralympics expanded, the system of classifying athletes was modified to reduce the number of categories. There are currently ten eligible disability categories, eight of which involve physical impairment and the others covering visual impairment and intellectual disability. The International Paralympic Committee has ruled that a minimum num- ber of athletes must participate for a category to be considered for the Paralympics, so groups have been conflated to achieve this. However, this operates against the severely disabled, since the uptake of sport within that group is small.

Olga Iurkovska, cross-country skier, at the 2010 Winter Paralympics.

More recently, two Paralympic-style multi-sports events have been developed for wounded, injured or sick armed-service personnel and veterans. These are the Warrior Games in the United States and the Invictus Games, which originated in the United Kingdom. Here, for the first time, sport has recognized those suffering from mental illness.

A few athletes with disabilities have made it to the actual Olympics. Wooden-legged George Eyser, a gymnast representing the United States, won six medals in one day in the 1904 St Louis Olympics, of which three were gold (parallel bars, long horse vault and 7.6-metre (25 ft) rope climbing), two silver (pommel horse and the four-event all-around) and one bronze (horizontal bar). More recently, blade-runner Oscar Pistorius made the semi-final in the 400 metres and ran in the South African team that made the final of the 4 × 400 metres relay at the London Games of 2012. Yet such exceptional disabled athletes are few and far between. For most disabled elite sportspeople, the Paralympics is the ultimate goal, with perhaps the long-term hope of a fully integrated Games at which Olympic and Paralympic athletes will compete at the same venues on the same day (albeit in separate events), as they have done at the Commonwealth Games since 2002.

Another set of international elite sport events is for those with the specific disability of deafness. In 1924 the World Silent Games held in Paris became the first regular, international multi-sport event for athletes with a disability (the Cripples Olympiad of 1911 in New York was a one-off). It was the idea of Eugène Rubens-Alcais, a deaf sports enthusiast, who in 1918 had founded the Sports Federation of the Deaf and Dumb. Since 1921 these games have been known as the Deaflympics, not the Deaf Olympics, although they have been sanctioned by the IOC. To qualify, athletes must have a hearing loss of at least 55 decibels in their better ear, and they cannot use hearing aids or cochlear implants in competition. To cater for their disability, races are started with a light and referees use flags rather than whistles. It is customary for spectators to wave rather than cheer or clap.

More relevant to athletes of all abilities are the Special Olympics for those with intellectual disabilities. Events are structured so that athletes compete with others of similar ability, with due regard to age and gender. The Special Olympics originated in a day camp that Eunice Kennedy Shriver organized for children with intellectual and physical disabilities. The first Special Olympics World Games were held in Chicago in 1968 with about a thousand North American athletes taking part. By 2003 more than 7,000 from 150 countries were participating in the Dublin event. Although the Special Olympics have secured official recognition from the IOC, it is perhaps the daily Special Olympics rather than the World Games that should be focused on. Some 100,000 events are held each year at local, regional and national level, involving about 5 million competitors. In recent years the Special Olympics have pioneered the concept of Unified Sports, which bring together sportspeople with and without intellectual disabilities as teammates. The goal is to break down stereotypes about people with intellectual disabilities. Some 1.5 million people worldwide now participate in unified sports.

WHO CLOSES THE DOOR?

Sport is a meritocracy, where the best win and those of inferior sporting ability lose, so it has often been seen as an area in which minorities and marginalized groups get a better chance to succeed than elsewhere in the economy. This does not detract from the fact that simultaneously obstacles have often been set up to prevent equality of opportunity, and we must not forget that sometimes the resistance to broadening opportunity can come from border guards within the group being discriminated against. A prime example was in the early twentieth century, when some female swimming officials would not select women for the Olympic team because they would be watched by male spectators. In those days many women also shared the broadly held male view that high-exertion, highly competitive, physical contact sport was unfeminine.

All the previous discussion should not blind us to the fact that the subcultures of the prohibited, victimized and discriminated against can influence their attitudes to access and their ability to succeed in sport. It is not always solely the oppressors who are to blame. The real problem with female sports participation in Australia (and perhaps elsewhere) today is with immigrant, non-English-speaking women. The rate at which they participate in sport is 8.4 per cent; that for Australian-born women is 26.7 per cent. I would argue that it is the attitude of men within the immigrant communities that has restricted the participation of such women. There are problems with the language barrier, but the main reason is cultural attitudes that state that women should not expose their bodies and that a daughter's role is in the household rather than on the sports field. In South Africa, in the first half of the twentieth century, black sports clubs voluntarily segregated themselves from each other on grounds of ethnicity, religion and even hair texture.

Something else that should be considered when analysing marginal groups is to distinguish between what happened because a person was black or female from what happened because they were from the working class. In Australia, for example, although there were special features relating to Aboriginal fighters (such as a non-defensive boxing style and a sharing of rewards with kinfolk), a history of getting punch-drunk, being exploited by managers and promoters, and dying in poverty applied equally to most white as well as black fighters.

17

PLAYING TOGETHER:
SPORTS CLUBS AND ASSOCIATIVITY

Annual folk football matches required a minimum of organization and had no need of clubs to supply participants; although players usually represented a particular area, teams were decided by birthplace, residence, family ties and sometimes marital status. Most pre-modern rural sports could be played on an ad hoc basis, when the participants felt the urge to play. Some sports events were organized more regularly by publicans looking to encourage a drinking clientele. None of these traditional sporting activities necessitated clubs for its operation. It was only when sports began to require a level of organization with written rules that clubs developed from the desire of people to collectivize their leisure activities. They enabled people with a common purpose to come together, provided a basis for agreeing common rules and regulations, created a framework for competitive interaction and secured a location for participation and sociability. There was a transition from occasional amusement to a system of organized clubs and regular sporting competitions. Some clubs that became custodians of written rules, such as Marylebone Cricket Club and the Jockey Club, rose to become the ruling bodies of their sports, in effect what might be termed 'meta-clubs'.

An emerging discussion of the origin of the sports club has revealed disagreements and differences internationally, but it is accepted that the club was central to the development of modern and, in some instances, pre-modern sport. The sports club as we know it emerged during the eighteenth century in Britain, initially in cricket, golf and horse racing before spreading to other sports and becoming the basic unit of modern grass-roots sport. It was part of a movement to new forms of associativity that scholars link to the intellectual ferment of the Western Enlightenment and the political and social revolutions that gave birth to limited constitutional governments, which protected the freedom of association and expression while limiting the powers of government over a wide range of activities. The voluntary associations that sprang to life coalesced not only around political, religious and economic ideas but around shared interest in sport. This was in contrast, it has been argued, to the situation in countries such as France and Germany, where the formation of clubs continued to require the explicit or implicit approval of the state. There, modern sports developed in ways consistent with the objectives of the state, most notably the need to maintain military preparedness; Britain, on the other hand, as an island nation, relied on naval power and did not require a large standing army or conscription.

When organizing themselves into institutions for the purpose of playing, British sportspeople had a long tradition of 'the club' to draw on because provincial and metropolitan life had a strong associational culture into which sport slotted relatively seamlessly. By the late eighteenth century the club was the major sporting institution in Britain. As a social institution it preceded the widespread development of sport, but sports promoters quickly adopted the idea as a mechanism of organization. When sport was exported from Britain in the late nineteenth century to its formal and informal empires, the club went with it as associated cultural baggage. One scholar, Stefan Szymanski, actually contends that modern British sport emerged directly from these new forms of associativity, although this is not the consensus opinion, which, while accepting that the club was essential to the emergence of much modern sport, believes that it still required assistance from other factors, in particular industrialization, urbanization and commercialization.

It must be acknowledged that there were forms of associativity in sport long before the British sports club. Medieval knights formed brotherhoods; German university students had an association life in their early eighteenth-century riding, fencing and dancing classes; and, above all, there were the shooting societies, of which some 3,000 of those formed before 1700 are still in existence in Germany, France, Belgium and the Netherlands today. Sports historians have now rejected the notion of origin moments for sports, so perhaps it is opportune to do likewise for sporting institutions. These early examples should be regarded as simply different forms of sports club, ones that failed to modernize and did not always survive. It may be that too much emphasis has been placed on the British club as an agent of modernization, especially given recent research that has downplayed the role of Britain in modernizing sport everywhere else.

Sport clearly did not invent the club, but borrowed the concept from an extant associational culture, adopting the format and adapting it to its own purposes. Sports clubs became the micro-unit behind the development of modern sport. But what if clubs had never existed? Clearly, sport has been played without the club as an organizational unit, so, in the absence of the club, sport would have continued, but would have developed differently. Team sports would probably have remained annual or irregular events with no leagues or knock-out cup competitions. Sports for individuals might well have progressed – gamblers would have seen to that – but perhaps less so the conviviality side of the sport, although landlords and publicans would still have sponsored competitions and provided facilities to attract a drinking clientele.

OPPOSITES DON'T ATTRACT

There has never been a legal requirement to establish a club in a particular way, a fact that has led to a variety of structures and organizational frameworks. Clubs are not a coherent body of organizations; they have different functions and structures, and hence cannot be embraced by a simple definition. Nor do all clubs have the same characteristics. From the earliest clubs in the seventeenth century, some were for those willing to exhibit the conspicuous consumption of time on what could be regarded as an unproductive activity. Such people were demonstrating that they were wealthy enough not to have to work all the time. These essentially middle-class clubs stand in contrast to working-class clubs, which developed from the 1880s in an attempt to bring together sufficient resources to enable their members to play sport. Moreover, clubs can have different cultures: they can be more or less regimented; have varying levels of sociability; be full of cliques or open; and play sport at different levels of competitiveness. Nevertheless, all share the fundamental aspect of being a collective, a members' organization that demonstrates associativity. Most membership clubs initially exhibited democratic participation, either in the decision-making directly or through a vote to elect committees to make decisions.

Playing sport is certainly at the core of sports club activity, but simultaneously the club can offer social goods such as fitness and camaraderie. Indeed, an important attraction of the sports club was the feeling of commonality that it could create, not just of playing sport together but from sharing a faith, a public-school education, a workplace, a drinking venue or a political orientation. This means there are many motivations for joining a club, and the task is to differentiate between the instrumental and expressive functions of sports clubs. The instrumental function is that of promoting a sporting activity – often outlined in the club's constitution as its primary goal – by the membership working together to acquire playing space, erect clubhouses and purchase equipment. Although instrumentality led to the establishment of clubs, the expressive functions of many clubs often became the cement that held the membership together via reinforcing a sense of identity, enhancement of status and the creation of social capital.

Social capital can be viewed as involving mutual support and obligations, social cooperation, trust and – of importance to a sporting organization – institutional effectiveness. Indeed, the establishment and operation of a sports club is a prime example of how, by developing relationships and working together, people can achieve more than they could simply by acting as individuals. Two aspects of social capital, the concepts of 'bridging' and 'bonding', perhaps have most relevance to sports clubs. Bonding social capital draws people together from a similar social niche and tends to reinforce exclusive identities, develop in-group loyalties and maintain homogeneity, whereas bridging social capital brings together people from diverse social divisions and tends to generate broader identities and wider reciprocities. The construction of bonding social capital infers the use of exclusionary practices to enforce a homogeneous group identity, in contrast to bridging capital's more inclusive agenda that cuts across class, gender and other boundaries.

Sports clubs generally served to consolidate existing collective identities, and almost all operated some form of restriction to ensure social homogeneity of membership, so bonding social capital dominated the bridging variety. For most of the social elite, sport was an opportunity for social differentiation, not conciliation, and was used to restrict rather than expand contact with social inferiors. In the late eighteenth century the twelve foundation members of the Royal Caledonian Hunt Club included four dukes, three earls and three baronets. As clubs descended the socio-economic scale, similar social exclusivity pertained. The members of the Alpine Club were overwhelmingly from the professional middle classes. In itself this does not mean that others were deliberately excluded, until we turn to the club's stated objective of facilitating 'association among those who possess a similarity of taste'. To be eligible, aspiring members had to possess experience of climbing in the Alps or 'provide evidence of literary or artistic accomplishments relating to mountains'. In the London golf scene, Northwood was the club for doctors, Woking for lawyers and Sunningdale for stock-exchange dealers. Moreover, the very existence of clubs catering primarily for adherents to particular faiths or to former pupils of particular schools and universities suggests that some form of social exclusivity was being applied.

ENJOYING THE CRAIC

Clubs also encouraged sociability and conviviality. Some perhaps took it too far; the Royal Caledonian Hunt Club's early minute books show that a wine committee was established in 1801 – 'good wine being absolutely essential for the Meetings of the Hunt' – but there was no racing committee until 1865.

Socializing with other members was a consistent feature of sports-club life. In Irish cricket in the late nineteenth century military bands played every Tuesday at the North of Ireland Cricket Club in Belfast. From its inception in 1888 the sporting paper *Scottish Referee* periodically included a section called 'The Social Circle' in which the various concerts and suppers of sports clubs were discussed. In the 1880s several of the early Scottish football clubs developed entertainment offshoots. Vale of Leven had a Dramatic Society, which performed before an audience of seven hundred in nearby Alexandria; Rangers set up a subcommittee to establish a Literary and Musical Association; and Queen's Park possessed a Musical and Dramatic Society. Most working-class angling clubs met in public houses and, as was explained to a parliamentary committee in

1878, 'had a jollification afterward', although the witness was careful to add, 'without exceeding the bounds of temperance'. Yachtsmen may have joined the Royal Cruising Club primarily for access to its navigational charts or the chance to win one of its annual awards, but it was an implicit condition of membership that they undertook 'to mix with fellow members whenever they meet afloat'.

A study of the Oxfordshire town of Banbury in the mid-twentieth century concluded that most sports clubs in the town existed less to enable the populace to engage in sport as an exercise in competitive athleticism, than as an occasion for social intercourse; and an examination of leisure organizations in the 1980s suggested that the leisure pursuit might actually be of secondary importance to the social side of a club's activities. Today in the lower sporting reaches there is Sunday pub football in which teams such as Real Ale Madrid play before indulging in a lunchtime drink. The conviviality of the dinners, dances, soirées, smokers for men, annual garden party and concerts not only served to draw individuals into social relationships – creating bonding social capital via friendship and enjoyment – but could also act as fundraisers. With the help of a supportive local press, they could also assist in creating a favourable image for the club, both in demonstrating approved, respectable behaviour to the outside world and in showing potential members how friendly and convivial it was. There was, however, a danger that the image created could be detrimental to the club and the sport. Much of the conviviality centred on alcohol, and sometimes behaviour became too boisterous. After a match in 1878 two members of the touring Queen's Park football team were fined £1 each by a Nottingham court for their disorderly conduct, and when Scottish clubs went on tour at New Year or Easter it was alleged that 'drunken orgies' often resulted, and that 'Lancashire hotel-keepers have a wholesale dread of Kilmarnock FC.'

SPORT WITH PRIVILEGE: THE AMERICAN COUNTRY CLUB

The history of the American country club, a lush landscape separate from everyday life, is one of private control over territorial space. It was more than a golf course and a clubhouse; it was a statement of exclusivity, a status symbol, a demonstration of conspicuous consumption, but one that most observers viewed from outside the gates.

By the late nineteenth century conditions in the United States were propitious for the emergence of the country club. City clubs for men, both the traditional social club and the newer athletic variety, had pioneered the organizational structure that it would adopt; summer resorts had provided urban elite families with collective leisure experiences with a connection to nature and the rural environment that they appreciated. These elites had also developed a taste for particular outdoor sports including tennis, equestrianism, croquet and golf, which at that time only they could afford to play. The trigger for the country clubs was the growing availability of commuter transport, which facilitated the development of suburban living in areas where land was available for sporting endeavour. This was seized on by speculative builders and developers, who saw profit in linking residential construction to the establishment of country clubs. They sited their housing either within the boundaries of a country club or in an adjacent estate, both of which enabled the elite to live in an enclave that included the club, separating them from the non-elite. This became a long-standing symbiotic relationship, with the club's presence raising land values and the occupants of the housing supplying a ready membership for the club.

The early country clubs adopted many of the practices of the city club, including the provision of indoor recreation facilities such as bowling alleys, cardrooms and billiard tables, as well as restaurants and bedrooms. However, they rejected the masculine bias and ethos of the city clubs and included family members in club activities, thus taking on the practices of the summer retreats. They also eschewed the idea of libraries; the country club was for sport and recreation, particularly outdoor physical activities, not intellectual pursuits. The earliest country clubs focused on equestrian sports: hunting, horse racing, carriage driving and – the one that became most popular because it required least space – polo. However, they soon became centres for multi-sport pursuit including archery, croquet, skeet-shooting, boating, tennis and golf, with curling, tobogganing, skating and ice hockey also featuring in northerly areas. Ultimately, horse sports lost out to golf in the internal struggle for land use, and the newer clubs never considered equestrian activities but, in warmer climes, brought in the swimming pool.

By 1901 there were more than 1,000 county clubs in the United States, covering all states and territories, sufficient to make the concept a national social institution but not enough to undermine the principle of exclusivity that was being marketed. In the next two decades the car began to play an important role in dictating the location of country clubs, especially in the smaller towns, where they became a pleasure ground for the more affluent families. Yet by the early 1930s the era of the country club, and indeed of the private golf club more generally, had peaked. In the previous decade both had expanded as the economy boomed with both individuals and the clubs themselves taking on debt to finance their membership and construction respectively, but the financial crash of 1929 and the ensuing Depression put paid to this. Membership shrank and perhaps a thousand clubs closed during the 1930s; others retrenched or became less private.

Even today numbers have barely recovered to the levels of the late 1920s, despite a boom of gated golf communities in the 1990s – this in a population that has tripled in size. Increased taxation on club fees and their removal as a tax-deductible business expense has not helped; neither has the increased geographical mobility of many Americans, which has reduced the desire to establish local roots. Moreover, the country club has become enmeshed in political argument, both from the left, who abhor the discrimination, and from the right, who claim a constitutional freedom to do what they want in a private club. It should be noted that discrimination was also practised in those clubs that had been created by Jewish and African-American entrepreneurs in response to being excluded from white country clubs.

A major change has been the emergence of corporations that own a number of country clubs and employ economies of scale in purchasing and economies of specialization in operating. In 1983 eight such organizations collectively owned or managed almost two hundred country clubs, and by 2020 one of them, ClubCorp (founded in 1957), had acquired or built 146 country clubs, with an aggregate membership of nearly 430,000. Associated with these profit-orientated enterprises was a greater willingness to end discrimination against minorities, a position that many independent country clubs have also adopted after social pressure and legal rulings.

LOTS OF SPORTS: THE EUROPEAN MODEL

Although the American country clubs offered multi-sport facilities, they were for the use of a restricted, wealthy membership. In contrast, many

European clubs, especially those in Spain, Italy and the Mediterranean, also catered for several sports but made them accessible to many more people by charging low membership fees. An early Spanish example was the Club Gimnàstic, which was set up in 1886 as a gymnastics club, but by 1922 had sections devoted to ten other sports, including soccer, fencing and Basque pelota. In more recent times several of the largest soccer clubs have also dominated competitions in other sports; Barcelona, Real Madrid, Panathinaikos and Olympiacos, for example, all have championship-winning professional basketball teams. Barcelona's Camp Nou complex includes two sports stadia, an indoor arena for basketball and other sports, and several practice fields. Real Madrid's Ciudad Deportiva also has an indoor arena, as well as member facilities such as tennis courts and a swimming pool. Other southern European clubs possess similar facilities, including Benfica's Caixa Futebol Campus in Lisbon and AC Milan's Milanello Sports Centre.

Sports clubs in the region have commonly cooperated with local and national governments to establish shared multi-purpose facilities for community sports and entertainment. One of the first major developments of this type was the Estadi Olímpic Lluís Companys, built in Barcelona in 1927, but it was Fascist Italy that epitomized the approach. There, the government supported the construction of huge stadia in Florence, Bologna and Rome for the 1934 FIFA World Cup, along with the multi-sport Foro Italico complex in Rome.

PART FIVE

MIXING OIL AND WATER: SPORTS, POLITICS AND POWER

The adage that sport and politics don't mix is often used to deflect criticism from those who object to discrimination in sport and to teams that represent regimes that are abhorrent (to them). Sport governing bodies argue that sport is apolitical and is not a suitable setting for the expression of political opinions or protest. They are doubly wrong. First, it should be emphasized that those who say that politics should be kept out of sport, or that the status quo should be preserved, are also making a political statement. Second, the reality is that, although they might not mix well, the two are deeply intertwined.

This section could have considered the efficacy of sport as soft-power diplomacy or the attitude of political parties towards sport. However, instead I will restrict the discussion to three major topics. The first chapter will look at how international sport has enabled small groups of athletes to become proxies for political systems and to represent much larger national communities, both for good and bad, and how – thanks to the media – some sporting events have gained a worldwide audience and thus are ripe for the publicity of protest. Finally, it will examine how politics has become the driving force behind the organization of some sports clubs and events for working-class people.

The second chapter examines human rights and sport. Theoretically everyone (at least, those of a Western liberal disposition) is in favour of human rights. The modern version of what such rights cover stems from the four freedoms promulgated by President Franklin D. Roosevelt in the early 1940s: freedom from want, freedom from fear, freedom of speech and freedom of religion. Then, in 1948, came the United Nations' Universal Declaration of Human Rights, which developed the concept to cover the pursuit of freedom, justice and peace for all, but which, significantly, was a declaration bearing only moral authority rather than a convention that had legal implications. To critics, the idea of human rights as commonly approached in the West ignores local cultural values: what is child exploitation to a human-rights activist is someone else's vital family income. More significant, to my mind, is that it is a concept disregarded by all governments when it suits them to do so.

In the final chapter we turn to the internal politics of sport, specifically the establishment of rules and the bodies that set and enforce them. Rules played a key role in creating modern sport, as regular competition with codified, written regulations gradually over-whelmed much traditional sport carried on under customary practices backed solely by oral tradition. The creation of codified rules led to bureaucracy, and in many sports there were political tussles as to which organization should be in charge and which code of regulations should be in place.

18

POLITICAL FOOTBALL: NATIONALISM, PROPAGANDA AND PROTEST

Sport is an ideal cultural medium for nation building and the promotion of nationalism. It is binary, emphasizing us versus them; it is simple, in that it requires no specialist knowledge to grasp the idea of loyalty to a national team; and it is universal, because everyone can support the national side. Sport can be used to demonstrate ideological strength, bring about a sense of national cohesion, and ultimately announce the arrival of a nation on the world stage.

This can be seen in nineteenth-century Australia. The Australian colonies had no aggressive neighbours to deal with, so there was no great war to bring the colonies together, with the corollary that there was no drain on resources into defence and away from other spending, such as sport. In some quarters sport has been seen as an alternative unifying force. Certainly, Australia came together on the cricket field (to play against England) before the colonies united politically to form the Federation of Australia in 1901. Many Australians had an inferiority complex vis à vis England, brought about by a feeling that either they were not wanted in the mother country or they had failed to make a success in life there. In Australia cricket became a litmus test to ascertain how immigrants and ensuing generations had fared in an alien environment and hot climate; beating England in its national game led to fewer press references to colonial degeneration and elicited new claims that the old stock had actually improved by being grafted on to Australian soil. No longer were the Antipodean colonials unsure whether they were Australians or southern hemisphere Englishmen. After the conclusion of the 1897/8 Test series, an editorial in the *Bulletin*, a journal that played a significant role in the encouragement and circulation of nationalist sentiment, maintained that 'this ruthless rout of English cricket will do – and has done – more to enhance the cause of Australian nationality than could ever be achieved by miles of erudite essays and impassioned appeal.' Indeed, the historian Bill Mandle has argued that the separate Australian colonies became unified on the cricket field, and the victories over the English showed them the value of cooperation and lent support to the movement for federation. Since then, sport has been how Australia – a relative nonentity in world politics – has attempted to find a place on the international stage.

Even before this, European gymnastics had been politicized, although not in the sense of having to beat an international opponent in the sporting arena. That became important to nations only when international sport competitions began, in the nineteenth century, a development accelerated by transport improvements. The first gymnastic ground was created in Berlin in 1811 for the Turners (gymnasts). The movement spread throughout the German Confederation states, and from 1815 onwards Turnvereine (gymnastics clubs) were founded where young men would meet to perform gymnastic exercises and engage in political discussion. The goal of the Turners was initially to end French occupation, over-throw the feudal order and unite the many small states into one German nation. Some states banned the movement, but many Turner societies were founded after 1842, when Prussia lifted its prohibition, and they were at the forefront of a revolution in the late 1840s that strove for freedom, equality and a united Germany. When the revolution failed, many Turners, fearful of imprisonment or worse, left their homeland for Switzerland, Britain or the United States, where they continued their gymnastic exercises and followed a political dogma that concentrated on the freedom of the individual and an opposition to religious indoctrination. Their influence, however, was much stronger in physical education than in the political arena.

As with the German gymnastic organizations, a strong politicization of the body emerged in the Czech lands of the mid-nineteenth century, combining gymnastics with folklore and anti-Habsburg and anti-Ottoman politics. The most significant movement involved the Sokol gymnastics associations, which identified and used sport with a nationalist ideological focus. Basically self-discipline, the pursuit of muscular improvement and gains in mental capability (all through sport) were subjugated to the political goals of the whole nation. In 1862 there were only seven clubs, but this had expanded to more than seventy (with some 7,000 members) by 1875. Membership had reached more than 100,000 before 1914. It could have been more, but some clubs left to join a Catholic gymnastic organization, their members angered by the anti-cleric attitude of the Sokol organization, and in 1897 social democratic activists were purged from Sokol and founded their own Workers' Gymnastics Association. Politics at play within a political organization – quelle surprise!

Then we have Ireland, where the GAA, founded in 1884, adopted a policy of Ireland first, which included banning its members from participation in what it termed 'garrison sports', those played by what it regarded as an occupying British army. As with the Turners and their gymnastics, Irish sports accompanied the Irish migrants who became part of the massive Irish diaspora. In 1890 two out of every five Irish-born people were living abroad, and between 1830 and 1914 almost 5 million went to the United States in search of a better life. Some of the immigrants chose to play American sports as a road to assimilation, but others opted to retain a distinctive ethnic identity and play hurling and, later, Gaelic football, which allowed them to retain their Irishness in this new environment. However, the games were more than just sports; they were nationalistic activities. Playing them enabled the Irish in America to express themselves as Irish nationalists and overtly lend support to the struggle for Irish independence, which was achieved in 1922.

The GAA itself entered the years following independence as the largest and most significant sporting organization in Ireland, a position of dominance that remained unchallenged until the later decades of the twentieth century. Yet it did not have everything sporting its own way. A clash of competing nationalistic ideologies occurred in the 1930s, when the Irish military revised its physical training systems, which had been based on Swedish or Ling gymnastics. After a successful trial it was decided to adopt the Sokol system as the best means to render recruits 'fighting fit'. Although it required musical accompaniment for displays, it was largely based on the use of a recruit's own body, alongside inexpensive equipment. In other words, it was both militarily and economically efficient. The GAA was aghast at the idea of the nation going 'foreign'. It had promulgated the idea that, as Ireland's premier sporting organization, it had played a pivotal role in securing independence, and it argued that playing the Irish sports of Gaelic football (which the GAA had invented) and hurling was the ideal training for warfare. Such sports were central to the sporting face of Irish nationalism. The Sokol system itself, of course, was imbued with nationalism, although not an Irish one. The GAA lost the argument, but gained some face-saving concessions as the Sokol system was modified for Irish consumption: when it was used for display purposes, the accompanying music had to be Irish, and Irish dancing was integrated into the system as a key component.

Sporting nationalism was a feature of the Soviet/Eastern European cluster that emerged in the twentieth century. Sport became an extension of the state apparatus, in the spheres of both mass display and the cultivation of elite athletes. During the early years of the new Russian state created by the Revolution of 1917, Soviet sport became entirely state-run, and within four years not a single private, non-state sports club remained. It remained that way until the collapse of Communism, both for utilitarian purposes and as an agent of social change. Its function was to raise health standards, socialize citizens into a new value system, and develop a sense of nationalism. During the 1930s the Soviet Union carefully and cautiously cultivated limited engagements with the emerging global sporting culture to shape an image for domestic and international purposes. The Soviets sought to project national strength through sporting endeavours, but were keenly aware that they had not yet developed the capacity to compete head-to-head in major spectacles with the world's leading sporting powers. They scrupulously avoided the Olympics during the 1930s for fear of what comparison with more athletically advanced nations might do to their national image.

At this time governments in both Fascist Italy and Nazi Germany intervened in the sporting sector to further their respective nationalist goals. The Italian football team – 'Mussolini's Boys' – was seen as the epitome of what Italian men could achieve in the name of the state and its political ideology; they won the 1934 World Cup (hosted by Italy, which may have helped), the 1936 Olympic Games and the World Cup again in 1938. Later the new Communist regime in China used sport to help the development of a nation state. Although government policy changed as circumstances altered and fresh challenges emerged, the

Spectators give the Nazi salute at the 1936 Berlin Olympics.

new Republic generally used mass sport to promote physical fitness and strength for economic and military purposes, and elite, competitive sport was seen as enhancing China's international standing as well as unifying the nation domestically.

International sport creates imagined communities. Teams of limited size represent the hopes of many more, and thus sport can give a nation pride, especially when the underdog comes out triumphant. Qualifying for the 2006 FIFA World Cup helped to unify the Ivory Coast after four years of civil war. However, there is an ugly downside to sporting nationalism, as reflected by the behaviour of many English soccer fans when they venture into Europe. In the European Championships in 2016 they used the fact of a Russian submarine venturing into the English Channel as an excuse to attack Russian supporters, although it must be said that the latter equally felt they had to assert their own nationalism and fight back or even provoke the English in masculine showdowns. Nationalism can induce fans to view others as fundamentally different, often in negative ways. In some instances, political leaders have built on sports nationalism to generate public support for aggressive foreign policies. Mussolini treated the 1934 World Cup final in Italy as a Fascist rally, and Hitler likewise the Berlin Olympics in 1936.

DON'T SHOOT THE POLITICAL MESSENGER

Nationalistic fervour is heightened every four years by the Olympic Games, which have placed the nation at the centre of affairs. Individual competitors cannot enter, but must be nominated by the Olympic Committee of their country. National flags are hoisted, national anthems played, and medals are listed by country in league tables. Sporting success at the Olympics has come to represent the benefits of particular political ideologies: and the reverse. Sporting failure has caused governments to rethink their sports policies, rather than their political ideologies, so as to restore their international image.

The Football War

On one infamous occasion sport was the trigger for the outbreak of war. Allegedly. Three weeks after El Salvador beat Honduras 3-2 in a World Cup qualifying match in June 1969, a conflict broke out between the two countries that cost more than 3,000 lives. It was a bloody struggle that is still remembered as the Football War, but in reality the fighting had been likely to occur irrespective of the match or the score. For decades Salvadoran farmers had migrated to neighbouring Honduras, where there was more land and fewer people; others had gone to work for the United States' fruit companies that operated there. In the mid-1960s domestic political pressure persuaded the Honduran president to begin to send thousands of Salvadorans home, where the government struggled to cope with the influx of returning migrants. Additionally, there were simmering sea and land border disputes between the two countries. It was a powder keg waiting to ignite. On the evening of the match (pun intended) El Salvador broke off diplomatic relations with Honduras, and within a month the former invaded its neighbour.

PELÉ (1940–)

Scorer of almost a goal a game in elite soccer (the best estimate is 1,281 goals from 1,363 matches), Edson Arantes do Nascimento, better known as Pelé, was a co-winner of FIFA's Player of the Century Award. He was also voted Athlete of the Twentieth Century by the International Olympic Committee, although as a professional he was not eligible for the Olympics during his career.

His father was a football player for the sports club Fluminense, and Pelé showed precocious talent at the game. He credits playing *futebol de salão*, an indoor game with limited space and only five players per side, with helping to develop his ball skills, making him think quickly in tight spaces, and allowing him as a youngster to play with and against men. When he was fifteen he made his debut with Santos, the Brazilian club he was to represent for eighteen years. Within a year he had been chosen to play for the national side in a 1-2 defeat by Argentina, in which he scored his first international goal, and he remains the youngest goal-scorer for his country. Ultimately he scored 77 goals for Brazil in 92 games. His last international match was in Rio de Janeiro in 1971, against Yugoslavia.

At club level, Pelé remains Santos's all-time leading goal-scorer, and he led them to victory in the 1962 and 1963 Copa Libertadores, a competition for the champions of each national league in South America, and in the 1962 intercontinental cup against the Portuguese club Benfica. He was the subject of transfer bids by European teams such as Real Madrid, Juventus and Manchester United, and even signed for Inter Milan before the Santos fans forced the club chairman to renege on the deal. Santos often went on tour to raise money, with Pelé being a major drawcard; in 1967 a ceasefire was even called in the Nigerian Civil War so that spectators from both factions could watch Pelé play for Santos in such an exhibition match. Towards the end of his career, and past his prime, he joined the New York Cosmos in the North American Soccer League, primarily to raise public interest in the game in the United States, although in his last season the team won the league. Like Santos, the Cosmos became a globetrotting club, and Pelé's appearances on tour swelled crowds throughout the world. Fittingly, his last match was for New York Cosmos against Santos in 1977.

Among football aficionados, it is Pelé's association with Brazil's exploits in the FIFA World Cup for which he is best remembered. When seventeen-year-old Pelé arrived in Sweden for the 1958 World Cup he was carrying a knee injury, but his teammates were insistent that he should play. However, he was held back until Brazil's third

Pele, in his number 10 shirt, playing in Brazil's 3-0 victory over Italy in Milan, 1963.

game, their last of the group stage, in which they defeated the USSR. Pelé thereby became the youngest player to take the field in the World Cup finals. He also became the youngest to score a hat-trick in the finals, which he did in the 5-2 victory over France in the semi-final. He then became the youngest player to participate in a World Cup final tie and, almost inevitably, the youngest to gain a winner's medal when Sweden was overcome 5-2. It almost goes without saying that he was voted the young player of the tournament. With six goals in just four games, he was the second-highest scorer in the finals, and was ranked second-best player in the tournament.

In 1962 Pelé was injured attempting a long-range shot in Brazil's second game, and he took no further part in the competition in which Brazil retained their world title. Four years later, in England, the team was eliminated at the group stage and again Pelé was injured, this time through deliberate fouls by brutal defenders from Portugal and Bulgaria. He vowed not to play in the World Cup again, but later changed his mind, and in the 1970 final he scored the opening goal in the 4-1 win over Italy and was declared the player of the tournament.

It is not clear why he became known as Pelé (the word has no meaning in Portuguese), but conventional wisdom has it that it was attached to him because, as a schoolboy, he constantly mispronounced the name of Bilé, goalkeeper for the local team Vasco da Gama. We do know why he wore the number ten shirt. When Brazil went to the World Cup in 1958 the Brazilian Federation failed to send in the players' numbers, so FIFA allocated them; he wore that number subsequently, whichever position he played in. He began his career as a striker playing up front, but also developed himself in a play-making role. In fact, he could play anywhere. When the coach of Brazil was asked who his best goalkeeper was, his answer was Pelé!

The relatively poor performance by Team GB at the Atlanta Olympics in 1996, where there was but one gold in the haul of fifteen medals, was seen by the prime minister, John Major, as a comment on his government. In an attempt to put the 'great' back into Great Britain, his response was to push money into elite Olympic sports and raise the government subsidy from £5 million to £54 million, much of it spent on allowing athletes to train full-time under the best specialist coaches, with state-of-the art equipment and facilities. The result? Sydney in 2000 brought 28 medals, eleven of them gold. When the Olympics came to London in 2012 the host nation won 65 medals – at a cost of just over £4 million each. Australia experienced something similar when its team won just five medals, none of them gold, at the Montreal Games in 1976. Money was poured into establishing the Australian Institute of Sport in Canberra with satellite, specialist branches in other states. Moscow in 1980 brought nine medals, two of them gold, and Los Angeles in 1984 garnered 24 medals, four of them gold.

Some countries don't even get invited to the Olympic party. Following their defeat in the First World War, no Germans, Austrians, Bulgarians, Hungarians or Turks were allowed to compete at the Antwerp Games of 1920, and there were no Japanese or Germans at the London Olympics of 1948.

Others turn down their invitations. Youssef Nagui Assad was one of the unluckiest potential Olympic athletes of all time. He was a physical-education teacher in Cairo and an international-standard shot-putter, although in 1968 his standard was not quite high enough and he failed to qualify for the Egyptian squad for the Mexico Games by just 2 cm (less than 1 in.). However, he was only 23 and time was on his side. He made it to Munich in 1972, but was ordered home because his government wanted to show solidarity with the Palestinian cause. In 1976 he made the team once more, but was again ordered home because his government joined the boycott to protest against New Zealand's rugby ties with South Africa. In 1980, now aged 35, he got his final chance, but his government decided to boycott the Moscow Games in protest against the Soviet Union's invasion of Afghanistan. On one side of his non-Olympic career there were boycotts of Melbourne in 1956 by Egypt, Iraq and Lebanon because of Britain's seizure of the Suez Canal; by the Netherlands, Spain and Switzerland because of the Soviet invasion of Hungary; and by China because of the IOC's recognition of Taiwan. On the other side, the Russians boycotted Los Angeles in 1984 not simply as 'payback' for the United States-led boycott of the 1980 Moscow Olympics, as many presume, but owing to security concerns about the American refusal to crack down on anti-Soviet protestors, and fears that U.S. intelligence agencies would seek to persuade Russian athletes to defect.

5 SEPTEMBER 1972: OLYMPIC VILLAGE, MUNICH

At around four in the morning on 5 September 1972 a group of Palestinian terrorists scaled the fence of the Munich Olympic village, where athletes were resident, and used a pass key to enter the building housing members of the Israeli team. A wrestling referee, awakened by the sound of voices speaking Arabic outside, tried to prevent them from entering his apartment but was shot dead, as were two other Israelis who resisted the intruders. Within an hour eight other Israeli athletes and coaches had been captured, and the terrorists, members of the Black September organization, had issued the demands to be met if they were to be released. Essentially these amounted to the freeing of more than two hundred Palestinian prisoners held in Israeli gaols, as well as the founders of the Baader-Meinhof revolutionary group who were imprisoned in West Germany.

Golda Meir, the Israeli prime minister, refused to consider any negotiation, and the terrorists rejected financial overtures from the German government. The only option left was a rescue attempt. It was a disaster. Under German law the military could not operate offensively on home soil, so the local police had to take responsibility. The initial plan was to have armed police crawl down the ventilation shafts and attack the terrorists, but since television cameras were covering the scene the terrorists were able to see the preparations being undertaken. These ended when the Palestinians threatened to shoot two of the hostages. The next idea was to pretend that the terrorists would be given safe passage by air out of Germany and shoot them as they walked to the helicopters that were to transport them to the airfield. This too was abandoned when the terrorist leader reconnoitred the route, became suspicious and demanded buses between the apartments and the helicopters. The third option was to kill them when they went to board the Lufthansa plane, using both snipers and police disguised as air crew. However, when the rescue ambush began the snipers missed their targets, thus giving the terrorists time to kill one group of Israelis by throwing a hand grenade into the helicopter that had transported them to the airfield; the other group was shot by another terrorist (although some believe they may have been caught in crossfire). Meanwhile the 'air crew' had fled the aircraft, realizing that theirs was a suicide mission. Three terrorists were captured; the rest were killed. The three were exchanged a month later for hostages held when a Lufthansa flight was hijacked by their supporters. Two of them were subsequently assassinated by agents of Mossad, the Israeli secret service.

The affair undermined the German reputation for efficiency. Security at the village had been deliberately lax, with an absence of armed personnel, so as to create the image of a carefree event. Athletes breaking the curfew regularly scaled the fence at night; indeed, some from North America had helped the tracksuited terrorists, believing they were fellow competitors. A tip-off from a Palestinian informer that an 'incident' was being planned was not acted on, nor was any practice undertaken of the response to an attack on the

'Black September' Terrorist at the Munich Olympic Village.

Israeli team while it was in residence, despite the event being thought not unlikely by security analysists. The snipers used in the rescue ambush were regular policemen with no professional firearms training; their weapons had no telescopic sights; they had no radio communication with each other or the operation coordinator; and there were only five of them to deal with eight terrorists.

As for the Games themselves, Avery Brundage, president of the IOC, insisted that they must go on, although, after severe public criticism of his statement, they were suspended for 34 hours. A memorial service was held in the Olympic stadium, after which the rest of the Israeli team left for home. The Algerian, Egyptian and Philippines teams also quit, as did several members of the Norwegian and Dutch teams.

When the Israeli team entered the stadium at the opening ceremony in Montreal for the 1976 Games, their flag was adorned with a black ribbon. However, not until 2016 did the IOC commemorate the victims, having rejected a campaign four years previously to hold a minute's silence at the opening ceremony in London in memory of the murdered Israelis on the fortieth anniversary of their deaths. There is a memorial tablet outside the Olympic stadium in Munich, and another plaque on the door of the building where they were captured.

CATHERINE 'CATHY' ASTRID SALOME FREEMAN (1973–)

As a female indigenous Australian, Cathy Freeman was discriminated against in a racist Australia, but ultimately became the face used as a means of reconciliation between whites and blacks. Contrary to a widely held view, she was not the first Aboriginal to win Olympic gold. That honour went to Nova Peris in field hockey at the Atlanta Games in 1996; coincidentally, Peris was Freeman's teammate in the 4 × 400 metres relay at Sydney in 2000, where they finished in fifth place.

Freeman's grandmother Alice Sibley was one of the so-called stolen generation, taken from her parents at the age of eight by an Australian government policy in the 1950s supposedly designed to help integration. As a consequence of this programme, in which Aboriginal children were removed from their parents and settled with white families, Freeman remained unaware of her ancestry on her mother's side. Her father, an Australia Rules footballer, left home when she was five and died of an alcohol-induced stroke at the age of 53.

Freeman began athletics at the age of five under the tutelage of her stepfather Bruce Barber. By her early teens she had amassed a host of regional titles in sprinting, long jump and high jump. By this time she was being coached professionally by Mike Danila, a Romanian immigrant to Australia, who entered her in the trials for the 1990 Australian Commonwealth Games team to compete in Auckland. She secured a place in the triumphant 4 × 100 metres relay team, making her the first Aboriginal Commonwealth Games gold medallist in track and field. She became Young Australian of the Year.

The pride Freeman takes in her indigenous heritage caused controversy in the next Commonwealth Games, held in Victoria, Canada, in 1994. When she won the 400 metres she did a victory lap carrying the Aboriginal flag, one not sanctioned for display under the Games rules. Arthur Tunstall, the unreconstructed secretary of the Australian Commonwealth Games Association, tried to snatch the flag from her and threatened to send her home, a view that outraged the public in Australia. Even his close ally Ray Godkin, president of the Association, noted that people ran around with the boxing kangaroo flag all

Cathy Freeman in the green and gold of Australia at the 2000 Sydney Olympics.

the time, and there were never any problems with that. After she later also won the 200 metres, Freeman was more circumspect and strategically waved both the Aboriginal and the Australian flags. The Aboriginal flag, in use at protests from the early 1970s, was officially recognized by the Australian government in 1995.

Freeman won silver in the 400 metres at the Atlanta Olympics in 1996, and in 1997 she won the same event at the World Championships in Athens. She was also awarded the prestigious Australian of the Year honour. Injury forced her out of competition in 1998 but she returned the following year, winning every race she entered, including the world championship again, this time in Seville.

Freeman became the celebrity of the Sydney Olympics, and showed the world a different face of Australia. She was chosen to light the Olympic cauldron, which she did wearing a white bodysuit similar in design to the white-and-green outfit in which she crossed the line to claim gold in the 400 metres some days later. These 'swift suits' were provided by Nike, as were her track shoes in the Aboriginal colours of black, red and gold. She also featured in a 75-metre-high (250 ft) electronic billboard for Nike products as part of her endorsements of AUS$1.2 million in that Olympic year. The Olympic reception following her victory in the final of the 400 metres stood in stark contrast to the day she had travelled to an athletics meeting aged thirteen. Waiting at Melbourne's Flinders Street station then, she had been ordered to move on by a group of middle-aged white women, when the whole adjacent seating area lay vacant.

As an admired and respected athlete, Freeman became a symbol of reconciliation between black and white people in Australia, and her image was used by the Council for Aboriginal Reconciliation to promote the case for harmony in the country. In 2008 the then prime minister, Kevin Rudd, issued a national apology to Australia's indigenous population for the way they had been treated. Freeman retired from athletics in 2003 and four years later established a foundation to work with remote indigenous communities to incentivize children to attend school. It is currently delivering educational programmes to 1,600 in-digenous children; it is, as Freeman herself remarked, not a 400-metre run but a marathon.

The FIFA World Cup has also had its boycotts. Although the host, Uruguay, won the inaugural Cup in 1930, they did not defend their title in Italy four years later in protest at the lack of European support for the Uruguayan tournament. Nor did they attend Germany in 1938 because – like Argentina, who also refused to participate – they objected to the holding of the event in Europe again, believing that it should rotate between South America and Europe, the two great homes of the world game. Football has also had problems with teams who refuse to play Israel. In the qualifying group for the Cup in 1958 Turkey, Indonesia, Egypt and Sudan all withdrew from matches against Israel on political grounds. Israel thus took the spot reserved in the finals for Asian and African teams without actually kicking a ball. This fell foul of FIFA's rules, since only a host country or a holder could be exempted until the finals, so Israel had to play against the best non-qualifier from Europe, which was Wales. They lost and Wales made the finals for the only time in their history. In later years FIFA shifted Israel to the European qualifying sector, where there was less political hostility towards the Jewish state.

Big events are accompanied by big publicity, so political protests and propaganda taking advantage of the Olympics and other mega-events are guaranteed to reach a worldwide audience. In 1908, at the London Olympics, the United States flagbearer refused to dip his flag to the British monarch. At the 1937 Tour de France, held during the Spanish Civil War, six Spanish cyclists raced wearing purple, red and yellow jerseys, the colours of the endangered Spanish Republic. They actually won two of the stages, bringing the Republican cause into the sporting limelight. The 1972 Munich Olympics saw the massacre of eleven Israeli team members by the Palestinian terrorist group Black September. Yet there can be a positive political aspect. Having the Aboriginal runner Cathy Freeman light the Olympic flame at the Sydney Games in 2000 did much for Aboriginal reconciliation.

Some protests are directed at the Olympics themselves. In 1972 Denver became the first Olympic host city to reject the Olympics after having been selected by the IOC. Despite strong support from Denver and wider Colorado politicians, chambers of commerce, and powerful economic groups, activists spearheaded a campaign that brought together environmentalists concerned about damage and destruction, and fiscal conservatives worried about the cost of the Games. They forced a referendum on the bond issue the state government was proposing to finance the project, and the public voted 60 per cent against funding. The Games were held in Innsbruck, Austria, instead. Since then, most organized protests have been before a bid was made, resulting in bids being headed off in several cities, most recently Calgary, Canada, where a bid for the 2026 Winter Olympics was rejected overwhelmingly in a public vote. In Boston, Massachusetts, the public rejected the 2024 Summer Games, despite the 'yes' side spending $15 million and those against just $10,000, when the financial implications for the citizens became apparent. In Rome the city mayor refused to support a bid for the same Games; Hamburg rejected applying after a referendum; and Budapest also pulled its application. In the bidding for the 2022 Winter Olympics, voters in Stockholm, Munich and Crakow all rejected the local bidders' aspirations, leaving only Beijing and Almaty in contention. The games were awarded to the Chinese capital, presumably – if it was assessed as it was supposed to be – because China's human-rights record was superior to that of its Kazakhstan rival.

WHO ARE YOU PLAYING FOR?

Early international sport could be haphazard in terms of eligibility to represent a country. Early Olympiads allowed joint teams for Australasia (as did the Davis Cup in tennis) and even pan-national teams in cross-country and tennis, in which a German partnered an Englishman in the men's doubles. In the first-ever cricket Test match between Australia and England at Melbourne in 1877, Englishman Billy Midwinter played for Australia, a country to which he had emigrated aged nine. Later that year he returned to England to play for W. G. Grace's Gloucestershire County Cricket Club. He was selected in the Australian team to tour England in 1878, and played some matches for them, before, when about to take the field at Lord's, he was allegedly virtually kidnapped by Grace, who took him to the Oval to play for Gloucestershire against Surrey. He opted out of the tour and remained with Gloucestershire until the 1882 season. He was chosen to tour with the England team visiting Australia in 1881/2, playing four Tests, but in 1882/3 he emigrated back to Australia and was selected to play against England the following season and then for the Australian tour of England in 1884.

As sport became international and competitions between nations developed, rules were required to determine eligibility to represent one's country. Although in most international team events entry has been by specific nationality, even tightened rules have been circumvented by the ease of nationality change offered by some sport-ambitious countries, by grandparent citizenship clauses and by threats of restraint-of-trade challenges, all of which allow flag-of-convenience athletes to represent nations other than those of their birth or residence. Elite athletes – particularly, at present, those who are African – have been offered financial inducements to switch nationality. In contrast, some athletes have been 'forced' to represent nations that they might not wish to. The amateur boxer Wayne McCullough had represented Northern Ireland at the 1990 Commonwealth Games in Auckland, where he won a gold medal and carried the Northern Irish flag in the closing ceremony. However, the Olympics was another matter. When Éire had separated from the United Kingdom, in 1922, the Irish Amateur Boxing Association was the body recognized by the IOC as having jurisdiction over Irish boxing, and – somewhat anomalously – it continued to select boxers from all over Ireland, both Ulster and the Republic. McCullough, who lived in the staunchly loyalist Shankill Road area of Belfast, was selected to represent Ireland at the Barcelona Games of 1992, where he won a silver medal. Had he won gold he would have had to listen to the anthem of a country alien to many loyalists. In the end that may not have concerned him too much, since, as the youngest member of the team, he had already carried the Irish flag at the Seoul Games four years previously.

WHAT ABOUT THE WORKERS?

At the micro level, clubs were political institutions that gave individual members the opportunity to stand for office, vote on policy and make speeches. When I tutored for the Open University in the early 1970s, one social-science module noted that even picking the local football team could be a political act. However, some clubs also entered the macro-level political sphere. Gaelic sports clubs always had a political underpinning: the cause of Irish nationalism. Such a motivation helped to attract politically conscious immigrants to the hurling and Gaelic football clubs established in London in the 1890s.

Apart from the pro-independence GAA affiliates, relatively little is known about politically orientated sports clubs in Britain. The cooperative wholesale and retail societies, often seen as a working-class political organization, recognized that sport could have a role in promoting a collective identity among its employees. As did many private businesses, they owned sports facilities for the use of their staff so as to demonstrate commitment to their workforce, create a sense of belonging and build loyalty; and, like most private businesses, they offered sporting opportunities to female workers. In common with some conventional businesses, although probably not a majority of those offering sports provision, they used sports days as family days, and, again, like some but not the majority, they used sport to integrate workers from their widespread operations network. Where they differed significantly from most conventional business was in holding cooperative demonstrations at sports events that drew large crowds, and in using the quality of their sports facilities and organization to offset the lower wages of the retail sector. More overtly political was the Clarion Cycling Club in 1894, a founder member of the socialist-inspired British Workers' Sports Federation (1923–35).

Those leading workers' sport in Britain sought to emphasize less competitive physical activities, such as recreational cycling, hiking and swimming, although later, in response to grass-roots pressure, there was a move to develop competitive team sports. However, labour sports societies could rarely compete in facilities and finance with traditional company or church teams. Although their overt political orientation (as seen in titles involving words such as 'workers', 'socialist' and 'labour') deprived them of external funding, they were not considered political enough to secure financial backing from the trade unions. In Britain, sports clubs never attained the level of political activity and awareness that was reached in Europe and Scandinavia. Finnish working-class sports clubs, for example, had purposes other than simply playing sport, and attempted to politically socialize their members. Such working-class sports clubs were not alone in having a political focus. Almost every political party in Finland and the social class they represented had its own sports club.

The interwar period was the global heyday of workers' sport, with two organizations in rivalry to promote the idea of working-class solidarity on the sports field, the ideology of internationalism and pacifism, and opposition to the commercialization of sport at the elite level. After the Russian Revolution of 1917 the international socialist movement divided into two antagonistic camps, one socialist, the other communist. This split, and its accompanying hostility, was reflected in the development of the two bodies striving for the international leadership of workers' sport.

The International Association of Physical Culture and Sport, informally known as Lucerne Sport International after the place of its foundation in 1920, was an international socialist organization, although it eschewed the term until 1926, when it renamed itself the Socialist Workers' Sport International (SASI, from the German name, Sozialistische Arbeitersport Internationale). At the time of its formation it consisted of six national federations with about a million members. Politically, it was supported by the International Federation of Trade Unions and the Labour and Socialist International, and in 1931 it claimed 1.8 million members from twenty countries. The communist International Association of Red Sports and Gymnastics Associations, usually referred to as Sportintern or, more commonly, Red Sport International (RSI), was founded in 1921. By 1924 it had over 2 million Russian members and sections in eleven other countries, but already it had become an auxiliary of the Communist International.

Both organizations held their own version of Workers' Olympics, although, being rivals, both excluded members of the other organization. However, they shared the idea of building mass participation through pageantry and artistic and cultural activities, as well as sport itself. They both saw the official Olympics as dominated by the privileged classes. SASI organized its first Workers' Olympiad in winter sports at Schreiberhau (now Szklarska Poręba, Poland), followed by summer games in Frankfurt. The next winter games were in Mürzzuschlag (Austria) and the summer ones in Vienna, where they attracted 80,000 athletes and some 250,000 spectators, both in excess of the official Olympics in Los Angeles in 1932. The festival eschewed national flags and anthems, with the socialist-inspired Olympics opting for flying the Red Flag and singing the 'Internationale'. RSI hosted its first Spartakiad in 1928, with summer games in Moscow and a winter version in Oslo. Another summer games followed in 1931 in Berlin, and a winter one in Oslo in 1936. A summer event was planned for Catalonia but was thwarted by the Spanish Civil War. The organization was dissolved in 1937 as the Soviet

Union became more concerned with internal dissidence and less with international communism. Following this, SASI welcomed ex-Red Sport athletes to its summer games in Antwerp in 1937 and the winter version in Janské Lázně, Czechoslovakia. A fourth Olympiad was scheduled for Helsinki in 1943, but obviously never materialized.

19

HUMAN RIGHTS
(AND WRONGS)

Discrimination seems to be endemic in sport as clubs often restrict membership to those who will fit in with the social preferences of existing members. Yet in South Africa discrimination was politically sanctioned. Even before formal apartheid, social segregation and the apportioning of space on racial grounds prevented black people from obtaining membership of the same clubs or playing in the same leagues as white sportspeople, but from 1948, when ethnically Dutch white forces (Boers or Afrikaners) gained the political majority, formal apartheid laws were passed and made progressively more severe. Almost every corner of life was affected by apartheid laws. Interracial marriage was banned; a work environment was created in which many important jobs became 'white-only'; and, while black South Africans were allowed to vote in designated homelands, they were barred from any real presence in national elections, so they had no recourse to politics for changing the system. Inevitably, sport became subject to apartheid. With no avenue to professional sports or high-level amateur sports, black people played sports only in isolation, often unknown to the international sporting community.

Although there was much internal black resistance to this, still not fully documented by historians, it was in the early 1960s that the leaders of the South African Non-Racial Olympic Committee began to press the outside world to intervene in the sports arena. The IOC prohibited apartheid South Africa from participating in the Olympics in Tokyo in 1964, and again in

1968 in Mexico City, after 32 other African teams said they would boycott the event if South Africa were allowed to attend. Two years later South Africa was expelled from the Olympics. However, rugby and cricket were more important to white South Africans than the Olympics, and it was not until those teams began to face international isolation that apartheid began to crumble. Of course it was not just sport that contributed to the political change, but sporting sanctions against white South Africans certainly played a part in forcing it to happen. Formal apartheid was renounced; South Africa returned to the Olympic Movement in 1992; and in 1994 the first non-white government took office.

Significantly, the new president, Nelson Mandela – who had spent 27 years in jail as a political prisoner – helped in sporting reconciliation when he donned a springbok rugby jersey (at that time still an emblem of white South African sport) to support the national team at the 1995 Rugby World Cup, held in South Africa. The crowd of 63,000 people – nearly all white – chanted the name of the man they had once feared and despised. When South Africa won the 1995 World Cup, there was a solitary black player in the side. When the triumph was repeated in 2007 there were two black players. In 2019, when the Springboks won the William Webb Ellis Cup for the third time, eleven of the 31-man squad were black, including the captain, Siya Kolisi, a man born the day before the formal repeal of apartheid.

ACTIVIST ATHLETES

In February 2019 the NFL agreed an out-of-court settlement with Colin Kaepernick, who had failed to secure even a third-string spot on the roster of any NFL team. This was not through lack of talent, but because of his decision in 2016 to kneel during the American national anthem as a protest against the oppression of black Americans, and especially against police brutality towards them. A wave of players followed suit, morphing the protest into an anti-Donald Trump one after the president waded in to denounce Kaepernick and his ilk. Trump's White House continually argued that the protest was unpatriotic and disrespectful towards the American flag and American troops. What Kaepernick did was not unique. Other elite American sportsmen have stood up (or knelt) to support issues on which they felt strongly. Muhammad Ali is perhaps one of the best-known American athletes to take a major political stand; he refused to be drafted into the Vietnam War – a refusal that involved prison time. He did so on the basis of his faith, he said, but he did note the cruel irony of asking black men to fight in Vietnam for a country that treated them as subhuman. More recently, NBA players such as LeBron James and the late Kobe Bryant helped the Black Lives Matter movement to pick up steam by wearing supportive shirts following the death of Eric Garner, who in 2014 was fatally choked by the police officers arresting him in New York.

MUHAMMAD ALI (1942–2016)

On 6 June 1964, just two weeks after first becoming heavyweight boxing champion of the world, Cassius Marcellus Clay Jr announced that henceforth he would be known as Muhammad Ali, an acknowledgement of his self-identification as a Muslim. He never registered this change legally, since that would have meant recognizing white authority. This allowed his critics leeway to refuse to respect his new name, and it was not until the early 1970s that 'Muhammad Ali' became generally used in newspaper reports. Popes change their names, actors adopt stage names and writers take pen names, but Ali knew that his new nomenclature was controversial because it was non-white and non-Christian, and signalled his allegiance to black nationalism. As an 'uppity black', he offended many whites in what was still a segregated nation, and as a believer in racial separatism he alienated large portions of the black community who sought integration via the civil rights movement.

Ali first fought as an amateur in 1954, winning on a split decision, and six years later he reached the final of the light heavyweight section at the Rome Olympics, winning gold, a medal some say he later threw away in disgust when on his return to Louisville he was feted by the city mayor but later refused service in a local segregated restaurant. He turned professional, and by 1964 he felt ready to challenge Sonny Liston for the world heavyweight title. Liston was a short-odds favourite, but Ali outmanoeuvred him and Liston quit after six rounds.

A rematch in 1965 lasted less than two minutes, with Liston controversially counted out.

Ali's belief in Islam was strong. He divorced his first wife for refusing to conform to its standards of behaviour, twice went on the hajj pilgrimage, and in 1967 refused – as a conscientious objector on religious grounds – to serve in the American army in Vietnam, famously remarking that 'no Viet Cong never called me nigger'. For this the boxing authorities stripped him of his titles and the political ones had him sentenced to gaol, although he stayed out on bail while the courts considered his appeal. As attitudes to the war changed he was allowed to box again in late 1970, and the Supreme Court quashed his conviction the following year. His actions made him an icon for the counterculture generation of the time.

The way was open for Ali to challenge for the world title again, but first he had to overcome Joe Frazier. He lost on points in their first bout – his first defeat in 31 contests – but won the rematch. He then took on the formidable George Foreman in 1974 for the title in Kinshasa, Zaire (now the Democratic Republic of the Congo), in what the promoter Don King labelled the 'Rumble in the Jungle', the most watched televised sports event to that date. African political leaders were keen to put their countries on the world stage by hosting international sports events. FIFA and the IOC shied away but boxing, with its plethora of competing ruling bodies, was willing to take the money – in this case a purse of $10 million, the most lucrative to that date. Ali publicized the fight as one between a black Muslim nationalist, anti-colonialist and black rights activist and a black representative of the American political establishment, a man who had waved the Stars and Stripes in the ring after winning gold at the Mexico Olympics. He taunted and evaded Foreman, tiring him before an eighth-round knock-out. Ali lost the title to Leon Spinks in 1978, but defeated him in a rematch, becoming the first heavyweight to win the title three times. He was 'the Greatest', but he failed to recognize when it was time to retire and lost the last two bouts of his career to Larry Holmes in 1980 and Trevor Berbick in 1981, taking his career losses to 5 from 61 fights.

Ali twice changed the style of heavyweight boxing. In his early career, in his own words, he 'floated like a butterfly and stung like a bee', using his speed and footwork to manipulate his opponents around the ring rather than participate in old-fashioned slugging matches. Later, when meeting powerful rivals he adopted his 'Rope -a-Dope' technique, in which he made them miss by bending his body or absorbed their punishment on his arms until they tired.

Time can change attitudes and behaviour. Ali himself disavowed the Nation of Islam and turned to Sunni Islam, becoming a supporter of racial integration; he returned to the Olympics in 1996, when he proudly carried the American flag at the opening ceremony of the Atlanta Games; and in 2005 in downtown Louisville, where he had once been turned away from a restaurant, the Muhammed Ali Center opened, devoted to the boxer's memory and causes. After retirement he devoted much of his time to philanthropy, using his name to raise millions for charities worldwide.

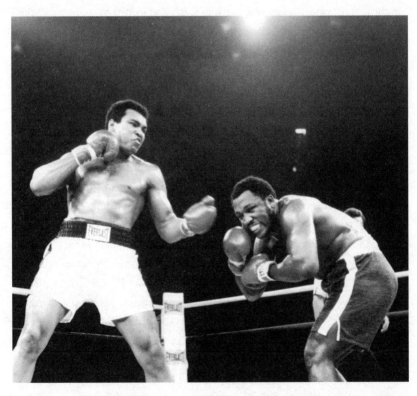

'The Thrilla in Manila 1975': Ali (in white shorts) on his way to victory over Joe Frazier in their third encounter.

These Americans were not alone in using their talent to protest against what they perceived as attacks on human rights. The silver medallist in the marathon at the Rio Games in 2016, the Ethiopian Feyisa Lilesa, crossed his wrists above his head as he finished, making a gesture of protest against the government of the country he was representing. He did the same at the awards ceremony, before – perhaps wisely – seeking political asylum. In the 1990s the Zimbabwean cricketers Andy Flower and Henry Olonga, one white, the other black, wore black armbands to protest at the way President Robert Mugabe was running the country. Neither of them ever represented their country again.

Perhaps the most famous protest is that from 1968 at the Mexico Olympics, where John Carlos and Tommie Smith made headlines across the world when they gave the black power salute on the medal podium. They were protesting against poverty, discrimination and inequality, and wore black gloves to symbolize strength and unity, beads to represent lynching, and no shoes to represent poverty. Not only were they expelled from the Games, but also their protest brought them death threats. Sports administrators (with a few exceptions) felt the civil-rights struggle had no place in the sports arena; college coaches and presidents professed that sport was more important than civil rights; and the public was persuaded that civil-rights activists in sport were 'radicals', a value-loaded term that inferred undesirability. Many in sport argued that the sector had given black athletes opportunities for economic advancement and that those who used it for political protest were being ungrateful. Many people forget that there was a third protester on the podium, the silver medallist Peter Norman, a white sprinter from Australia, who wore a human-rights badge in support of his fellow medallists. It was Norman who, when Carlos realized he had forgotten his own gloves, suggested that he share Smith's pair, one wearing a right glove, the other a left one. Norman suffered persecution for his actions too, but in 2012 he finally gained an official state apology from the Australian government, and in 2018 the Australian Olympic Committee bestowed a posthumous Order of Merit on him.

These three were not the first athletes to make a political protest. At the 1906 Intercalated Games in Athens, the Irish long jumper Peter O'Connor won a silver medal. He was an Irish nationalist, one of many seeking independence from Great Britain, but he had to represent Great Britain as mandated by the IOC. However, when the Union Jack was raised at the medal ceremony he climbed up the flagpole and waved a large green flag emblazoned with the words 'Erin Go Bragh' – 'Ireland forever'. His fellow nationalist and teammate Con Leahy held a similar flag at the base of the pole.

Part of the Olympic Charter says that it is a human right to be able to participate in sport. Indeed, as we have seen, South Africa was at one stage expelled for denying this to its black population. Yet for the period of the Games, athletes must sign away their rights and agree not to wear branded clothing of unauthorized sponsors when receiving medals. Nor, under Rule 59 of the Olympic Code of Conduct, can they post web diaries. In the opinion of the IOC, that would be tantamount to being a journalist, and only accredited journalists have access to Olympic Village and its stories. Moreover, an athlete might break a story, which would be unfair on the 'media partners' who have paid millions for exclusive rights. For 2021 in Tokyo the IOC has prohibited any political messaging including signs, armbands and gestures of a political nature during all ceremonies and events, and at the Olympic Village. Human-rights assessments are now part of the bidding programme for the Olympics and the FIFA World Cup (which explains some recent choices!). However, I suspect that, as with legacy requirements, it will be a matter of weasel words and lip service by the parties concerned.

No one can compel athletes to become activists, but some athletes disregard human-rights abuses in their legitimate desire to make a living. Nations with poor human-rights records attempt to use the lure of glamorous sporting events to 'sportswash' their reputations. Those sportspeople who played in apartheid South Africa or who, these days, pocket large sums of appearance money in Middle Eastern events usually excuse their actions on two grounds. First, and most justifiable, is that sport should

The hypocritical oath?

'The practice of sport is a human right. Every individual must have the possibility of practising sport, without discrimination of any kind and in the Olympic spirit, which requires mutual understanding with a spirit of friendship, solidarity and fair play . . . Any form of discrimination with regard to a country or a person on grounds of race, religion, politics, gender or otherwise is incompatible with belonging to the Olympic Movement.'
International Olympic Committee Charter, 28 January 2011

not be singled out when businesses of all types, including arms dealers, trade with abhorrent nations. Second, and this one flies in the face of all evidence, is that contact with such nations helps to change their outlook. Be honest: just say the money is more important than your conscience.

SPORT FOR DEVELOPMENT AND PEACE

A significant political development in the sports world over the past couple of decades has been Sport for Development and Peace, usually abbreviated to SDP. This involves the deliberate use of sport and physical activity to attain specific development objectives, usually in lower-income nations but sometimes in pockets of deprivation in higher-income ones. The objectives are generally focused on the areas of child and youth development, health, gender equality, social inclusion, educational development and post-conflict resolution. There can be a diverse set of entities involved, generally with no overarching control, ranging from United Nations agencies to faith schools.

The main international stakeholders have been intergovernmental organizations, especially agencies of the United Nations, whose involvement in SDP began in 2001 with the appointment of a special advisor in the area. The United Nations established an Inter-Agency Task Force in 2002 and a Working Group in 2004, resulting, in 2005, in a designated United Nations Office on Sport for Development and Peace (UNOSDP). There followed an outpouring of policy documents and resolutions, unfortunately not matched by action in the field. In a surprising move in 2017, the UNOSDP was closed and a new relationship established with the IOC. However, the latter has done relatively little, unlike (for all its faults) FIFA, which has financed a significant number of football-related SDP projects throughout the developing world. All these agencies suffer from the problem of whether the richer nations are using the clout of their funding to promote their own ideologies; is it in fact just a newer version of colonialism?

Some SDP projects impinge on education, health and other fields that are ultimately the province of government. This brings the problem of a hangover of colonialism, when one side thinks it knows best and the other rejects any imposition of ideas from outside. Then there is the basic problem of the prioritization of winning medals within the sports policies of emerging nations (one idea they have adopted from wealthier countries). Much more influential – in a positive way – in most countries have been non-governmental organizations, but they suffer from short-termism in continually having to seek funds to keep their projects afloat. Overall, SDP has been piecemeal in its impact: a good idea thwarted by politics and practicalities.

SUFFER THE LITTLE CHILDREN

Readers may have felt they were hard done by when they were punished at school for forgetting their sports togs. Some might feel that compulsory school sport was punishment in itself. However, these are minor complaints considering the way in which some children have been abused in the sports world. No doubt many professionals have felt exploited by their employers restricting their ability to change jobs and imposing limits on their earnings, but these are normally adults, capable of making life choices. In contrast, children involved in sport have no such discretion and can be subjected to severe exploitation.

Child labour in sport is often regarded as a relatively modern phenomenon, usually with exploitative implications: the children trafficked from Pakistan to virtual slavery in the United Arab Emirates as camel racers; the Communist bloc girl gymnasts having puberty deliberately delayed; and the teenage African footballers discarded when they fail to make the grade in Europe. Yet there have been historical precursors.

In mid-nineteenth-century Britain racehorse owners sometimes resorted to using child riders in an attempt to gain an advantage. The 'infant phenomenon' was legislated away by the Jockey Club's introduction of minimum weights, but no age limit was imposed until the 1960s, when it was set at fifteen. Children who wished to become jockeys faced a seven-year apprenticeship during which trainers were supposed to teach them the skills of jockeyship. Unfortunately, too many regarded the apprentice simply as cheap stable labour. Stories also abound of over-harsh discipline. The apprenticeship was reduced to three years by the 1970s, and an alternative to in-stable tuition began to be provided by the British Racing School at Newmarket and the Northern Racing College at Bawtry in Yorkshire. Making the grade remained as difficult as ever. Of the 187 apprentices registered in 1900, only 75 became jockeys and a mere 23

(12 per cent) continued as such for more than three years. A century later the director of the British Racing School estimated that nine out of ten failed to become full professional jockeys.

Another area of child labour was in golf, where caddying became a niche employment market for children that expanded significantly in the four decades before 1914. At many golf clubs playing without a caddy was socially unacceptable, even if not specifically regulated against. Before the invention of the golf bag in the 1890s it was impractical, but generally there was the implication that the manual labour associated with a round of golf should be done by someone other than the player. The majority of caddies were boys or young men, with a leavening of adults and, at weekends, schoolboys to meet the peak demand. In 1909 it was estimated that 20,000 boys were employed as caddies, and critics believed that most were living a 'casual, irresponsible and purposeless life'.

The state intervened indirectly in the labour market for caddies by introducing compulsory schooling and National Insurance. The last three decades of the nineteenth century were a period in which childhood was progressively lengthened as compulsory full-time schooling, introduced in 1870, replaced wage-earning as the accepted activity for many children. The age to which a child had to attend school had been first set at ten, but was raised to eleven in 1893 and twelve in 1899, although the last change was disregarded in many rural areas as recalcitrant employers and needy parents conspired to thwart its enforcement. The demand for boy bag carriers by members of golf clubs was a great temptation to poor parents looking to supplement the family income, to the extent that in 1902 the school inspectorate reported on 'children of nine, eight and even seven years old having been employed to drag clubs round the links'.

Caddies were paid relatively well for what they did. A school leaver in Dorset could earn almost as much as his agricultural labouring father for significantly less effort and time. However, critics considered such earnings demoralizing because they encouraged youths to have false ex-pectations of future income and because the nature of caddying, which required few transferable skills, offered little gateway to other gainful skilled employment (a survey undertaken in 1912 emphasized the 'blind alley' nature of the job). For some, albeit a minority, there was a future in golf. Nevertheless, even under the most optimistic estimations, less than 2 per cent of caddies became club professionals. Others might secure apprenticeships as club-makers or, as at the Royal Mid-Surrey club in Richmond, where the best caddies were also employed as green-men, they might progress to greenkeeping posts elsewhere. For most, however, caddying proved to be a dead-end job. Once given notice by the clubs at the age of sixteen, as was often the practice, especially after the coming of compulsory National Insurance, these boys drifted into the ranks of unskilled labour or the unemployed.

The work itself was not arduous, but it had to be undertaken in whatever weather golfers opted to play in, and their costumes might have been more suited to the elements than those of the caddies. Some clubs provided a shelter in which caddies could wait before beginning a round, but out on the course there was no protection from wind or rain. There was also a major moral problem. The caddie was effectively on a zero-hours contract and operated in a casual labour market where the demand for his services was dependent on the number of players on a particular day. Bad weather, transport disruption and the change in seasons meant that there was no guarantee of employment. Moreover, golfers tee off at intervals, so caddies could wait around for a while before picking up a bag, leading to a situation where, according to one critic, 'the regular caddie has about five hours' leisure five days a week, but nothing to do to fill them except idling or gambling'.

The question is whether such working and welfare conditions could be considered bad enough to amount to child exploitation and abuse. Clearly, the child caddie can be said to have suffered if we retrospectively apply the Convention on the Rights of the Child drafted by the United Nations in 1989. There was no way in which the golf clubs or members followed the principle that the best interests of the child should be of primary concern. Yet by contemporary standards caddies were not exploited economically. Although they were often competing with adults in the labour market, pay differentials and job opportunities generally reflected knowledge and experience, not age. The introduction of National Insurance actually led to positive discrimination in favour of younger caddies, but the increased enforcement of education legislation limited its impact on those still at school. For boys, the earnings were good, but there was concern that this gave them a false view of life and led many not to prepare for the years after caddying. Non-wage rewards were less generous, with generally inadequate food, shelter and sanitary arrangements. Some commentators saw possible health and moral problems in that the boys were often hanging around the club in all weathers waiting for employment, but worse than this was the fact that this might be in the company of adult males who, except at long-established clubs, were regarded as men of dubious character. It was feared that 'loafing habits' could be acquired while waiting for employment 'under insufficient supervision and in an uncivilized environment'.

In more modern times, we find the consequences of the international specialization of trade in sporting goods, in which developed countries buy goods made in less developed countries. In the early 1990s much of the world's output of footballs stemmed from young boys and girls hand-sewing panels of leather or synthetic materials. At the time the industry centred on Sialkot in Pakistan. A football could sell for £50, but the six-year-old Pakistani child who stitched it together was paid the equivalent of 10 pence. Even with distribution and marketing costs, and allowing for the press's gravitation to worst-case scenarios, this was a classic example of corporate capitalism exploiting market forces to its advantage. Capitalism has no moral principles where labour is plentiful and cheap; legally, the primary duty is always to shareholders, not the workforce. In some respects the situation of the children stitching footballs is reminiscent of that of the child caddies in Edwardian Britain, in that the children's earnings made a significant contribution to family income and that their social welfare was generally disregarded. But there were differences. Child stitchers could not earn nearly as much as their fathers, which was the case with rural caddies, and the point of production was not as fixed as in golf, so, with labour being abundant, employers could easily move to another village.

The outcry when the *Sunday Times* newspaper exposed the situation in Pakistan led to the Atlanta Agreement of 1997, which was signed by the Sialkot Chamber of Commerce and Industry, the International Labour Organization (ILO) and UNICEF, and which sought to eliminate the involvement of children under fourteen in making footballs. Because it was difficult to inspect home production, one aim was to allow football stitching only in premises that could be more easily monitored. The sports equipment manufacturers were not party to the agreement, but they did agree to purchase footballs only from companies that accepted ILO monitoring. Not until they were exposed did the multinationals see a need to change the system. Children certainly seem to have been absent from the monitored sewing centres since, but there are allegations of hidden production centres and that some children have moved into other trades, such as brickmaking, where conditions are even worse. The agreements were only with the major international sports goods companies, and applied only to the top grade of production. Moreover, there is no credible way of identifying whether or not a football has been produced by a child.

Child labour is illegal in India and Pakistan, but few seem to care that the law is infringed to produce sports equipment. Not the national or state governments, who simply accept the situation; not the multinational corporations, which subcontract the production of their wares to middlemen in those nations; not even the charity Save the Children, which argued that stitching footballs was not as bad as other trades; and certainly not the consumers who continued to buy footballs by the million.

Clearly, children need protection. They need it within sport to safeguard themselves from predatory coaches; they need it around sport to prevent exploitation in the supply of sports equipment; and they need it through sport, such as being taught how to swim to save some of the 17,000 Bangladeshi children aged between one and five who drown each year. Some steps have been taken. To help protect children from trafficking, FIFA now bans the transfer of under-18 footballers to other countries unless the parents have moved for non-footballing reasons or the player already lives within 100 km (62 mi.) of the new club; and the new club must meet criteria relating to education, living conditions and general support.

Every country in the world but one has signed the United Nations Convention on the Rights of the Child: the exception is the United States, which claims that to do so would contravene its constitution. This is the country where kids are made to play like adults in a $15 billion-a-year youth sports economy. In the past children played games; now they are forced to play sport, often with that obvious form of overt child abuse, the ugly parent screaming on the sidelines. When will UNICEF take this challenge on?

20

RUNNING OR RUINING THE GAME: RULES AND RULE-MAKERS

S ports need rules. Competitive sports require them to decide a winner, and ritual ones to show participants how to play their part. It is also rules that distinguish the sophisticated games of sport from the more naive ones of play. Participants in the latter have the freedom to improvise and alter how the game is played while it is in progress, but in sport the rulebook must be obeyed, at least for the duration of the event. Rules matter because they distinguish one sport from another. Rules matter because they can affect the diffusion of a sport; without standardized rules a sport cannot spread. Indeed, the distinguished intellectual Melvyn Bragg has claimed in his *Twelve Books that Changed the World* that it was the simplicity and brevity of the rules in the FA Laws of Football – initially just thirteen in all – that helped to make soccer the world game. Rules matter because they can tell us about the attitudes and prejudices of those who set them; we can learn what they thought of violence, equality, gambling, winning and losing, and even race and gender.

Rules fall into several categories. There are constitutive rules, both proscriptive and prescriptive, which set the formal rules of play and define the required equipment and facilities. These generally serve to make sport more difficult or complex, such as the offside rule in soccer and lbw in cricket. Auxiliary rules, which specify and control eligibility, come in two forms: participation rules and competition rules. The former consider who can participate in a sport. There is nothing inherent in the sports themselves to prevent the vertically challenged from playing basketball or entering the high jump, but those who set rules can determine who is actually allowed to play a sport. Complex rules about ancestry led to chivalric apartheid in German tournaments throughout the Middle Ages. The FA's attitude to female participation for most of the twentieth century also demonstrates that exclusion is a cultural creation.

Competition rules consider who can participate in particular events, and are set by the organizers of the league or championship. For an illustration, let's turn to golf and ask, 'How open is the Open Championship?' Golfers used to be able just to turn up, pay their entry fee and bash the ball down the first fairway. Well, in fact, they didn't. When the Open originated in the 1860s the players had to be caddies of good reputation with a letter from their employing club to say so. 'Caddy' at this time meant not a bag carrier but a professional player; no amateurs were allowed to play. This changed, however, and by the 1890s professionals and amateurs battled together. Then qualifying tournaments were brought in because of the increasing number of players who wanted to participate. There had been a move from subjectivity ('good conduct') to objectivity ('good play').

Finally, regulatory rules have nothing to do with the sport itself but are concerned with image management. They include that first official tennis notice of the All England Club, which requested gentlemen 'not to play in their shirt sleeves when ladies are present', or the dress codes enforced at many golf clubs, which have nothing to do with any ability to play the game.

Rules are there to prevent cheating. Not all knights were good guys, so rules of varying degrees of sophistication governed all medieval chivalric sporting activities, from the melee tournaments to the combats on foot. Interestingly, there were also rules governing the behaviour of spectators, so that their actions would not distract the participants. When there are no rules, by definition you cannot cheat, but once they are in place there will be those who seek an advantage by bending them. This leads to more rules. Those desperate to win will find ways around them, and the cycle of cumulative causation is perpetuated. Those who want to play fair have to play by the rules brought in to counteract the actions of those who don't.

In 1892 football pitches were given new markings as the penalty kick was introduced into the game. In vain Corinthian players such as C. B. Fry protested that only a cad would deliberately foul his opponent; some sides who subscribed to his view refused to score from penalties.

Nevertheless, they still had to play on pitches that had penalty areas marked out. The expansion of the rules of golf is a prime example of cumulative causation in which rule changes beget further changes in attempts at clarification. The first published rules of golf came in 1744 for the gentlemen who played on Leith Links in Edinburgh, and consisted of thirteen bald statements taking up just one page, with little subclause qualification. (Interestingly, nowhere does it say that the object of the game is to get the ball into the hole, so the next time you are having a bad day on the greens, just say to your opponent, 'I'm playing the Leith rules today.') By 1961 these 13 articles had swelled to 41, and they took up 54 pages of the *Golfer's Handbook* (not including an index of 22 pages, and 40 pages outlining particular decisions). The published rules of 1992 took up 85 pages, and a pocket-sized version of the current rules runs to 191 pages.

Rule-setting is a dynamic process, and few regulations are set in stone. Although the basic rules of the world's most popular sports were set by the early twentieth century, minor rule changes have occurred constantly to make sport safer, fairer and more entertaining. Helmets have become compulsory in horse racing; in baseball the pitching mound has been lowered to give the batter a better chance; and in basketball the time clock has been brought in. Any schema of rule formation must take account of the fact that sport has changed in character and that professional or elite sport is a different product from that which emerged during the 'games revolution' of mid-Victorian Britain. Moreover, the pressure leading to change in sport – and in its rules – have also altered. Commercial factors had a role in the nineteenth century, but they were much less significant than they are today, and the media at that time had little influence at all.

PLAYING REGULATIONS

The rules that govern how each sport is played have developed through several stages, beginning with the 'articles of agreement' that were common to most stake-money contests in the eighteenth and early nineteenth centuries. In essence they were 'play or pay' contracts between the contending parties and set out the particular terms of the intended contest, such as times, places, stakes and the means of settling disputes. For example, in the articles for a cricket match in 1727 between teams organized by the

Second Duke of Richmond and Mr Alan Broderick, heir to Viscount Middleton, one party insisted that the other could choose only men who had played in the team's last two matches; in return, his opponent allowed only men who had resided within 3 mi. (5 km) of the venue since Lady Day (the usual hiring time for new servants). These early rules were all one-off, specific to a particular contest, but gradually certain features became commonplace in challenges and match arrangements as participants saw the sense in building on what already existed. Rules for specific events were giving way to rules of sport. Standardization and universality were in the offing, but local and regional interests and circumstances remained influential. Named sets of rules emerged that were often voluntarily adopted for contests, such as the Broughton rules for boxing, issued in 1743 (see Chapter Six).

The next stage involved the development of governing bodies. By the 1820s, and in some cases much earlier, several sports had a recognized central organization. Coursing had the Swaffham Club, sailing the Cumberland Club, prizefighting the Pugilistic Club, archery the Toxophilite Society and cricket Marylebone Cricket Club (MCC). As new sports developed, so did national ruling bodies for them. Although the authority of a central organization was welcomed in most sports by those who sought the benefits of uniform regulations, there were always recalcitrants who preferred other versions. The next stage thus involved the development of mechanisms and processes to enforce acceptance of these rules more generally. These included licensing systems and the non-recognition of those who did not agree to the adoption of the rules. In the 1870s the Jockey Club developed the idea of 'recognized' meetings held under its rules, and any jockey, trainer or horse who participated in unrecognized ones was prohibited from the approved variety.

As sport became internationalized, pan-national organizations emerged to determine both the constitutive rules for a particular sport and also auxiliary rules for international competitions; to the chagrin of British rule-makers, global politics sometimes came into play. The establishment of the IOC in 1894 was an early sign that Britain's hegemony might be challenged, but it, unlike later organizations, did not threaten the autonomy of the British bodies that had pioneered rule-setting in their particular sports. In contrast, in soccer for example, although the home nations retain special voting rights, the power base of both FIFA and the

Union of European Football Associations (UEFA) is now rarely influenced by the founders of the game. In cricket – perhaps the imperial sport par excellence – the English authority managed to hang on to power until the late 1980s. An Imperial Cricket Council, comprising England, Australia and South Africa, had been set up in 1909, and, despite expanding to bring in other Test-playing nations, it remained virtually an offshoot of the MCC and firmly under the control of the parent body. By 1989, however, the political strength of the Asian bloc had forced the transformation of the group into the International Cricket Council; the initials remained, but the imperialism had gone. It was more than symbolic when in 2005 its headquarters was shifted from Lord's Cricket Ground to Dubai. Increasingly, the politics within the new organization led to the formal codification of regulations for international cricket, rather than a system based on unspoken and unwritten codes of behaviour.

RULES AND GAMBLING

Going back to our single page of golf rules in 1744, let me make a plea for a better understanding of the role of gambling in rule formation. At about the same time two other codes emerged: Jack Broughton's rules of the prize-ring (1743) and the cricket rules of the Conduit Club (1744). A possible reason for this congruence is that in 1740 an Act of Parliament set a minimum limit for prize money for any horse race. This led to a decline in the volume of horse racing, perhaps leading gamblers to ask what else they might bet on – with the answer being golf, pugilism and cricket. These gamblers were exhibiting 'conspicuous consumption', and there was little else to spend large sums of money on. However, although prepared to lose £1,000 on a cricket match, they were not willing to throw their money away. They therefore insisted on the formulation of a framework within which they risked their money, leading to the publication of written rules in those sports. In 1750 Parliament rescinded the prize-money legislation in horse racing, but the rules had now been put in place and were not going to be abandoned.

Since then gambling has influenced the rules of sport in two ways: one concerned with creating equality of opportunity to win; the other involving regulations to eliminate cheating and sharp practice. It is not conducive to gambling that the race should always go to the swiftest, the fight to the strongest, or victory to the most talented. Such predictability of outcome does not create a betting market, because every potential punter knows who will win. The commonest method of creating uncertainty of outcome was to make some participants run further than others, carry more weight, or play against a team with more players. Nevertheless, it should be stressed that, within this system of handicapping the better performers, most other rules of the sport continued to be applied; allowing the slower runners to trip the faster ones or the weaker boxers to carry cudgels was not contemplated. If the result is predictable, there is no betting market; equally, if corruption renders form and skill meaningless, bettors will withdraw. Although the fair-play movement attempted to ban gambling because of its perceived evil influence on sporting participants, the gambling industry itself has generally sought to protect the integrity of sport. Gamblers were more concerned with fair betting than with fair play, but, inevitably, the latter was a by-product of the former.

SPORT AND THE LAW

As a digression, it should be noted that historically sport has been used occasionally by the law to settle non-sporting disputes. Trial by combat was frequently resorted to in medieval times, and it is argued in some quarters that fencing as a sport emerged from such judicial duels. This was not the case only in Europe. Between 1622 and 1949 endurance contests were conducted irregularly in rural China to settle disputes over the distribution of public resources (usually water rights). The competitions included running long distances in iron boots heated on a fire, or leaping into pots of hot oil to recover coins. Competitors demonstrated bravery, but such manliness often cost them their lives.

Generally, however, it was the law that was used to settle sporting disputes, often over betting. This was especially true of England during the Georgian period, a time when there was a virtual absence of final authority within the sports themselves. The regulatory bodies, if they existed at all, were still uncertain of their powers and few, if any, had begun to recognize themselves as ruling institutions, even at the end of the era. As central rule-making authorities consolidated their positions, there was less recourse to the courts. Now the law is becoming interventionist once more, partly because trust in professionals has returned to late

Victorian levels and in some quarters the courts have been seen as the way to police their activities. This was not considered appropriate or necessary in the nineteenth century, when amateurs were in charge of sport and their decisions were accepted virtually without question. These days, the economic and financial implications of any judgments by sports authorities often lead to legal challenges. It is now clear to those running sport that informal understandings, however hallowed by tradition, count for little in law.

The law has forced changes to the rules of some sports, most significantly in those that were banned, such as cockfighting and bare-knuckle boxing. Once they became underground activities, they lacked central organization and codified rules. Prizefighting died in the mid-nineteenth century, prosecuted out of existence as a corrupt, illegal sport with no defenders in high places. When it was resurrected in the guise of boxing, bare knuckles were covered with gloves, fixed-time rounds were introduced and results could be determined on points rather than by exhaustion, all of which were acceptable to the law. More generally, the law has forced greater precision in those rules dealing with disciplinary procedures, so that transgressors cannot escape punishment on technicalities or because their legal or human rights were infringed.

Internal rule-setting is being influenced by the external imposition of rules. A major contribution of the law has been to bring the outside world into sport, forcing administrators to accept that sport is not a separate, isolated entity devoid of responsibilities for discriminatory policies, the rights of the labour force and the behaviour of players on the field. Handbooks of many sports now include clauses relating to discrimination. Selection policies for teams are a case in point. Human-rights legislation and a growing litigious tendency among athletes has encouraged sports associations to formally publish their selection policies and appeals procedures.

Although there is still a preference by both legal and sporting authorities to keep disciplinary procedures in-house, there is now more likelihood of the law intervening in cases of assault outside the rules of the game. On-field cheating such as simulated fouls, faked injuries or ball-tampering has not yet reached the courts, but off-field is another matter. In 2017 a scouting director for the St Louis Cardinals baseball team was sentenced to prison for hacking into the database of its rivals the Houston Astros. In

Britain in 2000 the Welsh team from Usk won the British village cricket competition, beating a team from Cornwall in the final. However, when one of the Cornish players decided to take his post-season holiday in Wales, he detoured to have a look at the victors' ground. To his surprise, as he entered Usk he found a road sign proclaiming that this was a 'historic *town*', albeit one with a population of just over 2,000 souls. The Cornish team lodged a protest and Usk had to hand over the title. This was not the end of the matter; Usk then appealed to the High Court on the grounds that the sign was just for tourists, but there the full majesty of the law upheld the view that Usk had breached the competition rules and should be disqualified.

FAIR PLAY

The notion of fair play and generosity of spirit among participants was largely alien to the ancient Greeks. Chivalrous sporting conduct dates back to medieval tournaments, but the concept of 'fair play' in sport emerged as part of the games revolution in mid-Victorian Britain. Consequently it spread internationally with the export of British sport and the accompanying cultural baggage of sporting ethics. Even parts of the world that were not pink on the map adopted British ideals. The French, for example, had 'le fair play' added to their sporting lexicon. By the 1890s fair play featured as one of the aims of the modern Olympic movement. It means more than simply adopting the norm of playing by the written rules of the sport, accepting what is prescribed and proscribed by the authorities. There were also unwritten rules that conveyed expectations about the manner in which the game ought to be played by true adherents of fair play. These denoted behaviour that was not specified in the written rules but which encompassed human virtues such as self-discipline, modesty, generosity, tolerance, respect and courtesy, characteristics that became embedded in the athletic ideology of muscular Christianity. To the real

Playing by the rules

'Serious sport has nothing to do with fair play. It is bound up with hatred, jealousy, boastfulness, disregard of all rules and sadistic pleasure in witnessing violence: in other words it is war minus the shooting.'
George Orwell, 'The Sporting Spirit', *The Tribune*, 14 December 1945

advocates of fair play, the ideological traffic was two-way; sport was also a classroom for the teaching of moral values that would transfer into the wider world, as reflected in vernacular phrases such as 'hitting below the belt' and 'it's not cricket'.

In its absolute, ideal form, fair play probably rarely existed except among the most Corinthian of players, but recent years have brought concerns that fair play and ethical sporting conduct have diminished. Whether there is still room for fair play in elite sport is often questioned. Reminiscent of the debate about the necessity to introduce the penalty kick in soccer, many commentators now believe that the high economic rewards for winners in elite sport have led the ends to justify the means. Professionals have integrated rule-bending into their on-field skills of deception, so that efficient deceit and tactical fouls are part of what counts as skilful performance in sport. Footballers are expected to commit a 'professional foul' (and accept the consequences) to prevent an opponent from scoring, and the law on altering the condition of the ball is routinely broken in cricket.

Much is still often made, particularly in works on the amateur ethos, of the so-called unwritten rules of sport: the sportsmanship that goes way beyond the rulebook. One problem with this that I found when preparing a report for the UK Sports Council in 2004 was a general reluctance to define what fair play actually was. It was implicit rather than explicit. References to the 'spirit of golf', the 'ethos of cricket' or 'Olympic ideals' inferred that those to whom the concepts were directed would intuitively understand what was meant. Possibly that is true in a general sense, but more precision is needed, particularly for new entrants to a sport, if discussion at cross purposes is to be avoided. 'Fair play' and 'sporting conduct' are nebulous concepts that can mean different things to different people and to different cultures.

The fair-play movement was concerned with what might be termed the 'nice' unwritten rules, such as not doing anything to put your opponent off and generally 'playing the game'. But there are also 'nasty' unwritten rules. Those who decry the lack of adherence to the unwritten rules of etiquette and fair play could take solace in the fact that other undeclared rules have fallen to the challenge of law and government policy. These were the ones that offered a darker aspect, the very opposite of fair play: in essence the 'nod and wink' associated with the discriminatory policies practised (but not openly espoused) by some sports bodies that kept Jewish people out of golf clubs or led to the non-selection of gay players for some teams. In the past such policies were rarely challenged, but now human-rights legislation, anti-discriminatory laws and the requirements of government and lottery funding have eroded some of the worst unwritten auxiliary rules.

WHOSE RULES?

Although a few early rule-makers, such as Jack Broughton, were accepted because of their experience and personality, most became rulers by virtue of their social position (and involvement in sport). The ruling bodies to which they belonged were not democratic institutions – as private clubs, they were at liberty to determine who could be members – so the rules of sport in the eighteenth and early nineteenth century were generally being developed by the aristocracy and the gentry. However, by the time the Football Association (1863) and the Rugby Football Union (1871) came into being, the social context had changed. The middle classes were becoming enfranchised both in politics and in sport. Certainly in the latter meritocracy was becoming more influential than social position, and democracy, in the form of club or association representation, was being enshrined in the constitutions of these rule-making bodies, which were in effect voluntaristic associations of voluntaristic associations. Apart from the IOC, which has some unelected, invited members, aristocratic involvement in the control of sport is now generally confined to figurehead patronage. Rules in most sports are made by elected representatives aided by paid administrators. Perhaps the bureaucracy involved occasionally hinders a quick response to a problem, but, politically, decisions are generally more acceptable (not just accepted) because they have been overtly discussed and debated, not just imposed by an oligarchy of self-selected individuals.

In this final section we will look at two contrasting case studies of rule-makers: the Jockey Club, which ran British racing for almost two centuries before having to cede power to a more representative organization; and FIFA, which has become an international non-governmental organization running what is often referred to as the 'world game'.

In 2002 the Jockey Club celebrated its 250th anniversary with a special race at one of its Newmarket meetings. It believed, as did most sports historians, that it had been founded in 1752, the date of the first mention of the club in Pond's *Sporting Kalendar*. In actuality, they celebrated far too late. Research has pushed the foundation date back as far as 1717, although it is not clear whether the 1752 club was a revival or continuation of the earlier one.

Whatever the real date, another myth that must be pricked is that at the time the Jockey Club controlled British racing. There is no evidence that at the outset it had any interest in doing so. At Newmarket, however, it was a different story, and there the Club attempted to control racing matters on the Heath, the vast stretch of land around the town that had been used from the sixteenth century as gallops, training grounds and racetrack. In 1758 it enforced compulsory 'weighing in' after a race, with any jockey who failed to do so being banned from riding again at Newmarket; and in 1771 it gave the stewards full authority to conduct racing affairs generally at Newmarket. Perhaps an indication of the power it had consolidated came in 1790, when, after the inconsistent running of his horse Escape, the Prince of Wales was informed that if he continued to employ Sam Chifney as his jockey, no gentleman would start against him at Newmarket. Although possibly aimed more at the servant than at the master, it showed that the Club would not be deferential if the integrity of the sport came under question. By this time it may have been seeking to formalize its influence in the wider racing world. In 1807 the *Racing Calendar* began to publish the results of certain 'Adjudged Cases', already decided by the Jockey Club, as a guide to local stewards throughout the country. Nine years later the Club published a note in the *Racing Calendar* that 'persons who may be inclined to submit any matters in dispute to the decision of the Stewards of the Jockey Club were at liberty to do so.' For the first time the Club was volunteering to intervene when requested to do so. Yet the number of cases published in the *Racing Calendar* remained low; a total of eleven in 1826 had risen to only nineteen by 1833, suggesting a limited take-up of the offer to adjudicate.

In 1832 the Club recommended 'for the sake of greater uniformity and certainty' the adoption of its rules to the stewards of other races, with the crucial accompanying statement that the Club would not adjudicate in disputes from elsewhere unless the Rules and Regulations of Newmarket had been in force. The bid for power was backed up both by social position and the force of law, although both had limited impact at the time. Beginning in 1835, the annual publication of the names of Jockey Club members in the *Racing Calendar*, an organ that commenced its list of racing abbreviations with D for Duke, E for Earl, M for Marquis and Ld for Lord, served to remind the racing world of the status of club membership. In a country that had limited democracy, social position was important both in its own right and for political patronage and influence. Additionally, the law was used to establish the Club's right to 'warn off' undesirable characters from the Newmarket courses and training gallops. But the situation was that until the 1860s, outside Newmarket and a minority of elite courses, the Jockey Club was ineffective; it had influence but little actual power.

A defining moment came in 1870, when the Club revised the rules of racing and drew a distinction between 'recognized' (that is to say, under Jockey Club rules) and 'unrecognized' meetings. Any owner, trainer, jockey or official who took part in unauthorized meetings would be disqualified from recognized racing. In the 1870s the Club used its power to restructure racing by ridding the sport of a mass of small-scale meetings that it felt did not contribute to the improvement of the thoroughbred, still an official rationale for horse racing. From 1877 all meetings wishing to be recognized by the Club had to provide a minimum of three hundred sovereigns in prize money for each day of racing, resulting in a dramatic decline in the number of authorized meetings. In effect the Club had abandoned any attempt to regulate lesser racing, concentrating instead on controlling the more significant meetings. The Club's grip on flat-racing was further tightened during the last quarter of the century when it introduced annual licences for jockeys, trainers, officials and racecourses; and warnings off were now reported to turf authorities in other countries, who, under reciprocal agreements, generally extended them to all racing under their control. Whereas Chifney in the late eighteenth century had been excluded solely from riding at Newmarket, malfeasant jockeys were now shut out of not just British racing but also many foreign meetings.

The Jockey Club began as an undemocratic organization, unrepresentative of racing in general and little changed over two hundred years or so. It remained fundamentally aristocratic and conservative, and even those more attuned to the concept of *noblesse oblige* began to feel that an exclusive private club could not speak on behalf of all the industry's stakeholders. The end was in sight for the Club having sole control of

British racing. In June 1993 monopoly became duopoly with the formation of the British Horseracing Board, which had a remit to run the commercial side of the sport while the Jockey Club was left with the role of regulator, in charge of race-day stewarding, discipline and security as well as having general responsibility for the rules. However, after a failure to take full cognisance of human-rights legislation, media publicity over corruption in the sport, and a conflict of interest via its ownership of racecourses, in 2007 it ceded all power to the newly created British Horseracing Authority. The Jockey Club, as the largest commercial group in the sport, now concentrates on making money to be ploughed back into the racing industry. It owns fifteen racecourses, training facilities at Newmarket and Lambourn, Berkshire, and runs the National Stud, which was transferred from the UK government to become a subsidiary in 2008.

Turning to soccer, the International Federation of Association Football (known as FIFA, from its French name) has been the ruling body of football (soccer), the world's most popular sport, since 1904. FIFA exerts control or influence over everyone who participates in football, from players to spectators, from coaches to club shareholders, from officials to sponsors. It has now transformed from being an international sporting body concerned with setting rules and promoting competition within Europe into a transnational organization pursuing cultural, humanitarian and development ambitions alongside UNESCO and UNICEF.

FIFA began as a Eurocentric organization keen to develop uniformity of rules in soccer and to promote international matches. Yet as early as the first years of the twentieth century, associations from North and South America, Australia, Africa and Asia joined, turning it into a more global organization. The greatest growth in membership came in the second half of the twentieth century as new nation states, often former colonies or breakaway territories, saw joining FIFA as a further symbol of political recognition. Today FIFA has more member countries than the United Nations, and has become one of the most financially powerful international non-governmental organizations. It has consolidated its position by securing from national governments regulatory privileges that have restricted state intervention in such matters as anti-competitive behaviour, control of employment relations, and internal governance. Even when the European Union did intervene over the Bosman affair, it then stepped back and allowed FIFA to reshape its own transfer rules.

From its origins FIFA adhered to three guiding principles covering membership, voting and general conduct. First, it accepted only one representative from any country. This persuaded many national football authorities to join because it strengthened their domestic political position, especially where they had been in competition with multi-sport organizations such as those from religious and socialist movements. Second, FIFA held to a democratic position of each member country having only one vote, with no extra votes granted to a member because of its footballing importance or longevity. This led to a swing in the balance of power from Europe as more and more African and Asian nations joined, leaving the Europeans in a minority in the organization they had founded, and often subject to bloc voting from other continents.

The third principle was to abstain from interference in the domestic politics of any nation. This allowed the organization to survive while around it the world was falling apart or there was antagonism between member states. For example, it allowed the quick return to the FIFA fold of Germany, Austria and Hungary, the defeated nations in the First World War, and it tolerated the Fascism of the 1930s, even consenting to the World Cup being played in Italy in 1934 despite a government change after the event was awarded to that country. In the third quarter of the twentieth century this policy led to severe criticism, as when FIFA took no action against corrupt politicians who viewed football as a power base (such as the dictatorships in Argentina, Brazil and Uruguay); turned a blind eye to the links between drug cartels and clubs (as in Colombia); and did nothing to prevent association presidents from being appointed from above (as in Eastern European Communist countries or some newly independent African nations). This policy has now changed, and towards the turn of the century a National Associations Committee was set up, to scrutinize all membership applications and intervene whenever politicians attempt to interfere in footballing matters. This internal police force is a unique institution in the sporting world.

It was perhaps the growing influence of the non-European sectors that forced FIFA to make good its initial tenet of promoting 'the game of association football in every way it deems fit'. This has led to the instigation of football development programmes across the globe, and in turn FIFA has been forced into becoming a fully fledged economic operator in order to finance these activities. It began by securing sponsorship from the likes of Nike and Adidas, and moved on to merchandising, but gains income primarily from selling the broadcasting rights to the World Cup, a trophy it instigated in 1930. In the period 2011–14 its income of $5.7 billion vastly exceeded its expenses of $2.2 billion.

Yet it could be argued that FIFA is not a typical profit-maximizing capitalist enterprise, because its surpluses are not distributed according to the size of shareholding, but rather to member associations either equally or according to need. Despite its entrepreneurial activity, FIFA remains a member organization, but it no longer needs the subscriptions of its members, which now account for less than 1 per cent of its income. As a consequence, even relatively wealthy member associations receive more money from FIFA than they contribute.

FIFA is still in control of world football, but it faces two major problems. First is how to deal with the factions and coalitions that inevitably occur in international organizations with representatives from across the globe. This has been aggravated by the formation of confederations within FIFA, which, although aiding administrative programmes, also serve to highlight divisions in what FIFA likes to term the football family. The first confederation was for Latin America as early as 1916, but the rest came after 1945, beginning with UEFA in 1954 and followed that same year by the Asian Football Confederation, the Confederation of African Football (1957), the Confederation of North, Central America and Caribbean Association Football (1961) and the Oceania Football Confederation (1966). They tend to act on behalf of their regions and push their own agendas through bloc voting and inter-confederation coalitions. European countries, the originators of FIFA, have 63 per cent of registered players and 68 per cent of registered teams but, because of the one nation-one vote principle, have only 55 votes among the 211 member associations. This is a potential area of conflict.

The second problem stems from FIFA's secrecy and lack of accountability – not unusual among organizations located in Switzerland. No member has any power of veto over its policies, which has given immense power to the Zurich officials who run its day-to-day activities. This had allowed corruption to fester within the organization – bribes taken in exchange for exclusive contracts, rampant tax avoidance and the like – but political authorities had been reluctant to intervene in the dealings of such a powerful international player that was apparently doing so much good around the world. Finally the volcano erupted, and in 2015 and 2016 federal agents in the United States filed criminal charges against several FIFA officials, resulting in a clear-out of the top echelons. However, recent events on the ethics committees, including the suppression or redacting of reports, suggest that transparency is still not at the forefront of FIFA's priorities.

PART SIX

SHOW US THE MONEY:
THE BUSINESS OF SPORT

Whether sport can be classified as 'big business' is a subjective call.
The costs of hosting huge events such as the Olympic Games and the
FIFA World Cup, large as they might appear to the lay observer, are
dwarfed by the turnover of global financial institutions and the
corporate giants of the petroleum industry. Yet, as we shall see,
sport certainly has become a major commodity in the contemporary
global economy, with sporting goods from shoes and sportswear,
to high-tech fitness computers and video games, to footballs and tennis
racquets generating a lucrative global trade, while mega events attract
millions of television viewers, an unparalleled audience for
the advertising industry.

As with big business, there is no template for what constitutes a
mega event, but, put simply, a sporting mega event is one that attracts
a huge audience, either in person or, more likely these days, on
television. The Olympics is unique among sporting mega events in the
number of participants, but, essentially, it is the audience that makes
an event mega. However, the definition of what is 'huge' is to some
extent a personal opinion. Everyone would accept the Olympics and
the FIFA World Cup as standouts in the category, but, after that, debate ensues and every commentator will have their own list. This author is no exception. If pushed to nominate a top three to add to the
Big Two, I would opt for the Tour de France, the American Football
Super Bowl and the Ryder Cup in golf. No one envisaged when they

started that these events would reach mega status. The early modern Olympics were not even standalone affairs, but accompanied international expositions (from which they borrowed the idea of a dizzying scale of spectacle and a kaleidoscopic range of activities), and the first World Cup had but thirteen entrants and needed no qualifying competitions. Yet, for varying reasons, cultural and otherwise, they have increasingly gripped the public imagination and ultimately, aided by the reach of television, achieved international cultural significance. A common feature of many mega events is that a sports organization owns the property rights to the event and allocates both hosting and broadcasting rights. Provided bidders can be attracted, this gives significant monopolistic power to the organization.

Most grass-roots sportspeople are true amateurs, involved in their sport with no regard for financial reward; indeed, playing sport can cost them money for equipment, club subscriptions and facility hire. At the opposite end of the spectrum are the professionals, that minority of sportspeople who are paid to perform. The most important thing for them is that there is a source of funding for their activities. In the eighteenth century this came from patrons who supported jockeys, pedestrians and prizefighters, both for gambling purposes and to demonstrate their status via conspicuous consumption. In the nineteenth century, especially from the 1870s in the case of team sports, an audience was willing to pay to watch contests, so promoters could sell tickets, pay players and make a profit. Today one might add sponsors and television companies, although they tend to be one step removed from directly paying the players.

21

SELLING THE GAME: SPORTS ENTREPRENEURS AND THE PRODUCTS THEY MARKETED

I f we start with the basics of a market for any goods, we must ask the following: what affects the demand for sport and what influences its supply? At the simplest level, demand is a function of five major variables: income and wealth, prices, population, time and taste. Income and wealth provide the means to purchase sporting goods and services. Price can have several influences: the price of all goods, but particularly those meeting basic needs (not usually including sport), affects disposable income; the effective demand for watching sport or purchasing sporting equipment will rise or fall with the price of those products; and price can be used as a rationing or segregation mechanism, as when differential amounts are charged to watch the same game from different vantage points, such as the grandstand or a corporate box. Demographic factors also have a role, and demand can be affected by population size, location and age structure: a larger population can mean a greater aggregate demand for sports products; a concentration of people provides a more accessible market; and the demand for different types of sporting activity can be influenced by the age distribution of the populace. Sport often occurs in specific time slots outside working hours. In the distant past it occurred annually, with folk football matches or the local race meeting often being held either after harvest or on a saint's day, this 'holyday' consequently being transmogrified into a 'holiday'. Later there was the Saturday half day or, for some, the midweek half day on which to play and watch sport; hence the name of Sheffield Wednesday Football Club.

Taste, perhaps better expressed as preference, allows for loyalty to certain clubs, the relative quality of the product being offered, such as league or cup fixtures rather than friendly matches, and even the choice of the sport to be followed. In combination these variables contribute to an explanation of why some sports flourish and others fade away; why commercial sport has become urban-based; and why many sports have developed a business orientation.

When looking at supply, there is much to be said for a factor of production approach that examines the use made of natural resources (conventionally labelled as 'land'), the labour force, monetary resources, entrepreneurship and technology. Such a method might be seen as old-fashioned, but it can force us to think about the historical drivers in the production of sport. There is an old economic adage – buy land, they've stopped making it – which emphasizes the fixed nature of this particular economic asset. In the crowded urban environment of industrializing Britain, land pressure may have forced the development of pitches of limited size, in contrast to folk football which could range several miles across the countryside. The supply of the sports labour force is less restricted than that of land and can be increased by demographic change, including population expansion and geographical mobility, and improved via training and skill development, a process referred to as human capital formation. More conventional capital formation involves investment in facilities to augment sporting output, and fundraising to finance such investment. We must ask, for example, who the patrons of the eighteenth-century pugilists and pedestrians were, and why they invested in the production of these particular forms of sporting output. For a later period it can be asked why the builders of Edwardian football stadia in Britain were not the local political authorities, as they often were in the United States and parts of continental Europe. How do we explain why the largest stadium in Britain before the First World War, at Hampden Park in Glasgow, was owned by Queen's Park, an amateur football club?

The factors of production outlined above are brought together by entrepreneurs. Such sports entrepreneurs could be individuals investing in sporting facilities, but might also, in the late nineteenth century, embrace directors, as advantage was taken of legislation to allow the formation of limited-liability companies in the sports sector; councils, which established municipal parks, bowling greens and golf courses to promote healthy activities; and even schoolteachers, who encouraged sport for its ethical values. Then there is the issue of how the factors were combined, conventionally referred to as technology, partly in the narrow sense of improved equipment and methods but also as a broader concept covering the development of leagues and other competitions.

As previous chapters have demonstrated, sport in the twenty-first century is not the same as sport in the sixteenth or even the twentieth century. The changes that have taken place can be analysed by the use of four more economic concepts: commercial widening, commercial deepening, product improvement and product development. Commercial widening occurs when more revenue is obtained from traditional gate revenue sources, such as the playing of more games or the expansion of stadium capacity when there is excess demand for the event being sold; in effect this is a business strategy of 'more of the same'. Commercial deepening involves the development of new revenue sources, such as sponsorship, merchandising, signage and media rights. Product improvement involves modifying the original sporting competition so as to attract larger audiences, either for one event or over a season. Such changes include the establishment of new competitions within the sport, the introduction of play-offs for promotion from one division to another, or playing on a Sunday. These developments add more events to the sporting calendar, but do not change the essence of the traditional game. Product development, on the other hand, can drastically change the nature of a sport and the way it is played. A prime example is in horse racing, where the development of sprints for two-year-olds replaced the traditional long-distance heats for older, staying animals.

THE SPORT PRODUCT

When we say sport is a product, we mean that it has become a commodity. This occurs when consumers are willing to pay to play or watch it. There are three categories of sport product: the player product, the spectator product and the associated product. All have a long socioeconomic history.

The player product can be divided into five further categories of games, equipment and costume, instruction and assistance, facilities, and clubs. To become a product the game requires formalization by the introduction of rules, so that participants know what is permitted and what is prohibited. Hence we find published jousting regulations in the mid-fifteenth century and rules for cricket, golf and prizefighting emerging in the eighteenth. Another form of game product came with the organization of matches, cups and league competitions in which the players, rather than the spectators, were the focus. The origins of many of these remain unrecorded, but in cricket inter-village and inter-club challenge matches for kudos, and sometimes money stakes, have been documented in the eighteenth century.

Recourse to equipment was essential to sports participation. There was a flourishing sports equipment industry in early modern Europe with, for example, strung tennis racquets and specialist non-martial jousting lances and armour. Costume was less necessary – the Greeks didn't even bother to dress – except as an identifier between opponents, but it did serve to show status and demonstrate conspicuous consumption. Early golf clubs had uniforms for formal dinners, but also for playing. Initially red coats had often been donned to warn walkers on the course that golfers were about, but uniforms were also an overt way of displaying one's prosperity and of differentiating club members from others; wearing a uniform constituted a demonstration of who you were. Some costume also functioned as protective equipment, as with medieval armour and American football helmets. Instruction and assistance came as goods (manuals, rulebooks and performance-enabling and -enhancing substances) and services (coaching, teaching and scientific advice). Even with a readership limited to a literate noble and bourgeois clientele, at least four hundred sports instruction manuals were published between 1400 and 1650.

Having somewhere to play is as essential as having the equipment. The early Greek gymnasia were loose ensembles of running tracks, areas of sand for combat sport training, equipment sheds and, of course, altars to the gods, all of which required dedicated space. During the Renaissance commercial operators responded to demand, and by the end of the sixteenth century there were more than two hundred public pay-as-you-go tennis courts in Paris. In the late nineteenth and early twentieth centuries the public sector also began to supply facilities including swimming pools, golf courses and sports pitches as part of the municipal socialism movement, and to attract visitors to resort towns. However, privately owned specialist facilities, which required payment for use, were already in existence in and around major cities. There were indoor riding arenas, bear- and bull-baiting arenas, cockpits, bowling greens, inns and taverns, and sports buildings erected specifically for ball games, while marathon pedestrian events gradually moved away from point-to-point challenges, with their varying terrains, gradients and surfaces, to measured courses and specialized running areas. Facilities were often provided by clubs, which, as we have seen, began so as to enable people with a common sporting purpose to come together.

While the market focus of the entrepreneurs in the player product sector is participatory sport, in contrast suppliers of spectator products are marketing to those who watch sport, either at the venue or, increasingly, on television or other electronic devices. They often made use of differential pricing, so that more might be charged for a better view or shelter from the elements; for example, well before the days of widespread gate-money sport, spectators at English racecourses were charged fees if they wanted to be separate from the masses and watch from the heights of a grandstand. When general charging developed, some football grounds responded to the demand by vastly increasing their capacity; even before the First World War Glasgow had the three largest football stadia in the world, with an aggregate capacity of more than 250,000.

Marketed to both or either of the player product and spectator product purchasers are associated sports products. These are goods and services that have been allied with sport in some way, but which are not necessary to the playing or watching of sport, although they can heighten the enjoyment. These include specialized sports newspapers

Anyone for scones?

Wimbledon tennis fortnight is the largest sporting catering operation in Europe. In 2015 its 1,800 staff served 350,000 cups of tea and coffee, 150,000 bottles of water, 207,000 meals, 235,000 glasses of Pimm's, 190,000 sandwiches, 150,000 Bath buns, scones, pasties and doughnuts, 130,000 lunches, 100,000 pints of draught beer and lager, 60,000 sausage baguettes, 40,000 chargrilled meals, 32,000 portions of fish and chips, 30,000 litres (52,800 pints) of milk, 28,000 bottles of champagne, 125,500 ice creams, 6,000 stone-baked pizzas and, of course, 142,000 portions of English strawberries and cream.

and magazines, the 'heritage' presented by sports museums, and branded merchandise other than equipment and costume. At the venues themselves, catering franchises and pouring rights have remained important contributors to revenue.

Like sport itself, sports products can be dynamic and subject to change. Player product output can be significantly affected by the development of new sports, as when Walter Clopton Wingfield's *Sphairistikè* was popularized as lawn tennis, which then demanded a range of new equipment including racquets, balls and nets. Sports equipment is improved either by simple modification or in a step change, as with the coming in the early twentieth century of the rubber-cored golf ball, which eclipsed the previous gutta-percha version within a short period and rendered it redundant. Player performance, a measure of quality, is improved

Technological innovation in sporting equipment:
the evolution of the shinty stick.

legitimately by better coaching methods or illicitly by the provision of performance-enhancing drugs. Finally, an increase in the number of participants is encouraged by the provision of additional facilities, such as the construction of swimming pools by Fascist governments in the interwar years, or by making participation compulsory, as in the English Victorian public schools.

Spectator products can be increased in the aggregate by developing new competitions, such as the media magnate Kerry Packer's World Series Cricket in Australia in the 1980s. Other mechanisms to do this include expanding the number of teams (and hence the number of games) in a competition, as was done by the early English Football League, which began with one division of twelve teams in 1888 but had increased to two divisions each with twenty teams by 1905/6. Innovation in the associated product area requires an ability to link the product with sport in some way, such as branded replica shirts, although perhaps some lateral thinking was involved when the football teams Manchester United and Glasgow Rangers offered own-label wines and beers to their fans. For those entrepreneurs not in the inner circle of player and spectator product producers, there was the sponsorship of new events, such as the French newspaper *L'Auto*'s financing of the inaugural Tour de France cycle race; or the issuing of publications that dealt solely with sporting matters, as when the *Sporting News* in 1886 became the first sports weekly aimed at a wide American audience.

CHARACTERISTICS OF THE SPORT PRODUCT

There are several distinguishing features of sport as an economic good. It can be non-durable and non-predictable, function as an intermediate or complementary product, and be consumed as a private or public good.

Unlike many consumables, the spectator product is non-durable. Once played, a game or match is over and cannot be stored for future consumption (except as a newspaper match report or for replaying on an electronic device, but then the result is known and the excitement perhaps dissipated). In contrast, producers of sports equipment are concerned with the durability of their goods, which they see as an important selling point: participants want reliability when they purchase a tennis racquet or golf club.

They also want predictability, in that the equipment, club member-ship or instruction manual will perform as stated. In contrast, spectator products should be unpredictable; the result and the quality should not be guaranteed. There is no script, no template and no identical replication. There is no homogeneity about sport. Even a replay of a cup tie with the same line-up of players as in the original match produces a different output. Nor can a result be predicted with certainty. Cast your minds back to the FA Cup of 2008. Who would have thought that my team, Barnsley, sitting just above the relegation zone in the Coca-Cola Championship, would have been capable of knocking out both Liverpool and Chelsea of the English Premier League? A scriptwriter might have given you the winner in the last minute, but this was football drama, not a drama about football. Indeed, 'uncertainty' is the selling point of the sport product. A maxim of sports economists is that the more unpredictable a contest, the greater the audience is likely to be.

Sport is generally regarded as a consumer good, but sometimes it can be regarded as an intermediate product; it all depends on the motivation of those involved. If you are playing for fun, sport is a consumer good, but when participation is not just for enjoyment, but a means to a different end (such as the desk-bound Victorian clerks seeking to improve their health by pushing their bodies hard in football and athletics), it is an intermediate good. Similarly, those who join sports clubs for status or to seek social capital can be considered to be consuming sport as an intermediate good. Spectator products, too, can be intermediate goods. If racegoers attend a meeting for relaxation, they are consuming the specta-tor (racing) product, but if their prime intention is to make money from betting, they might be considered as having purchased an intermediate good with their entrance fee.

Sport is very much a complementary product that the consumer buys in a personal package along with other consumer goods and services. Going to a sports event can also involve the travel product, the betting product, the catering product and the alcohol product. Complementarity can have economic consequences, something that is all too often ignored by economists when looking at the price elasticity of demand for sporting events. They fail to take into account the fact that consumers pay more than just the ticket price of the event itself. The purchasers also have (im-plicit) time and (actual) travel and other costs to consider when deciding whether to attend, and so population migration, transport developments, changing opportunity costs and the socio-economic status of potential fans can influence attendance. Indeed, for the EPL such variables have been shown to be more important than the ticket price itself.

Finally, we have the distinction between public and private goods, which is not about who supplies them but about whether their use is exclusive (private) or can be enjoyed by many without excluding other users (public). For example, a ticket for the 1912 Cup final in which Barnsley beat West Bromwich Albion can be seen as private, since if bought by one spectator it is not available for use by another, but the good feeling of winning the cup could be shared by all Barnsley fans, whether or not they were at the match, and hence can be considered a public one.

HOME OR AWAY? THE LOCATION OF PRODUCTION AND CONSUMPTION

In Britain, player products were first produced near the point of purchase; indeed, some were probably made by the players themselves from available raw materials. As demand increased, two quality segments emerged. At the high end of the market craft production dominated, but meeting the lower-quality demand of a mass market necessitated mass production. The aristocracy and landed gentry would purchase handmade, matched Purdey guns with good wood and fine engraving, for use at their shooting parties, while the rough shooter and clay-pigeon aficionados opted for mass-produced weapons with minor alterations made in local gun shops. Other manufacturers of sporting goods also opted for more mechanized production once it became feasible for their type of output, as with Duke's originally hand-sewn leather cricket balls and the replacement of the handcrafted golf ball stuffed with feathers by the cheaper and better-performing gutta-percha and, later, rubber-cored ones.

Whatever the method of production, centralization of output became the norm. In the United States, increased demand for player products was met first by imports (particularly from Britain, where the sports manufacturing industry had established itself) and later by domestic mass production. Once this occurred, a relatively small number of firms came to dominate the supply of sporting manufactures. By the end of the nineteenth century Spalding's was employing some 3,500 workers in five plants across the United States, and the Reach factory in Philadelphia was producing 18,000 baseballs a day. Major change came in the last quarter of the twentieth century, however, as Western sports goods 'producers' turned to the developing world for cheap, non-unionized labour who worked under minimal safety and environmental regulation. The output of much sports equipment became located far from its purchase and end use, a major change from the artisanal beginnings.

A few player products can still be considered locally produced, however. Swimming baths, golf courses and tennis courts have a fixed location, drawing their clientele primarily from a local catchment area. Participatory sports clubs, too, were – and still are – primarily locally orientated.

Whereas equipment and costume manufacture were feasible for centralized mass production, the spectator product was created at a multitude of local production points, although the 'delocalization' of spectator sport means that the consumption of spectator products has also diverged from being immediately located at the point of production to being consumed via electronic media away from the stadium or sports arena. Historically, though, team spectator sports production has always been tied to a local firm. This is still the case even when their market has extended to regional, national or even international dimensions.

Teams, especially, are seen as representatives of a locality, in a tradition that dates back to Roman chariot racing, Palio di Siena and British folk football. Promoters of team sports still present the team as being representative of the locality. Football, baseball and other teams have persisted as traditional firms, usually as a single unit with a single owner or small group of owners with a single major product line. Notwithstanding later tendencies to import players, capital and management, the site of production has remained local. The merger and consolidation movement that took place in both America and Britain in the late nineteenth century left spectator sport untouched, with sports competitions remaining as rivalries within networks of traditional local firms/clubs. Concentration of such production was not on the sporting agenda. Even today ownership of more than one club or franchise in the same competition is frowned on by the sporting authorities and treated with suspicion by fans. This has been less of a problem internationally; witness Manchester City FC, the owner of which, City Football Group, has clubs in several countries. Mergers of clubs have occurred. In Scottish football Inverness Caledonian Thistle was formed in the early 1990s from two neighbouring clubs, although this enraged many supporters of both. Indeed, such traditional rivalries forced the abandonment of a plan to reconstruct rugby league in England by merging local clubs. Clubs have moved grounds, but normally within limited distances, an exception being the franchise shifts that feature in American elite sport. Nevertheless, although relocations, mergers and franchise changes may have moved the site of production, it was still housed at a single, fixed point.

There have been other forms of spectator sport production that involved the producers taking their product to different localities, as with Formula One motor racing, the European and American golf tours, and the Jack Kramer professional tennis troupe (the precursor of the ATP tennis circuit). In the nineteenth century this came in England via the various professional touring cricket elevens, although generally they challenged sides who would have local support. In contrast, the Harlem Globetrotters in twentieth-century American basketball often took their opponents with them on the road.

IS THE BUSINESS OF SPORT DIFFERENT FROM 'REAL' BUSINESS?

Much of the economics associated with sport is conventional. Funds have to be raised, wages paid and resources allocated to the production process. Yet in some respects spectator sport has peculiar economics. Unlike in conventional business, each producer needs a competitor before a sellable product is available. As one pioneer in sports economics remarked, 'It is no good being heavyweight champion of the world if you have no one to fight.' No other form of commerce requires rivals to work together to produce a saleable product. It is no coincidence that as early as 1904 the traditional Glasgow soccer rivals Celtic and Rangers gained the soubriquet 'the Old Firm' because of the commercial revenue their clashes generated. It could be suggested that this is one reason why even today they do little to eradicate sectarianism from their respective followings.

Another peculiarity of sports economics is that while most manufacturers in the non-sport world sell the certainty of their output as being reliable, the uncertainty of the result is a bedrock of sport, so sports competitions are often organized to ensure this. Historically one way to bring this about was to exclude the better participants. The original

Doggett's Coat and Badge rowing races were limited to six selected watermen who had recently completed their apprenticeship, but when insufficient entries were forthcoming the regulations were relaxed to allow previous losing rowers to race. The commonest method of ensuring an uncertain result, however, was to bring in some form of handicapping and make some participants run further than others, carry more weight, have a disadvantaged starting position or play against a team with more players.

This has often been done by the relevant league operating as a cartel, something that is outlawed in most free-market economies to prevent companies from fixing prices and restricting competition. Yet this is precisely what has happened in most professional team sports. The sports industry has a history of regulations, determined by leagues, that have had an impact on the free movement of labour and prevented employees from choosing where they work or for whom. Equality of competition has been promoted by weakening the stronger teams and strengthening the weaker ones by such methods as salary caps, reverse-order drafts and various forms of revenue redistribution. Moreover, the leagues can impose restrictions on new entrants to the industry. In other businesses, if you can raise sufficient start-up funds you can become a new bank, oil company or whatever, but in sport your application to join a league can simply be refused, or you may have to join at the lowest level of the pyramid in a promotion/relegation system.

A final difference to note is that those who own teams at the elite level of commercialized sport are not always conventional in their economic behaviour. They may not seek to maximize profits but pursue what economists label 'utility'; in simple terms, they put winning cups and championships before making money. Within the parameter of not going bankrupt, utility maximizers will spend to create a winning team. Profit maximizers, however, are well aware that profit is determined not by revenue but by revenue minus costs. This has historically been seen as a major difference between European and North American sport. Certainly, my own work on English football, rugby and horse racing in the nineteenth century supports the view of the dominance of the utility motivation. County cricket clubs were dependent on distribution of revenue from Tests to keep themselves afloat; most soccer clubs were in debt; and horse racing existed only because owners were prepared to treat it as a hobby rather than a business. Little seems to have changed!

MARKET, TO MARKET: SPORTS ENTREPRENEURS

The linguistically challenged American president George W. Bush famously (but perhaps apocryphally) once remarked that the trouble with the French economy was that it had no word for entrepreneur. Economists do have a word, but in sport particularly they have generally used it very restrictively to infer a profit-seeking promoter of sport and its products. Yet these days the concept of 'social entrepreneurs' – people who seek social returns rather than (or as well as) operating surpluses – is in common parlance. It is time for a wider definition of the sports entrepreneur to encompass all who promote sport and its products. Hence I suggest that sports entrepreneurs are those who act as agents of change in the supply of sports products, and who attempt to increase the output of the industry, improve the consumer experience or raise interest in sports products by such means as developing new markets and creating new products. Interestingly, this definition vastly extends the range of people deemed to be sports entrepreneurs, to include some sportspeople, circus owners and theatrical impresarios, charity fundraisers and even criminals.

The definition says nothing about the size of the entrepreneurial venture. Nor should it. The establishment of the EPL might have had a greater impact on the sporting world than Alex Weir, the local golf professional at Turnberry in the pre-Trump years, who advertised his own brand of 'non-slicing drivers and brassies'. To my mind, both the key decision-makers in the major football institution and the individual craftsman in the golf-course pro shop are entrepreneurs.

This definition also says nothing about the qualities required to be a successful entrepreneur. Merely to attempt is to be entrepreneurial. The literature focuses on the successful entrepreneurs and pays little heed to those ventures that failed, yet, if risk-taking is a quality of entrepreneurs, there must have been failures. This must be incorporated into any discussion of entrepreneurship, since these failures may have pushed sport to develop in particular ways. An illustrative example is John Whyte's attempt to establish the Hippodrome, an enclosed racecourse, in London in the 1840s, which came three decades too early for the market, but showed the potential of such a development.

In many ways, sports entrepreneurs are no different from other entrepreneurs in that they are concerned with strategic planning, talent acquisition and public relations, but there are some differences, stemming from sport being a special form of industry because of the nature of the product and its economics not always being congruent with those of more conventional business. The concept of sports entrepreneurship can be made more meaningful by looking at the objectives and motivation of different types of entrepreneur, which I have categorized into four major groups.

First there are those who seek profit or non-salary income directly from sport. The most common of these are the producers and sellers of equipment and costumes, and those who promote a sports event and charge spectators to see it. The latter have not always been conventional sports promoters, but might include those who put on events to raise money for charity, and also sports professionals, such as the various cricket elevens that toured Britain in the nineteenth century playing matches for a share of the gate. Then there are 'sports entertainment' entrepreneurs, who promote events in which the sport itself is secondary to the entertainment value being marketed. A prime example is the American Edwin Cleary, who in 1905 organized football matches at Olympia in London. These were different from conventional games because they were indoors, under lights and on an artificial surface, none of which was acceptable to the football authorities of the day, but which were a novelty for spectators. More than three centuries earlier, in the late sixteenth century, European jousting tournaments lost their competitive edge and more attention was given to the accompanying float parades, the costumes of the participants and the general spectacle. There were also income-seekers associated with promoting gate-money sport, but their primary intention was to create a vehicle for gambling. Sport and gambling can work well together; having a bet can add to the excitement of the event, and the unpredictability of sport can create a lively betting market. Gambling interests had a long tradition of being involved in establishing sports events for betting purposes, and wagering, often with high stakes, featured extensively in eighteenth-century cricket, pugilism, pedestrianism, rowing, sailing and wrestling.

A second major entrepreneurial set also seeks to profit from sport, but indirectly. These include men such as Gus Mears, who helped to found Chelsea Football Club specifically to play at his Stamford Bridge ground, where he charged a high rent and monopolized the catering franchise. As far back as the eighteenth century, publicans organized bowls and cricket matches to attract a drinking clientele to their premises. Even earlier, minor entrepreneurs orbited around medieval tournaments: horse-traders, money-changers, quack doctors and bone-setters, blacksmiths and, of course, prostitutes, the last a continuing accompaniment to mega events today. A few centuries on, publicity and hopes of increased circulation lay behind pre-First World War newspaper proprietors organizing the Tour de France (*L'Auto*) and professional golf tournaments (*News of the World*). Several local authorities, particularly in England, constructed public golf courses specifically to attract holiday visitors to their towns. Then there were some employers who saw sport – once it had thrown off its disreputable image – as a means of lessening labour turnover. Creating works teams and providing sports facilities became regarded as ways of promoting loyalty to the firm as well as countering trade unionism.

A third group of entrepreneurs seek psychic income and personal or national kudos from sport. Their efforts can result in profit, but that is not the primary aim. Civic pride is a form of public good in which citizens of a town or region can bask in the reflected glory of a successful local sports team without necessarily having to pay to watch them – although many do. Sport has helped to enhance the status of urban areas. In late nineteenth-century Britain, having a football team inferred that you were a 'proper' town, so public benefactors put money into football clubs and their stadia along with funding libraries, museums and parks, all symbols of civic prosperity. Similarly, governments often invest in elite sport because they feel their citizens can bask in the reflected glory of gold medals won by their nation's athletes. Although sport has been used as a vehicle for charity fundraising, many of those promoting or sponsoring events gain personal kudos from their involvement. Kudos may also be a motive of those team owners who seek to maximize utility and fill their team's trophy cabinet.

A final category is that of entrepreneurs with not-for-profit objectives. Many market intermediate goods with the intention of using sport to achieve some non-sport goal: recreational groups (perhaps, historically, with religious, political or racial ties) forming sports clubs with social capital formation or conviviality in mind; the Canadian agricultural authorities, who revived ploughing contests in early twentieth-century Ontario with the aim of rehabilitating the agricultural sector and the countryside; and British municipal authorities in the late nineteenth century who aimed to improve the health and welfare of their electorate by providing parks (although not always for playing in), golf courses, swimming baths, bowling greens and other participant facilities. This development of sports facilities was part of the municipalization movement, which also involved local public ownership and provision of water, gas and electricity supplies, sewage systems and telephone exchanges. Most of these sports facilities operated on a pay-and-play basis, even if often subsidized by the local authority. Within five years of its opening in 1889, some 5,000 players a week were using Edinburgh's Braid Hills municipal golf course. The exemplar, however, is the southern English city of Bournemouth, which by 1914 had 33 bowling greens, twenty tennis courts, ten cricket fields, six football pitches, three croquet lawns and two golf courses.

DARK PRODUCTS AND DARK ENTREPRENEURS

Entrepreneurship in itself is not a value-loaded term, but there are 'dark entrepreneurs', people who besmirch the name of sport and undermine its integrity while promoting sport or attempting to improve its quality. They include those boxing promoters who fixed fights to create local heroes or to market racism, such as Hugh D. McIntosh, who staged a world heavyweight title fight in Australia in 1908 between the white champion, Tommy Burns, and black challenger Jack Johnson; the sports goods corporations and the Pakistani middlemen who made profits from the labour of young children hand-stitching footballs; the Nazi organizers of the 1936 Berlin Olympics, who used them to promote a racist ideology; and all those who supply illegal stimulants to sportspeople.

The dark sporting products these entrepreneurs sell or promote can be divided into four groups. Clearly, a product is a dark one if its exchange between producer and consumer breaks the law of the land. In Britain today the promotion of brutal animal sports such as dog- and cock-fighting is illegal, as is the hunting of foxes with dogs, so these events can be classed as dark products. Yet such animal sports and aspects of field sports have not always been deemed illegal, so a product can become a dark one at the stroke of a legislator's pen.

Then there are those products that are illicit only in a sporting context. There is a fine line – exploited by medical exemptions – between performance-enabling and performance-enhancing drugs; one is deemed appropriate for bringing athletes to the starting line, but the other is banned for giving them an unfair advantage. However, if products, such as dietary supplements or better footwear, improve athletic performance but have not been banned by the appropriate authorities, they are not dark products (unless they fall into the category below).

This third group contains those products that are subject to moral opprobrium. The problem here is that different subcultures might have different views, so is it simply the dominant one that prevails? The creation of a moral climate can lead to legislation to outlaw a particular product, such as the passing of the 2004 Hunting Act, which forbade the hunting of animals in England and Wales with a dog. Indeed, there has been an accretion of dark products over time, as society has become less tolerant of sports violence and violent sports. However, some dark products can be rehabilitated. Although training was viewed by Victorian sports administrators as cheating, now sports science is widely applied, often with governmental financial support, to gain marginal advantages.

A fourth group of dark products involves public perception that the integrity of a contest has been besmirched by competitors not trying; by taking performance-enhancing drugs; or by providing entertainment, sometimes choreographed – as in professional wrestling – rather than real sporting competition.

HAS MONEY RUINED THE GAME?

Many people involved in sport, particularly fans, are not happy with a situation in which they believe sport has sold its soul to business interests. The belief that sport is different from business, and therefore should not be operated in the same way, is a very common one. It is not totally different, of course, since – like business – sport is competitive, with participants seeking to win and success being rewarded. But sport can also be concerned with promoting enjoyment, exercise, health and fair play, and many would argue that these aspects disappear when money becomes involved. Additionally, business always wants to expand, and sports business is no different. The Olympics have become a huge global enterprise; the world cups in football, cricket and rugby have all increased the number of teams reaching the final stages; football teams no longer have to win their Premiership to enter the Champions League; and the first event of the European 2019 Professional Golfers' Association tour was in November 2018 in Hong Kong, with sports business here taking both geographical and chronological liberties.

Business demands value for money. For this reason sponsors put pressure on participants to play even when they are injured, which can pose a physical and mental threat to competitors. Business also wants to lessen the risk of investment, so there are demands by some club owners in Europe to protect their capital by abandoning the traditional quality-control of promotion and relegation and follow the major-league sports of the United States, guaranteeing that the league cartel will continue undisturbed.

Then there is television, where the money being paid for broadcasting rights has forced sports organizers to agree to change the timing, location and even rules of events. Another important aspect of television and sport is that, outside listed events in some countries, it is a free market in which the highest bidder wins: hence the complaints about cricket, rugby and football abandoning their traditional supporters and taking satellite television's 'blood money'.

This is part of the increasingly commercial attitude exhibited by sports organizers. Indeed, traditional supporters are now regarded as modern consumers, and if they cannot afford to attend then someone else will take their place. This is the working out of free-market forces. The same applies to the complaints about how much players are paid. Why do leading footballers in the UK get millions of pounds a year and nurses only a few thousand pounds? It's called the law of supply and demand. There is a limited number of talented footballers and several clubs willing to spend small fortunes to acquire their services. In contrast, there are thousands of men and women willing to become nurses despite the small rewards. Why should agents be paid so much? Because someone is willing to do it. And it's not just footballers. Look at the bonuses that were paid to bankers. It's obscene – nobody needs that level of income – but it's a result of the capitalistic economy.

As a historian, I have to ask if things really were better in the past. Sporting myths develop as nostalgia clouds recall, and all sports appear to have a 'golden age', usually beyond living memory. Many sports commentators allude to a previous era in particular sports, or sport generally, in which money played a less prominent role than it does now; in which genuine amateurism prevailed; in which drugs, violence and corruption were non-existent; and when everyone, both on and off the pitch, 'played the game'. Sports historians have shown that this was never really the case. In the so-called pre-commercialized sport of the eighteenth century, violence towards animals and fellow players featured strongly, and corruption was not uncommon because of the gambling that underwrote much sport. Then came the commercialization of the late Victorian years and its ethical consequences of shamateurism, deliberate foul play by professionals (remember the introduction of the penalty kick into soccer in the 1890s); gamesmanship; the use of drugs, especially for racehorses; and crowd trouble (soccer hooliganism was common even before the First World War). It should also be noted that the 'Golden Age' was one of class discrimination, and that much of the population was excluded from participation in sport simply because of their gender. The majority of the most cherished views about sport are simply not true. Fans talk about the good old days of football, and that supporters should 'reclaim the game', but football never belonged to the fans and at the elite level it has always been run with making money in mind. For instance, the Football League was formed in 1888 as an elite competition of twelve clubs to provide more money for leading soccer clubs in northern England and the Midlands.

In contrast to those who argue that money has ruined the game, I believe that in several aspects money has improved sport. Modern technology has helped improve decision making, and the increased rewards have produced fitter and more skilful players. Stadium facilities are far better than they used to be; just remember Wimbledon before it had a roof. For those who prefer to watch from home, television presentation offers a better view than the best seats at the ground, with the added attraction of expert analysis.

22

CITIUS, ALTIUS, FORTIUS
ET MULTO MAIORES:
MEGA EVENTS

The early Olympic Games were far from the mega events that they have now become. In contrast to the Games in 2004, when Athens welcomed 11,000 athletes from more than two hundred countries, the first modern Games there, in 1896, involved just four hundred athletes from a mere twelve countries. There were no official teams at the first Olympics, and – having paid his own way, like all the British competitors – the weightlifter Launceston Elliot opted to participate in several other events, thus becoming one of only three athletes who have competed in four different Olympic sports. He gained fourth place in the heavyweight Graeco-Roman wrestling but lost in the heats of the 14-metre rope climb and the 100 metres. However, he raised 71 kg (156½ lb) in the one-handed lift, thus gaining a place in the record books as Scotland's first Olympic gold medallist, although medals were not actually awarded until 1904. Moreover, as several of the pre-war Games were tied up with trade fairs, some competitors did not even know they were in the Olympics. I cite you, Donald Mackintosh, the Australian gold-medal winner in Paris in 1900 who did not appear on the official Australian medal list until the 1980s (see Chapter One).

The IOC, a semi-democratic institution in which for years the president has exerted enormous power, determines which city will host the Games, although not until the 1936 Games, when Berlin won 43-16 over Barcelona, was a vote necessary. The Berlin Games of 1936 were the first in which major new facilities were erected specifically for the Olympics; to the Nazi regime, cost was no object if their fascist ideology was glorified as a result. No such expenditure occurred at the first post-war Games, held in London in 1948. The organizers of what became labelled the 'Austerity Games' requested that overseas teams bring their own food, because Britain was under rationing at the time. British athletes were given blue and red ribbon to turn their vests into official uniforms, and prisoner-of-war camps were used to accommodate visiting athletes.

There was little commercialism at Berlin in 1936 – the sole sponsor was the Nazi Party. Today sponsorship, along with media contracts, has become a vital part of Olympic revenues, and both have put funding of the IOC (and by diffusion also that of the various national Olympic committees) on a firm footing. The Olympic movement has been able to cash in on two significant qualities of the Olympics that have made it marketable: its image as a model of health and fitness, fairness and sporting excellence; and the public awareness that there is no other sporting event of equal importance and with such global recognition. This sort of branding appeals to manufacturers and producers worldwide, and they

Rope tricks

All of us skinny-muscled children who, to the despair of our physical-education teachers, hated climbing ropes were probably unaware that the simple rope climb was an Olympic event from the first modern Games in 1896 through to Los Angeles in 1932. Competitors were originally judged on speed and style, but the subjective element was dropped and, from Paris 1900 onwards, it became a simple race to the top, starting from a sitting position and climbing using only arms and hands. In 1904, at St Louis, George Louis Eyser, a German-American gymnast, won despite competing with a wooden leg, having lost his real leg after being run over by a train. He gained six medals in one day, including a gold in the vault, an event that involved a jump over a long horse without the aid of a springboard. Another event involving a rope is the tug of war. Appearing for the first time at the Paris Games in 1900, it survived on the programme up to and including the Antwerp Games of 1920. Countries entered eight-man teams, but normally these were from specific clubs rather than compilations of individuals. They could also enter more than one team, which partially accounts for the result in the 1908 London Olympics, in which Britain secured all the medals courtesy of the City of London Police, the Liverpool Police and the Metropolitan Police 'K' Division.

have been prepared to pay to become linked to it. The Games of the 23rd Olympiad (known to those outside the Olympic movement as the 1984 Los Angeles Games) signalled the full acceptance of commercialism by the IOC. Television rights were sold for £287 million, more than double that for the previous Games in Moscow. The marketing programme attracted 35 commercial 'partners', 64 'suppliers' and 65 companies holding licences, with each category of commercial product being given designated rights and exclusivity, generating nearly £158 million in the form of cash, goods and services.

In 1948 the British Olympic Association took up the offers of some companies to supply goods and services to the team, but on condition that all a company could say was that it had supplied items *for use* at the Olympics; no product could be described or advertised as being 'Olympic', and no donor could use the name or photograph of a competitor in any advertisement or suggest that their gift had contributed to any medal-winning performance. Times change. When London was host again, in 2012, it was ambush marketers who were being restricted in order to protect the commercial sponsors. As part of London's commitment to meet the IOC host city contract, an Act of Parliament was passed effectively to curtail non-sponsors' freedom of speech by banning them from making any reference to the London 2012 Olympics, and to prevent the use of 'Games' or '2012' with other protected words, such as 'gold', 'silver', bronze', 'medal', 'London' or even 'summer'. A butcher in Weymouth, where the yachting events were held, was threatened with prosecution for selling sausages in the format of the Olympic rings. Although the Games are often criticized for their relationship with multinational corporations, it is the Coca-Cola and Nike money that allows them to be the mega events they are. Only if the sponsors start calling the shots should we become worried. There is not yet a Coca-Cola 100 metres or a Nike Marathon. Moreover, the IOC can rightly claim that the Games are the only international sporting event in which the competitors are not mobile advertisements and there is no in-venue advertising.

Media rights first became relevant for the Games in the 1920s, when, worried that gate money would not cover their costs, the organizing committees of both the Amsterdam and the Paris Games opted to sell exclusive rights to film some of the events. In fact, they went further and decided that all pictorial images should also be licensed and paid for.

Rights to image ownership were thus established that would yield millions in the long term.

Every city (in reality, every nation, because of the importance of state finance) that bids to host an edition of the Olympics claims that a profit will be made and a lasting legacy ensue, but the sad truth is that the Games always make an accounting loss and that the aftermath is often white elephants rather than enduring benefits. Montreal in 1976 was a financial fiasco, with an overspend of almost 800 per cent on initial estimates. Three decades later the people of that city were still paying off the debt, partly by a special tax on cigarettes; did anyone notice the irony of an unhealthy habit being used to pay for sports facilities? Sydney had a great 2000 Games as a community-building experience, but they went over-budget, there was an oversupply of housing and hotels and, afterwards, underused facilities out at Homebush, the main Olympic site. Gaining the Games did lead to the creation of modern infrastructure in Athens for 2004: a new airport, ring road and suburban trains. However, the cost significantly exceeded the budget, especially for security (twelve times the original estimate), and four years after the event Athens was paying £60 million a year to maintain its venues, few of which were being used. London's major legacy was the largest shopping centre in Europe, built on a site cleared as part of the Games' infrastructure planning. In Brazil many of the expensive arenas for the 2016 Games have been abandoned and are creating environmental hazards. It is rarely considered why, if a country didn't need a facility before the Olympics, it would need it afterwards.

The creation of a legacy has been a requirement of recent Olympic bids, but the feasibility is never fully assessed and there is no clawback of money if it fails to materialize in the manner promised. Although the Barcelona Games of 1992 helped to kick-start the regional economy, the story of Athens in 2004 is more typical. Despite some EU subsidies, the Greek national government was left with a bill equating to 5 per cent of the country's GDP. It had been hoped that selling off sites and buildings might bring in some funds, but there was little demand for the specialized sports facilities, and by 2008 all but one of the 22 venues were derelict. The Olympic Village also remained unsold and unused. When the economic crisis hit Greece in 2009, all hopes of realizing assets disappeared. Nevertheless, it must be pointed out that running a loss is not a bad thing in absolute terms, unless too much of the spending has flowed out of the host nation. As Sebastian Coe, who was knighted for his fronting of the London 2012 Games, made clear:

> Staging the Games provides seven years of opportunities for business . . . whether you are a clothing manufacturer in Bolton, a technology company in Cambridge, a sports equipment manufacturer in Swansea, a catering company in Aberdeen, a landscape gardener from Dorset or an entertainment group from Leeds, there will be thousands of opportunities to get involved in, and benefit from, the Games.

How can the Games run at a loss when crowd attendance and viewing figures are immense and the competitors are not paid by the organizers to perform? The basic reason is over-lavish spending, often 'forced on' the organizers by the IOC, exploiting its position as the sole seller of an event for which several buyers are competing. The main cost inflator has been not operating costs but capital expenditure on venues and infrastructure. In recent decades the IOC has increasingly insisted on top-line facilities, and it now also requires the national government of each bidding city to underwrite the costs of hosting the Games. Indeed, the basic economic rule of the Olympics is that the taxpayers, many of whom may have no interest in sport, foot the bill. Barcelona spent £6 billion on capital projects; Athens laid out about £8 billion on venues, infrastructure and security; and Beijing spent the equivalent of nearly £2 billion on new venues. This is because of the IOC's habit of playing off potential hosts against each other. Notably, when there was a shortage of suitable bidders for the 1984 Games, Los Angeles made do with existing venues, private financing and lots of volunteers – and made a surplus of $222 million.

Clearly, the economic benefits claimed at the time of bidding have not matched those calculated after the Games. But nations continue to bid – and indeed are willing to embrace corrupt practices to buy votes – so either the bidders have no sense of reality or history, or other benefits must be perceived. The four-year Cultural Olympiad, inaugurated for Barcelona in 1992, allows the host country to project its international image for longer than in the past. This has enabled the host to display its identity on a world stage, and to project that self-image to its domestic audience, using culture through a sporting lens for both domestic political

The Olympic Stadium of Barcelona.

and international-relations purposes. The opening and closing ceremonies are another arena of benefit for the host nation. The Sydney opening ceremony in 2000, for instance, featured a parade of the iconic Victa lawnmowers that had cut grass in the Australian suburbs for more than half a century, as well as a tribute to the Country Women's Association, an institution for the rural Australian matriarchy.

More influential has been the possibility of basking in the reflected glory from medals. History shows that home advantage has often delivered a superabundance of medals, thanks to crowd support and the ability to field a large team. Australia, for example, won 85 medals at the 1952 Helsinki Games, but on home territory in Melbourne only four years later the aggregate increased to 314. History almost repeated itself in 2002 at Sydney, where the home nation gained 630 medals, just under 50 per cent more than at the previous Olympics, in Atlanta. This does not always occur, however. Canada is the sole country to have hosted the Games without winning a solitary gold medal, and it did it twice, at Montreal in 1976 and again at the Calgary Winter Olympics in 1988. This did not stop the Canadians applying again, successfully, for the Winter Games of 2010 – this time with an avowed (and financed, to the tune of CAN$117 million) policy of getting back on to the podium. It was little surprise that this time, in Vancouver, the Canadians topped the gold-medal table.

Currently, there is no rush of potential hosts, but the IOC needs only two realistic bidders for extortionate demands to be made. There is always the likelihood of an ambitious nation wanting to announce its place on the world stage, as Brazil did in 2016 (and, almost simultaneously, for the FIFA World Cup in 2014). In the past Tokyo (1964), Seoul (1988) and Beijing (2012) have similarly used the Games to declare their arrival as economic powers.

THE WORLD GAME

The success of the Olympic football tournaments at Paris (1924) and Amsterdam (1928) tempted European football powers to consider a similar international competition for professional teams, the Olympics being restricted to amateurs at that time. However, despite their enthusiasm, they were concerned about the financial risk, and it was the Uruguayan government – keen to demonstrate confidence in its economy – to which FIFA allocated the 1930 event, having promised not only to bankroll the tournament but to build a new stadium to host it. As it turned out, construction delays meant that the first few matches had to be played on club grounds, but the FIFA World Cup (ultimately to become the second most watched mega event in the world) was underway. Owing to sporting politics, England and the other home nations did not participate.

The soccer World Cup shares mega-event status with the Olympics, but differs in that it is hosted by a nation (or even nations, as in 2002, when Japan and South Korea shared the event) rather than individual cities, and deals with only one sport. England may have invented soccer and given it to the world, but other countries put their own cultural imprimatur on the game. The World Cup enabled those cultures to be displayed beyond national boundaries. It allowed teams to demonstrate their distinctive playing styles, and, as international travel became more accessible, fans their devotion to a nation as represented by its football team.

The 1934 and 1938 events were both held in Europe, and Argentina and Uruguay boycotted the latter tournament. Brazil and Germany were the only bidders for the 1942 World Cup, but the Second World War broke out before any allocation was made and Brazil was awarded the 1950 event by default. From the 1950s FIFA adopted an informal policy of rotation between Europe and Latin America, which was extended to other continents, with World Cups in North America (1994) and East Asia (2002), although there was still intracontinental competition. Here there was an intermediary role for the various continental associations. The idea of rotation was formalized after the allocation of the 2006 World Cup to Germany, but abandoned a decade later when the tournament was awarded respectively to Russia for 2018 and Qatar for 2022, both controversially amid allegations of corruption.

The World Cup has become a money-making vehicle for FIFA, which uses its monopoly power to extract much of the financial benefits from the host country. It retains television and marketing rights and enforces conditions such as only FIFA-endorsed sponsors being allowed to advertise within 1 km (just over ½ mi.) of the stadia. If we look at the tournament held in Germany in 2006, we find that FIFA earned $2.4 billion from television and marketing and a further $200 million from the sale of VIP packages, producing a net profit for the organization of $1.9 billion. In contrast, the German host committee made after-tax profits of $80 million, mainly from ticket sales, which had to be shared with the Bundesliga, the national football federation and the German Olympic sports federation. Moreover, these profits have been subsidized by substantial national, state and city government expenditure on security ($120 million) and 40 per cent of the $1.9 billion spent on stadium upgrading. It is interesting to compare those figures with the respective direct profits accruing to FIFA and the host nation.

SUPER TROUPERS

That mega events do not necessarily have to have a major international dimension is illustrated by the American Super Bowl. In January 1967 the American football teams Green Bay Packers and Kansas City Chiefs played each other in the first World Championship Game, an annual fixture that soon became referred to as the Super Bowl. Yet at that first game more than 30,000 seats remained empty, an occurrence that the NFL commissioner Pete Rozelle vowed would never happen again. Thanks to his marketing efforts to make the game a 'must-attend' event, every subsequent Super Bowl has been a sell-out. By the mid-1970s it had attained mega-event status and Super Bowl Sunday was increasingly regarded as a national holiday.

The Super Bowl is now the most influential and lucrative entertainment behemoth in the national landscape, although – unlike the Football World Cup, which celebrates the world game – it remains a parochial spectacle. But what a spectacle! The half-time marching bands have given way to lavish shows featuring superstars of popular music. The Super Bowl leads Americans to gather to participate in shared rituals, including overt displays of nationalism. It is also a celebration (both in the profligate partying and the television advertising) of conspicuous consumption, a public demonstration of the American ability to buy things.

It is an American institution, the largest shared experience in the nation's cultural life. More Americans watch this sporting event on television than vote in elections or attend religious services. The United States television audience in 1967 was estimated at 24.4 million; it was 119.9 million in 2016. This rise in viewers has been reflected in the advertising rates charged by the broadcasters. At the first Super Bowl a thirty-second television advert slot could be bought for $40,000. Fifty years later inflation means that that sum would be worth $300,000, but it would now purchase only two seconds of commercial time. Although the Super Bowl dominates television ratings in the United States, the NFL harbours ambitions to become a global event, capable of rivalling, if not the Olympics, then certainly the FIFA World Cup final. It already suggests that it has a global television reach of a billion viewers, but this cannot be substantiated. More realistic estimates put the viewing figures outside the United States at around 150 million, mainly in Canada and Mexico, with most of the rest being Americans living overseas.

The Super Bowl itself has increasingly become a corporate event with huge entertainment tents – at between $750,000 and $1.5 million a shot – for hospitality before and after the game. The NFL has tied up the market. It handles all aspects of stadium operation, including parking, concessions, merchandising and even ATMs, which take only the credit or debit cards it approves. It also takes 100 per cent of ticket revenue and handles all ticket distribution and allocation. It owns or controls all commercial operations, including television rights and licensing agreements, and it demands that the host cities arrange for NFL transactions to be exempt from local and state taxes.

THE FRENCH REVOLUTION

Unlike the Superbowl, which is played in one stadium on one Sunday each year, the Tour de France cycle race takes up three weeks of the French summer as it wends its way around the country and, on occasion, beyond its borders. As we have seen, it began in 1903 as a specifically commercial venture designed to increase the circulation of the French sports paper *L'Auto*, but it served to help the French come to terms with modernity, technology and the mass media. For the French, it is more than a bicycle race; indeed, it is more than the several contests it embraces of the yellow jersey for the overall winner, the polka dot for king of the mountains, the green for the sprinter with most points, and the white for the best young rider. The media presents the Tour as an exploration of France's cultural heritage and history. The 1989 event, for example, offered 17,890 francs to the leader at the 1,789 km (1,112 mi.) mark to celebrate the 200th anniversary of the French Revolution, and the 1994 Tour went through the towns liberated from the Nazis fifty years before in the Normandy landings. Over time the Tour has acquired symbolic significance in France and has become a guardian of French cultural memory, helping to create a national identity and promoting the iconic heroic figures of the riders who manage the hard climbs and perilous descents of the Alps and Pyrenees to reach Paris, always the finish of the final stage. Every year millions of spectators line the roads to become part, albeit fleetingly, of a national cultural activity, to cheer their favourites and to admire the endurance of the riders.

The first race consisted of six stages over three weeks, totalling almost 2,500 km (more than 1,500 mi.). In effect, it took the idea of the six-day race hosted in a velodrome and transferred it to the French countryside. At the time of its inauguration, about 5 per cent of the French population owned bicycles, and many of those were interested in cycling as a sport and willing to purchase a newspaper to see how their heroes had fared. The Tour was an instant success for *L'Auto*, driving its main rival out of business and generally doubling its print run (and increasing its advertising revenue) during the month of the race.

Yet such revenues alone could not keep the race afloat. The Tour is an unusual commercial sporting venture in that it cannot charge roadside spectators for watching the race, so the organizers have focused on route-hosting fees, advertising and sponsorship, and, from the 1960s, television broadcasting rights. During the interwar years the organizers began to auction off the route to host cities and local newspapers. They also sold advertising space associated with the race, such as persuading local firms on the route to offer designated prizes as the race passed through their territory. On top of this, the Tour organizers sought major sponsors and official partners. In the 1930s the concept of a publicity caravan was developed in which vehicles preceded the riders, their occupants distributing samples and goody bags to spectators. By the 2010s companies were paying between €200,000 and €500,000 to be part of the caravan. In the 1960s around a third of the French population physically watched the Tour pass them at the roadside. Although this proportion has fallen, there are still more than 10 million (sometimes up to 15 million, depending on the route) such spectators each year.

Between the early 1950s and the late 1970s the financial turnover of the Tour doubled, 30–40 per cent coming from host cities and the rest from advertising and sponsorship. Even greater expansion was to come. In the three decades from the early 1980s, the turnover of the Tour increased twentyfold, a transformation attributable primarily to television contracts (boosted by competition between channels to gain the rights), which not only came to represent two-thirds of the Tour's revenue stream but tempted route cities and sponsors to pay more for the access to a wider audience. The Tour played its part in making its product more amenable to live telecasts (the first televising of the race had been edited film of the previous day's stage) by shortening stages and timing them to end in the late afternoon, to suit viewers. The organizers also broadened the boundaries of the Tour, involving more countries: Italy and Spain (first done in 1949), the Netherlands (1954), Germany (1965), Switzerland (1982), Luxembourg (1989), Ireland (1998) and England (2007). Such internationalization then influenced the invitations to teams, more and more of which featured foreign riders, the share of which has risen to over 75 per cent. The result: more than 20 million television viewers worldwide per racing day.

When the Tour resumed after the Second World War, *L'Auto* had already given way as the organizer to another newspaper, *L'Équipe*, which was followed by *Le Parisien libéré* and then a succession of sports-event organizers, culminating with the Amaury Sport Organisation. The last in particular has cemented itself as a dominant force in the cycling world, although it runs only the Tour and is a fully commercial entity, unlike the IOC and FIFA, which organize mega events but present themselves as ambassadors for sport rather than merely seeking profit.

DRIVING FOR SHOW, PUTTING FOR DOUGH

Competed for by European and American golfers, the Ryder Cup is unusual in professional sport because the participants play without financial reward using a team format in a game that is normally associated at the professional level with individual rivalry. It owes its existence to the ill health of a middle-aged English seed merchant. Advised by a friend to take up golf as an antidote to his stress, Samuel Ryder became addicted to the game. His passion for it led him to appoint the leading British professional Abe Mitchell his personal golf tutor in 1925; this was a sinecure designed to allow Mitchell time to practise and compete effectively against the Americans who were beginning to dominate the Open Championship. Ryder had a high regard for professional golfers, and sponsored matches and even tournaments to assist their development. His patriotism and love of golf came together in an offer to award a trophy for an international match between representatives of the British and American professional golf associations, the two leading groups of golfers in the world. He had funded a similar match at Wentworth, Surrey, in 1926 between British and American professionals, prior to the latter playing the qualifying rounds for that year's Open. Two years earlier he had sponsored a 72-hole four-ball match between two Americans and two British players, one of them Mitchell, and in 1925 he paid for a singles match between Mitchell and Jim Barnes, an Englishman who had emigrated to the States. The competition for the Ryder Cup itself, a 100-guinea gold trophy with the figure of Mitchell on top, began at the Worcester Country Club, Massachusetts, in June 1927, when the hosts trounced their visitors 9½-2½.

The initial Deed of Trust by which Ryder donated the trophy had stated that the cup should be played for annually, although this idea was quickly shelved and the competition became biennial, alternating with the Walker Cup for amateur golfers. In the six contests before the Second World War, the home team triumphed on five occasions, but the American victory at Southport in the last match before the war was a portent of their coming domination. The first post-war match, held in Portland, Oregon, ended in humiliating defeat for the British team by 11-1. Reminiscent of the mock obituary that had created the Ashes in cricket sixty years before (see Chapter Ten), one journalist wrote: 'Here, on November 2 1947, died British golf.' There was no resurrection. From 1947 to 1983 Britain gained a solitary victory, at Lindrick, South Yorkshire, in 1957, which brought a CBE for captain Dai Rees but no real change in the trend. American players were becoming uninterested; more significantly, so was American television.

Following another British defeat on home ground at Royal Lytham & St Annes, Lancashire, in 1977, the ninth in the last ten contests (the other being a tie), golfing folklore has it that overtures from the American golfing legend Jack Nicklaus to Lord Derby, president of the British Professional Golfers' Association (PGA), led to the British team being expanded to include players from elsewhere. Ten years earlier Bob Creasey of the United States PGA had written to the British PGA Executive requesting that the team be enlarged to include the Commonwealth countries, but, mindful of possible political difficulties and a smaller audience at the next match, the Executive had put off the decision until after the 1969 event at Birkdale, Merseyside. This resulted in a tie, and the idea had been shelved. The only change was the official recognition of Ireland in the team title from 1973. Nicklaus offered the suggestion of an alliance of English-speaking countries as another alternative, but the way forward was Europe-focused, with the new political alignments and golfing logic coming together. In the late 1960s a European golf circuit developed that began to attract top players. In 1970 the French Open was included in the Order of Merit for Ryder Cup points, and a year later the British and European tours were merged, essentially because it was believed that the British sponsorship market had reached its limit. This provided an opportunity for European and British players to compete regularly at the highest level.

Introducing European players was not an immediate panacea. In 1979 two Spaniards justified the European nomenclature, but the result was still a defeat. Two years later, at Walton Heath in Surrey, the Europeans, this time with a German and a Spaniard, were thrashed 18½-9½; in mitigation, their opponents were regarded as one of the strongest American teams ever, since all but one of the players either had won or would go on to win a Major. Nor was it a case of third time lucky, although the American win in 1983 was by the narrowest of margins. Then came a reversal of fortunes. The most European team to that date, with four Spanish players and a German, gained a win at the Belfry, Warwickshire, in 1985 – the date, according to team captain Tony Jacklin, that 'European golf came of age'. This was followed by the first ever European Ryder Cup victory on an American course, at Muirfield Village, Ohio, in 1987, before the cup was retained with a tie at the Belfry in 1989. The growing vigour of the European tour, perhaps aided by an expansion of prize money and no gaps in the weekly schedule of events, had increased the depth of the team. The match is no longer predictable.

COULD HAVE BEEN CONTENDERS

There are many other events that can be considered mega sports experiences, some of them similar to those discussed above. Indeed, there are several multi-sport miniature replicas of the Olympics, based on political allegiance, such as the Commonwealth Games, or geography, such as the Asian Games. The soccer World Cup has its lower-level regional imitators, which draw large crowds, especially in South America and Europe. The Super Bowl is the epitome of the finals play-off that is the culmination of a season's efforts in major competitions such as the Australian Rules Grand Final and the UEFA so-called Champions League. Although the primary event, the Tour de France is often considered one of the three Grand Tours in professional cycling, the others being the Giro d'Italia and the Vuelta a España.

Other team-sports mega events that deserve a mention are the world cups in both cricket and rugby union, although both are less lucrative than the FIFA version, and there has been little competitive bidding to host them. The International Cricket Council determined that England should host the first three Cricket World Cups, in 1975, 1979 and 1983, before handing it as a joint venture to India and Pakistan in 1987, after which an unofficial rotation system was introduced. The Rugby Union World Cup, held every four years since 1987, has had a strict hemispherical rotation, although this has been challenged recently by Japan's successful bid to host the 2019 event, a bid perhaps enhanced by the earlier award of the 2020 Olympics to Tokyo.

Turning to sports for individuals, both tennis and golf now feature in the Olympics (as they did before 1912), but the pinnacle events for the professionals and those watching are the four traditional tennis Grand Slams (Melbourne, Paris, London and New York), none of which has shifted location in a century, and the four golf Majors, of which the Masters is settled at Augusta's azalea-filled course and the other three – two in the United States and the 'British' Open – are on a roster to which clubs can apply. Despite the dollars available on the Desert Swing on the European Tour and the Fedex Cup on the American, such money cannot buy the status of a major.

Finally, there are the Formula One Grand Prix races. Although each race is part of a circuit (pun intended) with some twenty or so events on the schedule, each race is held in a different country and is essentially a mega event for that location. Competition for a race is strong, and the schedule has both expanded and changed, with venues being added or cut almost every year. In 1950 there were eight European venues, the ninth being in the United States; there are now 21 circuits, but only nine of them in Europe.

23

PLAYING FOR PAY:
THE PROFESSIONAL ATHLETE

Professionalism existed before the emergence of mass gate-money spectator sport. Admittedly, gladiators and chariot drivers performed before huge audiences, but these spectators did not pay to watch and the professionals were paid out of the pockets of those putting on the show. In Europe, by the mid-twelfth century, freelance knights were participating in sport for financial gain. In the fifteenth and sixteenth centuries there were professional real tennis players giving lessons and playing money-matches, and there were dancing, fencing and equestrian instructors on the staff of noble households.

Most professionals before the nineteenth century fell into one of five camps. They could be private tutors to the wealthy who wished to learn swordsmanship, riding and other sports associated with the nobility and gentry. Essentially, these were paid instructors rather than men earning their livelihood from competitive sport. Others, such as rowers, exploited a work skill. Professionalism in rowing actually pre-dated amateurism in that sport, although the participants did not devote themselves full-time to racing. They made their livings out of fishing or ferrying goods and passengers, but used their expertise in races as a means to additional income. The best of them could make substantial sums from prizes and betting, but for most participants regattas were an opportunity for a little extra money.

Other professionals were talented sportsmen whose patrons wished to wager on their abilities against those sponsored by other gamblers. It is likely that some pedestrians, jockeys and pugilists developed as sportsmen out of their servant tasks as messengers on foot or horseback, and body-guards. Cricket, however, was not a task of the household; if it had been, the aristocrats would not have played it themselves. Good cricketers found employment as estate workers so that their skill (particularly bowling, which was considered hard physical labour) could be used in matches arranged by their employers. In the eighteenth century the Duke of Dorset, for example, engaged the cricketers Brown and Miller as gamekeepers, John Minshull as a gardener and William Pattenden as a shepherd.

The fourth category was that of freelancers, who touted their sporting skill to whoever would pay them to play for their cricket team or ride one of their horses. Finally, there were entrepreneurial freelancers, who saw profit in operating and playing before a paying audience in gate-money fives and tennis-court venues, or setting themselves up as instructors in their sport. By the end of the eighteenth century the practice of making money from sport as a promoter or a performer was commonplace. The growing importance of gate money, albeit irregular and small-scale, led naturally to greater numbers of professional performers, and the best players were in increasing demand, so that the freelance professional sportsman became as common as the contracted version. Many of these sports labourers learned that they could make money through sport not only from winning prizes, but by giving tuition and exhibitions, and selling instruction books, portraits and memorabilia.

In the nineteenth century cricket provided entrepreneurial oppor-tunities for some of its players. William Clarke was a bricklayer turned cricketer who became the epitome of the Victorian self-made man. He was a working-class entrepreneur with an eye for the main chance. In 1837 he married the landlady of the Trent Bridge Inn and developed an attached cricket ground, attracted the county team to play there, and began to charge gate money. At the age of 48 he became a ground bowler at Lord's. As well as delivering his underarm lobs, he made the contacts to promote his All-England XI, a team that he led on tour around Britain for eleven years, playing thirty or more matches a year for money against sides of up to 22 players. Copycats followed in his wake, but all faded as cricket's gentlemen inaugurated the county championship, where the professionals could be kept in place by their amateur captain. Further sporting devel-opments in the nineteenth century provided even more entrepreneurial opportunities, such as those seized by professional swimmers who gained income as competitors, entertainers, promoters, teachers and coaches.

The nineteenth century also brought the rise of organized amateurism in sport and a consequent drive to control professionalism. It led to an ideological conflict between those who believed sport was for the participants alone and should remain amateur, and those who wanted entertainment sport in which professionals would demonstrate their skill before a paying audience. Eligibility to participate was determined by auxiliary rules, many of which in Victorian sport were designed to keep professionals (a category that often defined by class rather than any economic principles) out of amateur middle-class sport. Such rules were eventually swamped by the wave of commercialization as all but the most obtuse or stubborn recognized that the tide had turned. The scorn heaped on the professional sportsman was not usually from the fans, many of whom were working class themselves and perhaps would have liked to be pros if they had had the talent. The stigma came from those who did not like seeing their amateur ethos undermined, and from those who thought the spectators who paid to watch the professionals instead should have been playing sport themselves. At the elite level purity was a myth created by the proponents of amateurism (who were rarely working class), designed to keep sports exclusive for middle-class participants who could afford the time and expense required.

Except in a few sports, professionalism has become widespread at the elite level thanks to promoters who were prepared to purchase the services of talented performers and sports fans who were willing to pay to see them exhibit their sporting skill. Yet, for all the stars whose talents we admire, many more professional sportspeople operate lower down the sporting pyramid. The majority of golf and tennis professionals are not migrant professional athletes playing on the PGA or ATP tours, but rather those on less publicized and certainly less rewarding satellite circuits or making their living coaching members of the club that employs them.

THE MILLIONAIRES' CLUB (FOR SOME)

As we have just seen, teaching or coaching fees provide the basic income for most professionals. Turning to those who play competitively for a living, professionals have traditionally gained their economic rewards either from prize money, generally the province of individual sports such as golf and tennis, or from a contracted salary, the standard in team sports.

Successful participants at the ancient Olympics could be rewarded with amphorae of olive oil; medieval knights captured booty from their opponents; and in the eighteenth century pugilists, or more likely their patrons, issued challenges for head-to-head contests for money, hence the term 'prizefight'. However, in the nineteenth century, with the coming of a stricter amateur ethos, prize money in some sports was superseded by trophies, medals and ribbons (the common currency of awards at trade exhibitions), although this was resisted by working-class amateurs, who preferred to win clocks, tea sets and other goods that could be sold or pawned. I remember running in handicap races in the late 1950s in an attempt to augment the family's cutlery drawer. Nevertheless, competing for money did continue, with professional tournaments in many sports, gambling as the basis in several others, and sports goods entrepreneurs using sport to promote their wares.

The function of prize money seems obvious: to the winner goes the spoils. Yet experience showed that winner-takes-all-style tournaments did not bring in competitors of sufficient quality to be an attraction for spectators or broadcasting companies. One-offs may be successful, as was the golf match between the Americans Phil Mickelson and Tiger Woods in 2018, but they do not create sustained public interest. A balance has to be struck between this and sharing the prize money out equally, which would remove the economic incentive to win. This seems to have been worked out both in NASCAR races and on the American and European PGA tours, where studies of late twentieth-century events have shown that the differentials in prize money are sufficient for those who might not win still to perform as well as they can. The organizers of the Dubai marathon either still have something to learn or are exploiting the naivety or lack of organization among African runners. The winner of the Dubai Marathon in 2018, who ran it in 2 hours, 4 minutes and 45 seconds, received $200,000; the fifth-place runner won only $13,000, despite being just 8 seconds behind the winner: all this after more than 26 miles of endeavour!

Earnings from prize money cannot be guaranteed, so sometimes players have sought to smooth the income flows from tournament play by agreeing to share winnings over a season. Golf is a prime example. The Open winners Ted Ray and Harry Vardon, both from the island of

Jersey, agreed to pool their winnings on a tour of the United States in 1913, and George Duncan and Abe Mitchell (the latter one of the best golfers not to win a major title, and later captain of the first British Ryder Cup team) had a partnership that lasted thirteen years. One aspect that has changed in sport (but always existed in society) is that more now goes to those who already have a lot. Many of the professional circuits now hold end-of-season tournaments for those who have won most during the year, thus replicating on a much larger scale the climax to a tournament on the final day. Rory McIlroy, the Northern Irish golfer who plies most of his trade on the American tour, picked up $15 million for winning the FedEx tournament in 2019, and the eight professionals who made the end-of-season ATP finals divided $9 million between them.

Contracted players usually have a guaranteed income, at least for the duration of their contract. The earliest such professionals were the gladiators hired by Roman sports promoters. Also in individual sports, the pugilists, pedestrians and jockeys retained by patrons fall into this category as well. However, the majority of contracted professionals are in team sports, where, as with an industrial production line, it is essential to ensure attendance so that the team can perform.

Prize money and wages are not the sole source of income for the professional. Earnings can also accrue from endorsements and intellectual property rights. Today Cristiano Ronaldo, the star Portuguese footballer (although he plays there only in internationals), earns £365,000 a week from his club, but gets a further £73 million annually from other sources that wish to exploit his celebrity status. None of this is new, only the numbers have got bigger.

Income, of course, is relative. When hiring himself out as a professional cricketer in the 1780s, William Beldham received five guineas for a win and three if his team was defeated. Five guineas for three days' work in the 1780s was five times what a London artisan would have earned in the same time, and more than twenty times what an agricultural labourer might have had. The late nineteenth-century champion jockey Fred Archer's annual earnings were around the same as those of a surgeon. Today's large wages are sometimes begrudged by spectators when they feel the players don't justify their salaries in terms of effort, ability or loyalty (mainly to the team but, as recent events in the United States show, sometimes also to the flag). Yet those who feel that players are overpaid should remember that most professional sportspeople have short careers and have to make what they can while they can.

Many things can bring a sporting career to an end. Just take horse racing, where so much can go wrong. A non-exhaustive review of accidents in flat-racing in 1958 revealed that jockeys were injured by horses rearing in the parade ring, charging the starting gates, bolting, crossing legs, breaking blood vessels, running out at bends and striking the heels of another runner, as well as being pulled off by the starting gate and falling off because of a saddle slipping. In all sports, ageing muscles are eventually no longer compensated for by experience, and there is always the young gun emerging to challenge for the place in the team or in the order of merit. A few statistics can illustrate the brevity of life as a professional. My own research into professionals before 1914 shows that of the 187 apprentice jockeys registered in 1900, the typical career was between one and three years, with just six riders (3.2 per cent) lasting more than twenty years; in cricket, of the 222 players who debuted for the three leading teams in the 1880s, most had but one season at the top level and only seven (again 3.2 per cent) played for twenty years; and in the English Football League, of the 261 players who first signed professional forms in 1893/4, most did not survive more than two seasons and a solitary individual survived ten years. Golfers fared better, with the 2,692 professionals traced before 1914 having an average career of between thirteen and eighteen years – still not that long. In more modern times baseball players drafted into the minor leagues directly from high school averaged 4.38 years and just 1.46 years in the majors; if drafted from college, the respective figures were 1.7 years and 0.6 years.

Being paid to play sport is a childhood dream for many, but the reality is that professional sportspeople do not play; they work. Of course, you must have the ability, but talent alone is not enough to ensure success. You have to put in hours of practice, enhance your skill through coaching and specialist instruction, and be prepared to travel.

YOU'RE NOT GOING ANYWHERE

Professional sportspeople are different. They are different from other sports participants in being more talented, more skilled, bigger and faster (or any combination of these, depending on the sport); and they are different from normal workers in that many of them do not have similar employment rights. In contrast to most other occupations, the professional team sportsperson does not have the freedom to give notice, quit their employment and choose a fresh employer unless compensation is paid to their existing employer, who must be willing to accept the arrangement. Moreover, their employer can trade them to another employer either for cash or for another player, a rarity in conventional labour markets. Nevertheless, things are better than they used to be.

Historically, British professional sport operated a classic restraint-of-trade policy in the labour market. County cricketers either had to be born in the county for which they played, or had to have resided there for at least two years. If they wished to change employer, this could be done only by spending two years in their preferred county and thus being out of first-class cricket during that time. Soccer players in England and Wales were initially free agents, because professionalism was illegal and contracts could not be enforced, but when payment in the sport was officially recognized a major set of limitations on free labour mobility was imposed. One idea was that no player could represent more than one club in a season, although this soon gave way to a retain-and-transfer system. After the initial decision to join a club, a player was no longer free to select his employer, because that first club had an exclusive right to his services. At the end of each season clubs would produce a list of players whose services they wished to retain, and a second list of those they wished to transfer (for a fee) to other clubs. Players could not insist on being transferred, even if another club was willing to pay a transfer fee, and if a player refused to be transferred his career could be over. No wonder many footballers thought they were the last of the bonded men.

Things were similar in the United States. From the origin of the National League in baseball in 1876, a 'reserve' clause in player contracts restricted their ability to change club, something that had occurred commonly before. This was challenged in the courts, but with the unanticipated result that baseball became virtually exempt from anti-trust legislation. The exemption stemmed from a Supreme Court decision in 1922, which held that anti-trust laws did not apply to baseball because the laws governed only interstate commerce, and baseball was not a form of interstate commerce. Further decisions in 1953 and 1972 reinforced the initial Supreme Court view, and others in the 1950s made it clear that the exemption, somewhat illogically, applied only to baseball and not to other sports. The most common explanation of the situation is that the legal authorities acknowledged that baseball is a unique American cultural institution. A more prosaic version is that Major League Baseball was a sophisticated business organization with sharp lawyers who worked the levers of the American legal system. For many decades under the two-league, club-dominated system, players had little control over their careers.

The exemption did not apply to the NFL, but that still operated a reserve clause system under which clubs bound a player to his team for one year after his contract ended, although he could play in that additional year only if he had already signed a new contract. This catch-22 clause was successfully challenged in the courts in 1957, and was replaced for a while by a gentlemen's agreement not to sign players who had been under contract to another club. Given the character of many of these 'gentlemen', inevitably this broke down; then, under the Rozelle Rule (named after the NFL Commissioner), players were given the right to change club at the end of their contracts, but their new club had to compensate their old one with players of the same value as agreed by the clubs or determined by the Commissioner. Effectively, free agency had been turned into a trading arrangement, with the consequence that the movement of out-of-contract players was severely limited. Although the Rozelle Rule was declared illegal and free agency was restored in 1992, the imposition of a salary cap, agreed to by the players' union, limited the growth of salaries that a free market had promised.

This situation can be compared with European soccer, where for many years FIFA operated a global employment system in which a player could not transfer to another club once their contract had expired without the permission of their former club. This restraint of trade was successfully challenged by Marc Bosman in the early 1990s. The longer-term result has been a significant increase in players' income, with their share of club revenue across Europe topping 60 per cent.

15 DECEMBER 1995:
EUROPEAN COURT OF JUSTICE, LUXEMBOURG

On 15 December 1995 the European Court of Justice made its ruling in the case of *Union Royale Belge des Sociétés de Football Association* ASBL v. *Jean-Marc Bosman*, a decision that had a transformative effect on elite European football. Better known as the Bosman Ruling, it stemmed from legal action by a Royal Football Club Liège midfielder, Jean-Marc Bosman, when he was denied a transfer to another club.

Bosman's two-year contract with Liège expired in 1990. It had not worked out as he had hoped, and he wanted to move to Dunkerque, a French club. However, the Belgian club set his transfer fee at a level above what Dunkerque was willing to pay, giving Bosman only two options: stay with Liège or give up football. He stayed, but had his salary reduced by two-thirds, because he was no longer a member of the first-team squad. He felt this was unjust and took his case to law, arguing his treatment to be a restraint of trade inconsistent with the freedom of movement of workers as determined by EU legislation. No other workers in Europe had such strict limitations on their ability to change employer. The ruling of the Court of Justice consolidated three separate legal cases against Bosman involving the Belgian Football Association, Liège football club and the UEFA, the ruling body in European football. The line-up against Bosman indicated the realization that the verdict could change the face of European football.

The wheels of justice grind exceedingly slowly, and it took five years for a final decision to be made. The Court found in Bosman's favour and ruled that the existing regulations were a restraint on the operation of free trade. Henceforth players in effect became free agents after the cessation of their contracts. Clubs could no longer block a move or demand a fee from either the player or his destination club if he left at the end of his contract. There was to have been a transition period, but the lobbying of FIFA and UEFA so annoyed the judiciary that it was made instant, with the result that many clubs that had used their players as balance-sheet assets to secure bank loans found themselves in short-term financial trouble.

The first high-profile player to take advantage of the ruling was the Dutch internationalist Edgar Davids, who moved from Ajax to Milan the following year. In 1999 Steve McManaman left Liverpool for Real Madrid and became the highest-paid British footballer at the time. The rise in his and other players' wages was a direct consequence of the Bosman decision. If a transfer fee did not have to be paid, more money was available for the players; the age of the agent was about to take off.

A less well-known aspect of the Bosman Ruling was to stop national football authorities from restricting the number of 'foreign' players from the wider EU who could be fielded by any club. It also prevented UEFA from setting a quota on the number of non-nationals a team could name in its squad for European competitions. In 1994 the imposition of a rule limiting foreigners to just three forced Manchester United to count their Welsh and Scottish players as foreign, leading to the replacement of their first-choice goalkeeper, the Dane Peter Schmeichel, for a tie against Barcelona, which they lost 4-0. In 1999, in another tie against Barca, United fielded eight players who would have been considered foreign just four years before. In the EPL Chelsea became the first side to field an entire team of non-English players in their victory at Southampton on Boxing Day that same year. Quotas could still be applied, but only to non-European players.

Bosman himself gained little from the European Court of Justice's decision. He was not a good enough player to attract the richer clubs. In 1998 he received a compensation package of £312,000, but he struggled with depression and alcohol addiction. The height of his on-field achievements was a youth international cap for Belgium. Off the field he changed the game.

For many budding sportsmen, restrictions on mobility were imposed before they even signed for a club as, under the draft system, their employer was chosen for them. American college sports, at least in those that have major professional leagues, have in effect become minor leagues used for draft purposes. This stems from the fact that some sports, football and basketball in particular, have no minor-league system in which aspiring professionals can learn their trade. Recruitment has been geared to the college draft, and colleges are the only place where adequate coaching can be found.

Baseball, uniquely, will also draft straight from high school. The baseball draft, in which major-league clubs selected players in reverse order of their win/loss record the previous season, was established in 1964 in an attempt to reduce inequality in the distribution of talent across clubs, but also to lessen competition between clubs for amateur players, and hence their recruitment costs. Indeed, there was an abrupt decline in signing-on payments since, having lost the freedom to negotiate with any club, the only option for players unwilling to go to their designated club was to withdraw from the draft entirely for that year. Clubs were still willing to pay a signing bonus rather than lose a player they desired, but they no longer had to bid against other clubs.

Until 1974 each club relied on its own scouting, but that year a Major League Scouting Bureau (now the Baseball Bureau) was established to lessen the duplication of effort. This organization collected information on amateur players and provided regular reports to all major-league clubs. This centralization of scouting may have contributed to there being no statistically significant difference between clubs in their ability to discover talent. In fact, the whole system was less efficient than either football or basketball in recruiting players who eventually played at major-league level. Of the 506 players who were drafted as club first-round picks between 1965 and 1985, only 320 (63 per cent) made the grade, compared to virtually 100 per cent in the other sports. Of the 7,800 high-schoolers who were drafted between 1965 and 1980, only 992 actually played major league, just under 13 per cent. This is a cost to the clubs in wasted resources, but a horrendous life experience for those young men who thought they had a professional future in their chosen sport. The choice facing the aspiring professional is to accept an offer straight from high school with the option of going to college later in life – although with an awareness that ex-professionals are prohibited from playing college sport – or going to college, gaining an education and hoping to be drafted from college. The choice is not made any easier by the increased money within baseball, which has led to a reversal of the decline in signing-on bonuses. In 2003 the average first-round signing bonus for a high-school draftee was $1,877,083, a large sum to turn down when a career might be cut short by injury.

ALL FOR ONE: UNIONISM IN SPORT

Sport is not an industry suited to unionism. The units of production are small and geographically dispersed; there is a high degree of labour turnover; and generally high levels of job satisfaction. Moreover, unlike a production line, it is full of competing individuals, some much more talented than others. A major problem is for a union to be able to promote a commonality of interest that would embrace both journeymen and stars. To use the academic jargon, no sports union has been fully 'unionate', which means that they have to define themselves as a trade union (it is notable how many have preferred the nomenclature 'association' to 'union'); maintain independence from employers; consider collective bargaining and the protection of the interests of their membership as a core function; be prepared to use industrial action, including strikes; and identify with the broader labour movement.

The basis of sport is competition, with winners and losers, and generally this is borne out in the earnings of the players: the best earn more than the journeymen. To establish an association involving the stars requires some community of interest, as in British soccer (the abolition of the maximum wage and the retain-and-transfer system), golf (retaining the right to sell balls), major-league sports in the United States (free agency) and Australian Rules (the draft system). In many instances, the unions eventually won their battles, although it took time. A major victory came in American sports, where in the 1970s increased militancy, including strikes, ushered in free-agency rights with the courts holding that players were not bound to their club for life but only for the season after their contracts had expired. The door was opened to million-dollar salaries, and the average player salary of $51,500 in 1976 had risen to $2.9 million by 2008. The basic objective of many sports unions was to bring in the free market and eliminate employer-imposed restrictions on mobility and earnings, which contrasts with ordinary trade unions, which generally seek to impose their own restrictions on the labour market to prevent exploitation by employers in a free market. That said, both sets of unions wish to become monopsonic sellers of labour, so as to squeeze as much from employers as they can.

One way for professional sportspeople to look after their interests was to try to run sporting events themselves. In the 1840s various cricketing elevens toured Britain playing matches for a (not always equal) share of the gate. By the late nineteenth century the authorities of the various sports were now in full control, and self-help professionalism was frowned on. In the United States the Brotherhood of Baseball Players, formed in 1885, opted to establish its own league in 1890 after making no headway in its attempts to abolish the reserve clause. It lasted for just one season before being crushed by the financial power and political acumen of the rival capitalist-owned leagues. Yet there was one early success. By 1913 the British PGA had played a major role in establishing an incipient golf tour by organizing tournaments at national, regional and local level and actively seeking sponsorship for them. When tennis went open in the 1960s it stimulated the professional players to form associations to look after their interests. Eventually all elite tennis tournaments (except the Grand Slam events) were run by the Association of Tennis Professionals and the Women's Tennis Association.

EQUAL PAY FOR EQUAL WORK?

There were female professionals in several sports before 1914. Most early examples of women competing in sport for financial or other reward had been a novelty: smock racers, boxers and wrestlers offering titillation to a male audience. Later professionals were more serious and included swimmers and cyclists. Female swimmers made money as instructors, swimming-bath mistresses and occasionally entertainers, although these positions were often combined with a secondary source of income, as with Florence Ward, who was listed in the 1891 Census as 'professional swimmer and upholsters [sic] helper'. As a recreational sport for women, cycling had been aimed initially at the middle-class rider, but those who competed even as amateurs tended to have working-class backgrounds. By the mid-1890s in the UK there were more than thirty female professionals who received a base salary, prize money and other payments from cycle manufacturers. The first races were time challenges in endurance road events, typically of around 160 km (100 mi.) and taking the riders between seven and eight hours to complete. These led to six-day indoor events in London at such places as the Royal Aquarium and Winter Garden, and Olympia. Other professionals came from Italy, France and the United States to race against them. Such was their celebrity that some, such as

Clara Grace, regularly advertised the use of St Jacob's Oil (a mixture of turpentine, alcohol and ether) for relieving muscle pain.

In the wake of the second-wave feminist movement in America in the 1950s the Ladies Professional Golf Association (LPGA) and the Women's Tennis Association were formed, and since then there has been a general move for women's team sports to follow this shift towards professionalism, but it has been slow, sporadic and difficult, leading more often to semi-professionalism. Since the turn of the twenty-first century, however, there have been significant changes in the landscape of elite women's sport. In Britain there has been a move towards professionalizing domestic leagues, with national governing bodies offering central contracts to the most successful female players. The launch of the Women's Super League by the FA in 2011 heralded the start of a professional era for female footballers. The England cricketing authorities gave central contracts to female players in 2016, to allow them to play full time. The Rugby Football Union offered nine-month contracts to their elite women's squad in the run-up to the 2017 World Cup, and in 2019 announced full-time funding for players in the lead-up to the 2021 World Cup. The global picture is similar, with numerous examples across a range of sports demonstrating the increasing professionalization of elite-level women's sport, such as football in Argentina and, also in the southern hemisphere, Australian Rules football.

But what about the money? In 2019 the Victorian Open Golf Championship in Australia, a co-sanctioned event of the European PGA and LPGA Tours, was played on the same course (with length differences) on the same days for the same prize money. Such equal treatment is rare in professional sport. The first sport to offer equal prize money to men and women was tennis, thanks to action taken by nine courageous female players. In 1970 the Pacific South West tournament offered $12,500 to the winner of the men's event but only $1,500 for the women's title. This triggered a breakaway by the women to a special event organized by Gladys Heldman. The women took a risk with their careers – the United States Lawn Tennis Association (USLTA) refused to sanction the new tournament, which effectively barred them from playing in any officially sanctioned event in the world – but they persevered with what became the Virginia Slims Circuit, brought others on board, unionized and finally realigned with the USLTA. In 1973 the U.S. Open became the first major tennis tournament to offer equal prize money. This success was tempered by the fact that it took 28 years for the next Grand Slam tournament, the Australian Open, to follow suit.

Other prize-money sports have now begun to offer equal rewards. A global study in 2017 of 44 sports found parity in 35 of them, but large pay gaps still existed in such major sports as cricket, cycling, golf (where the total prize money on the PGA Tour is five times that of the LPGA one), soccer and basketball. What is it worth to be world champions in soccer? Well, when the U.S. women won the title in 2015 they aggregated $2 million, which contrasts poorly with the men's team's $8 million reward at the FIFA World Cup of 2014 – despite their being eliminated in the first round. When the women retained their title in 2019, the money had risen to $4 million.

BILLIE JEAN KING (1943–)

The former world number one female tennis player Billie Jean King did much to bring gender equality into the professional tennis arena. She won 39 Grand Slam titles: twelve in singles, sixteen in women's doubles and eleven in mixed doubles.

When tennis went open in 1968, King campaigned for equal prize money in the women's and men's games. After winning the U.S. Open in 1972 but receiving $15,000 less than the men's champion, she declared that she would not defend her title unless the prize money was equalized. To the surprise of many in the tennis world, in 1973 the U.S. Open became the first major tournament to offer equal prize money to men and women.

King had already challenged the American tennis establishment by involving herself in the development of the Virginia Slims Circuit. Nine players led by King rebelled against the USLTA, partly because of its support of unequal prize money, but also because the group felt that it was not promoting female tennis (it had organized no tournaments for women in 1970). Indeed, opportunities for women players were being reduced as the International Lawn Tennis Federation began sanctioning men-only tournaments: fifteen of them in 1970, all of which had previously been combined events. Gladys Heldman, founder and publisher of *World Tennis* magazine, helped the rebel nine to set up and publicize their own tour of eight professional tournaments sponsored by Virginia Slims, a brand of the tobacco company Philip Morris. The players were risking their careers, and indeed the USLTA suspended them, but by the end of the year the Virginia Slims Circuit had boosted its numbers to forty members, paving the way for the first full-year season of the Circuit in 1971. This was the year that King became the first sportswoman to earn more than $100,000 in a season.

The Virginia Slims Circuit later absorbed the International Lawn Tennis Federation's Women's Grand Prix circuit and became the Women's Tennis Association (WTA) Tour. The WTA, which has become the principal organizing body of women's professional tennis, was founded by King in June 1973, a week before Wimbledon, and traces its origins to the inaugural Virginia Slims tournament. It governs the Tour, in which more than 2,500 players from nearly one hundred countries now compete for $146 million in prize money. Despite criticism from the anti-smoking lobby, King showed loyalty to Philip Morris for

Billie Jean King, champion of women's tennis and of female tennis players.

kick-starting the modern era of women's tennis, by agreeing to join its board of directors in 1999.

In 1973 King's then husband, Larry King, co-founded World Team Tennis, a mixed-gender professional tennis league played in the United States. Billie Jean recruited the female players for the teams. It was the first professional tennis competition to grant equal status to each man and woman competing for their teams. Matches consisted of five sets, with each set featuring a different configuration (men's singles, men's doubles, women's singles, women's doubles and mixed doubles). The first league lasted until 1978, but then resumed as TeamTennis in 1981 (although the original name was reintroduced in 1992). Billie Jean King became commissioner and major owner of the league in 1984, following her retirement from tournament tennis competition; she retired as commissioner in February 2001. In March 2017 King sold her stake in the league, which had become a significant event in professional tennis.

It was also in 1973 that King took a calculated risk to publicize women's tennis – and earn $100,000. Bobby Riggs, ex-Wimbledon champion and number one male player in the 1940s, had become a tennis hustler who played in promotional challenge matches. Claiming that the women's game was so inferior to the men's that at 55 he could still beat the top female players, he challenged her. He had already beaten the Australian star Margaret Court, but in a televised match at the Houston Astrodome, King beat Riggs 6-4, 6-3, 6-3.

King retired from competitive tennis in 1984 to concentrate on her role with World Team Tennis, but she returned to the courts in the mid-1990s to play two seasons on the Virginia Slims Legends Tour to raise funds for AIDS charities. She was a tough, confident competitor, too aggressive for some, especially in her early career. However, when a selection of top players were asked in 1979 whom they would pick to come back from 1-5 and 15-40 down in the third set of a Wimbledon final, guess who most of them chose?

The problem is often said to be a socio-cultural one of discrimination, one that brings the prejudice of amateur sport into the economic arena. However, it is essentially one of economics and revolves around what is meant by 'equal work'. Too much attention has been focused by proponents of equality on the input aspect of the definition, and insufficient on the output. At the elite level successful sportswomen clearly put in as much effort as their male counterparts; in training hard, in developing skills and in pushing themselves to the limit. However, economists would ask about the marginal-value revenue product of all this effort. Simply put, how many spectators or television viewers does women's sport attract? If it can be demonstrated that the revenue raised by a female star is commensurate with that of a man, equal pay should follow (unless we then get back to social gender discrimination). Would the women pressing for equal pay in sport be prepared to give the same to junior and veteran athletes or elite disabled sportspeople? Unless sport becomes a social service, it is the market that determines rewards. This basic economic principle explains why in men's sport Premier League footballers earn more than field hockey players. Physical differences mean that men and women rarely compete together in a sport, but if they did, equality of reward should not be a problem as the prize money would be gender-blind. All this means that, if there is to be equality of reward in women's and men's sports, there has to be a cross-subsidization from the men's events to the women's. Commercial promoters do not see this as something they should take the responsibility for.

PART SEVEN

THE GOOD, THE BAD
AND THE UGLY:
THE PUBLIC IMAGE OF SPORT

I do not accept that sport breeds character, good or bad. I think it more likely that it accentuates existing character traits. Sport does not convert criminals into upright citizens; it may even encourage their drug-taking and make them run faster away from the law! If you cheat in life, you will try to cheat in sport. And if you are honest, you will not. Most people are complex individuals existing on a spectrum ranging from good to bad, and sport reflects this. Many of our sporting heroes have a dark side, as can be seen from the examples that follow, just a couple of the many that could have been chosen.

Harry Vardon was one of the greatest golfers of any era. He won the Open six times, finished second or third on six other occasions, and also – rare in the days when you had to cross the Atlantic by ship – won the American Open. Equally rare, he was awarded an honorary membership of the club where he worked. He was instrumental in the formation of the PGA, in effect the players' union, in 1902; he overcame the adversity of spending a year out of the game recovering from tuberculosis; he created the overlapping Vardon grip, still used by many golfers today (including this writer); and he has a perpetual trophy named after him, now awarded to the winner of the Race to Dubai on the European PGA Tour. Yet, for a long period of his career as a touring player he carried on an affair and within it fathered a child. All this came to light only after his death. Would it have escaped today's intrusive media?

Then we have Billy Meredith, the 'Welsh Wizard' of football. He was a hero to the fans of Manchester City, for whom he played 367 games, and also to the supporters of their city rivals Manchester United, for whom he made 303 appearances, and to the Welsh fans, whose country he represented 48 times, all this in the days when caps were much harder to come by. He played his final game at the age of almost fifty. More than 39,000 spectators attended his testimonial match in 1925 to acknowledge his service to his club. He used this adulation to raise money for charity to help the destitute of Manchester. He was admired by many for making a career in professional sport after spending eight years working underground in a Welsh coal mine, where he began as a pony boy aged just twelve. He was also a hero to his fellow players, for helping to found the Association Football Players' Union (the forerunner to the Professional Footballers' Association) to look after their interests. Yet, in the midst of this long career, he spent a year on the touchlines after being banned from football by the FA for offering a bribe to the Aston Villa captain in an unsuccessful effort to gain the 1904/5 league title for Manchester City.

Like Vardon and Meredith, sport itself has a Janus image. In this section we will look at a positive side of sport that is often overlooked by historians: its widespread involvement in charitable activities. We will also assess a more recent concern with sport's environmental impact and, finally, look at a major downside of sport, corruption by match-fixing and the use of performance-enhancing drugs.

Sport has a long-time involvement in charitable activities, much of it today associated with celebrity status. Professional athletes get lucrative endorsement contracts because of their ability to influence consumers' decisions. Charity work allows them to do likewise in the third sector. If a football or baseball star tells a child to study, it may have more impact than entreaties from anyone in the education industry.

It almost goes without saying that sport is bad for the environment. Nothing sport does has positive consequences, and at best sport participation and spectatorship can only be neutral. Sport itself was late in embracing environmental issues and sustainability. The focus here is on golf, a sport that for many decades has been in denial about its adverse effects on local flora and fauna.

Where there is prestige or money at stake, there will be corruption. Lest anyone think all is saintly in the world of disability sport, note that at the 2000 Sydney Paralympics it was claimed that only two members of the Spanish intellectually disabled basketball team actually met the criteria of having such a disability. The economic theory of corruption states that playing by the rules does not necessarily mean that participants accept them, merely that it is convenient to conform to them in a particular situation. However, if the benefits of corruption are seen to outweigh the costs and likelihood of being found out, the rules might be deliberately broken. Here we will consider two major forms of corruption, match-fixing and the use of performance-enhancing drugs. The latter used to include alcohol, which was seen as aiding strength, stamina and courage, although concern now centres on how drinking by sportspeople affects their non-sporting behaviour.

24

CHARITY BEGINS AT HOME
. . . AND AWAY

I n the 2007 Queen's Birthday Honours List one of England's outstanding cricketers, Ian Botham, was knighted for his services to sport . . . and to charity. He had raised more than £10 million for Blood Cancer UK. A link between sport and charity is not uncommon. The popularity of sport among participants and spectators has provided an ideal vehicle for charity fundraising via the creation of specific contests, the 'piggy-backing' on existing sports events for the purpose of making collections, the use of sports stars to raise the profile of particular charities, and the sponsorship of participants, from celebrities to primary-school children taking part in swims with support from grannies and neighbours. When earthquakes struck Pakistan in October 2005, the England and Wales Cricket Board and the England cricket team, who were on tour there, immediately donated £100,000 to a relief fund. Among a host of charities at the other end of the cricketing spectrum is the Primary Club, limited to players who have been out first ball in any level of the game, whose fundraising activities since 1955 have benefited sport for the visually impaired. Celebrities have also embraced sport for charitable purposes: the author and television star David Walliams raised £400,000 for Sport Relief in 2006 with a sponsored swim of the English Channel. Charities, in turn, have made use of sports stars, as when the England cricket captain Michael Vaughan, fresh from winning the Ashes, launched the 2005 Poppy Appeal for the British Legion. Sports celebrities have also made individual donations and initiated fundraising schemes. The international footballer

Alan Shearer gave the £1 million proceeds of his testimonial match to charity, and the Olympic oarsman Sir Steve Redgrave raised £5 million over five years for various children's charities. In 2009 there were more than five hundred personal charitable foundations run by professional athletes in the United States, dominated by those of the tennis player Andre Agassi and the golfer Tiger Woods, which had assets of $81 million and $48 million respectively.

Some of the money earned from American college football, in particular the post-season Bowl games, has gone to charity. The Peach Bowl has given more than $32 million and the Fiesta Bowl more than $12.5 million since 2000, and the Rose, Citrus and Alamo Bowls have spent millions in their communities on college scholarships for lower-income students, affordable housing and improving city parks in poor neighbourhoods. Also in the United States, in the four years from 2005, the NBA raised more than $105 million and provided nearly a million hours of voluntary service.

The global Homeless World Cup Foundation was established in 2001 with the aim of using soccer to alleviate homelessness, but it has widened its ambitions to include the promotion of social opportunities and access to support for those experiencing homelessness. Although based in Scotland, it now works in 450 locations and coordinates a network of partners in 74 countries, and in 2016 was estimated to have created $364 million in social capital.

The Football Foundation, which launched in 2000, is Britain's largest sports charity and awards grants to grass-roots clubs and organizations to help build and refurbish new and existing community sports facilities, such as changing pavilions, natural grass pitches or all-weather playing surfaces, for schools, local authorities and sports clubs. It gets its money from the EPL, and from the government Department for Digital, Culture, Media and Sport, and uses these funds to leverage more partnership funding. Up to 2019 the Football Foundation has awarded 17,000 grants worth more than £615 million towards improving grass-roots sport, using them to attract additional partnership funding of more than £817 million – in total, more than £1.4 billion of investment in the grass-roots game. It also delivers large-scale sport programmes, including the London Mayor's Sports Facilities Fund and Barclays' Spaces for Sports programme, which has created two hundred new or refurbished community sports sites across England. Moreover, the foundation is the delivery partner for a number of EPL and FA community schemes, including the EPL's Kit and Equipment scheme and the FA's schemes Grow the Game and Respect.

In Britain, two sporting events have been raising money for charity for many years: the London Marathon since 1981 and the FA Community Shield since 1907. The former is the largest single-day fundraising event in the sporting calendar, and up to 2020 had amassed more than £1 billion for charity. It is simultaneously a direct fundraiser for London charities and an intermediary facilitating the sponsorship of participating athletes, who run to support local, national and international charities, many adding to the challenge by running in fancy dress. The origins of the Community Shield – now the major charity match in England – lie in a dispute between leading amateur football clubs and the FA in which the former became disaffiliated and no longer able to hold the Sheriff of London charity competition, which required permission from the FA. Anxious that charity would not suffer, the FA instituted its own charity match, which is now generally held as a pre-season opener between the previous season's FA Cup victors and the winners of what is now the EPL. Proceeds are distributed to community-based initiatives and charities around the country, and revenue from gate receipts and match programme sales is given to the clubs who compete in the FA Cup, for onward distribution to charities and projects of their choice; the remainder is distributed to the FA's national charity partners. Another major British charity fundraiser is Sport Relief, a spin-off in 2002 from Comic Relief organized with the BBC. This biennial event raises money for tackling poverty and helping disadvantaged people both in Britain and in some of the world's most poverty-stricken countries. This is done via sport in a variety of forms, such as professionals donating match fees, auctions of sporting memorabilia, and celebrity races and events. In 2018 it raised £38.1 million.

GIVING WITH ONE HAND, TAKING WITH THE OTHER

Sport has always had both supporters and detractors; charity, however, is invariably seen as 'good'. Hence it made sense for sport to associate itself with charity in order to improve its image. During both world wars there was criticism that organized, commercialized sport continued to be played while men were dying at the Front, and that home energy should be devoted to the war effort. One reaction to this was that in Britain most Football League players agreed to donate up to 5 per cent of their wages to the National War Relief Fund, and a number of games were organized between League and army teams with the dual aim of raising money and stimulating recruitment. More recently, sports personalities have countered the image of the selfish, greedy professional by becoming ambassadors for charity, visiting disaster areas, establishing their own charities and making personal donations. Clubs, particularly in elite football, have seen charity as a way of restoring their links to local communities, allegedly broken by high ticket prices and the influx of foreign players, and in the United States it has been argued that charitable work has been important in bridging the gap between fans and athletes that had widened because of the latter's astronomical salaries and continued (and publicized) misconduct on and off the field. To mute the garish character of Super Bowl celebrations, the NFL began its 'A Party with a Purpose' in which cans of soup were distributed to the needy in the host city. This was later broadened to a partnership with the food company Campbell's in a 'Tackling Hunger Program' as part of a 500,000-can Super Bowl donation in 2002 with a further 6 million cans being donated later that year.

Charitable work has now in effect become a social obligation within sport. Most major-league teams in the United States have such work written into their mission statement, and their players are contractually obliged to become involved. Moreover, the leading sports agencies will not take on athletes unless they agree to establish a charitable foundation or volunteer their time and/or money towards charitable purposes; for them, favourable publicity brings in the endorsement dollars. This is not to say that the players do not want to do something that can improve lives, just to note that there are economic benefits to having a good reputation.

For some professional sportspeople, charity began at home because the unique nature of their employment meant involuntarily retired, injured and underemployed athletes often needed help. Horse racing is one of the oldest British sports and was one of the first to become involved with charity. Nineteenth-century trust funds named after the turf administrators Sir John Bentinck and Admiral Henry John Rous, set up by the racing authorities to aid distressed riders, were replaced in 1964 by the Injured Jockeys Fund, which has inevitably played a major role in this dangerous sport. Other in-house charities have included the Stable Lads Welfare Trust, the Jockey Club Charitable Trust, the Society of Equestrian Artists, several bodies dealing with retired racehorses, and the collective Racing Welfare charities. In cricket, although the Cricketers' Fund Friendly Society, established in 1857, has now disappeared after more than a century of assisting distressed players, its role has been taken over by the Professional Cricketers' Association Benevolent Fund. In golf and football the welfare gap was filled by the benevolent activities of the Professional Golfers' Association (from 1901) and the Association Football Players' Union (AFPU; from 1907). Even in the twenty-first century, the Professional Footballers' Association (successor of the AFPU) maintains a charitable function, helping to organize testimonial matches for the benefit of footballers' widows and children, as in the case of Cameroon star Marc-Vivien Foé, who died playing for his country in 2003 while on loan to English club Manchester City.

Fair play on the field and social justice off it: such notions of ethical behaviour should underpin both sport and charity. Yet the relationship between the two occasionally raise suspicions of dubious ethical practices. One major question is that of charitable status. In Britain there are currently more than 150,000 registered charities associated with sport, mainly small sports clubs but also the Football Foundation, one of the fifty largest charities in the country. Some of them involve what the National Council of Voluntary Organizations has labelled the 'charitization' of the public sector, as when local authorities have taken advantage of charity law to reclassify their sports and recreational facilities as arms-length organizations with charitable purposes, thus saving tax and rendering them eligible for National Lottery funding. All the major sports museums in Britain are run by charitable trusts, and organizations such as the cricket and golf foundations, ostensibly there to help disadvantaged children and young people participate in healthy, character-building activities, have the not-too-subtle secondary objective of producing a new generation of players. This contrasts with boys' boxing clubs in the early twentieth century, which were designed solely to help underprivileged children by offering them opportunities to build pride in themselves and to learn self-discipline.

Such charitable status is legal, but to my mind its use raises ethical questions about how such organizations were accepted as charities. I once applied for grants to study this subject area, but was unsuccessful, partly I suspect because the grant-awarding bodies themselves were charitable trusts. In Britain the standard test of being eligible for charitable status is based on Lord Macnaghten's revisions of the charity law in the 1890s, which simplified it under four heads: relief of poverty, advancement of religion, advancement of education and other purposes beneficial to the community. These remain the major categories, although there have been some additions, such as aiding the environment, promoting human rights and, of significance for sport, 'the advancement of amateur sport'. Prior to this amendment sport could qualify for charitable status only through attachment to other recognized charitable activities, in particular educational ones. However, the 2006 Charities Act included an important rider on 'public benefit', which now has to be demonstrated when charitable status is claimed, although, frustratingly, the concept has never been defined in statute law. In Australia the amateur sports clause has not yet appeared, and sports charities have to emphasize other aspects.

The benefits to the recipient, giver and facilitator of charity may be seen as generally positive, but sometimes the interaction between charity and sport has a negative effect. Examples include the RSPCA's attitudes to sports involving animals; charity involvement in boxing tournaments; the pressure to succeed, which may have contributed to the deaths and serious injuries of participants in charity endurance races; and the moral judgements made by charities on 'deserving' recipients. The London Marathon is a major charity, but it is also a business with an annual income of more than £7 million from sponsorship, television rights, entry fees and merchandising. Disputes over the payment of appearance money to elite runners in the London Marathon, the rationing of places in the event and the reservation of quotas for particular charities (who must purchase a five-year block of entries) somewhat tarnish the inevitably wholesome and 'good' image of charity.

Furthermore, the motives of those involved in sports charities are not always totally altruistic. Players obtain trips abroad, honorariums are paid to administrators, and psychic income is frequently obtained from favourable public relations. The integrity of those who seek a positive image through charitable activities can also be questioned when – as with many leading football clubs – the actions have not always matched the rhetoric of their annual reports. Indeed, many clubs that have enhanced their public image via 'football in the community' schemes contribute very little in resources to the projects.

As with charity in general, there are always complaints that too little money gets through to the actual recipients of sports aid. Sometimes this is because of inefficiency, as when in 2002 the Charity Commission found that in the case of the Charity Shield the FA had failed to meet its legal obligations under charity law by failing to specify what money from ticket sales went to charity, and by delaying payments to the charities nominated. As a result, the match was rebranded the Community Shield. On other occasions there have been qualms about possible corruption. This was certainly the case with Dick, Kerr Ladies, a women's football team set up in 1917 to raise funds for a local military hospital. They eventually travelled the world playing games for a myriad of charities, but there were accompanying allegations of both illegalities and excessive expenses.

FOOTBALL PAYS ITS WAY

To illustrate some of these points, we will explore the early relationship between British football and charity. Ten minutes into the football international between Scotland and England at Ibrox Park, Glasgow, in 1902, a wooden stand collapsed, plunging spectators 12 m (40 ft) through the broken boards. A total of 26 were killed and more than five hundred injured in what was Britain's first football disaster. The football authorities were quick to respond with financial aid to the victims. In Scotland the SFA immediately subscribed £3,000 to the Lord Provost's relief fund. In England the FA opened a relief fund with a donation of £500, requested clubs to play games to supplement that money, and arranged a special international match against Scotland with the gross proceeds going to the fund. In all, £3,000 was raised. In providing aid to those killed and injured at a football match, both associations were doing what might have been expected, but there were occasions when their generosity went beyond the boundaries of the game, and their accounts show donations to major charitable causes such as the Indian Famine Relief Fund (1897), the British victims of the South African War (1899) and the families of those lost when the *Titanic* sank in 1912. More generally throughout Britain, regional associations and individual clubs often responded to local disasters, tragedies and distress by playing matches or allowing collections to be made.

In April 1874 a football match was organized by the SFA between teams representing Glasgow and Dumbartonshire, raising more than £100 for Glasgow's Western Infirmary. This led directly to the creation of the Glasgow Charity Cup, which, before its demise in 1966, raised nearly £350,000 (over £14 million in 2019) for various charities and good causes, particularly those concerned with hospitals and medicine. A survey of the Cup's disbursements before 1914 shows that, although the three major city infirmaries received the bulk of the funds, there were also donations to hospitals offering treatment for ears, eyes and sexually transmitted diseases, to the maternity hospital, and to various hospices and convalescent homes, several dispensaries, nursing associations and the St Andrew's Ambulance Association. Such was the success of the Glasgow innovation that it spawned a host of imitators throughout Britain. By the end of the 1880s nineteen other Scottish charity competitions of note were being played, most of which continued for decades. Even more significant was the influence south of the border, where major charity cups were inaugurated in London, Sheffield and Birmingham, specifically modelled on the Glasgow example. In 1913 there were more than two hundred such competitions authorized by the FA or the SFA.

Yet was this unadulterated altruism? Not if we look at some of the stakeholders. First there was the question of power and control over charity football matches. The FA had cemented its authority over English football in the 1870s, and was effectively in charge of the game by the 1880s. Determined to keep charity football under its control, it passed regulations about when games could be played, who could participate and what should happen to the proceeds. No game was allowed – neither the final of a serious charity competition nor a burlesque involving pantomime artists – unless it was played under FA match rules. Then there were the patrons who lent their names to the charity tournaments, often providing the trophy for the winners. Although the efforts of these politicians, public figures and commercial interests were commendable, they cannot be seen as entirely altruistic. If newspapers and businessmen had been totally uninterested in promoting themselves, they could have donated cups anonymously. Instead, their names became inextricably associated with the competitions they sponsored in what was effectively a relatively cheap form of advertising; even when a cup cost over £100, it was a one-off payment that brought renewed publicity every year. Patronage of charity football kept the names of Members of Parliament in front of the electorate; for mayors it provided a legacy of their term of office. The donor's name continued to be associated with the event even when it was others who made the competition work.

Clubs often welcomed the opportunity to play in charity tournaments. Before the development of leagues with regularly scheduled matches, there was virtually a free market in fixtures. These were mainly friendly games that might be cast aside if one of the clubs progressed in a cup competition or obtained a better offer in terms of the quality of the opposition or expenses promised. Charity matches with a trophy attached meant that the clubs obtained meaningful fixtures, often with selected opponents rather than the random draw of cup competitions. Moreover, when leagues developed and professionalism was sanctioned, clubs increasingly began to flex their muscles. The Glasgow Charity Cup Committee had to concede neutral venues (1894), club alteration of match dates (1897) and permission for players tied to other clubs for SFA Cup matches to play in Charity Cup matches (1902).

As commercial considerations came to the fore in the sport, the charity ambitions of some clubs fell away. Celtic is a prime example. Although it was founded in 1887 to support local Catholic charities, within a decade it had become a limited company, was declaring dividends of 5 per cent, and had virtually ceased to donate to charity. The decline in the club's charitable donations dates from 1893–4, the season in which professionalism was formally adopted in Scottish football. Significantly, from this date all the competing clubs in the Glasgow Charity Cup – except Queen's Park, who remained staunchly amateur – immediately began to claim for players' wages. Unless offset by larger gates such extra costs resulted in less surplus available for charity; in 1903, for example, wages incurred during the Glasgow competition took 29 per cent of the £840 gate. By 1914 Alex Wylie, a long-standing trustee of the tournament, was complaining that players absorbed too much money from charity matches. More generally across Britain by the twentieth century clubs were less keen to play for charity, with the notable exception of pre-season practice matches, but those, of course, also served an important footballing purpose.

Charity fixtures gave players, as well as clubs, the opportunity to take part in meaningful fixtures, and professionals the chance to earn extra money, but the main charity impact for the latter was that players helped each other collectively through the benevolent fund of their union, financed partly by contributions from players and also through other fundraising activities, including benefit matches. Although the AFPU made little headway in its challenges to wage limitation and the retain-and-transfer system, its everyday benevolent work was a solid achievement. Between 1908 and 1914 hundreds of players and their families were helped with small but crucial sums towards funeral expenses, removal costs, furniture replacement and hospital fees.

Finally, there is the issue of fingers in the charity pie. There has often been concern that not enough of charity match proceeds goes to charitable purposes. In 1883 a Scottish newspaper criticized various charity-match organizers for 'allowing large numbers to sit down for tea', sometimes as many as seventy. They were reminded that 'charity funds are not association funds'. Increasingly over the next decade charity football was receiving warnings. A tournament at Coalville was investigated by the Leicestershire County Football Association because 'the amount given to charity was very small and the expenses very high'. Finally, at the end of the 1890s the FA set up a commission to formulate rules to sanction charity competitions and matches. Not all secretaries appear to have read those rules, however, and in early 1899 the Apsley and District Charity Competition was told that net gate receipts of just £4 18s were 'not sufficient justification for the existence of a competition described as a

---

No charity there?

The Coalville Charity FA was made subject to an investigation by the Leicestershire FA as 'the amount given to charity was very small and the expenses very high'; Ashton-under-Lyne Charity Competition Committee was asked for an explanation as to 'certain items on the balance sheet' and informed that 'the amount given to charitable institutions was small by comparison with the amount paid to the competing clubs, and that it was contrary to the ruling of the FA that a payment should be given to a secretary of a charity competition.'

Minutes of FA Emergency Committee, 7–14 September 1896,
29 May–10 July 1896

Football Charity Competition'. Further investigation revealed that less than £1 went to charity, mainly because the two clubs involved, Burton Swifts and Luton Town, had been guaranteed £40 to play.

CHARITY PLUS

In 1935 the U.S. tax authorities decided that corporations could deduct up to 5 per cent of their pre-tax income for charitable purposes. Although political right-wingers still considered such deductions theft from share-holders, the way was open for a rethink of the role of companies in civil society. Still, for many years social obligation remained an afterthought, if companies considered it at all. Sports organizations were no different. Slowly, however, in many countries, came a realization that corporate social responsibility (CSR) was not a zero-sum game. Rather than charitable works costing them money, there could be positive economic spin-offs for clubs and companies as their enhanced reputations encouraged an expansion of their customer base.

The core principle of CSR is that companies have responsibilities to society beyond the traditional maximization of profit. These include acting in a way that contributes positively not just to shareholders but to all stakeholders, including workers, customers and the local community. It is this last aspect that has been seized on by sports clubs and associations who have realized that teams and organizations, like individual sportspeople, can increase their social standing in the community through philanthropic activities. They can even win awards. The Football Is More foundation, established in 2011, now holds an annual international awards presentation, at which in 2019 the (Glasgow) Rangers Charity Foundation collected the Social Responsibility of a Football Club: Role Model Award.

In the past two decades – especially in North America, where elite sports teams are run more for profit than they are in Europe – profession-al sports executives have become increasingly concerned with the image, reputation and public perception of their teams and have attempted to integrate them into the communities they purport to represent. We can explore the delivery of CSR with two brief case studies: one of a leading British soccer club and the other a major sports organization in the United States.

It is more than thirty years since the City Football Group founded City in the Community (CITC) with just one employee; at the time it was one of only six community programmes run by football clubs. Today it has more than seventy employees working with some 40,000 people in Greater Manchester. Every CITC programme has been designed to improve health and education and promote inclusion. Below we look at a few of those in operation in 2018.

The CITC disability football programme is designed to increase participation of disabled people and raise awareness of the issues that affect people with disabilities. The programme has a number of different elements, including pan-disability football sessions, powerchair football, amputee football, multi-sport disability provision and disability awareness sessions. During the three years of the programme, 878 individuals took part. Health benefits were calculated for those participants who were considered to be 'retained' in the programme. The physical activity associated with the programme delivered a total benefit of £47,000 in savings to the National Health Service, associated with the reduced healthcare costs of physically active individuals; and £212,000-worth of additional years of healthy and productive life.

This gave an overall return on investment of £1.63 per £1 invested in the programme. Participants felt that they became fitter and healthier as a result of the programme's activities, and many parents and carers said this was one of only a few physical activities offered for disabled young people in Greater Manchester. Stakeholders also provided positive evidence of empowerment and improved confidence instilled in participants by the CITC programme.

CITC's Kicks programme is designed to give young people access to a range of diversionary opportunities, with the primary objective of reducing crime and antisocial behaviour (ASB). Kicks offers people aged twelve to sixteen access to football, dance, basketball, music and gym sessions on eight sites in Manchester, reaching up to five hundred young people per week. Analysis of the volume of ASB incidents showed a distinct impact in areas where Kicks was operational. Across all the sites in the study, ASB fell by 18 per cent compared to the twelve months before the start of the programme. This contrasted with a 1 per cent rise in ASB during the same period across Manchester as a whole. The net effect was that there were 696 fewer ASB incidents in the areas around Kicks sites than would have been expected. Analysis of these figures shows that the programme delivers total benefits of £79,000 of savings to public agencies for the cost of dealing with ASB incidents, and £61,000 of social benefits associated with reduced physical and emotional impact on direct victims of ASB. This gave an overall return on investment of £1.98 per £1 invested in the programme.

Although headquartered in Britain, Manchester City has taken stakes in several overseas soccer clubs, which they use to bring on players who might ultimately prove worthy of playing in the Premier League. The decision to invest in foreign clubs was a business one, but Manchester City has also exported its CSR policy, and similar projects to those mentioned above are now in place in Melbourne and New York City.

In the United States the NFL, one of the world's major sports organizations, committed itself to philanthropic activity more than 75 years ago, and in 1973 it established NFL Charities, the first league-wide foundation in professional sports in the U.S. It supports initiatives that provide education and youth services, designates funds to assist the personal charity foundations of current and former players, and awards sports-related medical research grants. Since it began, five other philanthropic themes have emerged. Youth programmes such as A Better Future are designed to stimulate young minds, encourage healthy lifestyles and produce a life-long love of sport, particularly American football. Community outreach programmes (Building Strong Ties) centre on creating opportunities for individuals and families to succeed socially and economically. The multicultural programmes (Understanding Each Other) celebrate the diversity of the nation while working to create educational and economic opportunities for 'all people in all communities'. Volunteerism (Lending a Hand) encourages NFL fans to join teams in projects that shape communities, and the health programme Cultivating Community Health focuses on creating a balanced and healthy lifestyle for individuals and families.

In essence, these clubs and organizations have engaged in strategic philanthropy, and CSR has become an important part of their business activities; doing good has been good for business. What this has shown is that a club can use its resources to achieve both profits and social benefits: that the two are not incompatible.

25

HOW GREEN WAS MY VOLLEY?
SPORT AND THE ENVIRONMENT

Pursuing sport requires space, and so inevitably it has environmental consequences, usually detrimental ones. Some sports actually make use of the natural environment. Seas, mountains and common land have provided sites for many sports because historically access to them was unfettered by problems of ownership. Yet in exploiting this environment sport can also degrade it; just look at the piles of rubbish deposited by those attempting to conquer Everest. This is more obviously the case with the various forms of hunting, shooting and fishing, those sports that involve the fauna of the natural environment. Other sports have found their space by constructing stadia in urbanized areas, but at significant environmental cost in terms of both input and output.

Sport is bad for the environment. Nothing sport does has positive consequences for the climate or the environment. At best, sport participation and spectatorship can be neutral; at worst it can be devastating. Consider the pristine snow scene ruined by skiers, snowboarders and, worse still, powered equipment. Yet it can snow again and obliterate the scenic damage until the winter-sports enthusiasts return. The green lobby are more concerned with permanent environmental damage, as with the huge carbon footprint of millions of football fans heading to stadia across the world every week to watch their teams, or the air travel necessary to operate and attract spectators to any sporting mega event.

The sport on which environmental activists have focused is golf, a land-hungry sport, in which a standard eighteen-hole course requires some 32–40 ha (80–100 ac) of land. This might not in itself be too bad environmentally if wildlife, both flora and fauna, were encouraged to inhabit the area. In practice, however, golf's environmental impact is negative because of its water use, land depletion and toxic contamination.

Augusta National Golf Club in Georgia, USA, is one of the most famous golf clubs in the world. It has also been one of the most criticized, not for the quality of its course – which ranks in the world's top ten – but for the conservatism of its members, which meant that no women were admitted to membership until 2012. Moreover, as a Southern social institution it insisted that all caddies be black, and did not admit black golfers to the club until 1990. Augusta at Master's time is as perfect a golf course as players, spectators and television viewers could want. It was built on the site of a former nursery, and flowers and trees, some of them inherited from the site's former use, have become part of the course's distinctive charm. Pine trees, dogwoods and azaleas are still the most identifiable plantings on the course. Many of the pines are more than 150 years old, and there are more than thirty varieties of azalea there. Magnolia Lane contains 61 magnolia trees planted before the Civil War; the 'big oak tree' behind the clubhouse was planted in the late 1850s; the wisteria on a tree near the clubhouse is believed to be the largest in the country; and the privet hedge at the club was imported from France in the 1860s and is the source of most hedges of its kind in the South. Each hole at Augusta National is named after the plant surrounding the green or the approach to the hole. Yet all this comes at an environmental cost. Its pristine nature means there must be no damage from insects or disease and requires pesticides, insecticides and other chemical aids to perfection. Thus an environmental badge of dishonour can be added to the Club's other sins.

The situation is worsened by Augusta being seen as the pinnacle of what can be achieved, and becoming the standard to which other golf clubs aspire. Too many courses want to look like Augusta at Master's time. Their clientele are not satisfied with being challenged by the wilderness, but want it tamed and presented as an aesthetically pleasing landscape. Golfers were not always so demanding. The original links courses in Scotland were, apart from the putting surfaces, almost as nature intended, but as golf moved south across the border and inland, away from the sand dunes, golf-course architecture emerged as a profession to create 'artificial' natural environments. The Scottish links wilderness became less appreciated than a romanticized rural England. Golf provided a means to enjoy the countryside, although in a form created by greenkeepers. The game was to be presented as a pastoral experience, but not too wild a one, culminating on each hole with that supreme object of suburban veneration: the perfect lawn. This view of what a golf course should be has become the standard for the rest of the world.

This has had significant environmental consequences. Keeping everything green on a golf course usually requires water, 3,000–5,000 cu. m (106,000–177,000 cu. ft) a day, equivalent to the daily consumption of 2,000 American families. Worse still, this is often required in places where water is a scarce resource. Keeping a course up to expectations also often requires chemicals: herbicides, fungicides, pesticides and fertilizers, on average 11–20 kg per treated hectare (10–18 lb per acre). (Large-scale commercial agriculture uses about 3 kg per hectare/2½ lb per acre.) These may help the course look nice, but they run off into water supplies and inadvertently kill more than they were intended to. And they are not just harmful to animals and birds. A study undertaken in 1996 by researchers at the University of Iowa of more than six hundred golf-course greenkeepers found an unusually high number of deaths from brain cancer and non-Hodgkin's lymphoma.

Added to the environmental problems where golf already exists can be that of the construction of courses in the developing world, as a response both to golf tourism and to increasing domestic demand from wealthier inhabitants for high-status leisure pursuits. This often involves the destruction of natural landscape, deforestation and the clearing of vegetation, leading to gullying and erosion.

WINNING THE GAME: SPORT AND SUSTAINABILITY

The environment emerged as a major international concern in the last quarter of the twentieth century, and sustainability became a catch-cry for protecting the future. Sport, however, came late to the sustainability party; indeed, for decades golf clubs in particular have been in denial about their sport's adverse effect on the environment.

Two main arguments dominate the issue of why sports organizations should concern themselves with the environment. Both centre on self-interest. One is that sound environmental stewardship is necessary to halt environmental degradation, maintain liveable environments and ensure the long-term health of the sports industry as a whole; the other suggests that taking informed steps towards environmental responsibility can result in substantial economic benefits through the more efficient use of resources and an enhanced image. To my mind, this last point of public image is key. Most of the world has accepted both that climate change is real and that future generations – our children and their children – will suffer if we don't get our environmental act together. It has become a political necessity for sport to jump on the environmental bandwagon.

The organizers of mega events, perhaps to assuage their guilt, now demand environmental statements from potential hosts. In 1991 the IOC Charter was amended to ensure that future Olympic Games must take account of the fragile nature of the environment, and in 1994 the United Nations Environment Programme created a sports and environment unit to evaluate the impact of hosting Olympic events. This may or may not have influenced decisions to award the Games to particular hosts. But it may all be window-dressing; there is no recorded instance of the IOC or FIFA or any other promoter of sporting mega events taking retrospective action to punish hosts who failed to meet their environmental targets.

That said, the Vancouver Winter Games of 2010 emphasized environmental sustainability. Many venues collected rainwater for irrigation, and captured heat from used bath and shower water; almost 70 per cent of the heating for the Olympic Village was provided by waste heat-recovery systems; and mass transit and cycling were encouraged as alternatives to using cars. Yet the organizers still had to import snow to ensure that the skiing went ahead on schedule. At the World Cup held in South Africa in the same year, 1.3 million plastic bottles were saved from landfill as Nike supplied shirts made from recycled bottles to several countries.

The London Marathon has raised millions of pounds for charity, but does this justify the environmental damage it causes? In 2018 Westminster Council, through whose streets the event is run, collected 5,200 kg (11,465 lb) of rubbish and 3,500 kg (7,715 lb) of recyclables, including 47,000 plastic water bottles left mainly by the runners. The next year the organizers changed some of their policies to become more environmentally aware. They reduced the number of drink stations from 26 to 19, and at three of those compostable cups were used instead of plastic bottles;

the plastic bottles themselves were 50–100 per cent manufactured from recycled materials; and race instructions for competitors were digitized rather than printed. However, most of this points to amelioration rather than sustainability.

What about golf, that environmental villain? Some courses have shown that it is possible to reduce the environmental harm by building where such construction would improve land use, such as on old industrial sites and landfills; by using recycled materials for paths and bunkers; by irrigating with treated effluent; and by using organic fertilizers and compost. Whether this catches on will depend on potential consumers being concerned about the environment. Although in a survey of 5,000 golfers in Canada in 2001 some 96 per cent said they enjoyed seeing and hearing wildlife when they played, 49 per cent still wanted tees, greens and fairways to be flawlessly green.

Still, it is fair to say that sport will not be the tipping point into environmental disaster. The world's ecosystems have much more to fear from industrial producers and insatiable consumers.

THE ENVIRONMENT STRIKES BACK

Whatever damage sport inflicts on it, the environment can fight back, specifically in terms of the weather, which is a factor beyond human control and exerts its influence on every outdoor activity. Just consider the Tour de France in 2019. While the good citizens of Paris (and some of the bad ones) were sweltering in temperatures of 40 degrees C (104°F), the nineteenth stage of the race was brought to a halt by a hailstorm and a landslide. At its worst, weather can kill. Nineteen people lost their lives

---

Organic golf

'[In a perfect world] The maintenance equipment would be charged by solar power. Recycled water would be used for irrigation, and used efficiently and sparingly. There'd be a great variety of wildlife habitats. This idea that you've got to make everything look like a miniature golf course with a green carpet is crazy . . . So let's get back to the rugged qualities of the game. People ought to read the history of golf.'

Brent Blackwelder, golfer and president of the American branch of Friends of the Earth, interviewed in *Golf Digest*, 23 March 2008

in the Fastnet yacht race in 1979, when a violent August storm struck the fleet, the appalling conditions compounded by a lack of adequate safety equipment or even radio transmitters to summon help.

Every year in Britain matches are called off because of frozen or waterlogged pitches. The worst example was probably in the winter of 1963, when there was no horse racing for eight weeks – horses got fat

---

14 AUGUST 1979:
OFF FASTNET IN THE ATLANTIC OCEAN

On Saturday 11 August 1979 a total of 303 racing yachts, with some 2,700 men and women on board, set sail in fair weather down the Solent from Cowes on the Isle of Wight. They were heading out to the Fastnet Rock off southwestern Ireland, from where they would sail back south of the Scilly Isles to the race finish at Plymouth, an overall distance of about 966 km (600 mi.). Little did they anticipate that they would be sailing into a nightmare. Since 1925, when ninety sailors in nine vessels had contested the first biennial Fastnet race, there had been only two fatalities: an owner swept overboard in 1931 and a Belgian skipper who had died from a heart attack in 1977. This comparatively good safety record was to be blown apart, literally.

For two days the wind held steady, rarely blowing above 25 kph (16 mph) or below 20 kph (12 mph), but then the clouds darkened and the barometer dropped. When the race started there had been a small depression over Nova Scotia, many hundreds of kilometres away, but within 48 hours it had crossed the Atlantic and picked up speed, with wind gusts of over 110 kph (68 mph) being reported at British coastal weather stations. Out at sea the wind built up massive waves, some of them walls of water over 12 m (40 ft) high. Although the organizer of the race, the Royal Ocean Racing Club, maintained that it was the skippers alone who decided whether or not to race, it did insist that all boats be equipped with safety harnesses, life jackets and rafts, fire extinguishers and emergency rations. Crucially, however, the vessels did not have to carry a radio transmitter, only a receiver capable of picking up marine weather forecasts.

It was on these receivers that the crews heard the BBC shipping forecast at 5.50 pm on the Monday evening. It warned them of a local gale measuring force 8 on the Beaufort scale. In the next forecast, at quarter past midnight on the Tuesday morning, the warning had been upgraded to a severe gale force 9. Four hours later some of the vessels encountered gusts of force 11, well over 100 kph (62 mph). All but the largest vessels became fragile toys at the mercy of the elements. More than a third of the boats were knocked so far over that their masts paralleled the water, and a quarter capsized totally, some rolling through 360 degrees. The yacht *Adrienne* rolled twice, the first time breaking a mast, half-filling with water and severely injuring a crew member, and the second time losing a man overboard. Fearing a third roll, the remaining men took to the life raft, one of 24 crews to abandon ship. Five of those vessels later sank. Boats without radio transmitters could not seek assistance; their crews faced the storm alone, often with pounding seas and howling wind making verbal communication impossible.

A Royal Navy helicopter comes to the rescue of the crew of *Camargue*, one of the victims of the hurricane that hit the Fastnet yacht race in 1979.

Emergency services, naval forces and civilian vessels from around the western side of the English Channel were summoned to what became the largest ever rescue operation in peacetime. This involved some 4,000 people, including the entire fleet of the Irish Naval Service, lifeboats, commercial boats and helicopters. The task facing the rescuers was immense, with more than three hundred boats taking punishment in an area of about 32,000 sq. km (12,360 sq. mi.). Nevertheless, lifeboats towed in nine yachts and escorted another nine to port; helicopters lifted 74 sailors to safety; and commercial vessels and other yachts picked up a further 62. They were the luckier ones. Six men were swept away when their safety harnesses could not take the strain and broke; nine others drowned or died from hypothermia in the cold; four spectators were lost from a trimaran that was accompanying the racing vessels. Three bodies were never recovered. It was the worst disaster in the history of yacht racing.

Remarkably, the race was not abandoned. The handicap winner was the *Tenacious*, owned and skippered by CNN founder Ted Turner, but the winner on elapsed time in the race was the *Condor of Bermuda*, skippered by Peter Blake, which broke the Fastnet record by nearly eight hours. An ill wind, as they say.

and bookmakers starved – and the third round of the FA Cup, normally held in the first week of January, was not completed until the middle of March. In contrast, but just as disruptive, was the hot, dry summer of 1976 in the UK, when the watering of sports turf was banned, golf courses and bowling greens were closed, and treated sewage was applied to football and rugby pitches. Further north, the weather has certainly undermined the very existence of the Scottish ski industry. Since the late 1980s the number of days with skiable snow at Scottish ski resorts has fallen by about 25 per cent, forcing their owners to invest in snow-making guns to augment supplies, and in fences to trap the snow and keep runs open. Both are expensive and eat into profit margins. Although some resorts have already diversified into summer activities such as paragliding and mountain biking, these may not be enough, and the centres might have to move to higher slopes where there is still adequate snow. This might present additional problems of access, safety and even increased wind chill.

Those responsible for organized sport have attempted to counter the elements in several ways: by altering the rules, by improving and changing playing surfaces, or by moving indoors. Changing the rules is relatively cost-free. In 1981 the cricketing authorities, attempting to regulate a game that is particularly susceptible to wet weather, enforced the covering of wickets before a match and during rain interruptions, a practice intended to prevent bowlers from gaining too much advantage or pitches from becoming unplayable. A major innovation to the one-day game came with the introduction in 1997 of the Duckworth-Lewis-Stern system, a mathematical formula that attempts to make allowance for weather interruptions as equitably as possible. Golf, on the other hand, allows a modicum of player power. The notion of 'preferred lies' on sodden fairways that cannot be drained effectively enables competitors to select a more suitable playing position. Following two deaths from lightning on a British golf course in 1952, players are also permitted to stop play of their own accord if they consider the conditions too dangerous. In football, rugby and tennis, however, it is the referee who has sole responsibility for calling off a match.

Football clubs at the elite level have increasingly made use of pitch covers and undersoil heating to combat wintry conditions. The key to playable pitches, however, is still good drainage. Until the 1970s winter sports pitches used methods borrowed from agriculture, but the soil compaction caused by football boots often prevented surface water from reaching underground drainage pipes, resulting in goalmouth mudbaths. The problem has largely been solved by using slit drains and creating a permeable root-zone layer, but labour-intensive solutions or the use of expensive equipment are seldom an option for smaller professional and non-league or amateur clubs. State-of-the-art weatherproofing can be afforded only by wealthier sporting organizations, partly because of the high cost of any technological application, but also because one investment decision can necessitate another round of capital expenditure. Underground heating pipes are viable only if the highest standard of drainage can also be obtained, and spending money to improve drainage may require the installation of irrigation systems to prevent the ground from drying out in a hot summer and to inhibit the need for end-of-season renovation.

Artificial playing surfaces, pioneered in North America during the 1970s, are a highly successful means of combating weather-related pitch and track problems, and are particularly useful on training grounds, practice areas and local council pitches, which are subject to intensive use. They are resistant to wear and tear and, unlike grass, can be repaired at any time of year. Different sports have responded in different ways. Hockey authorities have fully embraced the new technology and determined that elite games must be played on a water-based synthetic surface. Wimbledon is rare in sticking to grass for elite tennis tournaments, and at the recreational level that surface is restricted to a few select clubs. Top-grade cricket, however, has refused to countenance artificial surfaces, even though they are widely used for indoor practice, and golf restricts their use to winter tees at non-elite level, and for pathways and practice areas. Artificial surfaces in football have had a chequered history. Although the English and Scottish football leagues initially sanctioned artificial pitches during the 1980s and they were installed at several clubs as part of community sports-facility initiatives, they had been phased out by 1994 after complaints of abnormal ball bounce, injuries and unfair home-ground advantage. A decade later, however, both FIFA and UEFA changed their rules to encourage the use of the next-generation artificial surfaces.

The introduction of all-weather tracks in British horse racing highlights the way climate can affect potential viability. Although a relatively minor sport, racing is a sizeable leisure industry, employing more than 35,000 people in training, breeding and racing itself. Even the loss of one day's meetings can have financial implications for the industry, and the cancellation of ten Boxing Day fixtures in 1995 cost the sport about £5 million in lost levy contributions from the bookmakers. Longer periods of interruption could be devastating. In 1989, in response to concerns about the number of winter meetings lost to frost, snow and waterlogging, the Jockey Club approved artificial tracks at two courses, Lingfield Park in Surrey and Southwell in Nottinghamshire, followed in 1993 by another at Wolverhampton. Although some weather conditions – fog, flood and high wind – defeated even so-called all-weather tracks, fewer than twenty fixtures were lost in the first ten years, and now nearly one-fifth of all flat-race meetings take place on such courses. The substitution of artificial for turf surfaces is a more certain way of attaining consistent going as required by the Jockey Club, but it changes the tactical nature of flat-racing and has not been favourably received by those involved at the elite level. Nevertheless, all-weather courses have been the economic salvation of flat-racing as a whole because they have enabled a betting market to be maintained throughout the year. Such surfaces cannot currently assist National Hunt racing, however, having been banned in 1994 following a number of injuries and fatalities to horses and riders.

At the non-professional level, artificial surfaces have been adopted by local councils for use by children and recreational sports teams because they can't afford to maintain grass playing areas that cannot cope with bad weather or even just intensive use. The greater intensity of use that artificial surfaces can withstand also has economic relevance for multi-use recreational sport sites. Natural grass can typically accommodate about three hundred hours of play per year, and reinforced turf around eight hundred, but artificial turf can take more than 3,000. Moreover, the grass of such pitches is often full of pesticides and pollen, with the consequent risk to allergy sufferers and the health of the users more generally. But switching surfaces has its own problems; the rubber infill used in many pitches is toxic, and there is also a greater risk of burn injury.

A solution to weather problems for sports as diverse as swimming, tennis and bowls has been to move them indoors. Ironically, winter sports such as curling, ice hockey and ice skating, originally designed to make use of the outdoor environment, are normally held indoors to ensure adequate depth and uniformity of ice. Even climbing and skiing are moving indoors, albeit on a reduced scale, as entrepreneurs offer a mountain experience in an urban environment. Moving indoors has also proved beneficial to spectators, a group whose comfort in bad weather has not always been a major concern of sports organizers and promoters. Although grandstands were originally built to raise money from those who could afford to pay, major reports on many football stadia in the late twentieth century showed how dismal and decrepit they had become, offering shelter but little comfort and few facilities. Wimbledon, the sole grass-court Grand Slam tennis tournament, has been severely affected by rain on several occasions, prompting the tournament committee to sanction Sunday play as the only way of finishing on time. Although spectators were delighted by this decision, it cost Wimbledon money. This, together with pressure from television companies, finally persuaded the All England Club to incorporate a sliding roof into its plans for the redevelopment of Centre Court, in order to safeguard the commercial viability of the tournament.

In the eyes of aficionados, the methods used to overcome climatic problems sometimes change the whole nature of a sport. When all-weather tracks were introduced to British horse racing, there was an outcry from supporters who still believed that racing thoroughbreds was more concerned with improving the breed than providing a legitimate vehicle for gambling. The Duckworth-Lewis-Stern method of deciding one-day cricket matches in the event of rain interruptions was similarly frowned on by purists, just as the idea of a retractable roof at Wimbledon regularly brought forth observations that no one is a champion unless they have dealt with the weather. Golf correspondents and fans say the same about the Open Golf Championship. This school of thought holds that those who play sport must adapt their game to the elements: golfers and tennis players have to adjust their shots to the prevailing wind, rugby players must take account of wet turf and slippery balls, and marathon runners plan their race tactics according to heat and humidity. Battling the weather as well as the opposition is seen as part of playing sport.

In this section we have mainly focused on the situation in Britain, but in the long term all countries will have to consider how sport will be affected by climate change. Where the weather becomes wetter, it is probable that only the wealthiest organizations will be able to afford to weatherproof their facilities, while the majority of clubs, local authorities and schools will still have to face the elements. Clubs will be forced to spend on improving drainage, and some may attempt to move to more suitable ground. Where summers become hotter and drier, what priority will sport be given in the allocation of scarce water supplies? A third possibility predicted by climatologists is that extreme weather events may become more common, so regular severe storms will disrupt the play of golfers and sailors, among others.

26

SELLING OUT THE GAME:
MATCH-FIXING AND DRUG-TAKING

Although this chapter focuses on more modern sport, it should be emphasized that cheating and corruption are far from recent phenomena. Common perceptions of medieval sport have been unduly influenced by romantic ideas generated by the gothic revivalism of the nineteenth century, which emphasized the chivalry of tournaments and jousts. In fact, knights did cheat and were punished for their transgressions. Even earlier the prizes and kudos for winning in the ancient Olympics and other Greek games tempted athletes to cheat. Indeed, the host of bronze statutes honouring Zeus that lined the path through the sacred grove into the Olympic Stadium were paid for from the fines levied on cheating participants.

The uncertainty of the result is a bedrock of sport. Moreover, the fact that the result in a sports event cannot be predicted with certainty is what makes it so attractive to gamblers. For sportspeople to underperform deliberately or not play to win undermines the integrity of sport, as, of course, does the taking of performance-enhancing drugs to improve chances of victory. This is of concern not just to players, fans and promoters, but to the betting industry, which, despite outsider assertions to the contrary, has always been supportive of fair play in sport.

The difficulty for historians is finding evidence of corruption. When drug cheats are found out and match-fixers exposed, the information is sometimes publicized, but not always. Sporting authorities are reluctant to admit that corruption occurs in their sport, believing this might put off the paying public and sponsors. This code of silence is aggravated by the fact that in many countries neither doping nor match-fixing is a criminal offence. Worse still, from the historian's point of view, successful match-fixing or drug use is covert. No one boasts about beating the system, so we have no real idea about the extent of doping or match-fixing in sport.

How do we find out about corruption, then? For doping we are dependent on the statistics issued by testers, particularly the World Anti-Doping Agency, which reveals the proportion of positive tests, although these have been manipulated at times, particularly most recently by Russia, whose laboratories have lost their accreditation. Fortunately, in the case of match-fixing, the number-crunching capabilities of modern computers have enabled statisticians (mainly economists) to apply probability theory to large databases of sports results and assess whether some may have been pre-determined. It must be emphasized that not every unexpected result is because of match fixing; one of the delights of sport is its unpredictability. Even if obvious defensive lapses occur, blatant rule transgressions are ignored by the officials, or double faults are served in a tiebreak, it does not mean corruption has occurred. Both players and referees have off days and make unintended errors. However, large-scale data analysis can reveal patterns of behaviour that could raise suspicions of systemic corruption.

LESSENING THE GAMBLE

Sport and gambling can work well together – having a bet can add to the excitement of the event, and the unpredictability of sport can create a lively betting market – but there is always the temptation for fraud. Gamblers or bookmakers can find ways to persuade an individual or team to underperform in a particular event using threats, sex or money as their weapon. The knowledge that someone will not be trying gives them an edge in the betting markets. Gambling helped to create sport, but it could also destroy it.

Horse racing, a sport held together by betting, has always been susceptible to a jockey, trainer or owner deciding that a horse would not run on its merits. Knowing that a horse is not going to attempt to win gives bettors an advantage. In the 1980s an examination of every race

Handicap horse race in New Orleans, c. 1906.

in Britain over a four-month period found that 13.6 per cent of runners exhibited a marked difference between the morning forecast price and the actual starting price. Some of these would be in a negative direction as those in the know bet on horses other than those that were not being run on their merits. Of course, not all the others would turn out to be winners. All the data suggests is that there was the potential for profitable insider trading by those with superior knowledge (not publicly available) of the real probabilities, and that such betting practices were common in British racing.

Betting influences sports other than horse racing. In 2007, at a Polish tennis tournament, Nikolay Davydenko (top seed and fourth-ranked player on the ATP Tour) was one set up against Martín Vassallo Argüello, who was 87th in the rankings. Yet the in-play betting markets still favoured his opponent. Eventually Davydenko forfeited to his opponent in the final set. Later analysis has suggested that this was but one high-profile incident among a slew of match-fixing on both the men's and the women's tours. A study of nearly 50,000 contests between 2006 and 2013 suggested a tanking rate of about 1 per cent, after allowing for difference in skill. This has now been confirmed by an official report by the tennis authorities, which said there was a tsunami of match-fixing on the professional circuits.

In any sport that involves handicapping, a culture of corruption emerges in which beating the handicapper is a prime objective. Some deliberately reduced effort by athletes and horse trainers is intended as 'signal jamming', to confuse future opponents as to their true form and to outwit bookmakers, who may then offer longer odds on the under-performing participant in a future race. This is particularly relevant in handicap events such as Australian professional running, where ability may be hidden for two years or more. Here corruption is accepted as a norm, but a distinction is drawn between 'clean' cheating to beat the bookmakers and 'dirty' cheating, involving a betrayal of trust within the training stable by not sharing information on a planned coup or fix.

CHEATING WITH HONOUR

Two forms of gambling have allowed players to yield to the temptations of the gamblers without actually having to throw a game. With the development of Internet gambling has come 'spot fixing', where the bet might be on the time of the first corner or free kick in soccer, whether a bowler will bowl a no ball in cricket, or if a batter will strike out in baseball. All these allow players to underperform without necessarily affecting the result of the game.

More long-standing is 'point shaving', which occurs when athletes deliberately underperform to change the margin of victory or defeat in the context of handicap betting systems. Wagers are not on which team will win, but on which team will do better than the result suggested by the quoted 'spread' in the betting markets. Point shaving allows players to cheat with 'honour' – or, at least, without significant disutility. Their team can still win, but not by as much as the betting markets had predicted, so the team still gains the league points while the gamblers who offered the bribe win their bets and the players collect their pay-offs (only Joe Public loses out).

The first quantitative study of this was in American college basketball. It was based on the premise that successful point shaving was more likely for strong favourites (those favoured to win by more than 12 points), since reducing a winning margin from (say) 14 to 9 points is a less risky strategy than trying to win by only a few points, an objective that could backfire on the team. An examination of 44,120 NCAA Division I games between 1989 and 2005 for which spread betting data were available suggested that around 6 per cent of strong favourites had been willing to manipulate their performance, leading to a conclusion that about 1 per cent of all games involved gambling-related corruption.

WINNING BY LOSING

Although some games have been fixed by gamblers, others are arranged because of the structure of the sport's organization, specifically the operation of open leagues where promotion and relegation are in play. In March 1915 Manchester United were saved from relegation by a 2-0 victory over Liverpool. The referee reported a lack of enthusiasm by the Liverpool players, one of whom missed a penalty; another was remonstrated with by his teammates when his shot hit the Manchester crossbar. A subsequent FA enquiry found that several of the Liverpool players had been bribed. Additionally, these days, places in the league table can lead to entry in other lucrative competitions as well as bonus money from the league organizers. This may account for some of the match-fixing that has occurred on a significant scale in Czech, Turkish, Polish and Chinese football since the turn of the millennium. In Turkey 93 officials and players were indicted in relation to 19 matches; the biggest scandal in the Czech Republic involved 27 referees and 14 clubs; in Poland 638 games have been declared fixed; and in China the credibility of more than half of the First Division games in 2003 was questioned.

The structure of sports tournaments themselves can make trying to win a non-optimal strategy. Let us transport ourselves to 1994 and the National Stadium in Bridgetown, Barbados (or, even better, have a look on YouTube), where the home side was playing Grenada in the Shell Caribbean Cup in soccer. The score was 2-0 to the home side, which was cruising its way into the knock-out stages with the requisite two-goal margin needed to win its group. Then, unexpectedly, Grenada scored, meaning that – despite losing the game – Grenada would qualify for the finals on better goal difference. The Grenada team retreated to a mass defence to protect their goal. Here the peculiarities of the tournament structure came into play. Whether or not they were under the influence of rum no one knows, but the organizers had decided that all games had to have a winner, so games that were tied at 90 minutes had to go to sudden-death extra time, in which the first goal scored gave victory. Second, and most unusually, the extra-time goal would count double, meaning that the winner would be awarded a two-goal victory. The penny dropped with the Barbadian players, who realized that their best hope was to play for extra time, and two defenders inter-passed before one of them slammed the ball past his own goalkeeper, tying the game 2-2. The Grenadians then realized that if they too scored an own goal their consequent 2-3 defeat would still eliminate Barbados. For the last five normal minutes of the match spectators witnessed Grenada attempting to score in either goal while Barbados defended both ends of the pitch successfully, ensuring a drawn game and extra time in which they emerged as victors.

Another instance of the tournament structure having unanticipated consequences came in English football. Following the introduction of a second division into the English Football League in 1892, promotion and relegation were determined by play-offs involving the bottom two teams in the First Division and the top two in the Second. After each team had played three matches, Burnley and Stoke both had four points (two for a win in those days), while Newcastle and Blackburn both had two. Hence if Stoke drew its final game with Burnley, both teams were guaranteed First Division status, no matter the result of the Newcastle/Blackburn match. Whether there was any collusion is a moot point, but the game on 30 April at the Victoria Ground, Stoke-on-Trent, ended in a scoreless draw with allegedly not one shot at goal during the entire ninety minutes.

The structure of sumo tournaments in Japan has also led to corruption. At the elite championship level, six tournaments are held every year, each lasting fifteen days, with each of the fifteen qualifying wrestlers participating once a day. Rankings, which determined a wrestler's social status and monthly income, were revised after each tournament, taking into account each wrestler's wins and losses. During the tournament each victory was worth about three ranking points, except an eighth win, which offered eleven points. This non-linearity of rewards meant that in the crucial bout when a wrestler had seven wins he stood to gain much more than his opponent stood to lose, a situation that provided an opportunity for possible match-fixing. An analysis of 32,000 bouts involving

281 wrestlers between 1989 and 2000 revealed overwhelming evidence that some wrestlers were not pushing their weight in the final days of the tournaments. Approximately 26 per cent of all wrestlers finished with exactly eight victories and only 12.2 per cent with seven, whereas the statistical expectation would have been for a frequency of 19.6 per cent in both cases. Moreover, the loser in a 'rigged' match had an unusually high percentage of wins next time those two wrestlers met; in effect, matches were thrown in the expectation that a quid pro quo would ensue.

It has even happened at the Olympics. In London in 2012 eight badminton players were disqualified for not trying to win in the pool stages of the women's doubles. Where a team finished in their pool determined who they would face in the next stage of the competition, and losing was seen by those players as giving them a better chance to advance further in the competition.

The draft system operating in elite American sport offers temptation to more systematic corruption. As part of their drive towards competitive balance, several leagues have introduced the use of the reverse-order player draft. Essentially this gives first choice of eligible new recruits to the team that finished last the previous season. The team immediately above them gained second choice, through to the champions, who had last choice in the first round of selection. The cycle is then repeated for further rounds. Ironically, this offers a perverse initiative for teams to lose matches deliberately once any chance of making the play-offs for the title has gone. Losing their final matches of the season can improve their position in the draft and lead to a stronger side for the following season. The system creates what has been termed 'race-to-the-bottom incentives', as revealed in a study of three seasons of NBA basketball. In 1983/4, when a standard reverse-order draft system was applied at the end of the season, with due allowance for home-court advantage and the quality of the opposition, non-play-off teams were approximately 2.5 times more likely to lose than their play-off-bound counterparts. Next season, when the system changed to give each non-play-off team an equal chance of obtaining top draft choices via a lottery system, there was no difference in the relative performances of both groups, but for 1989/90, when a revised weighted lottery gave teams with the worse records greater probability (but not certainty) of obtaining higher draft choices, the ratio had risen again, to 2.2 times.

18 JANUARY 2000: CENTURION PARK, GAUTENG PROVINCE, SOUTH AFRICA

On the first day of the final Test match in the five-game series between South Africa and England at Centurion Park, South Africa crept to 155-6 in 45 overs before the rain came. The next three days were washed out, and the game was petering out into a boring draw. Hansie Cronje, the charismatic captain of South Africa, intercepted Alec Stewart, the England wicketkeeper, and asked him if Nasser Hussain, his England counterpart, might be interested in arranging a contrived finish, as occasionally happened in county cricket when the weather intervened. He suggested that South Africa would declare and both sides forfeit an innings, leaving a target for England to chase for victory. It was not as if the series were at stake, since South Africa had already taken a 2-0 lead.

At a meeting between Hussain and his senior players it was decided to wait and see how the morning's play progressed before responding. When play resumed, the overnight (from three days ago) batsmen had no problems on what was now a placid pitch. A run chase might be feasible. Hussain sent a message to ask if the deal was still on and to say that England would be willing to chase 250. Cronje did not haggle and declared at 249, leaving England 76 overs to reach their target. Traditionalists were aghast. This undermined the basis of five-day cricket, in which attrition and concentration were valued com-ponents. But many cricket fans and players thought it a magnificent sporting gesture, a brave and rare example of positive thinking in the sport, creating the chance to breathe some life into a dying match.

Technically England were not allowed to forfeit their first innings, so Hussain declared at 0-0. However, the rules did allow South Africa to forfeit their second innings. It was a thrilling game. England looked to have made it at 228-4 after 70 overs, but then panic set in with 4 wickets falling for only 12 runs. With tail-enders at the crease, 9 runs were required from thirteen balls. England made the target with 2 wickets and five balls to spare. Both teams had been in with a shout of winning, yet Cronje was not bothered about whether South Africa won or lost the match. What he did not want, it turned out, was a draw. He had been approached by Indian bookmakers who had too many bets riding on a drawn match. He had been promised R500,000 (£50,000) towards a charity of his choice to ensure a positive result. In the event he received only two payments, of R30,000 and R20,000, and a leather jacket as a present.

This came to light in April 2000 after an Indian newspaper reported that the Delhi police had recordings of telephone conversations between Cronje and a representative of an Indian betting syndicate discussing match-fixing schemes. The South African government set up a commission under Judge Edwin King to investigate corruption in their sport. While denying that he had ever been involved in match-fixing, Cronje admitted to bribing players to perform below expectations so as to aid spot-fixing bets rather than match results. The South African captain – a man who wore a bracelet inscribed 'What would Jesus do?' – acknowledged that 'in a moment of weakness, I allowed Satan to dictate terms to me, rather than the Lord.' In the opinion of several knowledgeable observers, the King Commission was shut down by the South African government before the full picture emerged, an unacceptable picture that would have reflected badly on the country. Tellingly, the judge refused to acknowledge that Cronje had been totally honest when giving his evidence. The South African Cricket Board gave Cronje a lifetime ban from playing or coaching cricket. He challenged the decision, but his appeal was dismissed. Subsequent investigations by reporters found that he had more than seventy illegal bank accounts in the Cayman Islands, possible evidence that his involvement in spot-fixing was larger than he had admitted.

After his ban from cricket Cronje took a job as an accounts manager with a South African company, and each weekend flew home as a non-paying passenger on a freight flight. On 1 June 2002 the plane never made it to the local airport, crashing into a mountain in bad weather. Pilot error was blamed, although conspiracy theorists believed the plane was sabotaged to shut Cronje up for ever.

In 2004 the South African Broadcasting Corporation ran a poll to find the 100 greatest South Africans. Hansie Cronje came eleventh. He remained an Afrikaner icon, a convincing leader who inspired loyalty even from those teammates he tried to bribe. To many white South Africans he remains a great man who made a mistake; to the Afrikaners among them his rise and fall constitute a metaphor for their own lost supremacy.

In contrast, another study found no evidence of tanking in the Australian Football League, the premier football competition in Australia, despite a reverse-order draft system being introduced in 1986 as the primary mechanism for assigning new players to clubs. This lack of tanking in the AFL can be explained by a relatively low marginal benefit from an improved draft position. One player of extra-high ability will have more impact in the NBA than in Australian football, since teams have five players on the basketball court but eighteen on the footy oval.

TAKE THE MONEY AND RUN (BUT NOT AS FAST)

Economists argue that economic actors seek to maximize what is termed 'utility', which can be gauged in financial terms, using both real and psychic income. The latter infers a value that individuals place on personal kudos, honour or other non-pecuniary rewards. At the level of the individual, the athlete or official essentially undertakes a personal cost-benefit analysis by assessing the relative influence of several factors. The individual has legal and illicit alternatives for action and chooses the course of action that, at the time, promises the greatest personal net utility. Any bribe or other reward must be high enough to render the utility higher than the expected disutility (which includes the chances of being caught and the penalty if found guilty) plus the value of the moral threshold.

Low earnings, absolutely and even relatively, are an obvious contributory factor to match-fixing. When players are paid badly to perform well, the alternative of being paid well to play badly could prove attractive. The Chicago Black Sox baseball players who threw the World Series in 1919 had not been paid the money promised to them as a reward for reaching the finals; the English footballers who fixed games in the 1950s were subject to maximum wage legislation that prevented them from earning their full economic rents; the low pay of Pakistani players was a contributory factor in the corruption problems of that country's cricket from the 1890s; and the perennial poor rewards for many British racehorse trainers tempted them to make use of inside information.

Another aspect of income affecting corruption decisions, particularly in individual sports, is the distribution of prize money. Where it is allocated asymmetrically it may incentivize players to try harder in an attempt to win more, but paradoxically it may also make a guaranteed sum as a bribe for underperforming an attractive alternative incentive. Where one player or team has more to gain from a result than their opponents, the opposition might be offered an incentive to lose, as for example in the sumo wrestling tournaments.

Third, the length of a player's contract can influence shirking. A study of Major League Baseball showed that some players who received new long-term contracts eased off the following season because they had job security (at least in the short run). The argument is not that they will deliberately lose specific games, but that at times during the season they will underperform, perhaps because of inadequate preparation for a game.

GETTING WORSE?

It has been suggested that match-fixing was common, almost expected and tolerated in eighteenth-century sport, but became less prevalent (or less overt) once the amateur ethic became established in Victorian times and emphasis was placed on maintaining the purity of sport. However, we simply do not know what the situation was, because of the nature of the evidence we have. Even if we restrict the analysis to recent years, evidence is rooted in opinion rather than comparative statistics. Declan Hill, an investigative journalist with a doctorate in sociology, believes that the war against match-fixers is being lost, predominately because of the globalization of the sports gambling market. This is also the view of a report solicited by the European Commission, which noted that scandals have multiplied in recent years and encompass all disciplines, all levels of sport and a wide range of countries. Looking just at Australia, recent research has suggested that in the past decade match-fixing has occurred in Victorian soccer, New South Wales greyhound racing, horse racing nationwide, national rugby league and, that cultural icon of Australia, Aussie Rules football.

DOES IT MATTER?

It must be specified how such undermining of 'sporting integrity' actually damages a sport beyond ethical rhetoric and condemnation. Too many of the reports on sporting integrity assume that it is a 'good thing' to keep sport free from competition corruption, but the adverse consequences of not doing so are rarely made explicit. Even when dire predictions are made, there tends to be no risk assessment, just statements that a calamity 'might' happen.

Can history enlighten us? Bold statements have been made by sports historians (including myself when younger) that corruption in nineteenth-century sport led to the decline of prizefighting, Cornish wrestling, open-water swimming contests and professional sculling. Yet no real evidence is ever produced to substantiate them.

Some football leagues in East Asia have lost hundreds of millions of dollars in sponsorship money because of corruption. Chinese football certainly lost followers through corruption. In 1994 a league system was launched in China modelled on Western soccer, but fears of relegation and the potential profits of promotion and championships led to a spate of match-fixing. Ultimately the league lost its reputation, fans protested and eventually stopped attending, and investors and sponsors withdrew their money from the clubs. Empirical investigations of fan support of Italian clubs found guilty of corrupt practices in the early twenty-first century suggest that home attendances fell by around 16 per cent relative to clubs that were not subject to punishment. Yet anecdotal evidence of widespread corruption in English football in the 1950s and early 1960s did not lead to the withdrawal of fans or sponsors, and there has been no decline of spectator interest in British horse racing, Japanese sumo, or American college and professional basketball. Stage cycle races in Europe have survived despite long-term allegations of both drug-taking and race-fixing.

Why have some sports gone under but others survived? Research (alas not yet done) into the now defunct professional sports mentioned above might reveal whether there is a level of corruption that acts as a tipping point and condemns a sport to spectator oblivion.

KEEP TAKING THE TABLETS

When I taught a class on sporting ethics and the use of drugs, I began by having all the students stand, before instructing them to sit down if they had had a beer (or any undefined recreational drug) the previous evening. This was followed by seating those who were on painkillers or other medication. The final group to take their seats were those caffeine addicts who had kick-started their morning with a cup of tea or coffee. The remaining students, few in number but upright in stance both physically and morally in their non-use of drugs, I labelled as 'social deviants'. It can be reasonably asked why, in a society where drug-taking is on the increase both recreationally and medically, we should expect sport to be drug-free.

Sportspeople resort to drugs for many reasons. One, of course, is legitimate therapeutic use. Like the rest of us athletes suffer from colds, upset stomachs and hay fever. The problem is that some of the medication to combat these conditions contains banned substances. If you had a cold and went to the local pharmacy for help, Sudafed would mean you failed a drug test but Actifed would keep you in the clear. The Scottish alpine skier Alain Baxter lost a bronze medal in the Salt Lake City Winter Olympics of 2002 by inadvertently ingesting methamphetamine from a nasal inhaler he had purchased in the United States. He had been unaware that the contents were different from those found in the British version.

Some athletes use restorative drugs to help them to overcome injury, because they allow them to continue to train or even compete during their recovery. These are what I would term 'performance-enabling drugs'. Then there are recreational substances that, apart from helping the athlete to relax, probably do not offer significant performance benefits, but nevertheless are frowned on by the ruling bodies of many sports who wish to protect the image of their sport from the 'social drugs culture'. However, the major drug problem in modern sport, particularly at the elite level, is that of performance enhancement, as competitors seek any marginal advantage over their rivals or to prevent their rivals from gaining an advantage over them (in the belief or knowledge that their competitors are using such drugs). It is a different form of corruption from match-fixing, because the winner is not predetermined.

The extent to which performance-enhancing drugs infiltrated (some might say invaded) athletics is illustrated by the final of the 100 metres at the 1988 Olympics in Seoul. Most readers will be aware that the original gold medallist, the Canadian sprinter Ben Johnson, was disqualified after testing positive for the steroid stanozolol. Less well known is the drug record of the other finalists. Carl Lewis from the United States was upgraded from silver medal position; he was later revealed to have failed three drug tests before the Seoul Games, but had been cleared to participate by the American Olympic authorities. The new silver medallist, Britain's Linford Christie, failed a drug test later that year and another in 1999. Of the remaining runners, another American, Dennis Mitchell, went on to win two world championship before testing positive for testosterone in 1998, and a second Canadian, Desai Williams, was later found to have been supplied with steroids by a team doctor. Then there is the man who finished last, the Jamaican Ray Stewart, who became a leading coach but who was banned for life in 2010 after trafficking banned substances to athletes. The bronze medal winner (after Johnson's disqualification), Calvin Smith from the United States, and the Brazilian Robson da Silva were the only runners in that final not to have been tainted with drugs. Yet this may not have been the 'dirtiest' race in history. That (dis)honour may go to the women's 1,500 metres final at the 2012 London Olympics. Six of the nine top finishers had already received or were later to receive bans for drug offences. Significantly, the three women who finished in the last places never failed a drugs test. The question of adequate punishment and negative reinforcement of inappropriate behaviour must be addressed. Johnson went on to fail two more drugs tests, and what of the 2017 world sprint champion, Justin Gatlin, a runner whose career has encompassed bans for two doping offences?

You're never too old to cheat

When he won the 90–94 age group sprint title at the U.S. Masters Track National Championships in July 2018, Carl Grove, a veteran American cyclist, set a new world record, only to test positive for epitrenbolone, a substance prohibited by the United States Anti-Drug Agency. Although the Agency declared that this violation of anti-doping rules was 'more likely than not' to have been caused by the consumption of a contaminated piece of meat the night before the race, the same in-competition urine test also revealed that a supplement the nonagenarian was using was contaminated with clomiphene, another prohibited substance.

Then there is stage cycling. There were allegations of doping in the Tour de France from its inception in 1903, a continuation of the use in endurance cycling of pain-dulling substances such as alcohol, strychnine, ether (soaked into handkerchiefs) and cocaine. Over time more sophisticated products were added to the cycle bag, and for sixty years or so such survival drug-taking was countenanced in the sport as a means to counter the tedium, pain and exhaustion. However, in 1965 a national anti-doping law was passed in France, and the police began to raid team hotels in search of prohibited substances. The reaction of most of the cyclists was to go on strike. They did likewise in 1998, when the police again became involved. The cyclists were part of a subculture within professional cycling that not only tolerated the taking of drugs, but actively promoted their use. Jacques Anquetil, a five-time Tour winner, argued that amphetamines were essential to get through a race in which riders had to be on their bikes almost every day for three weeks or so.

Although the volume of testing has expanded, delays in legal proceedings, the wish of the French authorities not to damage a major tourist attraction, and the development of new drugs and doping techniques have allowed doping to continue. A century of doping culminated in the revelation that the American Lance Armstrong, who had dominated the Tour between 1998 and 2005, has used erythropoietin (EPO) for much of his Tour de France career. He was not alone. Only one podium finisher during the Armstrong era – Fernando Escartín, who came third in 1999 – has not subsequently been tied to doping. Armstrong's disgrace has not ended allegations of drug-taking on the Tour. The history-making first two British winners of the race, Bradley Wiggins and Chris Froome, have been criticized, especially by European fans of the sport, for taking advantage of dubious (to some) medical exemptions to take drugs that are normally prohibited for riders.

How did we come to this? The use of natural or chemical substances to aid athletic performance is nothing new. The ancient Greeks used hallucinogens to give them a competitive edge; Roman gladiators and knights of old used stimulants to maintain their energy after injury; and late nineteenth-century athletes took nitroglycerine on sugar to dilate their coronary arteries and improve cardiac output. Thomas Hicks's use of drugs and alcohol to win the Olympic marathon in 1904 (of which more below) did not get him disqualified because, unlike a fellow competitor,

LANCE ARMSTRONG (1971–)

Lance Armstrong was a world-class road-racing cyclist and a cheat. He beat cancer to win seven consecutive Tour de France titles and a bronze medal at the Sydney Olympics, but later admitted to having based his cycling career on the use of performance-enhancing drugs.

Born Lance Edward Gunderson, he took the surname of his mother's second husband. He began his sporting life as a swimmer but moved into triathlon, in which he turned professional aged sixteen and won the national sprint-course championship in both 1989 and 1990. Two years later he joined the Motorola Cycling Team, and in 1993 he won ten one-day events and also the World Road Racing Championship. This was a precursor of future success, but in 1996 Armstrong was diagnosed with advanced testicular cancer, which had spread to his lymph nodes, lungs, brain and abdomen. Pioneering chemotherapy treatment put the cancer into remission. His final treatment was in December 1996, and by January 1998 he was in Europe training with his new team, U.S. Postal. Before his cancer Armstrong had ridden in four Tours de France, winning two stages although twice failing to compete the race. In 1998, however, he won four stages and the overall race. He went on to victory in the next six Tours, the last in the fastest pace to date of 41.7 kph (just under 26 mph). A major contributor to his success was that he changed the nature of the support behind his teams, getting suppliers to work together rather than, for example, developing frames, tyres and handlebars separately.

Armstrong then retired from professional cycling but made a comeback on the Tour, finishing third in 2009 when riding for Astana and 23rd (after too many crashes) for RadioShack in 2010. He then opted out of the sport permanently but took up triathlon again, finishing fourth at the XTERRA nationals and23rd in the World Championships. In 2002 he began to pursue qualification for the Ironman World Championships.

After his own cancer Armstrong did much for charity, including launching the Lance Armstrong Foundation to support people affected by cancer; the foundation has raised more than $300 million. He

competed in two New York marathons and also the Boston event
to raise funds personally. In 2001 he provided the funding to set up a
Texas charity, Wonders & Worries, to provide counselling and support
to children who have a parent with a life-threatening illness.

Then, in January 2013, in an interview with the American television
personality Oprah Winfrey, Armstrong publicly admitted that he had
taken performance-enhancing drugs, mainly erythropoietin, commonly
called EPO, during his successful Tour de France exploits. This confession was the culmination of two decades of rumours, assertions and
denials, years in which Armstrong had bullied members of his teams
also to resort to doping, successfully sued or settled out of court
with those who alleged that he had taken drugs himself, and poured
scorn on those riders who had been caught doping. His argument
was essentially that it was impossible to win a Grand Tour without
using drugs because the culture of cycling condoned such actions.
How could it really be cheating when everyone was doing it? Critics
felt that Armstrong's confession was partial, since he refused to name
other users or incriminate his personal cycling doctor, Michele Ferrari.
Nor did he explain fully how on 24 occasions of unannounced testing
he had been declared clean. Others argue that he had been painted
into a corner by a United States Anti-Doping Agency (USADA) report
in June 2012, which maintained that under the direction of Ferrari
Armstrong had taken performance-enhancing drugs, for which he had
paid the good doctor more than $1 million: and this was an attempt to
rehabilitate himself.

The accusations in the USADA report were based on blood samples from 2009 and 2010, Armstrong's comeback years, but also on
testimony from former teammates. In October 2012 he was formally
charged with running a massive doping ring and the USADA sought to
have him banned for life from all sports sanctioned by the World Anti-
Doping Agency (WADA). Armstrong chose not to appeal, saying that it
would not be worth the toll it would take on his family. He lost all his
endorsements, reportedly $75 million in one day. Companies that had
sponsored him demanded their money back, as did those athletes who
had been sued by Armstrong. He was stripped of his Tour de France
titles although, in implicit recognition of the pervasive drug culture in

the sport, they were not given to any other riders. The ensuing ban from WADA put paid to his triathlon ambitions, and he had to resign as the driving force of his foundation, which was renamed the Livestrong Foundation.

In a BBC interview in 2015, Armstrong declared that if he were back in 1995 (when he began doping), he would probably make the same decisions again.

who hitched a ride during the race, what he did was not against the rules. Until the late 1950s, with the exception of horse racing, the use of any drug in sport was not an offence, and there was little stigma attached to it. Any concern was over the possible health risks associated with effects on the central nervous system during sport-induced fatigue. Indeed, until then scientists and governments had seen drugs in sport as positive, as a way of reducing fatigue in sportspeople, as they had done for soldiers.

However, by the early 1960s there was a change in the official view of drugs in sport, linked with more general concern about drug use in wider society and the fact that sport itself was changing and drugs becoming more common. This was attributable partly to the growing kudos and economic rewards of winning, itself associated with a perverted form of nationalism as states saw successful sports performances as reflecting well on the nation. Much has been made of the drugs regimes of former Communist states, particularly East Germany and the USSR. The former won no gold medals in swimming at the 1972 Munich Olympics, but, thanks to a state-supported drugs policy, gained eleven at the following Games in Montreal. A similar policy became so prevalent in Russia that the entire team was banned from the 2018 Winter Olympics in Pyeongchang. Yet the United States, determined to display the superiority of the free world over those damned commies, has also been involved. In 1983/4 the U.S. ran secret 'no penalty' tests that revealed that over 20 per cent of their athletes were doping. Later, at the level of individual sports, those in charge did not want positive tests to give their sport a bad image, and doctors and testers were subject to influence so that that did not happen. American sport in particular demanded celebrities, particularly record-breakers, and it was easier to break records using performance-enhancing drugs than to run clean. Before condemning other nations too readily, Americans should remember the steroid abuse in the NFL in the 1970s and the testosterone-assisted home-run record-breaking feats in MLB in the 1990s.

THEY'LL GET YOU IN THE END

No sport is immune from the scourge of doping. When the WADA carried out its tests in 2017 it was not surprising that the sport with the highest rate of urine samples containing banned substances was bodybuilding, an activity in which many participants rely on drugs to shape themselves. However, in second place was bridge, a card game that is played sitting down, and which many would not even classify as a sport – a view clearly not shared by WADA. Yet bridge tournaments can be attritional, often lasting a couple of weeks, which tempts some players to take testosterone to improve their cognitive function. In 2019 the world number one, Geir Helgemo of Norway, was suspended for a year after testing positive for synthetic testosterone.

There is an ongoing race between drug developers and the testers, but WADA has one thing going for it: time. Lee McConnell is one of Scotland's most decorated track stars, but now, several years after she retired, she has two more medals. She was in the British women's 4 × 400 metres relay teams that finished fourth in the World Championships in 2009 and fourth again in 2011, but doping offences by members of the teams that beat them meant they were upgraded to bronze medals in both events. But not until 2017! She also had the relay bronze medal she won in the European Championships of 2010 upgraded to silver because of similar malfeasance. This was awarded to her in March 2019. However, she has given up hope of getting a medal from the 2004 Olympics, when the American Crystal Cox lost her relay medal for doping, but not the rest of the team.

There will be more to come; not for McConnell perhaps, but for other athletes who have been cheated out of their medals. The list of banned substances issued by the IOC continues to grow as pharmacological experts discover new performance-enhancing compounds. The IOC and similar sporting bodies are involved in a war, which, despite strong efforts to control the use of drugs, they appear to be losing, but only in the short run. As drug testing has improved, samples retained from earlier competitions have revealed previously undetected drug use. Samples from the 2012 London Olympics could be retested as late as 2020. There were nine positive tests in the run-up to and during London 2012. Since then the retesting scheme has uncovered a further sixty malfeasants, including 24 medallists. Seven of these were gold-medal winners, including the Russian racewalker Sergey Kirdyapkin, his compatriot the high jumper Ivan Ukhov and the Turkish 1,500 metres runner Asli Cakir Alptekin, who were stripped of their medals after rulings by the Court of Arbitration for Sport. Some people never learn. The Uzbek freestyle wrestler Artur Taymazov, who became the sixtieth athlete and seventh gold medallist to be disqualified, had already lost his 2008 Olympic gold in 2016 after a positive test for an oral steroid in the IOC's reanalysis programme. However, he still has his remaining gold from Athens 2004, safeguarded by the statute of limitations on retesting.

ALCOHOL AS A PERFORMANCE-ENHANCING DRUG

Thomas Hicks, an English-born athlete representing the United States, won the marathon at the St Louis Olympic Games of 1904 in a searing temperature of 30 degrees Celsius (86°F). At the 19-mile mark (just over 30 km in) he faltered on the hilly course and his coach fed him 1/60th grain of sulphate of strychnine as a stimulant (with a raw egg, to disguise the taste). Although it is a poison, the drug can stimulate the central nervous system if it is given in small doses. Another mile (1.6 km) on, the procedure was repeated but accompanied by a glass of brandy; this to a dehydrated runner who lost 10 lb (4.5 kg) during the race. He continued, finishing at walking pace and collapsing over the line, but a mile ahead of the second-placed athlete. This resort to alcohol as a performance-enhancing agent was following an established sporting tradition. Captain Robert Barclay Allardice, who gained fame in 1809 for winning a £16,000 challenge to run 1,000 mi. (1,610 km) in a thousand hours, consumed alcohol as part of his training regime to increase his strength and stamina. Another record-breaking pedestrian, Foster Powell, renowned for his walks from London to York and back in less than six days, drank wine and brandy with water during his perambulations. Pugilists, too, took advantage of alcohol. Bottle-holders at prizefights had brandy and water in readiness to be used as a stimulant during the long, bruising fights to exhaustion, and on occasions alcohol was also used to give the fighters extra courage, hence the phrase 'having bottle'.

Historically, the most commonly used performance-enhancing drug was alcohol. Its use by sportspeople should be seen in the context of a society in which many of the population used alcoholic drinks as thirst-quenchers or for physical stamina. Such drinks were seen as less dangerous than water, which was both scarce and unsafe in rural areas and even more contaminated in towns and cities. Moreover, it was generally believed that intoxicants imparted stamina; whenever extra energy was needed resort was had to alcohol, be it harvest workers being given up to a gallon (4.5 litres) of beer a day, or the regular imbibing of glassworkers and iron producers during their long, hot shifts.

Such ideas took a long time to change. At the end of the nineteenth century cricketers still resorted to alcohol during a day's play, and were being advised that when playing on a hot day 'beer and stout are too heady and heavy', 'gin and ginger beer is too sickly sweet' and that 'shandy-gaff, sherry or claret and soda are the most thirst-quenching, the lightest and the cleanest to the palate.' Fast bowlers in Australia were encouraged to train on a diet of beef and beer to gain strength and stamina. Scottish footballers in the 1890s were advised that if they overtrained, a little port or dry champagne at meals might be beneficial, thus following the line of the Oxford Boat Race crew of the time, who were allowed a glass of draught beer or claret and water with their lunch, two glasses with their dinner, and a glass of port with their dessert, but with champagne occasionally substituted for the other drinks when they had been doing very hard work, or showed signs of being over-fatigued and required a fillip.

Even when water supplies improved, alcohol continued to be recommended to athletes. There was a move towards less of it, but no absolute prohibition, and the 1880s brought advertisements professing the fitness-aiding qualities of alcohol. Grant's Morella Cherry Brandy claimed that it 'strengthened and invigorated the system', as was proved by Paul Boyton, who drank it while swimming the Straits of Dover. The health-giving qualities of alcohol were still being proclaimed in advertising campaigns in the interwar years, most notably in the Brewers' Society slogan 'Beer Is Best' and Guinness's explicit promotion of itself as being good for strength. But by this time sportspeople were being advised by the medicos not to consume intoxicants on any scale, since they were now considered detrimental to sporting performance.

Sports science research has shown that alcohol depresses the nervous system, impairs both motor ability and judgement, reduces endurance and, as a diuretic, can disturb electrolyte balance and cause dehydration, all of which are detrimental to effective sports performance. Yet, although generally alcohol has adverse effects on performance in sports that require fast reactions, complex decision-making and highly skilled actions, it can have a positive influence on performance where there is an advantage to be gained from its use as an anti-tremor aid (in, for example, aiming sports such as snooker, darts, archery and rifle-shooting) and an anti-anxiety drug. For some individuals it is simply the case that small amounts of alcohol can reduce feelings of insecurity and tension and improve self-confidence.

For teams, the psychological and other aspects of drinking together may have positive outcomes. Tactical discussions in the bar at the end of a day's play – common among cricketers – is one example. Team bonding, particularly in football, is another. Teams are collections of individuals who may not necessarily get along with each other. On top of personality differences, there is the friction brought about by competition for places. Older players may be wary of newcomers, unwilling to pass on the lessons of experience for fear that it might hasten their journey to sporting oblivion. The young bloods, aware that few of them will become established in the team, may not assist each other as much as the coach might desire. Alcohol is sometimes regarded as a panacea to these problems, in that drinking sessions are seen as a way of bringing teammates together. In the 1980s Liverpool Football Club, a dominant team of the decade, held social drinking sessions one Monday each month, policed by the senior players.

In horse racing, alcohol was seen as offering two specific kinds of help to jockeys. Many of them drank champagne before going into the sauna in the belief that it helped them to sweat. Traditionally, too, the French sparkling wine has been used to keep their weight down. In the early nineteenth century Frank Butler, the first Triple Crown winner, followed a diet of champagne to help restrict his weight to 8 st. 7 lb (54 kg). Later that century, Fred Archer, champion jockey for thirteen successive seasons, allegedly breakfasted on castor oil, a biscuit and a small glass of champagne for the bulk of his racing life. In more modern times Lester

Piggott, champion on eleven occasions, also used champagne in this way, but with the occasional gin and tonic as a change. Although nutrition research indicates that, because alcohol contains calories, drinking can impair any weight reduction programme even if food intake is reduced, the very small amounts jockeys took can be seen simply as a psychologically satisfying alternative to food.

For most participants, sport is a recreational stress reliever, but for elite athletes it can create stress, often producing severe pre-competition anxiety. Not all athletes can cope with this unaided, and some have resorted to anti-anxiety drugs, including alcohol. That sherry was a useful pre-match drink was a prevalent belief in rugby in the 1950s and '60s, and even as late as 1989 a sherry bottle was passed around the Leeds rugby-league dressing room before matches. The communal whisky bottle has also featured in football changing rooms before games. Darts players often resort to alcohol to calm their nerves. Leighton Rees, the Welsh international darts player who retired from the game in the 1990s, reckoned that a couple of pints of beer helped to steel him up for a match.

PLAYER MISCONDUCT

Alcohol has also created an adverse public image for sport because of occasional misbehaviour by players. Instances of sportspeople playing under the influence of drink are not unknown. James Cowan, captain and centre-half of Scotland, lost his place in the national football team following an inebriated performance against the auld enemy in the late 1890s; and what of the Heart of Midlothian goalkeeper who, in 1902, let in seven goals while being in what was described in the club minutes as a 'peculiar condition'? Cricketers were even more likely to lapse because of the long and (even in England) hot days in the field, which tempted them to accept drinks from admiring fans. In Australia the heat could be almost guaranteed, and in their inter-colonial fixture in 1857 New South Wales defeated a Victorian team in which some six or seven players allegedly were so intoxicated that they could hardly stand. No wonder their second innings total was a meagre 38 runs. As a Yorkshireman, I wish someone had prohibited that county's star left-arm spin bowler of the 1890s Bobby Peel from drinking. After over-imbibing during one match in 1897, Peel watered the wicket in unorthodox fashion and departed the game, never to play for Yorkshire again.

Sportspeople sometimes abuse alcohol. Populist press exposés of alcohol-fuelled misdemeanours by modern footballers provide a seemingly endless catalogue of hotel smashing, sexual impropriety and drink-driving. But misbehaviour by inebriated footballers is nothing new. In 1883 the *Scottish Athletic Journal* criticized the 'high jinks in hotels by footballer teams', which were 'becoming such a nuisance that something must be done to put an end to the gross misconduct which goes on'. Nobody can have heeded the plea, since two years later the same journal claimed that Scottish football team trips south of the border, usually at New Year or Easter, often resulted in 'drunken orgies'.

What we should acknowledge is that elite sportsmen are no different from other young men out on the town, except that they often have more money to spend and their activities are more likely to attract publicity. It is not just in Britain that the behaviour of male athletes in masculine flag-bearer sports warrants severe criticism. Excessive drinking has led to arrogant conduct, brawls and sexual assaults among athletes all over the world. Quite simply, young men, fame, high income and lots of free time are a recipe for social dysfunction. This has always been the case, but possibly the media has not always been so intrusive.

STOPPAGE TIME

Most sports historians think modern sport and its development are all that matters. This is an arrogant assumption, but unfortunately the dominant paradigm in sports history has become that of Western modernization, now regarded as central to interpreting the global sporting past. The idea of modernization infers that there must be something pre-modern, which implicitly (explicitly to some observers) must be inferior, or why should modern sport have become the dominant form? Consequently, we simply do not know enough about traditional sports, but there must have been hundreds of them throughout the world, albeit many that were extremely localized. Some traditional sports have survived, but we really have no idea how many have not. Whether those that have been revived can strictly still be termed 'traditional' is a moot point, given that we rarely know how exactly traditional sports were played; at best, they are a modern interpretation using the available evidence. Allied to the Western-centric thinking has been a failure to come to grips with indigenous ways of transmitting and understanding their own history. This could be hubris, ignorance or an unwillingness to retool: who knows?

There has been a general neglect in the literature of Western sports history of narratives from the non-Western world, unless they deal with modernized sport, such as baseball in Japan, soccer in Asia, cricket in India and the hosting of the modern Olympic Games. Recent research has made it clear that China's sports history has a very different narrative from that of the Western world. But, although in China sprinting on stilts and dragon-boat racing are still popular, as they have been for several millennia, the Chinese government's sporting ambition is to win the FIFA World Cup, and it is soccer, not any traditional Chinese sport, that is virtually a compulsory school subject.

Whereas traditional sports struggle to gain any presence in the European sporting calendar, relying on a few devotees to keep them alive, in Asia, the Near East and the Middle East many have survived and even thrived, sometimes with government support as their potential to attract tourists has become apparent. This may be their death knell, for what has so far kept them viable has been their authentic nature as practised by hundreds of thousands, even millions, of local inhabitants (but, of course, always in much smaller groups than that). Commercialism will undermine them, as might also economic development if it provides these locals with leisure and spending power, as it did long ago in much of the Western world.

There is an incalculable amount of research that could be done to cover the coexistence of traditional and modern sport and unravel the interaction between them. For example, if we look at the Middle East and the Arabian Peninsula we find that some cultural folk sports continue to be played, probably (although we cannot be certain) almost as they were centuries before, by nomadic tribes almost untouched by modernity. These include buzkashi, in which teams of players on horseback combine to carry a goat carcass across an open plain or field to a target area. Tracing the game's origin is difficult because several versions are played today, each emphasizing local traditions. Wedding celebrations and puberty initiations that bring together nomadic groups are often accompanied by games of buzkashi, and such gatherings facilitate military alliances, social connections and trading partnerships between tribes.

In contrast, one sport that is highly localized is camel jumping, which is practised only by male members of the Zaraniq tribe on the west coast of Yemen. The goal is to jump over as many standing camels as possible using only a small dirt ramp to assist the take-off. Camels also feature in a sport that has been a reaction to modernization, but ironically has also benefited from it. In Bedouin society, camels are important as a source of food, clothing and tents, transportation, fuel and companionship. Although

Kazakhstanis playing kokpar, a similar sport to buzkashi.

known as 'ships of the desert' for their transportation capabilities, camels were also used for combat and raiding. The need for swift combat animals led to breeding camels for racing as well. Camel races were an opportunity to display the animal's – and by implication the tribe's – combat ability in a non-military environment, such as at weddings, rainfall celebrations, religious feasts or competitions. The use of the camel fell away in the 1960s and '70s as the oil boom brought modern modes of transport to the desert. However, this sparked a desire not only to preserve, but to revitalize traditional culture as a symbol of contemporary patriotism and cultural identity, a move that was aided by the coming of television, which has vastly increased the audience for the sport. Other sports, such as cirit or jereed, in which a blunted javelin is used to knock opposing team members from their horses, have been revitalized in response to the threat of Westernization on native sporting culture, but also because they offer an attraction to tourists.

The concentration on modern sport has also led most sports historians either to ignore extant sport in colonial territories or to denigrate it as inferior to Western, introduced sport. Indeed, once an indigenous sport – Western or otherwise – had standardized rules imposed on it, it was deemed 'modern', 'scientific' and certainly an 'improvement' by Western scholars. Sports history as a discipline has not kept pace with the conceptual theories in the fields of colonial history and racial scholarship. Consequently, it has missed the opportunity to bring indigenous and traditional sports back from the margins of the subject area. There are a few encouraging signs, in that some sports historians have read outside their own subject area and realized that the field of history more generally has moved on and that more attention is now being paid to the concepts of deconstruction and post-colonialism. However, we must be careful not to swing the pendulum too far the other way simply to compensate for previous scholarly failings. Post-colonial histories rightly switch the emphasis from settler sport to the subaltern experience, so that indigenous sport is no longer regarded as inferior, but neither is it necessarily superior to modern sport. The two are simply different, perhaps sharing some common aspects such as enjoyment but also exhibiting marked differences in referencing particular cultures.

In the dawning of new forms of sports history, I hope there could be less concentration on the successful sportspeople and teams. We need greater recognition of the typical sporting experience: losing. Let us have histories of the also-rans, the fourth-place getters, the defunct clubs and the apprentice jockeys who never lost their weight allowance. Such a collection would provide a counterbalance in a world that is obsessed with winning. Another weakness in current sports history, perhaps also including this volume, is a relative failure to examine minority sports. It could be asked if this really matters, if few people are interested in them. Yet such an examination might have relevance for more popular sports if it were considered whether the spectators and participants in minority sports are different, rather than the sports themselves. We should also do more to evaluate why some people do not like sport, which would enable us to distinguish the cultural-specific from the sport-specific.

FINAL WHISTLE

Nothing has been covered in this book in the detail that it could have been. But I hope what this book has done is to give some idea of the questions sports historians have asked and will continue to ask about sport and the societies within which it takes place. Sport is more than the scores and results. Much of it deserves to be on the front pages of the newspapers – if there are still front and back pages online.

Sport can be good for the soul, but bad for the environment. It can inspire and offer aspiration, but, because there can be only one winner and many losers, it can also lead to despair and heartache. Sometimes true sportsmanship can be demonstrated, but cheating and corruption are an ever-present threat. An objective of this book has been to show that the words of the pro-sport lobby should not be accepted uncritically. Those, like myself, who love sport should not be blind to its deficiencies.

RECOMMENDED READING

The following is a brief list of books and articles that readers might find useful should they wish to delve further into any of the material presented in this book. For ease of reference, they have been separated into the same sections as the book itself.

SPORTS HISTORY

Christensen, Karen, Allen Guttmann and Gertrud Pfister, eds,
    International Encyclopedia of Women and Sports (New York, 2001)
Collins, Tony, John Martin and Wray Vamplew, eds, *Encyclopedia of*
    Traditional British Rural Sports (Abingdon, 2005)
Edelman, Robert, and Wayne Wilson, eds, *The Oxford Handbook of Sports*
    History (New York, 2017)
Hill, Jeffrey, *Sport in History: An Introduction* (Basingstoke, 2011)
——, Kevin Moore and Jason Wood, eds, *Sport, History and Heritage:*
    Studies in Public Representation (Woodbridge, 2012)
Hong, Fan, and Lu Zhouxiang, eds, *The Routledge Handbook of Sport*
    in Asia (Abingdon, 2021)
Levinson, David, and Karen Christensen, eds, *Berkshire Encyclopedia*
    of World Sport (Great Barrington, MA, 2005)
Murphy, Cait, *A History of American Sports in 100 Objects* (New York,
    2016)
Osmond, Gary, and Murray G. Phillips, eds, *Sport History in the Digital*
    Age (Urbana, IL, 2015)

Phillips, Murray G., ed., *Representing the Sporting Past in Museums and Halls of Fame* (Abingdon, 2012)

Polley, Martin, *Sports History: A Practical Guide* (Basingstoke, 2007)

Pope, S. W., and John Nauright, eds, *Routledge Companion to Sports History* (Abingdon, 2010)

Riess, Steven A., ed., *A Companion to American Sport History* (Chichester, 2015)

Vamplew, Wray, ed., *Sports History*, 4 vols (Abingdon, 2014)

——, and Mark Dyreson, eds, *Sports History*, 4 vols (London, 2016)

——, and Dave Day, eds, *Methodology in Sports History* (Abingdon, 2018)

——, Mark Dyreson and John McClelland, gen. eds, *A Cultural History of Sport*, 6 vols (London, 2021) [6 volumes]

SPORT THROUGH THE AGES

Arcangeli, Alessandro, ed., *A Cultural History of Sport in the Renaissance* (London, 2021)

Christesen, Paul, and Charles Stocking, eds, *A Cultural History of Sport in Antiquity* (London, 2021)

Fallows, Noel, ed., *A Cultural History of Sport in the Medieval Age* (London, 2021)

Huggins, Mike, ed., *A Cultural History of Sport in the Industrial Age* (London, 2021)

Mallinckrodt, Rebekka von, ed., *A Cultural History of Sport in the Age of Enlightenment* (London, 2021)

Renson, Roland, 'Contextual Essay: Traditional Rural Sports in Europe', in *Encyclopedia of Traditional British Rural Sports*, ed. Tony Collins, John Martin and Wray Vamplew (Abingdon, 2005), pp. 1–20

Riess, Steven A., ed., *A Cultural History of Sport in the Modern Age* (London, 2021)

Tomlinson, Alan, Christopher Young and Richard Holt, eds, *Sport and the Transformation of Modern Europe: States, Media and Markets, 1950–2010* (Abingdon, 2011)

Young, David C., '*Mens Sana in Corpore Sano*? Body and Mind in Ancient Greece', *International Journal of the History of Sport*, xxii/1 (2005), pp. 22–41

SPORTS

Booth, Douglas, *Australian Beach Culture: The History of Sun, Sand and Surf* (London, 2001)

Clements, Jonathan, *A Brief History of the Martial Arts* (London, 2016)

Collins, Tony, *How Football Began: A Global History of How the World's Football Codes Were Born* (London, 2019)

——, John Martin and Wray Vamplew, eds, *Encyclopedia of Traditional British Rural Sports* (Abingdon, 2005)

Day, Dave, 'London Swimming Professors: Victorian Craftsmen and Aquatic Entrepreneurs', *Sport in History*, XXX/1 (2010), pp. 32–54

Dyreson, Mark, and Jaime Schultz, eds, *American National Pastimes: A History* (London, 2015)

Hamilton, David, *Golf: Scotland's Game* (Kilmacolm, 1998)

Hardy, Stephen, and Andrew C. Holman, *Hockey: A Global History* (Urbana, IL, 2018)

Hofmann, Annette R., ed., special issue of *International Journal of the History of Sport*, XXX/6 (2013), on Skiing and Identity

Huggins, Mike, *Horse Racing and British Society in the Long Eighteenth Century* (Woodbridge, 2018)

Hughson, John, Kevin Moore, Ramón Spaaij and Joseph Maguire, eds, *Routledge Handbook of Football Studies* (London, 2017)

Johnes, Martin, and Matthew Taylor, eds, special issue of *Sport in Society*, XXXI/4 (2011), on Boxing, History and Culture

Lake, Robert J., and Carol A. Osborne, eds, *Routledge Handbook of Tennis: History, Culture and Politics* (London, 2019)

Riess, Steven A., ed., *A Companion to American Sports History* (Chichester, 2016)

Underdown, David, *Start of Play: Cricket and Culture in Eighteenth-century England* (London, 2000)

Vamplew, Wray, 'Sports Without Rules: Hunting, Shooting and Fishing in Edwardian Britain', *European Studies in Sport History*, II/1 (2009), pp. 34–51

——, and Joyce Kay, *Encyclopedia of British Horseracing* (Abingdon, 2005)

Van Reeth, Daam, and Daniel Joseph Larson, eds, *The Economics of Professional Road Cycling* (Berlin, 2016)

SPORTING LIFE

Guttmann, Allen, *The Erotic in Sports* (New York, 1996)

MacLean, Malcolm, ed., special issue of *International Journal of the History of Sport*, XXX/14 (2013), on The Sports Club in History

Mayo, James M., *The American Country Club* (New Brunswick, NJ, 1998)

Schultz, Jaime, *Women's Sports: What Everyone Needs to Know* (New York, 2018)

Vamplew, Wray, 'Success for All? Australia's (Un)Sporting Record', in *Australian Studies Now*, ed. Andrew Hassam and Amit Sarwal (New Delhi, 2007), pp. 361–74

SPORT, POLITICS AND POWER

Cauldwell, Jayne, and Darragh McGee, eds, special issue of *Leisure Studies*, XXXVII/1 (2018), on Human Rights and Events: Leisure and Sport

Chapman, Kenneth G., *The Rules of the Green: A History of the Rules of Golf* (London, 1997)

Kilcline, Cathal, ed., *Sport and Protest: Global Perspectives* (London, 2019)

Sikes, Michelle, Toby Rider and Matthew Llewellyn, eds, biennial Africa issue, *International Journal of the History of Sport*, XXXVI/1 (2019), on New Perspectives on Sport and Apartheid

Vamplew, Wray, 'Playing with the Rules: Influences on the Development of Regulation in Sport', *International Journal of the History of Sport*, XXIV/7 (2007), pp. 843–71

THE BUSINESS OF SPORT

Dyreson, Mark, and Peter Hopsicker, eds, *A Half Century of Super Bowls* (London, 2019)

Maennig, Wolfgang, and Andrew Zimbalist, eds, *International Handbook on the Economics of Mega Sporting Events* (Cheltenham, 2012)

Vamplew, Wray, 'Products, Promotion and (Possibly) Profits: Sports Entrepreneurship Revisited', *Journal of Sport History*, XLV/3 (2018), pp. 183–201

——, and Dilwyn Porter, eds, *Sport and Entrepreneurship* (London, 2020)

THE PUBLIC IMAGE OF SPORT

Collins, Tony, and Wray Vamplew, *Mud, Sweat and Beers: A Cultural History of Sport and Alcohol* (Oxford, 2002)

Corzine, Nathan Michael, *Team Chemistry: The History of Drugs and Alcohol in Major League Baseball* (Urbana, IL, 2016)

Dimeo, Paul, ed., *Drugs, Alcohol and Sport* (Abingdon, 2006)

Huggins, Mike, and Rob Hess, eds, *Match-fixing and Sport: Historical Perspectives* (London, 2020)

Millington, Brad, and Brian Wilson, *The Greening of Golf* (Manchester 2016)

Paramio-Salcines, Juan Luis, Kathy Babiak and Geoff Walters, eds, *Routledge Handbook of Sport and Corporate Social Responsibility* (London, 2016)

STOPPAGE TIME

Fan, Hong, and Liu Li, eds, special issue of *International Journal of the History of Sport*, XXXV/15–16 (2018), on Indigenous Sport History and Culture in Asia

Phillips, Murray G., Russell Field, Christine O'Bonsawin and Janice Forsyth, eds, special issue of *Journal of Sport History*, XLVI/2 (2019), on Indigenous Resurgence, Regeneration, and Decolonization through Sport History

ACKNOWLEDGEMENTS

Among the many colleagues across the world that I have benefited from working with over the years are Daryl Adair, Tony Collins, John Dewhirst, Heather Dichter, Mark Dyerson, Jane George, Grant Jarvie John McClelland, John O'Hara, Dil Porter and Dave Russell. Another who has provided help and inspiration is Stefan Szymanski. I especially acknowledge my collaboration and friendship with Mike Huggins, Gary James and Joyce Kay.

PHOTO ACKNOWLEDGEMENTS

The author and publishers wish to express their thanks to the below sources of illustrative material and/or permission to reproduce it:

Alamy: pp. 83 (PA Images), 290 (Everett Collection Inc), 293 (Allstar Picture Library Ltd), 305 (Everett Collection Inc), 381 (Keystone Press); Amsterdam City Archives: p. 29; Art Institute of Chicago: p. 148 (Gift of Mrs. Charles H. Schweppe and William McCallin McKee Memorial Endowment); The British Library: p. 56; Flickr: pp. 113 (George Eastman Museum), 140 (Janus Kinase), 192 (www.davidmolloyphotography. com), 195 (State Library of New South Wales), 215 (Arctic Warrior), 216 (Internet Archive Book Images), 250 (Boston Public Library); Getty Images: pp. 157 (Bob Thomas), 406 (Keystone); Library of Congress, Washington, DC: pp. 14, 94, 112, 163, 200, 204, 208, 221, 227, 257, 414; Metropolitan Museum of Art, New York: pp. 139 top (Purchase, 1896. Accession Number: 96.9.10), 197 (The Jefferson R. Burdick Collection, Gift of Jefferson R. Burdick. Accession Number: 63.350.202.43.50); Pixabay: p. 123 bottom (neildodhia); Shutterstock: p. 131 (Canadian Press); Smithsonian Institution: pp. 99 (Collection of the National Museum of African American History and Culture), 123 centre (Freer Gallery of Art and Arthur M. Sackler Gallery/Gift of Charles Lang Freer), 258 (Collection of the National Museum of African American History and Culture); State Library of New South Wales: pp. 16, 172; State Library of Victoria: pp. 169, 254; © The Trustees of the British Museum: pp. 55, 127,

INDEX

Page numbers in *italics* refer to illustrations